MEDIA AND ENTERTAINMENT LAW

MEDIA AND ENTERTAINMENT LAW

Peter Carey, LLB (Hons) (Nottingham), LLM (Texas), Solicitor, Charles Russell

Richard Verow, LLB (Hons), Solicitor, Octagon Worldwide Limited

JORDANS

2002

Published by
Jordan Publishing Limited
21 St Thomas Street
Bristol BS1 6JS

© The College of Law, Peter Carey and Richard Verow 2002

Peter Carey and Richard Verow have asserted their moral rights
in accordance the Copyright Designs and Patents Act 1988.

All rights reserved. No part of this publication may be
reproduced, stored in a retrieval system, or transmitted in
any way or by any means, including photocopying or recording,
without the written permission of the copyright holder,
application for which should be addressed to the publisher.

British Library Cataloguing-in-Publication Data
A catalogue record for this book is available from the British Library.

ISSN 1362–0762
ISBN 0 85308 747 4

Printed in Great Britain by Hobbs The Printers Ltd of Southampton

PREFACE

This book has been written primarily for use by students studying the Media and Entertainment elective on the Legal Practice Course at The College of Law. It is intended as a general reference work of an introductory nature.

In writing this book, we have necessarily been selective as to its content. We decided to look at areas of important background law applicable to the area. This is followed by a consideration of some of the important media and entertainment industries – advertising and sponsorship, newspaper reporting, music recording and publishing, and film and television programme making and distribution. We have set out the basic structure of the industries in question before going on to analyse particular legal and practical problems faced by legal advisers in these areas.

In discussing each of the industries, we consider the drafting of commercial contracts and specific documentation commonly found in each industry. We also look at certain aspects of litigation in media and entertainment practice, most notably in relation to defamation. Each area of discussion builds on the basics as covered on the LPC and detailed in other books such as the LPC Resource Books *Civil Litigation* and *Business Law and Practice* (Jordans) and *Commercial Law and Practice* (Jordans).

We are very grateful to the practitioners who have given their time to help us write this work. Our thanks especially to the firm of Harbottle & Lewis and, in particular, John Stutter for his general advice, Gerrard Tyrrell for advice on contentious matters generally and Medwyn Jones for film and television.

Thanks are also due to Howard Ricklow at Collyer-Bristow and Tim Cox and Richard Shillito of Crockers Oswald Hickson who have provided materials and made various helpful comments and suggestions. Special thanks to Melissa Button of the BBC's legal department for her expertise on the changes to defamation practice brought about by the Woolf reforms. Thanks also to Jo Sanders of Olswang for her guidance on media issues generally.

Peter Carey wrote Chapters 9–14 and 18–21; Richard Verow wrote Chapters 1–8, 15–17 and 22.

In the interests of brevity, we have used the masculine pronoun throughout to include the feminine.

PETER CAREY

RICHARD VEROW

CONTENTS

PREFACE	v
TABLE OF CASES	xi
TABLE OF STATUTES	xv
TABLE OF STATUTORY INSTRUMENTS	xix
TABLE OF EC LEGISLATION AND OTHER MATERIALS	xxi
TABLE OF ABBREVIATIONS	xxiii

Chapter 1		COPYRIGHT	1
	1.1	Introduction	1
	1.2	Sources of copyright law	1
	1.3	The subject matter of copyright	2
	1.4	Original literary, dramatic, musical and artistic works	2
	1.5	Databases	7
	1.6	Sound recordings, films, broadcasts and cable programmes	9
	1.7	Published editions	10
	1.8	Conditions for protection	11
	1.9	Duration of copyright	12
	1.10	Authorship	14
	1.11	Joint authorship	15
	1.12	Ownership of copyright	16
	1.13	Exploitation of copyright	18
Chapter 2		COPYRIGHT INFRINGEMENT	23
	2.1	Introduction	23
	2.2	Restricted acts	23
	2.3	Copying	26
	2.4	Issuing copies to the public	27
	2.5	Rental or lending of copies to the public	27
	2.6	Public performance	27
	2.7	Broadcasting	28
	2.8	Adaptations	28
	2.9	Secondary infringement of copyright	29
	2.10	Defences and permitted acts	31
	2.11	Civil remedies	35
	2.12	Criminal remedies	35
Chapter 3		MORAL RIGHTS	37
	3.1	Introduction	37
	3.2	Right to be identified as author or director	37
	3.3	Derogatory treatment	38
	3.4	False attribution	40
	3.5	Remedies	40
	3.6	Waiver of rights	40

	3.7	Right to privacy of certain photographs and films	41

Chapter 4	RIGHTS IN PERFORMANCES	43
	4.1 Introduction	43
	4.2 Performance rights	43
	4.3 Performers' rights	44
	4.4 Rights of persons with recording rights	47
	4.5 Duration	48
	4.6 Remedies	48
	4.7 Defences and exceptions to rights	49
	4.8 Exploitation	50

Chapter 5	COMMERCIAL CONTRACTS	51
	5.1 Introduction	51
	5.2 Reaching agreement	51
	5.3 Problems in formation	54
	5.4 Challenging agreements	55
	5.5 Remedies and termination	65

Chapter 6	THE MUSIC BUSINESS	69
	6.1 Introduction	69
	6.2 Composers and publishers	69
	6.3 The record industry	73
	6.4 The Musicians' Union (MU)	74
	6.5 Equitable remuneration	75

Chapter 7	GROUP MANAGEMENT	77
	7.1 Introduction	77
	7.2 Choice of business medium	77
	7.3 Appointment of a manager	77
	7.4 Terms of agreement	80
	7.5 Manager's warranties and obligations	85
	7.6 Artist's obligations	86
	7.7 Other provisions	88

Chapter 8	ARTISTS' RECORDING AGREEMENTS	89
	8.1 Introduction	89
	8.2 Sound recordings	90
	8.3 Duration of the agreement	92
	8.4 Artist's warranties and obligations	94
	8.5 Company's warranties and obligations	96
	8.6 Advances	100
	8.7 Royalties	101
	8.8 Other royalty rates	102
	8.9 Calculating royalties	105
	8.10 Accounting	107
	8.11 Departing members	108
	8.12 Termination provisions	109
	8.13 Post-termination	109

Chapter 9	DEFAMATION	111
	9.1 Introduction	111
	9.2 What is defamation?	111
	9.3 Libel or slander?	112

	9.4	Publication	112
	9.5	Words must be defamatory	113
	9.6	Words must refer to the claimant	115
	9.7	Defences	117
	9.8	Remedies	126
	9.9	Contentious considerations	128
	9.10	Summary disposal of claim	132

Chapter 10 — MALICIOUS FALSEHOOD — 135
	10.1	General	135
	10.2	Definition	135
	10.3	Defamation and malicious falsehood compared	137

Chapter 11 — OBSCENITY — 139
	11.1	Introduction	139
	11.2	Definition of 'obscene'	139
	11.3	The offences	140
	11.4	Defences	141
	11.5	Human rights	142
	11.6	Television	143
	11.7	Cinema exhibition	144
	11.8	Video recordings	144
	11.9	Obscenity and children	145

Chapter 12 — RACIAL HATRED AND BLASPHEMY — 147
	12.1	Inciting racial hatred	147
	12.2	Blasphemy	149

Chapter 13 — PRIVACY — 151
	13.1	Breach of confidence	151
	13.2	Data protection	152
	13.3	Human rights	156

Chapter 14 — CONTEMPT AND COURT REPORTING — 159
	14.1	Introduction	159
	14.2	Strict liability contempt	159
	14.3	Intentional contempt	163
	14.4	Contempt by publishing jury deliberations	164

Chapter 15 — FILM AND TELEVISION: PRE-PRODUCTION — 165
	15.1	Introduction	165
	15.2	UK television production	166
	15.3	Development	169
	15.4	Personnel	173

Chapter 16 — FILM AND TELEVISION: FINANCE AND PRODUCTION — 175
	16.1	Introduction	175
	16.2	Methods of finance	175
	16.3	Production agreements	180

Chapter 17 — FILM AND TELEVISION: RIGHTS AND CONTENT CLEARANCE — 187
	17.1	Introduction	187
	17.2	Rights clearance: copyright	187
	17.3	Moral rights clearance	191

	17.4	Performers' rights consents	191
	17.5	Copyright and Related Rights Regulations 1996: rights considerations	192
	17.6	Content clearance	192

Chapter 18 FILM AND TELEVISION: DISTRIBUTION AND EXPLOITATION — 195
- 18.1 Introduction — 195
- 18.2 Distribution — 195
- 18.3 Cinema — 198
- 18.4 Video — 199
- 18.5 Television — 200

Chapter 19 ADVERTISING: THE INDUSTRY — 203
- 19.1 Introduction — 203
- 19.2 What is advertising? — 203
- 19.3 The advertising media — 203
- 19.4 The advertising agency — 204
- 19.5 Advertising on television — 205

Chapter 20 ADVERTISING: SELF-REGULATION — 207
- 20.1 Introduction — 207
- 20.2 Broadcast advertising — 207
- 20.3 Non-broadcast advertising — 209
- 20.4 The ITC Code of Advertising Standards and Practice — 215

Chapter 21 ADVERTISING LAW — 221
- 21.1 Introduction — 221
- 21.2 Descriptions and prices — 221
- 21.3 Passing off — 225
- 21.4 Trade marks — 227
- 21.5 Copyright and moral rights — 230
- 21.6 Comparative advertising — 231
- 21.7 The law of contract — 238
- 21.8 Summary — 240

Chapter 22 COMMERCIAL ASPECTS OF SPORT — 241
- 22.1 Introduction — 241
- 22.2 The sponsorship agreement — 241
- 22.3 The sponsor's rights — 241
- 22.4 The sponsor's obligations — 245
- 22.5 The organiser's obligations — 246
- 22.6 Commercial conflicts and ambush marketing — 247
- 22.7 Merchandising and endorsement agreements — 249
- 22.8 Broadcast sponsorship — 249

BIBLIOGRAPHY — 251

INDEX — 253

TABLE OF CASES

References in the right-hand column are to paragraph numbers.

A&M Records v Video Collection International Ltd [1995] EMLR 25	1.12.4
Aiken and Others v Police Review Publishing Co Ltd (1995) unreported, 12 April, CA	9.6
Allason v Campbell and Others (1996) *The Times*, May 8, QBD	10.2.3
Allason v Haines [1996] EMLR 143, QBD	9.7.3
'Allo Allo' case, *see* Kaye v Robertson	
American Cyanamid Co v Ethicon Ltd [1975] AC 396, HL	9.8.2
Anglia Television v Reed [1972] 1 QB 60, CA	5.5.1
Anheuser-Busch Inc v Budejovicky Budvar Narodni Podnik [1984] FSR 413, CA	21.4.3
Armatrading v Stone (1984) unreported, 17 September, QBD	5.4.3
Associated Newspapers plc v Insert Media Ltd and Others [1991] 1 WLR 571, CA	21.3.1
Attorney-General v English [1983] 1 AC 116, DC	14.2.1, 14.2.4
Attorney-General v Guardian Newspapers Ltd (No 3) [1992] 3 All ER 38, DC	14.2.1
Attorney-General v News Group Newspapers Ltd [1988] 2 All ER 906, DC	14.3
Attorney-General's Reference (No 3 of 1977) [1978] 3 All ER 1166, CA	11.4.1
Attorney-General's Reference (No 5 of 1980) [1980] 3 All ER 816, CA	11.8
BBC v British Satellite Broadcasting Ltd [1991] 3 WLR 174, [1991] 3 All ER 833, ChD	2.10.2
Barclays Bank v O'Brien and Another [1994] 1 AC 180, HL	5.4.3
Barclays Bank plc v RBS Advanta [1996] RPC 307, ChD	21.6.3
Bassey and Another v Icon Entertainment plc and Another [1995] EMLR 596, ChD	4.3.4
Berezovsky v Forbes Inc and Another (2000) *The Times*, May 16, HL	9.9.2
Beloff v Pressdram Ltd and Another [1973] 1 All ER 241, ChD	2.10.2
Beta Construction Ltd v Channel Four TV Co Ltd [1990] 2 All ER 1012, CA	9.9.7
Blair v Osborne & Tompkins [1971] 2 WLR 503	1.12.3
Bourne v Walt Disney Co (1995) US App Lexis	1.13.5
British Horseracing Board v William Hill Organisation Ltd [2001] 2 CMLR 12, ChD	
British Horseracing Board Ltd, The Jockey Club and Weatherbys Group Ltd v William Hill Organisation Ltd [2001] All ER (D) 431 (Jul), CA	1.5.7
British Steel Corporation v Cleveland Bridge and Engineering Co Ltd [1984] 1 All ER 504, QBD	5.3.4
'Budweiser' case, *see* Anheuser-Busch Inc v Budojecky Budvar Narodni Podnik	
Byrne v Statist Co [1914] 1 KB 622, KB	1.12.2
CCC Films (London) Ltd v Impact Quadrant Films Ltd [1985] 1 QB 16, QBD	5.5.1
Campbell v Spottiswoode (1863) 3 B & S 769	9.7.2
Cape (Jonathan) v Consolidated Press [1954] 1 WLR 1313, QBD	1.13.3
Carlill v The Carbolic Smoke Ball Co [1893] 1 QB 256, CA	21.7.3
Central Independent Television, Re [1991] 1 WLR 4, CA	14.2.3
Charleston and Another v News Group Newspapers and Another [1995] 2 AC 65, HL	9.4, 9.5
Ciba-Geigy plc v Parke Davis & Co Ltd [1994] FSR 8, ChD	21.6.4
CILFIT v Ministry of Health [1982] ECR 3415, ECJ	1.5.5
'Clockwork Orange' case, *see* Time Warner Entertainment Co v Channel Four Television Corp plc	
Coca-Cola, Re [1986] 2 All ER 274, HL	21.4.1
Coco v A.N. Clarke (Engineers) Ltd [1968] FSR 415, ChD	13.1.1
Colchester Borough Council v Smith and Others [1992] Ch 421, CA	5.3.3, 5.4.4(5)
Compaq Computer Corporation v Dell Computer Corporation Ltd [1992] FSR 93, ChD	21.6.6
Condor v The Barron Knights Ltd [1966] 1 WLR 87, Bedford Assizes	5.5.3
Consorzio del Prosciutto di Parma v Marks & Spencer plc and Others [1991] RPC 351, CA	21.3.1
Coulson (William) & Sons v James Coulson & Co (1887) 3 TLR 46, CA	9.8.2
DPP v Whyte [1972] AC 849, HL	11.2.4
De L'Isle (Viscount) v Times Newspapers Ltd [1987] 3 All ER 499, CA	9.9.7
Denmark Productions Ltd v Boscobel Productions Ltd [1969] 1 QB 699, CA	7.3.4

Derbyshire County Council v Times Newspapers Ltd and Others [1993] AC 534, HL	9.7.2
Dimmock v Hallett (1866) 2 Ch App 21	21.7.4
Director General of Fair Trading v Tobyward Ltd and Another [1989] 2 All ER 266, ChD	21.2.3
Donnelly v Rowlands [1971] 1 All ER 9, DC	21.2.2
Donoghue v Allied Newspapers Ltd [1938] Ch 106, ChD	1.4.2, 1.10.1
Douglas, Zeta Jones and Northern & Shell plc v Hello! Ltd [2001] FLR 982, [2001] UKHRR 223, CA	13.3
EMI Music v Evangelous Papathanassiou [1987] 8 EIPR 244	2.2.2
Eastham v Newcastle United Football Club Ltd and Others [1964] Ch 413, ChD	5.4.4(5)
Elton John v Richard Leon James [1991] FSR 397	5.4.3
Emaco & Electrolux v Dyson Appliances Ltd (1999) *The Times*, February 8, ChD	21.6.6
Esso Petroleum Co Ltd v Harper's Garage (Stouport) Ltd [1968] AC 269, HL	5.4.4, 5.4.4(5)
Esso Petroleum v Mardon [1976] QB 801, CA	21.7.4
Exxon Corporation v Exxon Insurance Consultants International Ltd [1982] Ch 119	1.4.2
Fisher v Bell [1960] 3 WLR 919, QBD	11.3
Football League v Littlewoods Pools Ltd [1959] Ch 637	1.4.1
Francis Day & Hunter Ltd v Bron [1963] Ch 587, CA	2.2.1
Francis Day & Hunter Ltd v Feldman [1914] 2 Ch 728, CA	1.8.2
Francis Day & Hunter Ltd v Twentieth Century Fox Corporation Ltd [1940] AC 112, PC	1.4.2
Fraser and Others v Thames Television and Others [1984] 1 QB 44, [1983] 2 All ER 101, QBD	13.1.2, 15.3.1
Fuentes Bobo v Spain (Application No 39293/98) (2000) unreported, 29 February	13.3
Gamerco SA v ICM/Fair Warning (Agency) Ltd [1995] 1 WLR 1126, QBD	5.5.3
'George Michael' case, *see* Panayiotou v Sony Music Entertainments (UK) Ltd	
Gleaves and Others v Deakin and Others [1980] AC 477, HL	9.3
Godfrey (Lawrence) v Demon Internet [2000] 3 WLR 1020, QBD	9.7.5
Goldsmith v Pressdram Ltd [1987] 3 All ER 485, CA	9.9.7
Goldstar Publications v DPP [1981] 2 All ER 257	11.2.4
Grappelli and Another v Derek Block (Holdings) Ltd and Another [1981] 2 All ER 272, CA	10.1
Green v Broadcasting Corporation of New Zealand [1989] 2 All ER 1056, PC	1.4.1, 1.4.3
Hadley v Baxendale (1854) 9 Exch 341	5.5.1
Handyside v United Kingdom [1976] 1 EHRR 737, ECHR	11.5
Harman Pictures NV v Osborne and Others [1967] 1 WLR 723, ChD	15.3.4
Hartt v Newspaper Publishing plc (1989) *The Times*, November 9, CA	9.5
Hawkes and Son (London) Ltd v Paramount Film Service Ltd [1934] Ch 593, CA	2.2.2
Horrocks v Lowe [1975] AC 135, HL	9.7.2
Hospital for Sick Children (Board of Governors) v Walt Disney Productions Inc [1966] 1 WLR 1055, ChD	1.13.5
Hubbard and Another v Vosper and Another [1972] 2 QB 84, CA	2.10.2
Hulton (E) & Co v Jones [1910] All ER Rep 29	9.6
Independent Television Publications v Time Out Ltd [1984] FSR 64	1.4.1, 1.4.2
J.C. Williamson Ltd v Metro-Goldwyn-Mayer Theatres Ltd [1937] VLR 67, 140	1.13.5
Jersild v Denmark [1994] 19 EHRR 1, ECHR	12.1.4
Jennings v Stephens [1936] Ch 469, CA	2.6
John v MGN Ltd [1997] QB 586, CA	9.8.1
Joyce v Sengupta and Another [1993] 1 All ER 897, CA	10.2.2
Jude's Musical Compositions, Re [1907] 1 Ch 651, CA	1.13.3
Kaye v Robertson and Another [1991] FSR 62, CA	10.2.1, 10.2.2, 10.2.3
Kelly v Cinema House Ltd [1928–1935] MacG Cop Cas 391	1.4.2
Knupffer v London Express Newspapers Ltd [1944] AC 116, HL	9.6

Case	Reference
LA Gear Inc v Hi-Tec Sports plc [1992] FSR 121, CA	2.9
LB (Plastics) v Swish Products [1979] RPC 611, HL	2.2.1
Ladbroke (Football) Ltd v William Hill (Football) Ltd [1964] 1 WLR 273, HL	1.4.1, 1.4.2, 2.2.2
Lion Laboratories Ltd v Evans and Others [1985] 1 QB 526, CA	2.10.5
Loutchansky v Times Newspapers Ltd and Others [2001] 3 WLR 404, CA	9.7.4
Lucas-Box v News Group Newspapers and Others [1986] 1 WLR 147, CA	9.7.1, 9.9.5
Lumley v Wagner (1852) 1 De GM & G 604	5.5.2
MGN Pension Trustees Ltd v Bank of America National Trust and Saving Association and Credit Suisse [1995] EMLR 99, ChD	14.2.1, 14.2.3
McCartan Turlington Breen v Times Newspapers Ltd [2000] 4 All ER 913, HL	9.7.4
McDonald's Corporation v Steel [1995] 3 All ER 615, CA	9.7.1
McDonald's Hamburgers (McDonald's Golden Arches Restaurants Ltd) v Burger King (UK) Ltd [1986] FSR 45, ChD	21.6.4
Mad Hat Music Ltd and Another v Pulse 8 Records Ltd [1993] EMLR 172, ChD	4.3.4
Magill TV Guide (1991) 4 CMLR 586	1.4.1, 2.1
Mail Newspapers plc v Express Newspapers plc [1987] FSR 90	1.11
Mandla and Another v Dowell Lee and Another [1983] 1 All ER 1062, HL	12.1.1
Merivale v Carson (1887) 20 QBD 275	9.7.2
Missing Link Software and Another v Magee and Others [1989] FSR 361, ChD	1.12.2
Moore v News of the World Ltd and Another [1972] 1 QB 441, CA	3.4
Newsgroup Newspapers Ltd v Mirror Group Newspapers [1989] FSR 126	1.4.2
Newstead v London Express Newspapers Ltd [1940] 1 KB 377, CA	9.6
Nordenfelt v Maxim Nordenfelt Guns and Ammunition Co Ltd [1894] AC 535, HL	5.4.4(3), 5.4.4(5)
Norowzian v Arks Ltd and Others (No 2) [2000] FSR 363, CA	1.4.3
O'Shea (Kerry) v MGN Limited and Free 4 Internet Limited (2001) unreported, 4 May	9.6
O'Sullivan v Management Agency and Music Ltd and Others [1985] QB 428, CA	5.4.3
Panayiotou and Others v Sony Music Entertainment (UK) Ltd [1994] EMLR 229, CA	5.4.4(5), 5.5.2, 8.7.2
Partridge v Crittenden [1968] 2 All ER 421, DC	21.7.2
Peach Grey & Co (a firm) v Sommers [1995] 2 All ER 513, QBD	14.2.2
Performing Right Society Ltd v Harlequin Record Shops Ltd [1979] 1 WLR 851, ChD	2.6
Pharmaceutical Society of Great Britain v Boots Cash Chemists (Southern) Ltd [1952] 2 QB 795, QBD	21.7.2
Prior v Lansdowne Press Pty Ltd [1977] RPC 511, Supreme Court of Victoria	1.11
Proetta v Times Newspapers Ltd [1991] 4 All ER 46, CA	9.9.6
R v Anderson and Others [1972] 1 QB 304, CA	11.2.2, 11.2.3, 11.4.2
R v Bow Street Magistrates' Court, ex parte Choudhury [1991] 1 All ER 306, DC	12.2
R v Calder and Boyars Ltd [1969] 1 QB 151, CA	11.2.4, 11.4.1
R v Central Independent Television plc [1994] 3 WLR 20, CA	9.8.2
R v Hicklin (1868) LR 3 QB 360	11.2
R v Horsham Justices ex parte Farquharson and West Sussex County Times [1982] QB 762, CA	14.2.1
R v International Stock Exchange ex parte Else (1982) Ltd and Another [1993] QB 534, CA	1.5.5
R v Lemon; R v Gay News Ltd [1979] QB 10, CA	12.2
R v Taylor (Alan) (1994) 158 JP 317, CA	11.3
Ravenscroft v Herbert and New English Library Ltd [1980] RPC 193, ChD	2.2.2
Ray v Classic FM [1998] FSR 622	1.12.3
Reynolds v Times Newspapers Ltd and Others [1999] 3 WLR 1010, HL	9.7.4
Royal Aquarium & Summer & Winter Garden Society Ltd v Parkinson [1892] 1 QB 431, CA	9.7.3
Rubber Improvement Ltd and Another v Daily Telegraph Ltd; Lewis and Another v Daily Telegraph Ltd; Lewis and Another v Associated Newspapers Ltd [1964] AC 234, [1963] 2 All ER 151, HL	9.5, 9.5.2

Savory Ltd v The World of Golf [1914] 2 Ch 566, ChD　　　　　　　　　　　　　　　　1.13.2
Schroeder (A.) Music Publishing Co Ltd v Macaulay (formerly Instone) [1974] 1 WLR 1308,
　　[1974] 3 All ER 616, HL　　　　　　　　　　　　　　　　　　5.4.4(1), 5.4.4(3), 5.4.4(4),
　　　　　　　　　　　　　　　　　　　　　　　　　　　　　　　　　　　　　　　5.4.4(5)
Schweppes Ltd and Others v Wellingtons Ltd [1984] FSR 210, ChD　　　　　　　　　　2.2.2
Shevill and Others v Presse Alliance SA [1995] 2 AC 18, ECJ　　　　　　　　　　　　9.9.2
Silvertone Records v Mountfield [1993] EMLR 152　　　　　　　　　　5.4.4(5), 8.1.1, 8.5.1
Sinanide v La Maison Kosmeo (1928) 139 LT 365, CA　　　　　　　　　　　　　　　　1.4.2
Smith v Land and House Property Corporation (1884) 28 Ch D 7　　　　　　　　　　21.7.4
Spelling-Goldberg Promotions Inc v BPC Publishing Ltd [1981] RPC 280, CA　　　　　 2.3.2
Sports and General Press Agency Ltd v 'Our Dogs' Publishing Ltd [1916] KB 880, KBD　　1.6
'Stone Roses' case, see Silvertone Records v Mountfield
Sunday Times v United Kingdom Government (1979–80) 2 EHRR 245, ECHR　　　　　　14.1

Tate v Fullbrook [1908] 1 KB 821, CA　　　　　　　　　　　　　　　　　　　　　　1.4.3
Tate v Thomas [1921] 1 Ch 503　　　　　　　　　　　　　　　　　　　　　　　　1.10.1
Telnikoff v Matusevitch [1991] 4 All ER 817, HL　　　　　　　　　　　　　　　　　9.7.2
Thomas v Bradbury, Agnew & Co Ltd and Another [1906] 2 KB 627, CA　　　　　　　9.7.2
Time Warner Entertainment Co v Channel Four Television Corp plc [1994] EMLR 1, CA　 2.10.2, 17.6
Times Newspapers Ltd and Another v MGN Ltd [1993] EMLR 443, CA　　　　　　　2.10.5
Tolley v Fry & Sons Ltd [1931] All ER Rep 131　　　　　　　　　　　　　　　　　9.5.1
Turner (Ernest) Electrical Instruments Ltd v Performing Right Society Ltd; Performing Right
　　Society Ltd v Gillette Industries Ltd [1943] Ch 167, CA　　　　　　　　　　　　　2.6
Tyburn Productions v Conan Doyle [1991] Ch 75　　　　　　　　　　　　　　　　　1.2.1

University of London Press Ltd v University Tutorial Press Ltd [1916] 2 Ch 601, ChD　　1.4.1, 1.4.2, 2.2.2

Vodafone Group plc and Another v Orange Personal Communications Services Ltd [1997] EMLR
　　84　　　　　　　　　　　　　　　　　　　　　　　　　　　　　　　　　　　21.6.3

W (Wardship: Publication of Information), Re [1992] 1 FLR 99, CA　　　　　　　　　9.8.2
Wagamama Ltd v City Centre Restaurants plc (UK) Ltd [1995] FSR 713, ChD　　　　21.4.2
Walford and Others v Miles and Another [1992] 2 AC 128, HL　　　　　　　　　　　5.3.2
Walter v Steinkopff [1892] 3 Ch 489, ChD　　　　　　　　　　　　　　　　　　　1.4.2
Warner v Gestetner Ltd [1988] EIPRD 89　　　　　　　　　　　　　　　　　　　1.12.3
Warnink (Erven) BV v J. Townend & Sons (Hull) Ltd and Another [1979] AC 731, HL　 21.3.1
Warren v Mendy and Another [1989] 1 WLR 853, CA　　　　　　　　　　　　　　5.5.2
Warwick Film Productions Ltd v Eisinger and Others [1969] 1 Ch 508, ChD　　　　　2.2.2
Watson v Prager and Another [1991] 3 All ER 487, ChD　　　　　　　　　　　　5.4.4(5)
Williamson Music Ltd v The Pearson Partnership Ltd [1987] FSR 97　　　　　　　　2.2.2
Wingrove (Nigel) v United Kingdom (1997) EHRR 1, ECHR　　　　　　　　　　　　12.2
Wiseman v Weidenfeld & Nicolson [1985] FSR 525　　　　　　　　　　　　　　　1.10.1
Withers v General Theatre Corporation Ltd [1933] 2 KB 536, CA　　　　　　　　　　5.5.1
Woodward and Others v Hutchins and Others [1977] 2 All ER 751, CA　　　　　　　13.1.3
Wright, Layman & Umney Ltd v Wright [1949] 66 RPC 149, CA　　　　　　　　　21.3.1

Youssoupoff v Metro-Goldwyn-Mayer Pictures Ltd (1934) 50 TLR 581　　　　　　　　9.3

Zang Tumb Tuum Records Ltd and Another v Holly Johnson [1993] EMLR 61　　5.4.4(5), 8.5.2

TABLE OF STATUTES

References in the right-hand column are to paragraph numbers.

Banking Act 1987	21.1	s 5(1)	1.6.1, 1.6.2
Bill of Rights 1689		(2)	1.6.2
Art 9	9.7.3	s 6	2.7
Broadcasting Act 1990	1.4.1, 11.2.1, 11.3,	(1)	1.6.3
	9.5.2, 20.2.1, 20.4,	(3)	1.10.3
	22.8.1, 15.1, 15.2.1, 16.2.2, 17.6	s 7	1.6.4, 2.6
s 6(1)(e)	9.5.3	s 9	1.10, 1.10.1
s 8(2)	9.5.3	(1)	1.11
s 43(1)	11.6	(2)	1.9.2, 1.12.4
s 162(1)(a)	11.6	(a)	8.2.2
s 164	12.1.2	(aa)	1.10.2
s 166(1)	9.3	(ab)	1.10.2
British Nationality Act 1981	1.8.1	(c)	1.10.3
		(d)	1.10.4
		s 10	1.11
Cinemas Act 1985		(2)	1.10.3
s 1(1)	18.3.1	s 11	1.10
Consumer Credit Act 1974	20.4, 21.1	(1)	1.11
Consumer Protection Act 1987		(2)	1.12.2, 1.12.3
Pt III	21.2.4	s 12	1.9.1
s 20	21.2.4	(2)	1.9.1
(2)	21.2.4	(3)	1.11
(6)	21.2.4	s 13A(3)	1.9.2
s 24(3)	21.2.4	s 13B	1.9.2
Contempt of Court Act 1981	14.1, 14.3	s 14(2)	1.9.3
s 3(1)	14.2.4	(5)	1.9.3
s 4(1), (2)	14.2.3	s 15	1.9.4
s 5	14.2.5	s 16	2.1, 2.9, 2.10.1
s 8	14.4	(2)–(4)	2.2.1
s 10	13.1.4	ss 16–21	2.2.1
Sch 2	14.2.2	ss 16–26	2.9
Copyright Act 1911	1.2	ss 16–76	2.1
Copyright Act 1956	1.2	ss 17–20	2.8
Copyright, Designs and Patents Act		s 17(2)	2.3.1
1988	5.2.4, 1.2, 1.2.1, 1.4.4,	(3)	1.4.5
	1.12.3, 2.7, 2.9.2, 2.9.5,	(4)	2.3.2
	4.2.2, 4.2.3, 4.3.4, 4.4, 4.6.1, 4.7,	(5)	2.3.3
	8.4.2, 15.2.2, 17.2.1, 17.3	s 18(2)	2.4
Pt II	4.1, 4.6.2, 8.1.2	s 18A	2.2.1
Pt IV	3.1	(1)	2.5
s 1(1)	1.3	(2)(a)	2.5
(b)	1.6	(b)	2.5
(3)	1.3, 1.8	s 19	2.6
s 3	1.4	ss 19–20	4.3.3
(1)	1.4.2, 1.4.3, 1.4.4, 1.5.3	s 20	2.7
(2)	1.4	s 21(1)–(3)	2.9
(3)	1.4	s 22	2.9.1, 15.3.4, 17.3
s 3A	1.5.3	s 23	2.9.2, 17.3
(2)	1.5.4	s 24	2.9.3
s 4	1.4	s 25	2.9.4
(1)	1.4.5	(2)	2.9.4
(2)	1.4.5, 1.4.6	s 26	2.9.5
		s 27	2.9.6

Copyright, Designs and Patents Act 1988 *cont*	
s 28 *et seq*	2.2.1
ss 28–76	2.10.1
s 28(2)	2.10.2
s 29	2.10.2
(3)	2.10.2
s 30	2.10.2
(1), (2)	2.10.2
s 31	2.10.3, 17.2.1
(3)	2.10.3
ss 32–44	2.10.2
s 51	1.4.5
ss 57–63	2.10.4
s 57(1)	1.9.1
s 62	17.2.1
ss 77–89	3.1
s 77	3.2.1, 3.6
(1)	15.2.2
s 78	3.2.1
(4)	3.2.1
s 79	3.2.2
s 80	3.3.1, 3.3.2, 3.6
(2)	3.3.1
s 81	3.3.2
s 82	3.3.1
s 84	3.4
(1)	3.4
s 85	3.7
(2)	3.7
s 87	3.6
(4)	3.5
ss 88, 89	3.1
s 90	1.13, 1.13.1, 1.13.2, 1.13.3
(1)	1.13.3
(3)	1.13.1, 1.13.2
s 91	1.13.1
s 93A	2.5
s 93B	2.5
s 93C	2.5
ss 94, 95	3.1
s 96	2.11
s 97	2.9
(2)	2.9
s 104	2.9.6
(4)	1.9.1
s 105	2.9.6
(1), (2)	2.9.6
s 107	2.11, 4.6.2
ss 108–110	2.11
s 116 *et seq*	2.2.1
s 153	1.8
(1)	1.8
s 154(1)	1.8.1
(4), (5)	1.8.1
s 155	1.8.2
(1)	1.8.2
s 159	1.8.2
s 173	1.11
s 175(1)	1.8.2
s 176(1)	1.13.1
s 178	1.4, 1.10.2, 2.8
s 180(1)	4.2.1
(2)	4.2.2
(4)	4.1
s 181	4.2.3
ss 182–184	4.3.1
s 182(1)(a), (b)	4.3.3
(2), (3)	4.3.3
s 182A	4.3.1
(1)	4.3.2
s 182B	4.3.1
(1)	4.3.2
s 182C	4.3.1
(1)	4.3.2
s 182D	4.3.1, 4.3.3
(5)	4.3.3
(7)	4.3.3
s 183(a), (b)	4.3.3
s 184	4.4
(1)(a), (b)	4.3.3
ss 185–188	4.4
s 185(2)	4.4
s 186(4)	4.4
s 189	4.7
s 190	4.7
(4)–(6)	4.7
s 191(3)	4.5
s 191B	4.3.2
(2)	4.3.2
ss 191C–191D	4.3.2
ss 191F–191G	4.3.2
s 191G(2)	4.3.2
(5)	4.3.2
s 191H	4.3.2
(2)	4.3.2
s 191I	4.3.2
s 191L	4.3.2
ss 194–196	4.6.1
s 197	4.3.3, 4.6.2
s 198	4.6.2, 4.7
(1)(a)–(d)	4.6.2
(2)	4.6.2
s 198A	4.7
ss 199–202	4.6.2
s 204	4.6.2
s 206	4.2.3
s 208	4.2.3
s 236	1.4.5
Sch 1	17.3
Sch 2	4.7
Courts and Legal Services Act 1990	
s 8	9.8.1
Criminal Justice and Public Order Act 1994	18.4.4
s 85(3)	11.3

Table of Statutes

Data Protection Act 1984	13.2.1, 13.2.2, 13.2.3
Data Protection Act 1998	13.2.1–13.2.8
s 31	13.2.7
Sch 3	13.2.5
Defamation Act 1952	
s 3(1)	10.2.3
s 5	9.7.1
s 6	9.7.2
s 10	9.7.4
Defamation Act 1996	9.4, 9.7.3, 9.7.6
s 1	9.7.5
(1)(b), (c)	9.7.6
(5)	9.7.5
s 2	9.7.6, 9.9.3
(4)	6.9.3
s 8	9.10
(3)	9.10
s 9	9.10
s 13	9.7.3
s 14	9.7.3
European Communities Act 1972	2.9.6
Financial Services Act 1986	21.1
Human Rights Act 1998	12.1.4
Indecency with Children Act 1960	
s 1(1)	11.9
Law of Libel Amendment Act 1888	12.2
s 3	9.7.3
Legal Aid Act 1988	
Sch 2, Pt II, para 1	10.2.2
Obscene Publications Act 1959	11.4.3, 11.6, 11.7, 11.8
s 1(3)	11.2, 11.2.2, 11.2.4
s 2	11.3, 11.4.1
s 4	11.4.1
Obscene Publications Act 1964	11.3, 11.4.3
Partnership Act 1890	
s 1	7.2
Police and Criminal Evidence Act 1984	11.3
Protection of Children Act 1978	11.9
s 1	11.9
Public Order Act 1986	
s 17	12.1.1
ss 18, 19	12.1.2, 12.1.3
s 21	12.1.2, 12.1.3
s 22	12.1.2
s 25	12.1.2
Race Relations Act 1976	
s 3	12.1.1
Rehabilitation of Offenders Act 1974	9.7.1
s 8	9.7.1
Supreme Court Act 1969	
s 69	9.9.7
Theatres Act 1968	
s 4(1)	9.3
Trade Descriptions Act 1968	21.2.2
s 3(1)	21.2.2
s 5(2)	21.2.2
s 18	21.2.2
s 24(1)	21.2.2
s 25	21.2.2
Trade Marks Act 1938	21.6.3
s 4(1)(b)	21.6.3
s 24(1)(b)	21.4.4
Trade Marks Act 1994	21.4.1, 21.4.2, 21.4.3, 21.6.3
s 1(2)	21.4.1
s 2(1)	21.4.2
s 3(2)	21.4.1
s 9	21.4.2
(1)	21.4.2
(3)	21.4.3
s 10	21.4.2
(4), (5)	21.4.2
(6)	21.4.2, 21.4.4, 21.6.3
s 11	21.4.4
(2)	21.5.1
s 12	21.4.4
s 14	21.4.3
s 15(1)	21.4.3
s 16(1)	21.4.3
s 18	21.4.3
s 31	21.5.1
s 56	21.4.3
s 92(1), (2)	21.4.2
Video Recordings Act 1984	12.2, 17.6, 18.4.4
s 2(3)	18.4.4
s 9	18.4.4

TABLE OF STATUTORY INSTRUMENTS

References in the right-hand column are to paragraph numbers.

Broadcasting (Independent Productions) Order 1991, SI 1991/1408	15.1
Civil Procedure Rules 1998, SI 1998/3132	9.9.1
Part 24	9.10
Part 36	9.9.6
Sch 1, RSC Ord 82, r 3	9.5.1
Control of Misleading Advertisements Regulations 1988, SI 1988/915	20.3.1, 20.4, 21.2.3, 21.6.9
reg 6	21.2.3
Control of Misleading Advertisements (Amendment) Regulations 2000, SI 2000/914	21.6.3, 21.6.8, 21.6.9
Copyright and Related Rights Regulations 1996, SI 1996/2967	1.2, 4.2.1, 4.3.1, 17.5
Copyright and Rights in Databases Regulations 1997, SI 1997/3032	1.5.2
reg 13	1.5.5
Duration of Copyright and Rights in Performance Regulations 1995, SI 1995/3297	1.2, 1.10, 4.2.1
Personal Pension Scheme (Advertisements) Regulations 1990, SI 1990/1140	21.1
Price Indications (Method of Payment) Regulations 1991, SI 1991/199	21.2.4
Price Marking Order 1991, SI 1991/1382	21.2.4
Video Recordings (Labelling) (Amendment) Regulations 1995, SI 1995/2550	18.4.4

TABLE OF EC LEGISLATION AND OTHER MATERIALS

References in the right-hand column are to paragraph numbers

Directives

EC Directive 84/450 relating to misleading advertising (OJ 1984 L 250/17)	21.2.3, 21.6.9
EC Directive 85/552/EEC on Broadcasting	20.2.3
EC Directive 89/104/EC on Trade Marks Harmonisation	21.6.3
EC Directive 89/552/EEC on Transfrontier Television Broadcasting	11.6, 20.4
EC Directive 92/28/EEC concerning the advertising of medicinal products for human use	20.4
EC Directive 92/73/EEC on Homeopathic Medicinal Products	20.4
EC Directive 92/100 on Rental and Lending Rights	6.5, 8.2.4, 15.2.2, 17.5
EC Directive 93/98 on Copyright Harmonisation	15.2.2
EC Directive 95/46/EC concerning the protection of individuals with regard to the processing of personal data	13.2.1
EC Directive 96/9/EC (the 'Database Directive')	1.5.2
Recital 16	1.5.4
EU Directive on Comparative Advertising 97/55/EC	21.4.4, 21.6.1, 21.6.3, 21.6.9

Conventions and Agreements

Berne Copyright Convention	1.2.1, 3.1
Brussels Convention on Jurisdiction and the Enforcement of Judgments in Civil and Commercial Matters 1968	9.9.2
Art 2	9.9.2
Art 5(3)	9.9.2
Convention for the Protection of Human Rights and Fundamental Freedoms 1950 (European Convention on Human Rights)	14.1
Art 8	13.3
(2)	13.3
Art 10	9.8.2, 11.5, 12.1.4, 12.2
(2)	12.2
Convention for the Protection of Producers of Phonograms against Unauthorised Duplication of their Phonograms (the Phonogram Convention)	1.2.1
EC Treaty 1957 (as amended by the Treaty of Amsterdam)	
Art 81(2)	5.4.4
European Convention on Transfrontier Television	20.2.3, 20.4
International Convention for the Protection of Performers, Producers of Phonograms and Broadcasting Organisations 1961 (the Rome Convention)	1.2.1
Paris Convention for the Protection of Intellectual Property	21.4.3
Universal Copyright Convention	1.2.1

TABLE OF ABBREVIATIONS

ASA	Advertising Standards Authority
AURA	Artists United Recording Association
BACC	Broadcasting Advertising Clearance Centre
BBFC	British Board of Film Classification
BCASP	British Codes of Advertising and Sales Promotion
BCC	Broadcasting Complaints Commission
BECTU	Broadcasting, Entertainment, Cinematographic and Theatre Union
BPI	British Phonographic Industry
CAP	Committee of Advertising Practice
CDPA 1988	Copyright Designs and Patents Act 1988
CLA	Copyright Licensing Agency
CRRR 1996	Copyright and Related Rights Regulations 1996
DA Notice	Defence Advisory Notice
DGFT	Director-General of Fair Trading
ECHR	European Convention for the Protection of Human Rights and Fundamental Freedoms
ECJ	European Court of Justice
E&O	Errors and omissions
IMF	International Managers Forum
ITC	Independent Television Commission
MCPS	Mechanical Copyright Protection Society
MU	Musicians' Union
OPA 1959	Obscene Publications Act 1959
PA 1890	Partnership Act 1890
PACT	Producers Alliance for Cinema and Television
PAMRA	Performing Artists' Media Rights Association
PPL	Phonographic Performance Ltd
PRC	Performers Registration Centre
PRS	Performing Rights Society
RA	Radio Authority
the Rome Convention	International Convention for the Protection of Performers, Producers of Phonograms and Broadcasting Organisations 1961
UCC	Universal Copyright Convention
VPL	Video Performance Ltd
VRA 1984	Video Recordings Act 1984
WGGB	Writers Guild of Great Britain

Chapter 1

COPYRIGHT

1.1 INTRODUCTION

Copyright is a property right. It is a right to stop others from copying works without permission. There are many categories of copyright work which include applications as diverse as architecture, dress design and computer software.

It is important to consider copyright in the context of intellectual property generally. The practical overlap between copyright, trade marks, passing off and the law of confidence is substantial. The law of contract is also of particular importance when considering the terms and enforceability of any contract which deals with copyright and any other intellectual property rights.

1.2 SOURCES OF COPYRIGHT LAW

The Copyright Designs and Patents Act 1988 (CDPA 1988) is the principal statute governing UK copyright law. This statute has been amended by the Duration of Copyright and Rights in Performance Regulations 1995 and the Copyright and Related Rights Regulations 1996. This legislation applies not only to UK citizens but to many other nationals by virtue of the reciprocal protection granted in various international conventions. The CDPA 1988 is supplemented by case-law which has developed and interpreted the statute. The CDPA 1988 is the most recent copyright statute. The previous Copyright Acts of 1911 and 1956 are of considerable practical relevance. References in this chapter and in Chapters 2 to 4 are to the CDPA 1988 unless otherwise indicated.

1.2.1 International copyright protection

The CDPA 1988 is applied to authors from foreign countries by statutory instrument. The CDPA 1988 generally applies only to countries which give reciprocal protection to UK works. The countries specified in the statutory instrument are all members of one or other or both of the international copyright conventions.

Two international copyright conventions lay down minimum standards of protection for copyright owners between those countries which have ratified the conventions. These are the Berne Convention and the Universal Copyright Convention (UCC). Both have many members, and some countries, such as the UK, have ratified both treaties. Whilst both conventions lay down general rules for copyright protection, there are some important differences for the formalities of protection. Under the UCC, the copyright work must contain the © copyright symbol along with the name of the copyright proprietor and the year of first publication. There is no requirement for such a mark under UK law, although it is essential for wide international protection. International aspects of copyright infringement are beyond the scope of this book. The UK courts will not usually hear disputes where no infringement has taken place within the UK (*Tyburn Productions v Conan Doyle* [1991] Ch 75),

Chapter 1 contents
Introduction
Sources of copyright law
The subject matter of copyright
Original literary, dramatic, musical and artistic works
Databases
Sound recordings, films, broadcasts and cable programmes
Published editions
Conditions for protection
Duration of copyright
Authorship
Joint authorship
Ownership of copyright
Exploitation of copyright

although contracts may require claims to be settled in accordance with UK law and in the courts of England and Wales.

The International Convention for the Protection of Performers, Producers of Phonograms and Broadcasting Organisations 1961 (the Rome Convention) gives international protection to makers and producers of sound recordings as well as performers and broadcasters. The Rome Convention (in conjunction with the Convention for the Protection of Producers of Phonograms against Unauthorised Duplication of their Phonograms (the Phonogram Convention)) requires the use of the ℗ symbol, together with the year of first publication, and the names of the owner of the producer's rights and of the performers, on the packaging and usually on the recording itself as well. The ℗ symbol is the equivalent of the © symbol for other copyright works.

1.3 THE SUBJECT MATTER OF COPYRIGHT

There are detailed rules that need to be considered to determine whether copyright subsists in a given work.

As a starting point, s 1(1) of the CDPA 1988 provides that copyright may subsist in:

'(a) original literary, dramatic, musical or artistic works;
(b) sound recordings, films, broadcasts or cable programmes; and
(c) the typographical arrangement of published editions.'

This book is particularly concerned with (a) and (b) above.

Unlike for other forms of intellectual property (eg patents, registered design rights and trade marks), there is no registration requirement for copyright to subsist in a work. The position is different in other countries, such as the USA, where rights should be registered for full protection. There are various qualifying provisions which must be met for copyright protection under UK law (s 1(3)), which are discussed at **1.8**.

Ownership of copyright is quite distinct from ownership of the material which records that copyright work. Although a consumer buys a book, the rights in the actual copyright work are those granted by the author and publisher over the work.

1.4 ORIGINAL LITERARY, DRAMATIC, MUSICAL AND ARTISTIC WORKS

Literary, dramatic, musical and artistic works must be recorded in writing or otherwise (s 3(2)). Writing is defined as any form of notation or code (s 178). It does not matter if the work is recorded by or with the permission of the author (s 3(3)); copyright subsists immediately. There is no notice requirement under UK law, although international law has different requirements. A prudent author dates and names a work and puts it in safe keeping. Section 3 of the CDPA 1988 (discussed at **1.4.2–1.4.4**) elaborates on the meaning of literary, dramatic and musical works, and s 4 (discussed at **1.4.5–1.4.6**) on that of artistic works. The courts have considered the requirement for 'originality' as it relates to literary, dramatic, musical and artistic works.

1.4.1 Originality

Literary, dramatic, musical and artistic works must be 'original' to acquire protection. The question therefore arises as to what is original. In *University of London Press v University Tutorial Press* [1916] 2 Ch 601, it was held that 'original' does not mean that the work must be the expression of original or inventive thought. Except in the case of works of artistic craftsmanship, there is no requirement that a work should have any artistic or literary merit in order to obtain copyright protection.

In *Ladbroke (Football) Ltd v William Hill (Football) Ltd* [1964] 1 WLR 273, the court said that the word 'original' requires only that 'the work should not be copied but should originate from the author'.

An author needs to show he has expended his own skill and effort in order to justify protection. This requirement should be of little concern for most categories of work as they will obviously have the necessary originality. Skill and effort may lie in the selection and the obtaining of information, or the generation of information and ideas in the first place. This means an author may use the same source of information as another to create his own work, but he must not copy from another; he must use his own skill and effort.

Copyright is not a monopoly right. Two people could, in theory, write exactly the same tune or book quite independently of each other. If it could be established that one author had not copied or known about the other's work, then the copyright in the work which was published first in time would not be infringed by the second. Both would be original. Copyright prevents one person from benefiting from another's skill and labour or directly copying another's work. This can cause problems, as in *Independent Television Publications v Time Out Ltd* [1984] FRS 64, the result of which meant that no one else could publish TV schedules as the information could only be obtained from one source – the copyright work. This situation has since been rectified by the Broadcasting Act 1990 and the decision in *Magill TV Guide* (1991) 4 CMLR 586.

Whilst original works require skill and effort to justify protection, that protection extends only to the language or composition or the chosen form of expression. It is often said that copyright does not protect ideas but only the expression of ideas (see, eg, *Football League v Littlewoods Pools Ltd* [1959] Ch 637). The television presenter Hughie Green took action against a New Zealand broadcaster who broadcast a programme which was very similar to his own programme *Opportunity Knocks*. He failed to stop the broadcast of the programme because his programme was too imprecise to qualify as a literary or dramatic work. Essentially, all that was copied was the idea for the programme (*Green v Broadcasting Corporation of New Zealand* [1989] 2 All ER 1056).

1.4.2 Literary works

Section 3(1) provides that 'literary work' means any work, other than a dramatic or musical work, which is written, spoken or sung, and includes a table or compilation and a computer program.

A common example of a literary work is a book – it may be a work of fiction or a textbook. Articles in a newspaper or magazine benefit from protection as literary works. Since a literary work does not need to have any particular literary merit, copyright protection is not limited to novels, poems, articles or the lyrics of a song.

Case-law has established categories of information which may be protectable such as examination papers (*University of London Press v University Tutorial Press* [1916] 2 Ch 601); pools coupons (*Ladbroke (Football) Ltd v William Hill (Football) Ltd* [1964] 1 WLR 273); television programme listings (*Independent Television Publications v Time Out Ltd* [1984] ERS 64); and letters and business letters (*Donoghue v Allied Newspapers Ltd* [1938] Ch 106). The protection is enhanced by the recent introduction of the Database Right.

Names and slogans

Various categories of works have been refused protection as literary works on a de minimus principle. In *Exxon Corporation v Exxon Insurance Consultants International Ltd* [1982] Ch 119, the claimant invested considerable time and money in finding a suitable name for its oil business only to find the defendant insurance business using the same name. In a subsequent copyright infringement action by the claimant, the court held that the word 'Exxon', even though it was original, did not qualify as a literary work. The name was simply an artificial combination of letters that provided no information, no instruction and gave no pleasure.

Accordingly, the titles of books and magazines will not usually qualify for protection as literary works.

In *Francis Day & Hunter Ltd v Twentieth Century Fox Corporation Ltd* [1940] AC 112, it was held that the copyright in the words of a song was not infringed by the use of the song's title as the title of a film. The film did not use any other parts of the song. In this case, the use of the title was not in itself substantial enough to constitute an infringement, especially when the song title was used in a very different context.

In such circumstances, a claimant may have recourse under the law of passing off or it may be appropriate to register a trade mark. In *Ladbroke (Football) Ltd v William Hill (Football) Ltd* (above), it was said that, whilst as a general rule titles will not be protected, in a proper case a title would qualify for copyright protection. Similarly, there will rarely be copyright in an advertisement slogan such as 'youthful appearances are social necessities, not luxuries' (*Sinanide v La Maison Kosmeo* (1928) 139 LT 365). Advertisements may be capable of copyright protection as literary or artistic works (see *Newsgroup Newspapers Ltd v Mirror Group Newspapers* [1989] FSR 126) and, where appropriate, films, sound recordings and broadcasts also qualify.

Storylines

It is difficult to infringe copyright in a novel simply by adopting the same story. Whilst repeating the story or information used may result in a very similar creation, unless the two are the same or substantially the same and provided they are sufficiently original, copyright can exist in both works with no question of infringement. Two film makers proposing to make films of the life of World War One flying ace 'The Red Baron' can do so as long as one does not copy the other's film or script.

Copyright protection for characters

Common ideas and themes do not merit copyright protection of their own (see *Kelly v Cinema House Ltd* [1928–1935] MacG Cop Cas 391). However, the author of a story may be able to claim copyright protection for particular elements of the story such as the character and order of incidents. A character existing in myth or legend, such as Robin Hood, will not warrant protection except to the extent that the precise dialogue written by the author of the work is reproduced elsewhere. A character created for the story or work in question may merit copyright protection. The approach suggested in *International Copyright Law and Practice* (looseleaf, Sweet & Maxwell) is to consider:

(1) whether the character as originally conceived was sufficiently developed to command copyright protection; and
(2) whether the alleged infringer copied the development and not merely a broader, or more abstract, outline.

A film or work recounting the exploits of a fictional English spy could not stop another producer or writer from using a similar theme. However, a producer or writer who creates a similar character doing similar things may, in the right circumstances, infringe the character's copyright. Alternative means of protection may be available through artistic and dramatic copyright, passing off and trade mark protection.

News

A useful illustration of the difference between ideas and the expression of ideas can be seen with the reporting of current events. Whilst information itself is not subject to copyright, the actual expressions used to report the information are protected as literary or other copyright works.

In *Walter v Steinkopff* [1892] 3 Ch 489, one news service copied the form of another's news verbatim. As a result, there was an infringement of copyright. Where it is simply the information which is used and not the actual form or material itself, there is no copyright infringement. Provided the actual expression of the news items is not copied from someone else's reporting, no problems should arise.

In the case of news items, there will usually be other sources available. If the information is publicly available (and there is no question of breach of confidence or contract) then there is no reason why the news item cannot simply be re-cast in another form (which will in itself attract copyright protection) and be conveyed in that new form.

1.4.3 Dramatic works

Section 3(1) of the CDPA 1988 defines a 'dramatic work' as including a work of dance or mime. Elements of a work may qualify for different copyright protection as a literary work, musical works and dramatic works. A dramatic work which contains musical elements may be protected under dramatic, literary and musical categories. Copyright protects the dramatic elements (stage directions, etc) separately from the literary elements (script). A dramatic work is one which is capable of being performed, for example, by acting or dancing. A dramatic work is distinct from the literary elements of the work.

Once again, a de minimis principle applies. In *Green v Broadcasting Corporation of New Zealand* [1989] 2 All ER 1056, the Privy Council held that the features which constituted the 'format' of a television show, which were simply accessories used in the presentation of, and additional to, other dramatic or musical performances, did not attract protection. A dramatic work must be one which is capable of being performed and, in this case, there were no sufficient materials to constitute a dramatic work. The features of the show for which protection was sought did not form a cohesive whole capable of performance. The format of *Opportunity Knocks* consisted of the use of a clapometer and various catchphrases which the court held did not amount to a dramatic work for the purposes of copyright protection. In *Tate v Fullbrook* [1908] 1 KB 821, a character's acting style and the scenic effects used in a comedy sketch were not protected as dramatic works since they were not capable of being printed and published. It appears that here, as in *Green*, there was insufficient certainty in the dramatic format for which protection was sought. The recent decision of *Norowzian v Arks Ltd and Others (No 2)* [2000] FSR 363 confirms the general approach where a dramatic work was defined as 'a work of action, with or without words or music, which is capable of being performed before an audience'.

The licensing of TV format rights is important for the international exploitation of many familiar TV game shows and situation comedies. Effectively, a form of gentlemen's agreement is in place between major TV producers and broadcasters ensuring that formats may be exploited by producers. This exploitation takes the form of a contractual licence by the owner of the format to the third party who wishes to use it. Accordingly, the protection is based as much in contract as in copyright law. Producers and broadcasters are advised to record the format with which they are dealing in as much detail as possible in order to establish its protection as a literary or dramatic work. The names of characters particularly associated with the show may also be protected using trade mark or passing off protection, and by adopting appropriate licensing and merchandising arrangements. Special protection for formats has also been suggested in a DTI consultative paper.

1.4.4 Musical works

The CDPA 1988 defines a 'musical work' as a work consisting of music, exclusive of any words or action intended to be sung, spoken or performed with the music (s 3(1)). The copyright for the music of a song is distinct from the literary copyright in the lyric and, indeed, any dramatic copyright if the music is accompanied by a dance or other type of performance. Copyright in musical works is in the composition itself. Quite separate rights arise in respect of any sound recording or broadcast of a musical work. There are separate copyrights, perhaps in separate ownership, for music, lyrics and recording.

1.4.5 Artistic works

Section 4(1) defines an 'artistic work' as:

> '(a) a graphic work, photograph, sculpture or collage, irrespective of artistic quality;
> (b) a work of architecture, being a building or a model for a building; or
> (c) a work or artistic craftsmanship.'

Most artistic works are protected irrespective of artistic quality. The result of this is that as long as some effort is expended making the artistic work original it is protected – personal taste will not matter. Section 4(2) defines a 'graphic work' as including a painting, drawing, diagram, map, chart or plan, and any engraving, etching, lithograph, woodcut or similar work.

Section 17(3) provides that copying an artistic work includes the making of a copy in three dimensions of a two-dimensional work and the making of a copy in two dimensions of a three-dimensional work. Copyright in works of architecture may be infringed in this fashion. The law of copyright infringement as it relates to dimensional shift infringement is complicated by the relationship between copyright and unregistered design law. By virtue of CDPA 1988, s 51, copyright in a design document is not infringed by making an article using that design document unless the finished article is itself a work of artistic craftsmanship. It is possible to rely on unregistered design law for a cause of action as three-dimensional objects (but not their surface decoration) are protected regardless of merit as long as they are original, although the remedies available under unregistered design law do not include prosecution for criminal offences. If copyright subsists in an article, s 236 operates to suppress the unregistered design right in favour of the copyright. The problem remains in establishing exactly which three-dimensional articles warrant protection as works of artistic craftsmanship.

1.4.6 Photographs

A photograph is defined as being 'a recording of light or other radiation on any medium on which an image is produced or from which an image may by any means be produced, and which is not part of a film' (s 4(2)). Single frames of a film are capable of protection as part of a film. The definition is wide enough to cover holograms. No artistic merit is required for copyright protection. Although photographs may not be copied, the scenes they represent can be independently photographed.

1.5 DATABASES

1.5.1 Introduction

Until (and including) 27 March 1996, 'databases' (broadly, collections of information such as directories) were protected under English law by copyright as a compilation if the compilation involved sufficient skill and labour according to the usual copyright requirements.

1.5.2 The new Rules

Databases created after 27 March 1996 will now only get copyright protection if they satisfy extra rules: Copyright and Rights in Databases Regulations 1997, SI 1997/3032, implementing EC Directive 96/9/EC (the 'Database Directive'). The 1997 Regulations came into force on 1 January 1998.

1.5.3 What is a database?

Under s 3A of the 1988 Act, a database is a collection of independent works, data or other materials which are:

(a) arranged in a systematic or methodical way; and
(b) individually accessible by electronic or other means.

A database should be considered as distinct from its contents – akin to the structure of a computer program.

Section 3(1) of the 1988 Act has been amended to add 'database' to the list of, potentially 'literary', works and to exclude it from categorisation as a compilation.

1.5.4 Copyright protection

Under s 3A(2) of the 1988 Act, the rules for full protection of a database by copyright are:

- as with any other literary work, a database must be original; but
- a database literary work will only be original if, by reason of selection and arrangement of the database contents, the database is the author's 'own intellectual creation'. No aesthetic, qualitative or other criteria are applicable (Database Directive, Recital 16).

So, this apparently increases the copyright threshold for 'databases' as defined.

1.5.5 The Database Right

This right is separate from the copyright, if any, in the database. The right exists in a database where there is:

> 'a substantial investment in obtaining, verifying or presenting the contents of the database' (reg 13, Copyright and Right in Databases Regulations 1997, SI 1997/3032).

It lasts for 15 years from the end of the year of creation of the database.

This right saves many if the arguments that have gone on in the past about the protection of databases. The right applies to databases whether held as paper records or in electronic form.

The database right was successfully used at first instance in the *British Horseracing Board v William Hill Organisation Ltd* [2001] 2 CMLR 12, ChD. The defendant was using information derived from the claimant's database on the horse races taking place that day and the runners and riders in those races. The defendant used the information without consent in order to operate its internet betting service. The claimant succeeded in its infringement action.

Later, the Court of Appeal released its judgment in *British Horseracing Board Ltd v William Hill Organisation Ltd* [2001] All ER (D) 431 (Jul), CA.

After re-précising the facts and decisions – with great credit given to and almost verbatim from the original judgment – the Court of Appeal concluded:

> 'It is not in dispute that this court, not being a court of last instance, has a discretion, and we have been reminded of what the European Court of Justice said in *CILFIT v Ministry of Health* [1982] ECR 3415 at 3430:
>
>> "Finally, the correct application of Community law may be so obvious as to leave no scope for any reasonable doubt as to the manner in which the question raised is to be resolved. Before it comes to the conclusion that such is the case, the national court or tribunal must be convinced that the matter is equally obvious to the courts of the other Member States and to the Court of Justice. Only if those conditions are satisfied, may the national court or tribunal refrain from submitting the question to the Court of Justice and take upon itself the responsibility for resolving it."
>
> We have also been referred to the remarks of Sir Thomas Bingham MR in *R v International Stock Exchange ex parte Else Ltd* [1993] QB 534 at 545:
>
>> "I understand the correct approach in principle of a national court (other than a final court of appeal) to be quite clear: if the facts have been found and the

Community law issue is critical to the court's final decision, the appropriate course is ordinarily to refer the issue to the Court of Justice unless the national court can with complete confidence resolve the issue itself. In considering whether it can with complete confidence resolve the issue itself the national court must be fully mindful of the differences between national and Community legislation, of the pitfalls which face a national court venturing into what may be an unfamiliar field of, the need for uniform interpretation throughout the Community and of the great advantages enjoyed by the Court of Justice in construing Community instruments. If the national court has any real doubt, it should ordinarily refer'".

On that basis, the Court of Appeal felt:

- it could not say that it could resolve the issues with complete confidence, nor
- that there was no scope for any reasonable doubt, still less
- that the matter was equally obvious to the courts of other member states.

So, the Court of Appeal ordered that the relevant questions be referred to the European Court of Justice (ECJ).

Finally, pending determination by the ECJ even though the Court of Appeal could not say it with 'complete confidence' the Court of Appeal said this:

'If the interpretation question to which this case gives rise had to be determined without the luxury of a reference we think it likely that we would support the conclusions of the judge for the reasons which he explains.'

1.6 SOUND RECORDINGS, FILMS, BROADCASTS AND CABLE PROGRAMMES

Sound recordings and films are, in most cases, 'derivative works', ie they are based on other copyright works. Broadcasts and cable transmissions are often derivative works as either they consist entirely of previously recorded films or sound recordings, or they are live transmissions of copyright works. Broadcasts and films may also be of subject matter which is unprotectable under copyright or performers' rights legislation (such as sporting events). The sale of broadcast rights to sporting events is based on contract law and a simple licence to enter property. In the absence of a contractual restriction on tickets, there is nothing to stop spectators or photographers from taking photographs or filming events (*Sports and General Press Agency Ltd v 'Our Dogs' Publishing Ltd* [1916] KB 880).

Originality is not a criteria for the protection of sound recordings, films, broadcasts and cable transmissions (s 1(1)(b)).

The distinction between derivative works and the underlying rights is important. A simple example is the recording of a song. There is a copyright in the song itself and copyright in the sound recording of the song. The song itself is the underlying work. The permission of the copyright owner of the underlying rights (in this example, the song) must be obtained prior to use of the underlying work.

1.6.1 Sound recordings

A 'sound recording' is defined in s 5(1) as:

'(a) a recording of sounds, from which the sounds may be reproduced; or

(b) a recording of the whole or of any part of a literary, dramatic or musical work, from which sounds reproducing the work or part may be produced',

and this is regardless of the media on which the recording is made or the method by which the sounds are reproduced or produced.

1.6.2 Films

A 'film' is defined as a recording on any medium from which a moving image may by any means be produced (s 5(1)).

This clearly covers video recordings and is wide enough to embrace new technology such as CD-ROMs, interactive media and the visual aspects of computer games.

Section 5(2) provides that copyright will not exist in a sound recording or film which is a copy of a previous sound recording or film.

1.6.3 Broadcasts

A broadcast is defined in s 6(1) as a transmission by wireless telegraphy of visual images, sounds or other information which:

(a) is capable of being lawfully received by members of the public; or
(b) is transmitted for presentation to members of the public.

Copyright will not subsist in a broadcast which infringes the copyright in another broadcast or cable programme.

1.6.4 Cable programmes

A cable programme is defined in s 7 as any item included in a cable programme service. 'Cable programme service' is defined as a service consisting wholly or mainly in sending visual images, sounds or other information by means of a telecommunications system, ie by electronic means.

There is no copyright in a cable programme which infringes copyright in a broadcast or other cable programme.

1.7 PUBLISHED EDITIONS

Copyright also subsists in the typographical arrangement of published editions. A published edition is defined as: 'the whole or any part of one or more literary, dramatic or musical works'.

These provisions are aimed at giving a publisher of a work (whether in or out of copyright) some protection in the typesetting and arrangement of the published work. This can be seen as a reflection on the time and effort which publishers put into formatting and typesetting works prior to publication. No copyright subsists in the typographical arrangement of a book which reproduces the arrangement of a previous edition. Copyright will not subsist indefinitely in any given typographical arrangement.

1.8 CONDITIONS FOR PROTECTION

There are three main conditions which must be satisfied before any work will qualify for copyright protection. Copyright does not subsist in a work unless the qualifying requirements are met (s 1(3)). The relevant requirements as to qualifying conditions for all works are contained in s 153. Copyright does not subsist unless qualifications as to:

(a) the author; *or*
(b) the country of first publication; *or*
(c) in the case of broadcasts, the country from which the broadcast was sent,

are met (s 153(1)).

These conditions are not cumulative. A work qualifies for copyright protection if it falls within (a), (b) or (c) above. The author of a copyright work is frequently asked to provide a contractual warranty confirming that he is a 'qualifying person'. This ensures protection for the work or at least a breach of contract claim if the warranty is incorrect.

1.8.1 Qualifying authors

A work qualifies for copyright protection if the author was at the 'material time' a 'qualifying person' (s 154(1)). A 'qualifying person' is defined as a British citizen, a British dependent territories citizen, a British national (overseas), a British overseas citizen, a British subject or a British protected person within the meaning of the British Nationality Act 1981, or an individual domiciled or resident in the UK or another country to which the relevant provisions of the Act extend, or a body incorporated under the law of a part of the UK or of another country to which the relevant provisions of the Act extend. The Act applies to most countries in the world.

The 'material time' in relation to a literary, dramatic, musical or artistic work is defined in s 154(4) as:

'(a) in the case of an unpublished work, when the work was made or, if the making of the work extended over a period, a substantial part of that period;
(b) in the case of a published work, when the work was first published or, if the author had died before that time, immediately before his death.'

The material time in relation to other descriptions of work is defined in s 154(5) as:

'(a) in the case of a sound recording or film, when it was made;
(b) in the case of a broadcast, when the broadcast was made;
(c) in the case of a cable programme, when the programme was included in a cable programme service;
(d) in the case of the typographical arrangement of a published edition, when the edition was first published.'

1.8.2 The place of first publication

All types of works, except broadcasts and cable programmes, qualify for copyright protection under s 155(1) if they were first published in:

(1) the UK, or
(2) another country to which the relevant provisions of the CDPA 1988 have been extended.

It is also possible for works to qualify for protection where they were first published in a country to which an order has been made under s 159 of the CDPA 1988.

Under s 155, a work must be published to qualify for protection. 'Publication' is defined as the issue of copies to the public (s 175(1)). Publication is also defined to include making copies available to the public by means of an electronic retrieval system. In *Francis Day & Hunter v Feldman* [1914] 2 Ch 728, the sheet music of the song 'You Made Me Love You (I Didn't Want to Do it)' was printed in the USA. Copies were sent to the UK and six copies were placed on sale in a shop in Charing Cross. The issue was whether this was sufficient to constitute publication. The anticipated demand for the song was small, and it was held that this was a good publication in the UK because it was intended to satisfy such demand as there was. However, a publication 'which is merely colourable and not intended to satisfy the reasonable requirements of the public' does not constitute publication.

1.9 DURATION OF COPYRIGHT

There are various rules for the duration of copyright which depends on the type of work under consideration. These periods have been amended by the Duration of Copyright and Rights in Performances Regulations 1995, which came into force on 1 January 1996, and which increase copyright protection to 70 years (see **1.9.2**).

1.9.1 Literary, dramatic or musical works

Copyright lasts for 70 years from the end of the calendar year in which the author dies (s 12).

Copyright in a work of unknown authorship expires 70 years from the end of the year it was written, or 70 years from the end of the year it was made available to the public (s 12(2)). A number of presumptions operate to counter this potentially perpetual copyright. Section 57(1) provides that copyright is not infringed if it is not possible to ascertain by reasonable enquiry the identity of the author, and it is reasonable to assume that the copyright has expired or the author died 70 years or more before the beginning of the calendar year in which the act in relation to the work was done. Section 104(4) also contains a presumption that where a work is anonymous, the publisher of the work as first published is presumed to be the owner of the copyright at that time.

1.9.2 Sound recordings and films

Copyright lasts for 50 years from the end of the year in which a sound recording was made and, if not released immediately, the copyright will expire at the end of the period of 50 years from the end of the calendar year in which it was released. Section 13A(3) provides that a sound recording is 'released' when it is first published, played in public, broadcast, or included in a cable programme service. Unauthorised acts are ignored.

Section 175 defines publication as being the issue of copies to the public.

The term of copyright in films is increased to 70 years from the death of the last to survive of the principal director, the author of the film screenplay, the author of the film dialogue and the composer of music specifically created for and used in the film (s 13B).

The meaning of 'author' is extended beyond the definition in s 9(2) to include the principal director of the film. This does not apply to films made on or before 30 June 1994.

1.9.3 Broadcasts and cable programmes

For broadcasts and cable programmes, copyright expires 50 years from the end of the calendar year in which the broadcast was made or the programme included in a cable programme service (s 14(2)).

Section 14(5) ensures that the copyright in repeats of broadcasts or cable programmes expires at the same time as the copyright in the original. Accordingly, no copyright arises in respect of a repeat broadcast or cable programme where such is included in a service after the expiry of copyright in the original broadcast or programme.

1.9.4 Typographical arrangement

The copyright in the typographical arrangement of a published edition expires at the end of the period of 25 years from the end of the calendar year in which the edition was first published (s 15).

1.9.5 Revived copyright

Copyright in works which had expired before 1 July 1995 subsists as if the regulations had been in effect at the date the work was made. This will affect the works of authors who died between 1925 and 1945. The provisions for ownership of the extended or revived copyright are as follows:

- in relation to existing works, the person who is the owner at 1 November 1995 owns the extended copyright;
- for a revived work:

    (a) where copyright was subject to an exclusive licence immediately before expiry of copyright, ownership vests in that licensee; and
    (b) in any other case, the person who was the owner immediately before expiry shall be first owner of the revived copyright;

- in relation to an existing work where the owner at 1 November 1995 is the owner by virtue of an assignment of the copyright and the assignment terminates earlier than the date on which the subsisting copyright expires, the person to whom copyright would have reverted thereafter shall, on 1 November 1995, be the first owner of copyright in that work, even though the date of termination of the assignment falls after 1 November 1995.

An agreement relating to:

(a) extended copyright entered into before 1 November 1995; or
(b) revived copyright prior to expiry of copyright,

makes provision for vesting of ownership of the extended or revived copyright upon the coming into existence of that right ownership of the copyright vests in accordance with that agreement.

Copyright is not infringed where:

- an act is done in relation to a copyright work pursuant to an agreement entered into before 1 January 1995;
- copies of a work are issued to the public where the copy was made before 1 July 1995 and copyright did not subsist at that time; or
- a restricted act is performed in pursuance to an arrangement made at a time when the name and address of a person entitled to authorise the act could not be ascertained by reasonable enquiry.

1.10 AUTHORSHIP

Authorship and ownership are distinct concepts in relation to copyright. The author of a work means the person who creates it (s 9). The author of a work is the first owner of any copyright in it (s 11). The author of certain works (as distinct from the owner) is entitled to the moral rights in the work, the benefits of which remain with the author despite the fact that someone else may initially or subsequently own the work. Moral rights are discussed further in Chapter 4.

1.10.1 Authorship – literary, dramatic, musical and artistic works

The author of a work is the person who creates it (s 9). Accordingly, it should usually be obvious who is the author of a given work. For example, with a novel, the author of the work will be the person who writes the novel. In relation to a piece of music, the composer will be the author of the work. A person who contributes titles, ideas, scenic effects and catch-lines, as in *Tate v Thomas* [1921] 1 Ch 503, may not be an author for copyright purposes. It is a question of fact and evidence as to whether the contributions were given any material form or were ideas. In *Tate*, the contributions of the claimant were insufficient to hold that he was a joint author (see further *Wiseman v Weidenfeld & Nicolson* [1985] FSR 525).

The position of 'ghost writers' will usually be governed by a contract between the person who provides the material for the work and the actual writer of the work. In the absence of any such agreement, the position is that the author of the work is the person that fixes it and gives it form. However, where a work is simply dictated to a secretary or shorthand writer, the author is the person dictating the work and not the person transcribing it (see *Donoghue v Allied Newspapers Ltd* [1938] Ch 106).

For the purposes of copyright, the author of a photograph is the photographer.

1.10.2 Authorship – sound recordings and films

The author of a sound recording is the producer (s 9(2)(aa)). The authors of a film are the producer and the principal director (s 9(2)(ab)). Accordingly, a film is usually a work of joint authorship (see **1.11**). The producer is defined as the person who makes the arrangements necessary for the creation of the work (s 178).

1.10.3 Authorship – broadcasts and cable programmes

The person making the broadcast, invariably a company, is its author. In the case of a broadcast which relays another broadcast by reception and immediate re-transmission, the person making the first broadcast is the author. Section 6(3) provides that the person making a broadcast is the person transmitting the programme if he has responsibility to any extent for its content and, further, any person who makes the arrangements necessary for the programme's transmission. Broadcasts will often involve more than one party and, strictly speaking, there may be two makers of a broadcast for the purposes of the legislation. In such a case, the work will be treated as a work of joint authorship (see s 10(2)).

In the case of a cable programme, the person providing the cable programme service in which the programme is included is the author (s 9(2)(c)).

1.10.4 Authorship – typographical arrangements

In the case of the typographical arrangement of a published edition, the publisher is the author (s 9(2)(d)).

1.11 JOINT AUTHORSHIP

Many works will not be the result of one person's endeavours. A work of 'joint authorship' is defined in s 10 as a work produced by the collaboration of two or more authors in which the contribution of each author is not distinct from that of the other author or authors.

If one person writes lyrics and the other the music for a song, then that is not a work of joint authorship. If both authors collaborate and assist with the ideas for both lyrics and music, then that is a work of joint authorship. In each case, there will be two separate copyrights in the work: the copyright in the lyrics, and the copyright in the music. If one person simply provides the materials to record the work, such as paper and pen or a tape recorder and cassette, that person may own the materials on which the work is 'recorded' but not the copyright itself.

The duration of copyright in a work of joint authorship expires at the end of the period of 70 years from the end of the calendar year in which the last author dies (s 12(3)).

In *Prior v Lansdowne Press Ltd* [1977] RPC 511, three people claimed to be joint authors of a work, two of whom actually contributed to the writing and the other acted as a compiler of the work. Whilst the three were free to arrange ownership of the work as they wished, the actual writers were the authors for copyright purposes. Copyright distinguishes between joint authorship and joint ownership. As far as ownership is concerned, the parties can reach any agreement they like. The question of authorship relates to the contribution to the work. In joint authorship, each individual author must be an 'author' for the purposes of s 9(1). Each author must have been responsible to some degree for reducing the work to a material form.

It is clear from s 173 that if copyright in a work is owned by more than one person jointly then the agreement of all the owners is required for any exclusive dealing with the work. The author of a work under s 11(1) is the first owner of any copyright in it. Quite how ownership is divided will vary. Joint authors may be either tenants in common or joint tenants. The law usually presumes they are tenants in common.

In *Mail Newspapers plc v Express Newspapers plc* [1987] FSR 90, a husband agreed that the claimants could publish wedding photographs, but the defendants published them instead. The claimants claimed an infringement of their exclusive rights. The defendants argued that the husband and the wife were joint owners of the copyright and, as joint owners, they both had to consent to any dealings with the photographs. The court held that both the owners had to consent to the exploitation of the work. Despite this, the defendants were prohibited from publishing on the grounds of breach of confidence.

1.12 OWNERSHIP OF COPYRIGHT

1.12.1 Author as first owner

The author of a work is the first owner of the copyright in the work. Subject to the discussion at **1.11**, the person who creates the work – whether it is a song or a novel or a painting – owns the copyright in that work. It is that person who can deal with the copyright in the work. Authors frequently sign contracts granting rights to individuals and companies. These agreements may entitle others to some or all of the rights in a work.

1.12.2 Employees

There is an exception to this general rule. Section 11(2) provides that where a literary, dramatic, musical or artistic work is made by an employee in the course of his employment, the employer is the first owner of any copyright in the work, subject to any agreement to the contrary. It is not enough that a literary, dramatic, musical or artistic work is made by an employee; it must also be made in the course of employment. If a work is made in the course of employment, then the employer will be the first owner of any copyright in the work, subject to an agreement to the contrary.

In industries which employ creative people such as the advertising, music, and film and TV industries, it is in the interests of the employer (and indeed the employee) to set out at the beginning of their relationship the arrangements which are to exist between them regarding works produced. Express assignments or licences of copyright are usually taken. Particular problems can arise where employees devote time to creating works in what they may well regard as being their 'spare time'. Cases turn on their own facts, and particular regard will be had to such matters as working hours, use of the employer's facilities, and whether the contract is viewed as a contract of service or a contract for services.

In *Byrne v Statist Co* [1914] 1 KB 622, an employee was on the regular staff of a newspaper but made a translation of a work in his spare time and for a separate fee. He was held to own the copyright in the translation because translations were not part of his normal duties. Where there is any doubt as to whether the employer owns the copyright, either an express assignment of rights should be taken or, alternatively, the employee should be joined as a claimant in any proceedings.

If an employee chooses outside his normal office hours to develop competing works, for example works of a similar nature to those that he would normally be employed to produce, then there may be a breach of contract or a breach of a fiduciary duty which prevents the employee from asserting that the work was not created in the course of employment (see *Missing Link Software v Magee* [1989] FSR 361). Copyright would then vest in the employer. Any attempt by the employee to deal with the work would amount to conversion or theft in addition to a possible copyright infringement.

1.12.3 Commissioned works

Where a work is commissioned from an independent third party, ownership of copyright should be dealt with at the time the work is commissioned. In the absence of an employer/employee relationship, s 11(2) does not apply. Express contractual provision should be made dealing with the copyright. The CDPA 1988 makes no express provision for commissioned works. A written agreement evidencing any dealing with copyright is preferable, although not always essential.

A court may decide the commissioning party has a beneficial interest, as in *Warner v Gestetner Ltd* [1988] EIPRD 89, where the court held that there had been a beneficial assignment of copyright in a number of drawings.

Alternatively, there may be an implied licence of copyright. A licence will not be implied between parties simply because it is reasonable to do so, rather it must be the intention of the parties.

In one case, an architect was commissioned to draw building plans for the purpose of obtaining planning permission for some houses. The site was subsequently sold with the benefit of planning permission, and the plans transferred to the purchaser. The original commissioner and the purchaser both had an implied licence to use the plans for the purpose of building the houses. The court restricted the implied licence to use of the plans for building houses on the site in question. If the purchasers had attempted to use the plans to build houses to those specifications on another site, they would have been prevented from so doing (see *Blair v Osborne & Tompkins* [1971] 2 WLR 503). A licence of copyright should be obtained in writing on terms agreed between the parties.

The problem arose in *Ray v Classic FM* [1998] FSR 622, where the claimant developed a copyright database for the defendants. The defendants licensed the work overseas, and the claimant claimed it had no right to do so. The consultancy agreement between the parties contained no express terms as to ownership of the work. The claimant successfully claimed the defendants' rights were limited to a licence of copyright for the UK.

1.12.4 Ownership of other works

The author of sound recordings, films, broadcasts, cable programmes or typographical arrangements will be the first owner for copyright purposes. The arrangements necessary for creating the copyright work may be undertaken by someone on behalf of, or as agent for, another party. In this situation, the principal, not the agent, is the owner of the copyright in the resulting work. Such a situation may arise where a company asks a third party to make the necessary arrangements on its behalf. It is a question of fact as to who undertakes the necessary arrangements for authorship to be established under s 9(2). (See further *A&M Records v Video Collection International Ltd* [1995] EMLR 25.)

1.13 EXPLOITATION OF COPYRIGHT

Most copyright owners want to exploit their rights. This may be done on a 'bulk' basis by collection agencies such as the Performing Rights Society or Phonographic Performance Limited. On the other hand, copyright owners often have individual needs and will exploit works individually. Copyright is a form of personal property and may be dealt with by assignment, by testamentary disposition or by operation of law (s 90). Copyright is exploited by way of assignment or licence.

The first and subsequent owners of copyright works have a number of options as to the manner of exploitation of the copyrights. For example, they may decide:

- to keep their rights and not exploit them in any way; or
- to exploit the copyright material themselves (although this inevitably involves a third party's co-operation at some stage to print, distribute or sell the work); or
- to assign rights to a third party; or
- to license third parties to do otherwise prohibited acts in relation to the work.

Copyright may be divided and exploited in a number of ways. The method of exploitation essentially depends upon the medium and not the choice of the individual owner. The ways of dividing and exploiting rights are extremely important, especially when considering the most effective way of exploiting particular works. An author may be advised to appoint a UK publisher to exploit his novel within the UK, but that publisher may not be the best placed to exploit the novel in the USA. Likewise, the UK publisher may not be the best placed to exploit the film rights or the dramatic rights in the novel. As technological advances take place, the author may have to decide who should exploit the CD-ROM and other electronic rights. Great care must be taken in defining the rights, territory and duration of the agreement.

1.13.1 Assignments and licences

An assignment is usually an outright sale of rights, whereas a licence is a contractual permission to use rights subject to ongoing obligations. An assignment may also be by way of gift or testamentary disposition. The distinction between an assignment and a licence must not always be entirely clear. An assignment of copyright is not effective unless it is in writing and signed by, or on behalf of, the assignor (s 90(3)). The assignor will usually sign the document himself although, in the case of a company, s 176(1) requires the company seal be affixed to satisfy this requirement. Whoever signs a document must have authority to do so, and this authority should be checked where an agent is dealing with copyrights.

Assignments and licences may be limited in a number of ways. The dealing may be limited to:

- one or more, but not all, of the things which the owner has the exclusive right to do; and/or
- part, but not the whole, of the period of copyright protection (s 90).

An assignment or licence may thus be absolute or partial. Under s 90, the way rights are divided is not limited to categories of exploitation but can extend to the length of time for which a right is to be assigned or licensed. If an assignor attempts to divide rights territorially it takes effect on a licence of copyright. The Act makes no explicit provision for territorial division by assignment.

An assignment may be of future as well as existing copyright (s 91), and in such cases, it is usual to specify that the assignment takes effect on a present assignment of future copyright.

1.13.2 Form of assignment

Although s 90(3) requires an assignment to be in writing to transfer the legal and beneficial title, the content of the document which forms the assignment is not specified by the statute. An assignment may be in very simple words or it may be a more complicated document containing a number of obligations. There are various problems that can arise with both assignments and licences, even though the s 90 requirements may have been followed. An assignment by the original owner is often also referred to as a 'grant of copyright'.

The question of whether copyright has been assigned, and what form of words will suffice to do this, is sometimes problematic. A receipt stating that a sum of money was received 'inclusive of all copyrights' was deemed sufficient to assign the copyright in a number of card designs (see *Savory Ltd v The World of Golf Ltd* [1914] 2 Ch 566).

It is usual commercial practice to include a more comprehensive assignment which also deals with various obligations, warranties and indemnities, together with the extent and duration of the rights granted and the consideration. An assignment from the author of certain categories of work may also contain an assertion or waiver of the author's moral rights. There is a full discussion of moral rights in Chapter 3.

An effective assignment removes the copyright or part of the copyright from the control of the assignor. The assignor can, if necessary, be restrained from subsequently doing anything which infringes the rights of the assignee. If the rights to publish a novel are assigned by an author, that author cannot then grant the same rights to someone else without being in breach of contract and the subsequent publication being an infringement of copyright.

1.13.3 Licences

A licence of copyright is a contractual right or permission from the owner of the copyright to do certain acts. A licence is not absolute in the same way as an assignment. The distinction between licences and assignments is not always clear. A licence does not pass title in the copyright. A licence is a contractual right which generally ends if the contract is breached or expires or terminates.

A licence may be distinguished from an assignment in a number of ways.

(1) Ownership of rights is not transferred: an assignment gives a property right, a licence a contractual right.
(2) An assignee has the right to sue to protect his copyright. A licensee does not usually have this right.
(3) After assignment, the owner will usually have no more rights in the work.

(4) A licence may be exclusive or non-exclusive by its nature, an assignment confers ownership.
(5) A licence may be conditional on the performance of obligations by the licensee which, if breached, will lead to the termination of the licence.
(6) On a licensee's insolvency, rights usually revert to the owner, whereas an assignee retains rights.
(7) Assignments must be in writing (although an agreement to assign may be oral).
(8) An assignee has the right to alter the work by way of correction and additions. A licensee does not automatically have such a right.
(9) Both assignments and licences may provide for the payment of a royalty to the copyright owner. The payment of a royalty may in fact point to the document being a licence. This point has been considered in a number of cases. A presumption against assignment may arise wherever there are continuing obligations between the parties. The case of *Jonathan Cape v Consolidated Press* [1954] 1 WLR 1313 concerned the grant to a publisher of the exclusive right to publish a work in volume form. This was held to constitute an assignment. Conversely, in *Re Jude's Musical Compositions* [1907] 1 Ch 651, an agreement to publish in 'volume form', subject to payment of a royalty, constituted a licence. An agreement to publish a work subject to the performance of conditions is likely to constitute a licence.

There are occasions when the distinction is particularly important. A licensee who wishes to sue is precluded from doing so as he has no title; only an assignee can sue, although an exclusive licensee does have such rights. Where there are continuing obligations on the assignee, such as an obligation to make royalty payments, there may be a presumption of a licence rather than an assignment.

Because of the difficulties which have arisen in distinguishing between the two, great care should be taken in drafting the necessary contracts between the parties. Where any continuing obligations are envisaged, appropriate restrictions such as limitations on the right to assign the benefit of the contract and termination provisions should be included in the contract. This ensures that, even though property has been transferred, there may still be a re-assignment of rights in certain circumstances. This has become the norm for assignments and licences.

Types of licence

There are various types of licence. A licence may be exclusive or non-exclusive and may sometimes be expressed to be 'irrevocable'. An exclusive licence is one which (under s 90(1)) authorises the licensee, to the exclusion of all other persons, including the licensor, to exercise a right that would otherwise be exercisable by the licensor. Such a licence must be in writing. The holder of a valid exclusive licence has the same rights as if the licence were an assignment. Rights are also concurrent with the copyright owner.

A bare licence requires no formalities – it need not be in writing – yet will bind the copyright owner who granted it and any assignees except a bona fide purchaser for valuable consideration without actual or constructive notice (s 90). A licence can even be implied from circumstances, for example where an advertising agency designs a company logo, the company has an implied licence to use the logo. A licensee cannot usually restrict any other exploitation of the work by the licence owner unless the licence is exclusive licence. A licensee has no direct right to assert the copyright against third parties; it must act through the licensor.

Occasionally, a licence may be referred to as a 'sole' licence. This means the rights holder and the licensee can exercise the rights. This is in contrast to an exclusive licence, which also excludes the rights holder from exercising the rights granted.

1.13.4 Drafting the documents

Although the form of an assignment or a licence is prescribed, its contents are not. The most important consideration for an assignor or licensor is to transfer that which is intended and no more. This means that care must be taken with the rights definition in the agreement. A useful guide is for an assignee to assign as few rights as possible to accord with the parties' intentions and give the contract business efficacy. Except in the case of an outright assignment, the owner may retain control over other rights and exploit them as it sees fit.

Most agreements deal with the exact rights granted, the territory and duration of the agreement. There should also be terms dealing with the exclusivity of the agreement. Basic warranties as to ownership and the 'basic' copyright warranties should be considered. Good title must be established, and account may have to be taken of the contractual matters discussed elsewhere in this book, such as duress and restraint of trade. Terms for payment should be included unless the dealing is by way of gift. Various boiler-plate and termination provisions should always be included.

Basic warranties

There are various basic warranties in a licence or assignment of copyright, which may include the following:

(1) the work is written by a qualifying person;
(2) it is original; and
(3) it is not defamatory or in breach of any third party rights.

Additionally, assignments and licences may be made with full or limited title guarantee.

1.13.5 Construction of contracts: assignments and licences

As technology has developed, so have the ways in which copyright is exploited. This has had an important effect on the assignment and licensing of rights. Early cases involved the granting of film rights in novels and plays where, at the time of drafting the licence or assignment, innovations such as sound had not been not envisaged. One dispute involved the exploitation of a film by means of video where such rights did not exist at the time of the original assignment of performers' rights (see *Bourne v Walt Disney Co* (1995) US App Lexis).

The starting-point in the construction of any contract is the document itself. If the words used in the contract are clear and precise, then in the absence of fraud, mistake or other contractual circumstance, the contract stands. Despite what appears to be a perfectly clear document, disputes may arise where a novel form of exploitation is developed which did not exist at the time of the agreement. A current example is the development of multimedia products which incorporate various copyright works. It is often unclear whether an original assignment or licence was intended to include the right to exploit copyright in this way. This is a matter of interpretation.

The interpretation centres upon the form of words used by the parties in their agreement. If the words are wide enough to cover the new rights (for instance, CD-ROM exploitation) and those rights were at the least in the contemplation of the parties at the time of the agreement, then clearly those rights pass. A claimant may seek to open up the document to wider consideration. Whilst a court looks to the document as a whole for its meaning, it is possible to use extrinsic evidence as an aid to construction of the contract by looking at what was properly in the consideration of the parties at the time of the agreement. In *Hospital for Sick Children (Board of Governors) v Walt Disney Productions Inc* [1966] 1 WLR 1055, the court had to consider the grant in 1919 by Sir James Barrie of a licence in all his literary and dramatic works to the defendants for the duration of the copyright term 'in cinematograph or moving picture films'. The court held that the proper construction of these words rested upon the view of the parties at the time of the agreement. The wording of the document itself provided no assistance (the words used being so wide) so the court looked at matters in the contemplation of the parties at the time of the agreement. Since silent films were the only means of commercial exploitation in the cinema at the time of the licence, a narrow view was taken and the talking rights were excluded from the licence.

Similar disputes may arise over licences granted to put films on video formats as new formats are constantly being developed. Widely drawn definitions clauses in agreements cause problems for licensors, who now give more careful thought to the definitions in licences.

It appears that contracts will be construed in one of the following ways.

(1) The assignment will be interpreted by what was in the minds of the parties at the time it was drafted, as evidenced by the words used in the agreement and facts that were then relevant (the majority view in *Hospital for Sick Children* (above)).

(2) The agreement must be looked at in the light of circumstances and conditions surrounding the agreement, as long as the parties have knowledge of the relevant circumstances and conditions. This may involve looking at the state of the art at the time of the agreement (see *J. C. Williamson Ltd v Metro-Goldwyn-Mayer Theatres Ltd* [1937] VLR 67, 140).

There are further important considerations when there are insolvency issues. In such circumstances, the distinction between assignments and licences is important as this may determine the right of the copyright owner to the return of the property as opposed to merely ranking as an unsecured creditor.

Chapter 2

COPYRIGHT INFRINGEMENT

2.1 INTRODUCTION

The owner of copyright is entitled to exploit his works very much as he sees fit, with the proviso that he does not do so in breach of, for example, EC law, as in the *Magill* case. It is important to establish exactly what rights a copyright owner has, how those rights are infringed, and equally what defences are available to third parties faced with infringement proceedings. Copyright is infringed if a person does an act within the exclusive rights (set out in s 16) without the permission of the copyright owner. There are two categories of civil copyright infringement, known as primary and secondary infringements. There are also various criminal offences which can arise where rights are infringed.

The categories of primary infringement relate to the exclusive rights to acts which only the owner of copyright can do or authorise, known as the acts restricted by copyright. These rights are dealt with in ss 16–21 of the CDPA 1988. Acts of secondary infringement involve dealing with or making commercial use of infringing copies of a copyright work. Secondary infringement is dealt with in ss 22–27.

There are various permitted acts dealt with in ss 28–76 which provide defences to infringement.

2.2 RESTRICTED ACTS

2.2.1 Exclusive rights

The exclusive rights set out in s 16 are the basis of protection for copyright owners. They are:

- the right to copy the work (s 17);
- the right to issue copies to the public (s 18);
- the right to rent or lend works to the public (s 18A);
- the right to perform the work in public (s 19);
- the right to broadcast or send a cable transmission (s 20); and
- the right to make adaptations of the work (s 21).

Copyright will be infringed where any of these acts are done without the consent of the copyright owner (s 16(2)). An act restricted by copyright may be done in relation to the work as a whole or any substantial part of it (s 16(3)). An infringement of copyright may take place not only where the whole of a work has been copied, but also where something less than the whole but none the less 'substantial' has been copied. The question of what amounts to a 'substantial part' of a copyright work is discussed at **2.2.2**. Section 16(4) provides that the restricted acts are subject to permitted acts (s 28 onwards) and the copyright licensing provisions of the CDPA 1988 (s 116 onwards). The latter provisions are beyond the scope of this work.

Chapter 2 contents
Introduction
Restricted acts
Copying
Issuing copies to the public
Rental or lending of copies to the public
Public performance
Broadcasting
Adaptations
Secondary infringement of copyright
Defences and permitted acts
Civil remedies
Criminal remedies

Matters may be complicated where, in an action for copyright infringement, it is alleged that the defendant has copied a work or a substantial part of it but the defendant denies that in fact copying has taken place. Where an allegation of infringement is disputed, the courts have then to decide two elements that must be present:

(1) there must be sufficient objective similarity between the infringing work and the copyright work, or a substantial part of it, for the former to be properly described, not necessarily as identical with, but as a reproduction or adaptation of the latter;

(2) the copyright work must be the source from which the infringing work is derived (per Diplock LJ in *Francis Day & Hunter Ltd v Bron* [1963] Ch 587). This case and the test adopted by Lord Diplock made the possibility of subconscious copying a possibility. If, in substance, there is a similarity it must be proved that the defendant had access to the claimant's work, in which case, a presumption will be raised that the defendant had copied the other work. In such a case, the defendant must rebut that presumption. If one author arrives by independent work at the same result as another author, there will be no infringement.

The House of Lords in *LB (Plastics) v Swish Products* [1979] RPC 611 adopted the approach of the court in the *Bron* case. A number of factors will be relevant: the degree of familiarity between the works; the characteristics of the claimant's works; the objective similarity between the works; the inherent possibility that any similarity is due to coincidence; other factors which may have influenced the defendant; and, finally, evidence with respect to the defendant's state of mind.

2.2.2 Substantial part

The copyright in a work is infringed where someone other than the copyright owner does any of the restricted acts in relation to the whole or a substantial part of a work. Whilst it is usually obvious what constitutes the whole of a work, the question of what constitutes a substantial part of a work can be problematic. The approach the court has adopted is that the question of what constitutes a 'substantial part' is a qualitative not a quantitative question. *Hawkes and Son (London) Ltd v Paramount Film Service Ltd* [1934] Ch 593 concerned a newsreel that contained 20 seconds of a 4-minute piece of music. The newsreel was held to infringe the copyright in the music. However, the inclusion of such a piece of background music in a piece of film would now be permitted as incidental inclusion. In *Ladbroke (Football) Ltd v William Hill (Football) Ltd* [1964] 1 WLR 273, Lord Pearce said that the question as to what is substantial must be decided by quality rather than quantity. Additionally, the parts of a work copied will not amount to a substantial part if the parts copied were not in themselves original. The claimant in *Warwick Film Productions Ltd v Eisinger and Others* [1969] 1 Ch 508 owned the copyright in a book which was essentially a compilation consisting of various court transcripts, an introduction and various appendices written by the claimant. Because of the amount of skill and effort the claimant had expended on the work, it was held that copyright subsisted in the collocation. However, the defendant copied parts of the work which had been taken from court transcripts. Accordingly, the court held that there was no substantial qualitative taking, since the claimant had merely copied those parts himself.

In *Ravenscroft v Herbert and New English Library Ltd* [1980] RPC 193, the defendant wrote a novel entitled *The Spear*. A prologue to each of the chapters in the novel was based on the story of *The Spear*, as told in the claimant's work. The defendant author admitted using these excerpts, but denied taking a substantial part of the work. It was held that the defendant had used more than common source material and, as such, had infringed copyright. Although it is open to another author to research common sources to develop a work, where the efforts of another are used, including their arrangements, or their efforts are simply adopted with colourable variations, this amounts to a breach of copyright.

In *EMI Music v Evangelous Papathanassiou* [1987] 8 EIPR 244, the court considered the similarities between the defendant's piece 'Chariots of Fire', and the claimant's piece 'City of Violets'. There was not sufficient objective similarity between the works for infringement. The court reached this decision after hearing expert evidence from musicologists. The experts convinced the court that the similarities in the pieces were commonplace in music and not copied. The quality of evidence adduced in copyright litigation, together with the court's assessment of the similarity, frequently holds sway in such cases.

Parodies

Parodies are a category of work which clearly owes something to the original work that is being parodied. Copyright works are often the subject of comical or satirical treatment. In essence, a parody of a copyright work is treated no differently than any other alleged infringement. The question is whether there has been a 'substantial taking' from the claimant's work. Parodies rely for some of their effect upon the association with the original work and, because of this, they are very susceptible to attack as infringing works. A parody will not usually incorporate the whole of a work, but rather an element of it which may be sufficient to identify the original and infringe the exclusive rights of the copyright owner. An attempt at parody will not of itself remove the work far enough away from the original.

Whether the parody is of a song, musical or dramatic work, the test will be the same. In *Williamson Music Ltd v The Pearson Partnership Ltd* [1987] FSR 97, the Rogers and Hammerstein song 'There is Nothin' Like a Dame' had been parodied in an advertisement. In this case, there was a substantial taking of the music but not the lyrics for copyright purposes.

In *Schweppes Ltd and Others v Wellingtons Ltd* [1984] FSR 210, the claimants claimed infringement of their tonic label. The defendants had used the phrase 'Schlurpps' instead of the claimants' 'Schweppes'. The defendants argued that their label was a joke in the nature of a caricature; however, it was held that the fact of a parody constituted no defence in an action for infringement of copyright.

Sampling

Sampling involves taking the whole or part of a sound recording. It may be a snatch of melody or a drum beat or sound. If the sample taken is of the whole or a substantial part of the copyright work, it may infringe that copyright, even though it has its own copyright protection. Samplers must take care not to use identifiable pieces of copyright material. Any sound recording which uses identifiable elements of other musical works or sound recordings may infringe copyright. It is usual for samplers to obtain a licence to use extracts from other copyright works.

Guidelines

The following guidelines may be useful in determining whether infringement has taken place.

(1) Even short extracts of works may, when assessed qualitatively, be vital parts of a work and thus substantial. Even though there may be only a fleeting resemblance between two works, such as a melody line, or the selective use of scenes, incidents and language from another work, this does not preclude infringement of copyright.

(2) The courts adopt a de minimis approach to some uses for copyright purposes, such as the use of a name or title, and will not hold that infringement of copyright has taken place. Alternative remedies such as passing off, defamation or trade mark infringement may be pursued.

(3) The fact that the work in question is short does not preclude a conclusion of copying or substantial taking.

(4) Some very simple ideas may only be represented in a limited number of ways – such as a photo of a view or a commonplace instruction. In such cases, a court will be reluctant to hold that infringement has taken place.

(5) A similar theme or plot for a literary work may be unprotectable as an idea – although care must be taken to avoid copying any text or dialogue. The similarities must be of the unprotectable elements of the work: broadly speaking, the idea rather than the expression of the work.

In spite of all this, a good general guideline is that set out in *University of London Press v University Tutorial Press* [1916] 2 Ch 601: 'what is worth copying is worth protecting'.

2.3 COPYING

2.3.1 Literary, dramatic, musical or artistic works

Section 17(2) provides that copying in relation to any literary, dramatic, musical or artistic work means reproducing the work in any material form. This includes storing the work in any medium by electronic means.

At its simplest, copying will be very easy to prove: for example, where a compact disc is recorded onto a cassette, or the pages of a book are copied using a photocopier. In the case of artistic works, copying also occurs if a two-dimensional copy is made of a three-dimensional work, or a three-dimensional copy of a two-dimensional work.

2.3.2 Films, television broadcasts and cable programmes

In addition to the copying of the work as a whole or any substantial part of it, s 17(4) establishes that copyright in a film, television broadcast or cable programme is infringed if a photograph of the whole or any substantial part of any image forming part of the film, broadcast or cable programme is made. The producers of *Starsky and Hutch* were able to prevent the defendants from publishing a single frame from an episode infringing their copyright (*Spelling Goldberg Promotions Inc v BPC Publishing Ltd* [1981] RPC 280).

2.3.3 Typographical arrangements

Section 17(5) states that the copying of a typographical arrangement of a published edition means making a facsimile copy of it.

2.4 ISSUING COPIES TO THE PUBLIC

In the case of this restricted act, the issuing to the public of copies of a work means the act of putting into circulation copies not previously put into circulation in the UK or elsewhere (s 18(2)). This restricted act does not apply to the subsequent distribution, sale, hiring or loaning of copies nor to any subsequent importation of such copies into the UK. However, the rental of copies of sound recordings, films and computer program to the public is prohibited.

2.5 RENTAL OR LENDING OF COPIES TO THE PUBLIC

The rental or lending of works to the public applies to literary, dramatic, musical and artistic works as well as films and sound recordings (s 18A(1)). Rental means making a copy available for use on terms that it will be returned for direct or indirect commercial advantage (s 18A(2)(a)). This covers video rental shops. Lending means making a copy of the work available through an establishment accessible to the public for use on terms that it will be returned but otherwise than for direct or indirect commercial advantage (s 18A(2)(b)). This covers public libraries.

There are other provisions affecting authors' rental rights. In s 93A an agreement for film production between an author and a film producer is presumed to transfer any rental right the author has to the film producer. This is the case unless the agreement provides otherwise. The rental right may arise because the author's work is included in the film.

The author of a literary, dramatic, musical or artistic work and the principal director of a film have a right to equitable remuneration for the rental of their work (s 93B). An agreement cannot exclude or restrict the right to equitable remuneration under the section. There are no guidelines as to what constitutes an equitable amount. Either party may apply to the Copyright Tribunal to determine the amount payable. It is also possible to vary any agreement as to the amount payable or vary a previous decision of the Tribunal (s 93C).

2.6 PUBLIC PERFORMANCE

The performance of a literary, dramatic or musical work in public is an act restricted by copyright (s 19). 'Performance' of a work includes delivery of lectures, addresses, speeches and sermons, and, in general, includes any mode of visual or acoustic presentation, including presentation by means of a sound recording, film, broadcast or cable programme of the works.

The playing or showing of a sound recording, film, broadcast or cable programme in public is a restricted act.

When will a performance not be in public? It appears that a monetary limitation is not sufficient to ensure that the performance is private. If payment is made to see a performance, the economic rights of the copyright owner are being affected, since an opportunity to exploit the work is being lost and, accordingly, the performance will be in public. For a performance not to be a public performance, it appears that the performance must be limited to a domestic situation. Playing records or having friends round to watch a film at home will not be a public performance of the work. If the film or music is played in a hall of residence at a university, however, it constitutes a public performance. If there is a degree of recurrence or regularity about such performances, a licence would also be required from the relevant licensing authority or copyright owner. (See further *Jennings v Stephens* [1936] Ch 469, *Performing Right Society Ltd v Harlequin Record Shops Ltd* [1979] 1 WLR 851, *Ernest Turner Electrical Instruments Ltd v Performing Right Society Ltd; Performing Right Society Ltd v Gillette Industries Ltd* [1943] Ch 167.)

Music played in shops, over telephones, in waiting rooms and in reception areas constitutes a public performance for which licences are required. The playing of videos to guests in hotels or the transmission of cable or satellite programme services to guests will also constitute a public performance, and a licence will be required. The administration of the performance right in music is usually assigned by composers and publishers to the Performing Rights Society (PRS), which deals with the licensing of public performance and broadcast rights on behalf of its members. In practice, the right to perform a copyright work is of tremendous value.

2.7 BROADCASTING

The broadcasting of a work or the inclusion of a work in a cable programme service is an act restricted by copyright (s 20). The owner of the copyright in a literary, dramatic, musical or artistic work, sound recording or film, or a broadcast or cable programme may prohibit others from broadcasting the work or including it in a cable programme service. This section does not apply to copyright in the typographical arrangements of published editions.

'Broadcast' is defined in s 6 of the CDPA 1988, and 'cable programme service' in s 7.

2.8 ADAPTATIONS

Making an adaptation of a literary, dramatic or musical work is restricted by copyright. Section 21(3) defines an 'adaptation' in relation to a literary or dramatic work as a translation of the work; a version of a dramatic work in which it is converted into a non-dramatic work or, as the case may be, of a non-dramatic work in which it is converted into a dramatic work; or a version of the work in which the story or action is conveyed wholly or mainly by means of pictures in a form suitable for reproduction in a book, newspaper, magazine or similar periodical. In relation to a musical work, 'adaptation' means an arrangement or transcription of the work.

An adaptation is 'made' when it is recorded in writing or otherwise. Section 21(2) states that the doing of any of the acts specified in ss 17–20 or s 21(1) in relation to an adaptation of the work is also an act restricted by copyright in a literary, dramatic or musical work. For the purposes of s 21(2), it is immaterial whether the adaptation has been recorded in writing or otherwise at the time the act is done.

'Writing' is defined as including any form of notational code, whether by hand or otherwise, regardless of the method by which, or medium in or on which, it is recorded (s 178).

Under s 21(2), where an adaptation of a work has been made, subsequent dealing with it will infringe the other exclusive rights of the copyright owner.

2.9 SECONDARY INFRINGEMENT OF COPYRIGHT

As well as the infringing acts restricted by the copyright in the work under ss 16–20, there is another category of infringing act known as 'secondary infringement'. The category of secondary infringement generally relates to commercial use of a copyright work, and such infringements are usually performed – although not necessarily by the same party – in relation to a work in which the copyright has already been infringed under one of the s 16 restricted acts. Secondary infringers are often also prosecuted in the criminal court.

In contrast to the position under ss 16–21, secondary infringers under ss 22–26 must know or have reason to believe that they are dealing with infringing copies of a work.

In *LA Gear Inc v Hi-Tec Sports plc* [1992] FSR 121, it was stated that the test as to what a defendant 'has reason to believe' is an objective one. It requires a consideration of whether the reasonable man, with knowledge of the facts that the defendant had knowledge of, would have formed the belief that the item was an infringing copy. This is important because, under s 97, if it can be shown in an action for infringement of copyright that at the time of the infringement the defendant did not know, and had no reason to believe, that copyright subsisted in the work to which the action relates, the claimant is not entitled to damages.

There is provision in s 97(2) for the court to award damages notwithstanding the defendant's lack of knowledge if the infringement is flagrant and the defendant has benefited from the infringing activity. In such a case, the court may award 'such additional damages as the justice of the case may require'.

Sections 22–26 set out the acts that constitute secondary infringement of a work.

2.9.1 Importing infringing copies

Importing an infringing copy of a work without the permission of the copyright owner, other than for private or domestic use, constitutes secondary infringement (s 22).

2.9.2 Possessing or dealing with infringing copies

Copyright in a work is infringed where, without the permission of the copyright owner, a person possesses, sells or lets for hire, or offers or exposes for sale or hire, exhibits or distributes, or distributes otherwise than in the course of a business to such an extent as to affect prejudicially the owner of the copyright, an infringing copy of the work (s 23).

2.9.3 Providing the means for making infringing copies

Anyone who provides the means to make infringing copies is liable (s 24).

Copyright is also infringed where a person without permission transmits a work by means of a telecommunication system (this does not include broadcasting or inclusion in a cable programme service) if an infringing copy will be made at the point where the transmission is received.

2.9.4 Permitting the use of premises for infringing performance

If copyright in a literary, dramatic or musical work is infringed by a performance at a place of public entertainment, any person who gave permission for that place to be used for the performance is also liable for the infringement.

Section 25(2) explains that 'places of public entertainment' includes premises which are occupied mainly for other purposes, but are from time to time made available for hire for the purposes of public entertainment. This might include a room in a pub which is occasionally used for performing plays or for live bands to perform (s 25).

2.9.5 Provision of apparatus for infringing performance

Supplying the apparatus to infringe the copyright in a sound recording or film or to receive visual images or sounds conveyed by electronic means will result in liability for the person who supplied the apparatus or any substantial part of it. An occupier of the premises who gave permission for the apparatus to be brought on to the premises may also be liable, as may any person who supplied the copy of the sound recording or film used to infringe the copyright (s 26).

2.9.6 Infringing copies

An article is an infringing copy if its making constitutes an infringement of the copyright in the work in question. An article is also an infringing copy if it has been imported into the UK, and making it in the UK would have constituted an infringement of the copyright in the work (s 27).

The question may arise as to whether an article is an infringing copy. It must be shown that the article is a copy of a work and that copyright subsists in the work, in which case it is presumed until the contrary is proved that the article was made at a time when copyright subsisted in the work. These provisions do not apply if the copyright work may be lawfully imported into the UK under any of the provisions of the European Communities Act 1972. This applies particularly to the doctrine of 'exhaustion of rights'. Effectively, once a copyright work has been put on the market within the EC with the owner's permission, the owner cannot restrict the subsequent sale of those goods. The exhaustion of rights principle does not apply where the articles in question infringe the copyright in a work.

Secondary infringement by way of a public performance of the work does not occur if the person who gave permission 'believed on reasonable grounds that the performance would not infringe copyright'.

CDPA 1988, ss 104–105 contain various presumptions relating to the proof of authorship and other matters in proceedings.

In relation to literary, dramatic, musical and artistic works, where an author is named on the published work, he is presumed, until the contrary is proved, to be the author of the work (s 104).

Similar presumptions are made for sound recordings which bear the name of the copyright owner and year of first publication (s 105(1)) and for films which bear the name of the author or director, the name of the copyright owner at the date of issue and year of first publication (s 105(2)).

These presumptions can help to avoid the cost of proving title to copyright works.

2.10 DEFENCES AND PERMITTED ACTS

2.10.1 Introduction

The provisions of s 16 take effect subject to the 'permitted acts' contained in ss 28–76. If a person can establish that what has been done in relation to the copyright work in fact falls within these provisions, there will be no infringement of the copyright in the work.

There are various categories of permitted acts grouped together under a number of headings.

2.10.2 Fair dealing

The first of these categories deals with the concept of fair dealing. This applies in a number of contexts, namely fair dealing for the purposes of research and private study, and fair dealing for criticism, review and news reporting.

The permitted acts centre around the concept of 'fair dealing'. This is a concept that has troubled the courts on numerous occasions – for example, in a case involving the film, *A Clockwork Orange* (*Time Warner Entertainment Co v Channel Four Television Corp plc* [1994] EMLR 1) discussed further below. The copying of the work in question must be of the whole or a substantial part of the work to be an infringing act in the first place. The question of what amounts to a substantial part of a work and the application of the fair dealing defence are different issues.

The defence is only available as set out below.

Fair dealing for research and private study

The provisions of s 29 permit fair dealing with a literary, dramatic, musical or artistic work for the purposes of research and private study. Copying in these circumstances does not infringe any copyright in the work.

The application of the provisions is not without difficulty. There is no rule or indication as to the amount of work which may constitute fair use of the work. The application of the rules clearly relates to the quality as well as the quantity of the material used. It is clear that, in certain circumstances, a work may be copied.

The making of multiple copies or habitual copying of a work (because, for example, it is part of a syllabus) amounts to infringement. In the latter case, different rules apply and the copying should be licensed.

It is also clear that copying may be done by another person on behalf of the researcher as long as that copying does not result in copies of substantially the same material being made for more than one person at substantially the same time (s 29(3)). The making of copies for research or study is thus limited to single and not multiple copies.

There are extensive provisions in ss 37–44 setting out the conditions upon which librarians (who may not be protected by s 29) may make copies of works for others. There are also provisions in ss 32–36 dealing with copyright works, and use and reproduction by educational establishments.

Fair dealing for the purposes of criticism, review and news reporting

Section 30(1) provides that fair dealing with a work for the purpose of criticism or review, of that or of another work or of a performance of a work, does not infringe any copyright in the work. A copyright acknowledgement must be given. Section 30(2) states that fair dealing with a work (other than a photograph) for the purposes of reporting current events does not infringe copyright in the work. No acknowledgement is required if reporting takes place by means of a sound recording, film, broadcast or cable programme. If no particular category of work is mentioned, the act does not infringe copyright in any category of work (s 28(2)).

Fair dealing in this context is also problematical. The basis is that copyright will not be infringed if *either* the use does not amount to a substantial part *or* the fair dealing provisions apply. The question of what amounts to a substantial part is a vexed one. The fair dealing defence adds a significant weapon in cases of alleged infringement.

In *BBC v British Satellite Broadcasting Ltd* [1991] 3 WLR 174, the defendants used excerpts from the claimants' World Cup football coverage in their news broadcasts. BSB gave an acknowledgement – which the legislation does not require – to the BBC for use of the excerpts. The court held that the use of the excerpts, even though it was of the interesting bits, mainly goals, amounted to fair use within the meaning of the CDPA 1988. The limitation on the use suggested by the court related to the timing of the showing of the excerpts. As long as an item is current, its use will be covered by fair dealing.

The court will look at a number of factors in considering fair use. Lord Denning, in *Hubbard and Another v Vosper and Another* [1972] 2 QB 84, described fair dealing as 'a matter of impression'. The factors to be considered include the following.

- The amount of the work used will clearly be important. Fair dealing is not a carte blanche to reproduce copyright works.
- The status of the work reproduced may also be important. If the material in question is confidential in nature, a claimant may have other remedies, but the availability of a defence of fair dealing may also be limited. In *Beloff v Pressdram Ltd and Another* [1973] 1 All ER 241, the reproduction of the contents of a 'leaked' memo could not be fair dealing. In contrast, the criticism of a work that is already in the public domain (even though not readily available to the public in this country) can, in principle, amount to fair dealing (see *Time Warner Entertainment Co v Channel Four Television Corp plc* [1994] EMLR 1).
- The purpose of or the motive behind the copying may also be relevant. The fact that the publication is for commercial gain may not be relevant – a reviewer may be keen to help sell copies of his paper – but if the use of the work will compete

with the copied work, then that may be unfair. This applies whether the copying is for research or for criticism and review.

The *Time Warner* case illustrates s 30 well. The defendants had produced a programme that included excerpts from the claimants' film *A Clockwork Orange*. The claimants had taken the film out of circulation in the UK because of incidents of copy-cat violence after its original release. Until recently, the film has not been on authorised release in the UK since 1974, although it has been available within the EC. The defendants bought a copy of the film in Paris and used extracts in their documentary. A total of 12 extracts were used, amounting to 12½ minutes, or about 8%, of the film itself and 40% of the programme.

The defendants appealed against an injunction prohibiting broadcast. The Court of Appeal lifted the injunction on a number of grounds.

(1) The fact that, at the time, the film was not commercially available in the UK did not mean the fair dealing defence was unavailable.
(2) The claimants claimed that the programme misrepresented the film as a whole, as the clips chosen were mainly violent ones. The court did not consider it necessary that the clips used were representative of the film as a whole. The fact that the criticism or review covers only one aspect of a work does not mean that the defence cannot be used.
(3) The total length of the extracts used did not in this case go beyond the bounds of fair dealing. The question was a matter of fact and impression for the court. If use amounts to an 'illegitimate exploitation of the copyright holder's work' then it may be unacceptable.
(4) The claimants contended that the purpose of the film was not criticism or review of the film, but criticism of the decision to withdraw the film from circulation. The court held that this did not appear to be the case, as the producers of the programme regarded the film as a work '… of long-term social significance'.

2.10.3 Incidental inclusion

Section 31 permits the showing, playing, broadcasting or inclusion in a cable programme service of anything which was incidentally included in the making of an artistic work, sound recording, film, broadcast or cable programme.

Section 31(3) states that a musical work, words spoken or sung without music, or so much of a sound recording, broadcast or cable programme that includes a musical work or such words, shall not be regarded as incidentally included if it is deliberately included.

This exception exists to permit programme makers and news broadcasters to show works that might otherwise be protected by copyright.

A typical example might involve a film crew doing interviews or filming footage on the street. A number of works which are protected by the laws of copyright may be included in the film, such as buildings, advertising hoardings, music from cars or shops, and even other TV broadcasts.

The exception to this is the use of musical works – most usually, records played over the radio – where the inclusion is deliberate. Thus, a film maker is presumed to have control over his set to the extent that any musical work playing in the background would then have to have clearance. Even a live film broadcaster could find itself in infringing copyright. It will be a question of fact as to what constitutes deliberate inclusion. However, the existence of the PRS and PPL and the block licensing regimes should make most broadcasters' breaches merely technical ones for which permission is granted under the terms of the block licence. The inclusion of any copyright work should, nevertheless, be carefully considered.

2.10.4 Other provisions

There are various other permitted acts (ss 57–63) which apply to certain categories of works, for instance, literary, dramatic and artistic works, as follows.

(1) Section 57 covers acts done in relation to anonymous or pseudonymous works where it is not possible to trace the author and it is reasonable to assume that copyright no longer exists.
(2) Section 58 is important for journalists using a recording of spoken words. As long as the recording is a direct record which is not prohibited by the speaker or copyright owner, and the owner of the recording allows the use, then the words may be used. This is most likely to be relevant where an interview has taken place. The interviewee has copyright in his spoken words, and permission is required for their use. As long as the conditions are satisfied, the interview may be used.

2.10.5 Public interest defence

The public interest defence is not a statutory defence. This defence has been developed by the courts in a number of cases involving the publication of material which has been obtained illicitly. One example concerned the publication of *The Thatcher Diaries* (*Times Newspapers v MGN Ltd* [1993] EMLR 443). Serialisation rights had been granted to *The Times*. The *Daily Mirror* obtained and published excerpts from the book prior to its serialisation. In its defence to an action for breach of copyright and breach of confidence, the defendants alleged that publication was in the public interest. It was held that the publication could go ahead as there were matters of legitimate public interest in publication. The claimants were left to a remedy in damages at a full trial or sooner settlement.

The defence applies in both the law of confidence and the law of copyright. In essence, a defendant argues that disclosure of the information in question is necessary.

The reasons vary, but the defence has applied where the publication relates to an iniquity (although a wrongdoing is not essential), to religious matters and to persons in the public eye. The courts have also stated that there is a difference between what is interesting to the public and what is in the public interest.

The commercial interests of publishers and broadcasters must be distinguished from the public interest, which might be best served by giving the information to the police or some other responsible body.

A leading case, *Lion Laboratories Ltd v Evans and Others* [1985] 1 QB 526, concerned the publication of information relating to the reliability of intoximeters. The defendants argued successfully that it was in the public interest for the information to be published. The defence is a useful 'addition' to the fair dealing provisions of the CDPA 1988.

The defence is also a useful tool to defeat an application for an interlocutory injunction. The courts are reluctant to restrain free speech, even though a breach of copyright or confidence may be involved.

2.11 CIVIL REMEDIES

The remedies for infringement of copyright include damages, injunctions, delivery up and account of profits (s 96).

2.12 CRIMINAL REMEDIES

In addition to the various civil remedies which are available for primary and secondary infringement of copyright, there are criminal remedies contained in ss 107–110. These remedies are available for similar infringing acts to copyright owners, performers and those who have the benefit of an exclusive recording contract with a performer. The categories of infringement of copyright and performers' rights broadly relate to illicit commercial exploitation of works without the permission of the copyright owner or the performer.

Chapter 3

MORAL RIGHTS

3.1 INTRODUCTION

This chapter considers moral rights, which were introduced into UK law by the 1988 Act. Moral rights exist alongside the copyright in certain types of work. Moral rights, generally, remain with the author of a work or pass to the author's estate on death (s 95). Unlike copyright, moral rights cannot be assigned (s 94), although they are frequently waived. Moral rights apply to joint authors (s 88) as well as to the whole or part of a work (s 89).

Moral rights are dealt with in Part IV of the CDPA 1988 under ss 77–89. Moral rights are divided into four categories as follows:

(1) the right to be identified as the author or director of a work – this is often known as the 'paternity right' (s 77);
(2) the right to object to derogatory treatment of a work – sometimes known as the 'integrity right' (s 80);
(3) the right to object to false attribution of a work (s 84); and
(4) the right to privacy of certain photographs and films (s 85).

These rights are new to UK law. They were introduced to bring UK law into line with the Berne Copyright Convention. The rights conferred by ss 77, 80 and 85 subsist for as long as copyright subsists in a work. In this respect, the moral rights are dependent upon the existence of copyright. The s 84 right subsists until 20 years after a person's death.

The existence of moral rights raises an important additional element in the negotiation and drafting of certain agreements. Unfortunately for many authors, the sale of rights is often accompanied by the insistence of the purchaser on the waiver of moral rights.

3.2 RIGHT TO BE IDENTIFIED AS AUTHOR OR DIRECTOR

3.2.1 Identification

The author of a copyright literary, dramatic, musical or artistic work, or the director of a copyright film, has the right to be identified as the author or director of the work. The right to be identified as author or director must be asserted. Generally, the right must be asserted in writing. The assertion may take place in an assignment of the copyright in the work by including a statement that the author or director asserts his right to be identified. Alternatively, the right may simply be asserted in writing by the author or director. In the latter case, a letter or other assertion by the author or director should be signed and sent to the person who will be dealing with copyright in the work.

If the right to be identified is asserted by the author or director, various people will be bound by such an assertion. Upon an assignment of copyright containing an

Chapter 3 contents
Introduction
Right to be identified as author or director
Derogatory treatment
False attribution
Remedies
Waiver of rights
Right to privacy of certain photographs and films

assertion of moral rights, the assignee and anyone claiming title to copyright through the assignee will be bound, whether or not they have notice of the assertion of rights (s 78(4)). Where the right is simply asserted in writing by the author or director, anyone to whose notice that assertion is brought will be bound by it.

An author's right of paternity may be asserted as follows:

> **The Author asserts his moral right of paternity to the Publisher, its assignees and licensees in accordance with sections 77 and 78 of the CDPA 1988.**

It is common for an author to stipulate that every published copy of a work bears a notice stating:

> **The right of the author to be identified as the author of this work has been asserted in accordance with sections 77 and 78 of the CDPA 1988.**

Assuming an author or director fulfils the formal requirements and asserts his rights, if his work is published commercially, performed in public, broadcast or copies of the work are issued to the public, the author must be identified. Practically speaking, this means that the author of a book will be named on the cover of the book. If a film is based upon a book, then the author should be identified or given a credit in the film. Authors and directors are well advised to insist upon the s 77 right in any dealings with their copyright works.

3.2.2 Exceptions

There are various exceptions to this right. The right is not infringed in a number of situations (s 79), for example:

(1) it does not apply to computer programs, typefaces and any computer-generated works;
(2) it does not apply to employees whose employer is the first owner of the copyright in the work, or the director of a film where the director is not the author of the film for copyright purposes;
(3) it is not infringed where any of the defences to infringement apply (for example, fair dealing with the work or incidental inclusion of a work);
(4) it does not apply to any work made for the purposes of reporting current events; and, further,
(5) it does not apply in relation to the publication in a newspaper, magazine or similar periodical, or an encyclopedia, dictionary, year-book or other collective work of reference where the work was made for such a purpose, or the work was used with the author's consent.

3.3 DEROGATORY TREATMENT

3.3.1 Meaning

The author of a literary, dramatic, musical or artistic work and the director of a film have the right not to have their work subjected to 'derogatory treatment'. Section 80(2) defines treatment of a work as meaning 'any addition to, deletion from or alteration to or adaptation of the work, other than a translation of a literary or dramatic work or an arrangement of a musical work'. The treatment of a work will be derogatory if it amounts to 'distortion or mutilation of the work or is otherwise prejudicial to the honour or reputation of the author or director'.

It appears from s 80 that derogatory treatment must be in some way prejudicial to the reputation of the author. Although the author of a copyright work has assigned or otherwise dealt with the rights in the work, this does not give the new owner of copyright a carte blanche to deal with the work in any manner he thinks fit. The alteration of a story-line or significant alterations to the traits of main characters in a film based upon a book could amount to derogatory treatment of the work. It should also be borne in mind that an author may consent to or waive any right to object to derogatory treatment. Indeed, producers acquiring rights in novels or screenplays often obtain a waiver of the s 80 right as a matter of course. An employee author or director has the right under s 82 (assuming that the right has not been waived or consent is given to an act) not to have his work subjected to derogatory treatment as long as he is identified as author or director, either at the time of the infringing act or he has previously been identified in published copies of the work. An employee is thus able to object to derogatory treatment of his copyright work although he does not have the right to be identified as the author of a work. The right to object to derogatory treatment is dependent upon having been identified as the author or director of the work at some point.

Most commercial agreements which deal with the copyright in a work also contain waivers of the s 80 moral right. The British singer George Michael obtained an injunction asserting his 'integrity right' in some of his compositions. The singer alleged that some songs he recorded with Wham! had been subjected to derogatory treatment when they were remixed and amended in other ways.

The rights under s 80 are infringed by commercial publication or the issuing of copies to the public of a work that has been subject to such derogatory treatment.

3.3.2 Exceptions

Various exceptions to the s 80 right are detailed in s 81. The right does not apply:

(1) to computer programs or computer-generated works; or
(2) to works made for the purpose of reporting current events; or
(3) to publication of a work in a newspaper, magazine, periodical or encyclopedia or other reference work where the work was made for such a purpose, or was used with the author's consent;
(4) where a work is altered to avoid committing an offence, complying with a duty imposed under an Act of Parliament, or, in the case of the BBC, avoiding the inclusion in a programme broadcast of anything which might offend against good taste and decency or which is likely to encourage or incite crime or lead to disorder or be offensive to public feeling. In such cases, a disclaimer should be included explaining that the author's or director's work has been altered in such a way.

There are no exceptions for fair dealing and, accordingly, despite the fact that a defence of fair dealing may be available in an action for infringement of copyright, an author or director may still have a cause of action under s 80 for breach of moral rights.

3.4 FALSE ATTRIBUTION

A person has a right not to have literary, dramatic, musical or artistic work falsely attributed to him as author. A director also has a right not to have a film falsely attributed to him. Section 84(1) defines attribution as 'a statement (expressed or implied) as to who is the author or director of a work'. This right is infringed where copies of a work containing such a false attribution are issued to the public. The rights may be further infringed where such a falsely attributed work is performed in public or broadcast where a person knows, or has reason to believe, that the attribution is false. There are also categories of secondary infringement where, in the course of business, a person deals with or possesses copies of the work.

The right to object to false attribution was contained in earlier copyright legislation. In one case, *Moore v News of the World Ltd and Another* [1972] 1 QB 441, the claimant obtained damages for false attribution of ownership where a reporter working for the *News of the World* made up quotations 'for an interview with the claimant'. In this case, the claimant also successfully pursued a libel action against the defendant. The remedy available under s 84 for false attribution is clearly useful where an author's name is attached to a work which is not his. Such an attribution may also amount to a passing off. The false attribution right exists until 20 years after a person's death. It is also possible that, where a work is adapted (perhaps in the transition from novel to screenplay to film), the work changes so fundamentally that in addition to a claim that this amounts to derogatory treatment, attaching the author's name to the final film also amounts to false attribution.

3.5 REMEDIES

The remedy for breach of moral rights is damages and injunctive relief. Defences to an action will include consent or waiver of moral rights in a work. In addition, s 87(4) states that the general law of contract and estoppel also applies where there are any dealings with moral rights. Authors and directors are advised to record any agreement relating to their work in writing, thus avoiding any later disputes.

3.6 WAIVER OF RIGHTS

There is no infringement of moral rights if consent has been given (s 87). Any waiver of rights should be in writing signed by the person giving up the rights. A waiver may be specific or general, and may relate to existing or future works. A waiver may also be conditional or unconditional, and may be expressed to be revocable. A form of waiver may read:

> **The Author irrevocably and unconditionally waives his moral rights under s 77 and s 80 of the CDPA 1988.**

A waiver may also be informal, in which case, the general law of contract or estoppel applies.

3.7 RIGHT TO PRIVACY OF CERTAIN PHOTOGRAPHS AND FILMS

The owner of copyright in a photograph is the photographer. The only exception to this exists for employees acting in the course of employment. Copyright in the photograph may be assigned or licensed by the owner. Whilst the copyright in the photograph may be assigned or licensed by the photographer, s 85 contains additional provisions to protect people who commission photographs or films for private and domestic purposes. It is unclear whether or not such commission must be for value. Such a person has the right not to have copies of the work issued, exhibited or shown in public or broadcast in public. Anyone who does or authorises the doing of any of those acts will infringe this right to privacy. Section 85(2) contains exceptions to the right where infringement will not occur. One example is incidental inclusion of such a photograph or film in an artistic work, film, broadcast or cable programme. The s 85 rights are enforceable by the commissioner of the work and not the subjects of it, although the subjects may have other remedies in contract or tort.

This right to privacy is of limited use to protect public individuals whose photograph has been taken. The work must have been commissioned and must be for private and domestic purposes to be of any use. Clearly, a newspaper wishing to publish wedding photographs which it obtains from the photographer at the wedding without the consent of the commissioner (perhaps the bride's or groom's family) could be liable for infringement of moral rights, despite the fact that the position in copyright law as to ownership is clear. As with the other moral rights, no infringement occurs where the person entitled to the right has consented or waived his right.

Chapter 4

RIGHTS IN PERFORMANCES

4.1 INTRODUCTION

This chapter is concerned with the existence and protection of performers' rights. The exploitation of performers' rights is generally a matter of contract law. Such contracts may be on standard terms and conditions, as negotiated by the Musicians' Union or Equity on behalf of their members, or may be a bespoke recording contract signed by a new pop group with a record company.

The rights of performers – musicians, singers and actors (amongst others) – and those with whom they contract, to control and exploit their performances are of particular importance in the entertainment industry. The performance is an integral part of the 'product' which is exploited.

Section 180(4) provides that performance rights exist quite independently of copyright and moral rights in any works and any other rights or obligations other than those arising under Part II of the CDPA 1988. There is a distinction between the performance right in a copyright work (the right to perform a song in public) and the rights of the person who sings or performs that song. There are similarities in the form and duration of protection granted by performers' rights and copyright. Performers' rights are of particular importance to individuals who do not also own the copyright in the works performed.

As well as defining the ambit of performers' protection, Part II details the civil and criminal remedies available to performers and those with whom they have exclusive recording contracts.

4.2 PERFORMANCE RIGHTS

4.2.1 The rights

The CDPA 1988 (as amended by the Copyright and Related Rights Regulations 1996, SI 1996/2967 (CRRR 1996), and the Duration of Copyright and Rights in Performances Regulations 1995, SI 1995/3297) sets out the regime for protection of performers' rights. The regime creates (in CDPA 1988, s 180(1)):

- statutory civil rights for performers by requiring their consent to the exploitation of their performances;
- rights for those with whom performers have exclusive recording contracts in relation to recordings made without their consent; and
- related offences which prohibit dealing with or using illicit recordings.

4.2.2 Meaning of 'performance'

A performance is defined in s 180(2) as any one of the following:

- a dramatic performance (which includes dance and mime);

Chapter 4 contents
Introduction
Performance rights
Performers' rights
Rights of persons with recording rights
Duration
Remedies
Defences and exceptions to rights
Exploitation

- a musical performance;
- a reading or recitation of a literary work; or
- a performance of a variety act or any other similar presentation.

The performance in question must be a live performance by one or more individuals. It is important to note that the performance in question does not need to be in front of an audience – it can be in a studio or in a theatre or concert hall. There is also no qualitative test. The performance can be mundane or spectacular and original.

If the performance in question is also the first fixation or recording of a new work, then the work may also qualify for copyright protection.

It is worth noticing the extent of the rights in question. Whilst protection clearly extends to actors, musicians, singers, dancers, etc, there are individuals who do not benefit from protection. The rights clearly do not extend to sportsmen as they are not, for the main part, performers as defined in the Act. Whilst ice dancing in the Torvill and Dean mode may well qualify as a performance, a footballer or athlete will not be able to stretch the definition of 'performance' to include his sporting endeavours. Notwithstanding this, a performer's consent is usually taken from sportsmen taking part in a recorded or broadcast event. Of course, if a sportsman takes part in a pantomime, then that performance is protected. In the main, any remedies sportsmen have rely on common law rights such as passing off or defamation, or on the registration of a trade mark. Sportsmen are best advised to take tight contractual control over commercial exploitation of their name and likeness.

4.2.3 Qualifying for protection

The only performances which qualify for protection are qualifying performances (s 181). These are performances given by a 'qualifying individual' or taking place in a 'qualifying country' as defined in s 206:

- a 'qualifying individual' means a citizen or subject or an individual resident in a qualifying country;
- a 'qualifying person' is a qualifying individual or corporation formed in the UK or another qualifying country which has a place of business in the qualifying country at which substantial business is carried on;
- a 'qualifying country' means the UK or another EC Member State, or a country which is a party to a convention relating to performers' rights to which the UK is also a party. Section 208 allows the protection of the Act to be extended to other countries if a statutory instrument designates it.

4.3 PERFORMERS' RIGHTS

4.3.1 Infringing acts

Infringement of a performer's rights occurs where any person does any of a number of acts without the permission of the performer.

A performer's rights can be infringed by:

- making a recording of or transmitting live a qualifying performance;
- exploiting a recording of a qualifying performance by using it to show or play in public, by broadcasting it or by including it in a cable programme service;

- importing, possessing or dealing with an illicit recording of a qualifying performance.

Infringement only occurs if each act is done without the performer's consent.

A 'recording' is defined as a film or sound recording which is made:

(1) directly from the live performance;
(2) from a broadcast of, or a cable programme including, the performance; or
(3) directly or indirectly from another recording of the performance.

More specifically, ss 182–184 deal with the restricted acts in relation to a performer's rights.

The CRRR 1996 amended the CDPA 1988 to insert a new s 182 and new ss 182A, 182B, 182C and 182D.

The new sections are, for the purposes of exploitation, divided into performers' property rights and performers' non-property rights. Performers' property rights may be assigned and licensed, whereas, with non-property rights, a form of consent is required before exploitation. Most agreements need to deal with the legal distinction to ensure that all rights are passed over to permit exploitation. Accordingly, the rights are dealt with separately below (**4.3.2** and **4.3.3**) to reflect the legal distinction, whereas the practical point is to ensure drafting covers both rights.

4.3.2 Performers' property rights

A performer's property rights are infringed when someone, without the performer's consent:

- makes, otherwise than for his private and domestic use, a copy of a recording of the whole or a substantial part of a qualifying performance (s 182A(1)) – the reproduction right;
- issues to the public copies of a recording of the whole or a substantial part of a qualifying performance (s 182B(1)) – the distribution right;
- rents or lends to the public copies of a recording of the whole or any substantial part of a qualifying performance (s 182C(1)) – the rental and lending right.

Performers' property rights may be dealt with by way of assignment or testamentary disposition or operation of law as personal or movable property (s 191B). In the same way as copyright, an assignment may be partial so it applies:

(1) to one or more, but not all, of the things requiring the consent of the performer; and
(2) to part, but not the whole, of the period for which the rights subsist (s 191B(2)).

Future performers' property rights may also be assigned (s 191C). It is also possible to grant an exclusive licence of a performer's property rights (s 191D). An assignment must be in writing (s 191B(3)) as must an exclusive licence (s 191D(1)).

In agreements concerning film production between a performer and a film producer the performer is assumed, unless the agreement provides to the contrary, to transfer the rental rights in his performance in the film to the film producer (s 191F). Most agreements will deal with this point explicitly. Although the rental right may be transferred, the performer retains the right to equitable remuneration for the rental of the film containing his performance (s191G). The right to equitable remuneration may not be assigned by the performer other than to a collecting society (s 191G(2)) and it may not be waived (s 191G(5)).

An organisation such as the PAMRA may perform this function by collecting money for actors and musicians. The amount paid as equitable remuneration is to be agreed by or on behalf of the person to whom it is payable although applications to the Copyright Tribunal under s 191H are possible. Indeed, it is possible to go to the Tribunal to vary an agreement between parties or a previous decision of the Tribunal (s 191H(2)).

An action for infringement of a performer's property rights is actionable by the rights owner (s 191I) and by an exclusive licensee (s 191L).

4.3.3 Performers' non-property rights [NOT ASSIGNABLE]

A performer's non-property rights are infringed where someone, without the performer's consent:

- makes a recording of the whole or any substantial part of a qualifying performance directly from the live performance (s 182(1)(a));
- broadcasts live, or includes live in a cable programme service, the whole or any substantial part of a qualifying performance (s 182(1)(b));
- makes a recording of the whole or any substantial part of a qualifying performance directly from a broadcast of, or cable programme recording including, the live performance

otherwise than for private and domestic use (s 182(2)).

In the case of s 182 infringements damages will not be awarded if the defendant can show on reasonable grounds that consent has been given (s 182(3)).

Rights are also infringed where someone, without the performer's consent:

- shows or plays in public the whole or any substantial part of a qualifying performance (s 183(a));
- broadcasts or includes in a cable programme service the whole or any substantial part of a qualifying performance (s 183(b));
- imports into the UK other than for private and domestic use (s 184(1)(a)) or in the course of a business possesses, sells or lets for hire, offers or exposes for sale or hire, or distributes (s 184(1)(b)) a recording of a qualifying performance which is, and which that person knows or has reason to believe is, an illicit recording.

An illicit recording is a recording of the whole or any substantial part of a performance which was made otherwise than for private use without the performer's consent (s 197).

Under s 182D, where a commercially published sound recording of the whole or any substantial part of a qualifying performance is played in public or included in a broadcast or cable programme service, the performer is entitled to equitable remuneration from the owner of the copyright in the sound recording. The right cannot be excluded or restricted (s 182D(7)). The Copyright Tribunal may vary or determine the amount payable by way of equitable remuneration (s 182D(5)).

This means record companies now have to pay the artists a share of the income they receive by virtue of ss 19 and 20 of the CDPA 1988 which is collected by PPL.

Performers now have another income stream which did not previously exist. As far as the record companies are concerned, this is an income stream they may seek to control and use to recoup advances and recording costs. Performers on the other hand will be keen to ensure they receive this money direct, thus avoiding recoupment. The PPL accounts for this income directly to performers who register with it either directly or through AURA.

The requirement that the infringing act must be done in relation to the whole or a substantial part of the performance is similar to the infringement of copyright works. The test is a qualitative one and not a quantitative one. Reference should be made to **2.2.2** on this point.

4.3.4 Consent

The question of whether or not 'consent' has been given for exploitation of performers' non-property rights is fundamental to exploitation of these non-property rights. A singer may agree to perform live for a promoter. If that promoter also, without the singer's knowledge, records and subsequently sells the recording of the performance, the singer's rights will be infringed. If the promoter simply records the concert for his own domestic use, then there will be no infringement.

Assuming that the same performance is recorded, but this time the singer has been notified in advance of the intention to record the performance and agrees either by his conduct or because there is a written agreement consenting to the arrangement, then he cannot claim the promoter is infringing his rights.

Although the CDPA 1988 does not specifically require consent to be in writing, this is obviously preferable. Consent may be inferred by conduct, such as where a recording is made with a performer's knowledge. There may also be a question of the amount of any payment to be made in return for the consent. This fact in itself should not preclude the exploitation of the recording. All contracts with performers must deal with and obtain the consent of the performer to record and also to exploit his performance. The absence of terms dealing with these matters can cause problems, as in *Bassey and Another v Icon Entertainment plc and Another* [1995] EMLR 596 and *Mad Hat Music Ltd and Another v Pulse 8 Records Ltd* [1993] EMLR 172.

4.4 RIGHTS OF PERSONS WITH RECORDING RIGHTS

Prior to the enactment of the CDPA 1988, it was only the performers who had enforceable rights in their performances.

Sections 185 to 188 of the CDPA 1988 create rights for those who have the benefit of exclusive recording contracts with performers.

Section 185 defines an 'exclusive recording contract' as a contract between a performer and another person under which that person is entitled exclusively to make recordings of the artist's performances for commercial exploitation. Commercial exploitation means 'with a view to the recordings being sold or let for hire, or shown or played in public' (s 186(4)).

Infringement of the rights relating to exclusive recording agreements relate to use of the whole or any substantial part of a recording in the following circumstances:

(1) showing or playing in public (s 187); or
(2) broadcasting or including in a cable programme (s 187); or
(3) importing into the UK other than for private or domestic use, or in the course of business possessing, selling or letting for hire, offering or exposing for sale or hire, or distributing, illicit recordings. The requirements of knowledge for these offences are similar to those set out under s 184.

A live broadcast is not an infringement of the rights of the person with an exclusive recording contract, although the broadcast of a recording will be an infringement of those rights.

Recording rights may be assigned (s 185(2)), although a performer may exclude such a possibility in any recording contract.

Consent is also important when considering recording rights infringements. Either the person with the benefit of the recording rights or the performer may consent to the making of the recording. Section 186 makes it clear that rights are infringed if consent was not obtained, unless the defendant can establish that he believed on reasonable grounds that consent had been given.

In the situation where a record company has not consented to the recording but the performer has, the record company will have to rely on its contract with the performer for an effective remedy.

4.5 DURATION

Performers' rights last for 50 years from the end of the calendar year in which the performance takes place if a recording of that performance is released during that period, or for 50 years from the end of the year of release (s 191). A recording is released when it is first published, played or shown in public, broadcast or included in a cable programme service (s 191(3)).

4.6 REMEDIES

4.6.1 Civil remedies

The principal remedies are those of injunction and damages for breach of statutory duty (s 194).

Additional remedies provided by the CDPA 1988 allow:

(1) an application for delivery up of illicit copies of a performance (s 195);
(2) seizure of illicit copies which are exposed or otherwise immediately offered for sale or hire as long as prior notice is given to the police (s 196). This right does not apply to anything offered for sale at a permanent place of business.

4.6.2 Criminal remedies

The offences relating to performers' rights are contained in s 198. These offences are very similar to those created by s 107. The s 198(1) offences are committed by a person who (without consent):

'(a) makes for sale or hire; or
(b) imports into the UK otherwise than for his private or domestic use; or
(c) possesses in the course of a business with a view to committing any act infringing the rights conferred by [Part II of the CDPA 1988 (the provisions relating to performers' rights)]; or
(d) in the course of a business—

   (i) sells or lets for hire, or
   (ii) offers or exposes for sale or hire, or
   (iii) distributes,

   a recording which is, and which he knows or has reason to believe is, an illicit recording.'

It is also an offence to show, play in public or broadcast a recording of a performance without sufficient consent (s 198(2)).

Offenders under s 198(1)(a), (b) or (d)(iii) are liable on summary conviction to imprisonment not exceeding 6 months or a fine, or both. On indictment, they are liable to a fine or imprisonment for up to 2 years, or both. The other offences are liable on summary conviction to a fine not exceeding level 5 or imprisonment not exceeding 6 months, or both.

An illicit recording is a recording of the whole or any substantial part of a performance made without consent. A recording made for private purposes is not illicit (s 197).

There are provisions relating to delivery up (s 199), search warrants (s 200) and corporate liability (s 202). There is also a separate offence relating to false representation of authority to give consent (s 201). A person guilty of this offence is liable on summary conviction to up to 6 months' imprisonment or a fine not exceeding level 5 on the scale, or both. An order may be made for forfeiture or destruction of illicit recordings (s 204).

It is the duty of local weights and measures authorities to enforce the provisions of s 198 (s 198A).

4.7 DEFENCES AND EXCEPTIONS TO RIGHTS

In certain circumstances, consent may be given by the Copyright Tribunal on behalf of a performer. An application to the Copyright Tribunal can be made where either:

(1) the identity or whereabouts of a performer cannot be ascertained by reasonable inquiry; or
(2) a performer unreasonably withholds his consent.

The Copyright Tribunal has power to make a suitable order for payment in the absence of agreement between the parties (s 190(6)). The criteria upon which the Tribunal may base its decision are set out in s 190. The Tribunal will not give consent where it is apparent that the performer is withholding consent for the protection of a legitimate interest. It is for the performer to show his reasons for withholding consent. If the performer does not give evidence, the Tribunal may draw such inferences as it sees fit (s 190(4)).

In any case, there are a number of factors which the Tribunal must take into account:

(1) whether the original recording was made with the performer's consent;
(2) whether the recording is lawfully in the possession or control of the person proposing to make the further recording;
(3) whether the making of the further recording is consistent with the obligations of the parties to the arrangements under which, or is otherwise consistent with the purposes for which, the original recording was made (s 190(5)).

It is important that any consent given by the performer covers the method of exploitation proposed for the work in question. The terms of any consent contained in a contract should be carefully considered before use is made of the performance in any new or unanticipated media. Similar considerations apply as with the construction of copyright licences discussed at **1.12**.

The CDPA 1988 provides, in s 189 and Sch 2, for a number of permitted acts which may be done in relation to a performer's rights. These are similar to the permitted acts done in relation to copyright works. There are 20 sections dealing with the various permitted acts, which include the following:

(1) fair dealing for the purposes of criticism or review;
(2) incidental inclusion of a performance or a recording;
(3) various exceptions allowing the playing, showing and recording of works, including performances for educational establishments;
(4) free public showing or playing of broadcast or cable programmes.

4.8 EXPLOITATION

Most performers will, during the course of a professional career, sign a number of contracts. Contracts which relate to a performance, whether it is simply a live concert or a sound recording release, fall broadly into two categories: standard terms and individual contracts. The former category accounts for most of the day-to-day dealings between performers and businesses. For instance, the actors' union Equity has negotiated standard or collective terms with the BBC and the ITC relating to minimum fees and conditions of employment for its members. The Musicians' Union has reached similar agreement with these broadcasters. The agreements provide for the payment of a basic fee for limited transmission rights. If further exploitation of a work is proposed, then repeat fees may be payable, together with fees for transmissions overseas and for other exploitation of the performance, such as video release.

Individual agreements are likely to be the subject of greater negotiation. Such agreements typically relate to longer-term exclusive contracts, such as for the services of a pop group or a well-known actor.

The terms of these collective and individual agreements are discussed where relevant in the music, and film and television sections of this book.

Chapter 5

COMMERCIAL CONTRACTS

5.1 INTRODUCTION

This chapter introduces a number of important considerations in the negotiation, documentation and challenge of entertainment contracts.

Chapter 5 contents
Introduction
Reaching agreement
Problems in formation
Challenging agreements
Remedies and termination

5.2 REACHING AGREEMENT

5.2.1 General considerations

The basic structure of a commercial contract should include a statement of the parties, any recitals and the operative part of the document.

The operative part may contain a list of defined terms, any conditions precedent, the agreed rights and obligations of the parties, a list of representations and warranties, as well as the usual standard or boiler-plate terms. These matters are dealt with fully in the LPC Resource Book *Commercial Law and Practice* (Jordans).

When negotiating rights and other matters in the media and entertainment business, the negotiator should ensure that all the points in the following checklist are dealt with in the basic terms of the contract:

- who the parties are;
- what rights are being granted;
- how exclusive the rights are;
- when or for how long the rights can be exercised and how the contract may terminate;
- where the rights can be exercised; and
- payment terms.

Each of these points is considered in turn below.

5.2.2 Parties

The contract should state clearly who the parties are and their capacity to enter into the contract.

5.2.3 Rights

The rights clause is fundamental and is often a grant of intellectual property rights such as copyright. The grant of rights may also relate to an individual's services such as those of an actor or a musician.

An agreement must specify what rights are being granted; it may (but does not have to) specifically reserve rights not otherwise granted. A specific reservation of rights is very common where a category of rights has already been granted to a third party and the rights owner does not want this fact to be in doubt.

The division of rights varies between different entertainment businesses and, when negotiating a contract, regard has to be had to prevailing practice as well as the specific contract in point.

A rights clause can cause problems if it is not carefully drafted. For example, the rights clause may be too wide, impinging on other deals. Developments may take place which make new forms of exploitation possible. A recent example is the rise of electronic publishing and multimedia applications. It may not be clear who actually owns the rights to publish a work in electronic form as many contracts do not deal with these rights as they did not exist until recently.

Rights clauses often do not deal with these new methods of exploitation, and difficulties of interpretation ensue, which may be resolved by negotiation or legal action as well as consideration of the contract and the intention of the parties. The leading cases in this area are the copyright cases referred to in Chapter 1.

5.2.4 Exclusivity

If the agreement is to take effect as an exclusive licence of copyright, the provisions of the Copyright Designs and Patents Act 1988 must be complied with (as discussed in Chapter 1).

Exclusivity is very important whatever rights or services are being considered. An actor's services must be exclusive for certain purposes during the filming and promotion of a film; an actor promoting a product may have to agree to provide an exclusive service which may mean he cannot appear in other adverts.

There are potential legal problems with such arrangements since such exclusivity may amount to restraint of trade. It can also lead to breach of the freedom of goods and services provisions of the EC. An exclusive agreement may also be anti-competitive – which is likely where the distribution of goods or the exploitation of rights is concerned.

5.2.5 Term

The 'when' of an agreement is its duration. The term of an agreement may be a specified period of time, although an indefinite period may be used with a notice period exercisable by either party to the agreement to end the contract.

Dealings with intellectual property rights are often tied to the length of protection given by law.

If a contract deals with the personal services of an actor or musician, the term may vary between a day and a number of years.

The term of an agreement may be extended by an option clause allowing one party to give notice to the other extending the agreement on agreed terms. In this context, an option is a contractual term allowing a party to acquire a right or to extend the term of an agreement. Options are frequently found in entertainment agreements where an initial fixed period is followed by a number of contractual 'option' periods allowing an extension of the original term. A common alternative is for a lengthy fixed term with a number of 'opt out' provisions at agreed intervals.

All option clauses in agreements should set out the method by which, and the time-limit within which, they should be exercised. An option should also contain its own separate consideration upon exercise. Options when exercised should constitute valid binding contracts themselves. An option which is contingent upon terms of the subsequent contract being agreed may not constitute a binding contract at all, but may simply be an agreement to agree or an agreement to negotiate, both of which are unenforceable.

If an option is included in a contract, the person with the benefit of the option must call for its performance by notice in accordance with the terms of the agreement. There is only a right, not an obligation, to demand performance.

A right of first refusal, or a pre-emption right, gives a party the ability to make an offer on such terms as it sees fit which the other party may choose to accept (or not) as it sees fit.

Some contracts grant 'matching' rights to a party. Upon termination, the party with the matching rights is entitled to match any offer the other party has obtained for the contract.

5.2.6 Territory

Most entertainment contracts contain a territorial restriction.

The territorial limits commonly start with the world or the universe. They may also be restricted by language and country or 'territory'. It is very common for rights, whether they are the rights to services or intellectual property rights, to be divided in this way. A rights owner may try to maximise income and protect exclusivity by striking deals in a number of territories.

Legal problems relating to exploitation in this way may arise from the EC rules on freedom to provide goods and services, as well as competition law and the restrictions it can impose on contracts.

5.2.7 Payment terms

Contractual payment terms vary enormously. The contract may provide for a fee, a royalty or a profit share. A fee is normally a lump sum payment, which pays for all the rights under the contract.

A royalty payment is a percentage of income or the sale price of the product in question. Royalty rates can be altered and recalculated in many ways, as discussed in Chapter 8. If there is a royalty, there may also be an advance against royalties, which represents a payment on account of future earnings. Such an advance is always recoupable from future royalties although it is rarely returnable. This means that until enough royalties are earned to cover the amount of the advance from income from sales, no royalty is paid.

The contract may pay a share of profits. This may be a share of gross profits or net profits (as defined in the agreement), which usually means that once all the defined expenses are covered any profits are shared in an agreed way. In addition, there may be a guaranteed minimum payment due, whether the contract generates gross or net profits or not.

5.3 PROBLEMS IN FORMATION

5.3.1 General considerations

The terms necessary for the existence of a binding contract must be established by the parties to the contract. Although a contract may be oral, ideally the terms should be set out in a written agreement which is signed by both parties. There may be problems in formation where, before a full agreement is reached, the parties are negotiating terms. Negotiations should generally be conducted 'subject to contract'.

5.3.2 Lock-in and lock-out agreements

The terms of an agreement should be comprehensive and certain. Occasionally, situations arise where parties suggest that an 'agreement to agree' is entered, or that they will 'negotiate in good faith', or that one party will not negotiate with anyone else. Such agreements must be carefully drafted if they are to be enforceable.

An agreement to agree or a duty to negotiate in good faith is contractually uncertain and therefore not binding on the parties. An agreement between the parties that one of them will not negotiate with anyone else for an agreed period of time is enforceable, provided consideration is given. This is a lock-out agreement. In such a case, the party agreeing to the restriction is not obliged to negotiate, they are simply saying that they will not go elsewhere. An agreement which requires them to negotiate with the other party, a lock-in agreement, is unenforceable being void for uncertainty (see *Walford and Others v Miles and Another* [1992] 2 AC 128).

5.3.3 Renegotiation

Contractual renegotiations are common. The terms of a valid existing contract should be adhered to, as failure to do so by either party may result in a claim for breach of contract. There may be different reasons for a renegotiation. The artist may simply feel that he deserves more money, or he may have been advised that his contract is unenforceable on a legal ground such as restraint of trade. All renegotiations should be conducted 'without prejudice' to reserve a position in case of litigation.

If one party threatens proceedings for breach of contract and then subsequently settles the dispute, that party may not be able to reopen that dispute at a later date before the courts. Public policy prohibits the settlement of a previous dispute being reopened at a later date (see *Colchester Borough Council v Smith and Others* [1992] Ch 421).

If a contract is successfully renegotiated, the new agreement should be recorded in writing to reflect its terms. A novation agreement or a variation should be executed to alter the previous agreement.

5.3.4 Letters of intent and heads of agreement

One party may not be willing to commit itself to a full agreement. This may be for a number of reasons, for example because it wants to take more time to review the prospects of an artist or the viability of a project. A letter of intent may, in fact, be a binding contract if all the necessary elements for a contract are present. A letter of intent written 'subject to contract' may not be binding. It has been said that 'there can be no hard and fast answer to the question of whether a letter of intention is a binding agreement: everything must depend upon the circumstances of the particular case' (*British Steel Corporation v Cleveland Bridge and Engineering Co Ltd* [1984] 1 All ER 504).

A person who signs a letter of intent must consider the obligations to which he is being committed and whether or how he may be called upon to perform those obligations. Payment for work undertaken on the basis of a letter of intent may be recovered on the basis of a quantum meruit.

A head of agreement may be a binding or non-binding document and is a useful short-form method to record the basic commercial terms of the agreement.

5.3.5 Independent advice

Although all the factors necessary to constitute a binding contract may be present, there may be other matters to consider before signing an agreement. Particular problems arise whenever artists enter any form of contract. Advice should always be taken on the terms of the contract. There are a number of minimum terms agreements in the entertainment industry. These agreements have been negotiated between various unions (such as Equity and the Musicians Union) and major employers (such as the BBC).

The quality and availability of professional advice may be an important factor in any subsequent attempt to challenge a contract. Many agreements contain a specific declaration that the artist has been given independent professional advice. Paying for such advice is often a problem for impecunious artists. Managers and record companies may advance the artist the amount of their removable professional fees against future income.

An independent adviser should explain the contract and the reasonableness of the obligations imposed. If necessary, terms should be varied by negotiation. All advice should be recorded in writing. If a client refuses to accept advice, that fact should also be recorded in writing.

If there is a later challenge to an agreement and one party can point to the fact that independent advice was taken, it is harder to establish that the artist did not understand the extent of his commitment. Independent advice is of particular value in cases where undue influence is alleged.

5.4 CHALLENGING AGREEMENTS

5.4.1 Introduction

Contracts in the entertainment business are occasionally susceptible to challenge. Some common reasons for such challenges are considered below.

5.4.2 Contracts with minors

The entertainment industry attracts young aspirants. Whilst all inexperienced artists need to be carefully and independently advised, minors or infants need special consideration. A minor is a person under 18 years of age. Any agreement with a minor is voidable at the instance of the minor on attaining the age of majority.

However, it is less likely that the contract will be voided at that time if the artist has either positively affirmed the contract (for example, by continuing to fulfil his contractual obligations) or done nothing to dispute the contract within a reasonable time ('reasonable time' will vary according to the circumstances). The same will apply if the contract is manifestly advantageous to the artist, or if the artist had taken independent legal and financial advice prior to signing and so can be said to have understood fully the terms of the agreement. In general, the court will consider all relevant circumstances, and it is by no means the case that a contract can be voided solely because the minor has reached his eighteenth birthday.

To reduce the risk of the contract being terminated, the terms of the contract should be reasonable and allow a reasonable financial return for the minor. The contract should be for the minor's benefit so that it provides in some way for adequate training and other aids to a successful career. In addition, the terms of the contract should be properly explained to the minor, and preferably also to his parents or guardians, so that there can be no scope for future misunderstanding.

Where the contract provides for a guarantor of the performance of the minor's obligations, and the contract is held to be unenforceable against the minor, the guarantor is not obliged to fulfil the contract but may find himself liable to compensate the other party for loss caused by the non-performance of obligations by the artist. A guarantor should take independent advice on his obligations before committing himself and should ensure that those obligations cease when the minor attains the age of majority. As a rule, no one should guarantee the performance of a third party if he can reasonably avoid doing so.

There are a number of regulations concerning the employment of minors in the entertainment industry which are beyond the scope of this book.

5.4.3 Undue influence

A court will not hold someone to a bargain if undue influence can be established. This is an equitable doctrine. If a person enters an agreement where undue influence is presumed, the inference is that no free and deliberate judgement has been exercised upon entering the agreement and the agreement will be set aside.

A presumption of undue influence often arises with the existence of a fiduciary duty. In order for the presumption to arise, the party seeking to avoid the contract must prove that the other party involved acquired an influence over his mind which precluded his free consent. However, in cases where there is a fiduciary relationship, undue influence is presumed. A fiduciary relationship exists where one party relies on the guidance or advice of the other. There are certain categories of relationships which are by their very nature fiduciary. For example, the relationships between solicitor and client, doctor and patient, and trustee and beneficiary are all fiduciary relationships. In the entertainment industry, this category may include the relationship between a manager and an artist.

Cases concerning undue influence have been concerned particularly with the relationship between husbands and wives and lenders (see, for example, *Barclays Bank v O'Brien and Another* [1994] 1 AC 180). Where undue influence is presumed, rather than proved, the party seeking to avoid the contract must prove that the contract is manifestly disadvantageous to that party.

It is possible to rebut the presumption most easily by showing that the weaker party took independent advice. In the context of an artist's contract, this should involve the terms of the agreement being explained to the artist by a truly independent third party adviser. One solicitor should not act for both parties in a negotiation (to avoid any conflict of interest) even if there appears to be complete accord between the parties. A separate solicitor from a different firm should be instructed. If the presumption of undue influence is to be rebutted successfully, it will also help if the independent adviser is experienced in the appropriate area of law. The 'weaker' party should also understand the terms of the agreement.

The relationship between artist and manager is one that may give rise to a presumption of undue influence. In the correct circumstances, it is also possible for the relationship between an artist and his record or publishing company (or, rather, the individuals involved in those companies) to give rise to such a presumption.

Not all relationships between an artist and a manager or a record company executive are fiduciary. This will be a question of fact. The age and experience of the artist and the extent to which the other party has taken control or otherwise of the artist's career are relevant factors. Coupled with this, the agreement entered into must involve some form of conflict of interest on the part of the other party. Accordingly, the artist must enter into an agreement with the party whose advice is being relied upon, which agreement is to some extent disadvantageous to the artist.

Examples

Armatrading v Stone (1984) unreported, 17 September, QBD

The singer/songwriter Joan Armatrading entered into a management agreement with the Copeland Sherry Agency. The defendant was a partner in that firm. Initially, the Copeland Sherry Agency represented the claimant as her manager. However, during the term of the initial management agreement, the claimant was effectively represented by the defendant, Stone. When the initial agreement expired in March 1976, the claimant and defendant discussed between them employing the defendant as the claimant's personal manager. They both met a solicitor who prepared a draft agreement which they both signed. The bill for the agreement was sent to the defendant, and it appears that the solicitor was effectively acting for the defendant. The claimant did not receive, nor was it suggested that she should obtain, independent legal advice. One of the terms of the new management agreement was that the manager's commission should be perpetual for contracts negotiated or signed during the period of the management agreement. The agreement was to be for 5 years and the management commission was 20% of all earnings.

The claimant successfully claimed that the agreement should be set aside on the grounds of undue influence. Towards the end of the 1976 agreement, she took independent legal advice and it became clear that she had not understood the commission clause and, in particular, the post-termination commission provisions of the agreement. In this case, the claimant was able to establish undue influence because she had not formed an independent judgement after full, free and informed thought.

O'Sullivan v Management Agency and Music Ltd and Others [1985] QB 428, CA

The claimant, Gilbert O'Sullivan, signed management, publishing and recording agreements with companies controlled by his manager. His manager never suggested that the singer should take independent legal advice, and the evidence showed that at the time the agreements were signed the singer was commercially naive and trusted the manager implicitly. It transpired that the agreements which he signed with his manager's companies were not as advantageous as if they had been arm's length with independent third parties.

Because of the relationship between the singer and his manager, the agreements were presumed to be the result of undue influence and were voidable. In this case, the claimant recovered the copyrights in his compositions and the master tapes, and was also awarded damages based on an account of profits plus interest. In awarding damages, the court took some account of the time and effort that the defendants had spent in promoting the claimant. Essentially, the amount the claimant received was the difference between the arm's length rate he could have received with an independent company and the rate actually received from the defendants.

Elton John v Richard Leon James (1991) FSR 397

The facts of this case were very similar to the *O'Sullivan* case. The claimant entered publishing agreements before signing a management agreement with the same company. Despite the fact that at the outset of the relationship the publishing and recording companies were not managing the claimant, a fiduciary relationship arose. The agreements were not the subject of negotiation although they were explained to the claimant by the defendant. However, no independent legal advice was taken on the original contract. The facts of this case showed that the claimant placed trust and confidence in the defendant and, accordingly, a presumption of undue influence arose.

It was held that the defendant had breached its fiduciary obligations and was ordered to account to the claimant for elements of its profit.

5.4.4 Restraint of trade

Many contracts are exclusive arrangements between the parties. An artist usually appoints only one manager. The artist is signed to one record company and one publishing company exclusively for all recorded performances and compositions. The reason given for the exclusive nature of many agreements is the risk and investment undertaken by the recording or publishing company in signing both established and unknown artists. A degree of exclusivity is acceptable in a contract, and most contracts involve a degree of exclusivity.

Restraint of trade is usually understood to mean or to involve a restriction on a person and his future ability to carry on a trade or profession. Such restrictions were originally regarded as unacceptable because of the monopolies they created in providing services or skills in industry. Restraint of trade makes all contracts or covenants which restrict trade unenforceable unless they are reasonable as between the parties and not injurious to the public interest. A distinction must be drawn between those contracts which are in restraint of trade and those which regulate the normal commercial relations between the parties to a contract.

Artists, individuals and businessmen often seek to challenge agreements not because they restrict them from carrying on their business once the agreement has ended (although some agreements contain post-contractual restrictions) but because during the course of the agreement they are committed exclusively to another party (usually a record or production company). That other party is not committed to them in a similar way. The company may not be obliged to record, exploit, publish or release an artist's compositions or recordings. During the course of the agreement, the artist cannot, it is argued, effectively carry on his business and as a result is prohibited from earning a living.

An artist's recording contract will commit the artist to a particular record company for an initial period which may then be extended for a number of option periods. During each period, there is usually a certain product requirement. The total period of such contracts may be anything between one and 10 years and involve the artist in a continuing obligation to record and perform, and thus provide recordings for the record company to exploit if it chooses.

Whenever an artist is exclusively contracted to another party, such as a record company, it may be open to the artist to challenge the agreement on the basis of restraint of trade.

The present law is largely based on the speeches of the House of Lords in *Esso Petroleum Co Ltd v Harper's Garage (Stourport) Ltd* [1968] AC 269. This case set out some of the main principles of the doctrine of restraint of trade.

(1) Is the contract in restraint of trade?

The House of Lords refrained from laying down a rigid approach as to what constitutes a restraint of trade and stated that 'the doctrine of restraint of trade is one to be applied to factual situations with a broad and flexible rule of reason'.

At one end of the scale, there are contracts which 'merely regulate the normal commercial relations between parties' and, at the other end of the scale, there are contracts where the doctrine undoubtedly does apply. Examples of the latter include contracts where an employee restricts his ability to compete against his employer after he has left his employment, and contracts where the seller of a business agrees not to compete against the buyer of that business. The contracts with which this work is concerned, such as recording contracts, may also fall within this category. When considering a contract, all of the terms are important. If 'contractual restrictions appear unnecessary or to be reasonably capable of enforcement in an oppressive manner, then they must be justified before they can be enforced' (*Schroeder (A.) Music Publishing Co Ltd v Macaulay (formerly Instone)* [1974] 1 WLR 1308).

One way of looking at this is to consider whether the agreement is aimed at the absorption or the sterilisation of an artist's services. In other words, a certain amount of protection is permissible, but it must be limited to the amount necessary for the protection of a commercial interest.

(2) Does it protect a legitimate interest?

The term which is in restraint of trade must protect a legitimate interest. What amounts to a legitimate interest for a record company in imposing restrictions in a recording contract varies. However, it seems that the commercial needs of the company in its desire to sell as many records as possible will be paramount. Such commercial considerations relate to the need to make a profit and a high quality product, and the ability to make informed and reliable business decisions based on the availability of products, as well as the ability to recover its investment in the contracted artist and any other artists.

A record company, like any other business, needs to be able to plan ahead for marketing, manufacturing and distribution purposes. Similar considerations will apply to publishing companies and managers involved in the entertainment business where exclusively signed performers seek to challenge those agreements. These considerations all amount to a legitimate business interest.

(3) *Is it reasonable between the parties and is it in the public interest?*

The term must also be reasonable between the parties and in the public interest (*Nordenfelt v Maxim Nordenfelt Guns and Ammunition Co Ltd* [1894] AC 535). In *Nordenfelt*, it was also stated that the claimant's motives in challenging the contract are not material.

If a term is to be reasonable between the parties, the restraint must be no more than is necessary for the adequate protection of the person in whose favour it is created. The balance is between protecting an investment and achieving a good return, and allowing the artist to pursue his career.

A number of terms should be scrutinised, for example the duration of the agreement, particularly with regard to any options to extend the term; provisions for assignment of the obligations and the ownership of rights created under the agreement; the consideration involved; provisions for terminating the agreement; and any obligations to promote and manufacture the product of the agreement. The fact that certain terms are not included in the agreement may be important, as is the relative bargaining position of the parties, their age and the availability of professional advice. The test laid down in *Schroeder* was 'is the agreement taken as a whole fair?'.

Not only must an agreement be reasonable as between the parties, but it should also satisfy the public policy test. The guiding principle is that 'everyone should be able to earn a living and give to the public the fruits of his particular abilities'. As long as the agreement does not conflict with this aim, it will satisfy the public policy requirement.

When considering an agreement it is necessary, first, to decide whether the contract is one that attracts the doctrine of restraint of trade at all. Secondly, if it is established that the contract is in restraint of trade it must then be determined whether it protects a legitimate interest and whether it is reasonable.

(4) *Effect of an agreement being in restraint of trade*

If a contract is found to be in restraint of trade, it appears that the contract is voidable or unenforceable (*Schroeder*). A voidable or unenforceable contract ceases to exist for future purposes at the date of judgment. Prior to that date, the record or publishing company will retain the advantage of the contract.

It is possible that an offending clause could be severed from the contract. Severance involves separating the void part of the contract from the valid part. In principle, the courts will apply the 'blue pencil test' and sever an illegal promise only if this can be done by cutting words out of the contract so that the meaning of the remaining part of the contract is not affected. The court will not rewrite the contract, although it will delete offending terms provided that the other terms of the contract can remain sensibly intact. In principle, with exclusive entertainment contracts, the terms on which the parties will seek a declaration will be central to the contract and, accordingly, if the court is unwilling to rewrite the contract, the severance of those terms will leave no contract at all.

In claims involving restraint of trade and undue influence, it is common for the defendants to allege laches and/or acquiescence in the action.

Laches involves a delay in coming to court to seek a remedy for the alleged wrongdoing. The delay must not be one that takes the claimant outside the limitation period. However, even within a limitation period, action should be taken as promptly as possible. It is important to consider the length of the delay and the nature of acts done during the interval before action is taken which might cause a balance of injustice to one party or the other in the remedy sought.

In principle, a person should not be deprived of his legal rights unless he has acted in a way which would make it fraudulent for him to assert his rights.

(5) Application of the doctrine

The restraint of trade doctrine has been invoked in a number of cases involving performers and writers. It has also been used in cases involving sportsmen (see, for example, *Watson v Prager and Another* [1991] 3 All ER 487 and *Eastham v Newcastle United Football Club Ltd and Others* [1964] Ch 413), as well as in frequent cases involving employees.

Some examples of the application of the doctrine in the entertainment field are set out below.

MUSIC PUBLISHING

Schroeder (A.) Music Publishing Company Ltd v Macaulay (formerly Instone) [1974] 1 WLR 1308, [1974] 3 All ER 616

This case involved a young and unknown songwriter who entered into an agreement with a music publishing company. The agreement engaged the songwriter's exclusive services for a period of 5 years. The agreement was in the standard form used by the music publishing company. The songwriter assigned the full copyright for the whole world in each of his original songs created at any time during the period of the agreement. The publishers paid £50 to the songwriter as a general advance against royalties. When the first £50 was recouped from royalties, the publishers would then advance a further £50 which would be recouped from royalties in the same way. These advances would continue throughout the initial 5-year period of the agreement. However, if the total royalties advanced to the songwriter equalled or exceeded £5,000, the agreement would be automatically extended for another 5 years. The music publishers could terminate the agreement by giving the songwriter one month's written notice. The songwriter was unable to terminate the agreement in similar fashion. Furthermore, the publishers were under no obligation to exploit any of the songwriter's compositions.

The songwriter sought a declaration that the agreement was contrary to public policy as being an unreasonable restraint of trade, and as a result was void.

This was an exclusive agreement which allowed the publishers to do as they wished with the copyrights. However, the songwriter could not assign any of his copyrights elsewhere during the term of the agreement. The agreement was in the publishers' standard form and was expressed to be non-negotiable.

The court held that all the terms of the agreement had to be considered. The court had to decide whether the bargain made was fair. In other words, the court had to decide whether the restrictions contained in the agreement were both reasonably necessary for the protection of the legitimate interest of the publisher and commensurate with the benefits that the songwriter received. In this case, the restrictions in the agreement were not fair and reasonable as they combined a lack of obligation on the part of the publishers with a total commitment from the songwriter. The publishers were not required to publish any of the songwriter's compositions. The songwriter could earn nothing from his abilities as a composer if his works were not published. The agreement amounted to an unreasonable restraint of trade contrary to public policy and was therefore void.

In reaching its decision, the court noted that under the agreement as originally drafted, the songwriter was tied to the publishers and could not recover the copyright in his works which the publishers refused to publish. Although the court did not consider that for the agreement to be reasonable the publishers should enter into a positive commitment to publish future works by an unknown songwriter, it felt that there should be some general undertaking to use their reasonable or best endeavours to promote the songwriter's work. There should also be some provision enabling the songwriter to terminate the agreement. The evidence in this case showed that there was no justification for the agreement being so one-sided.

The test of fairness is '... whether the restrictions are both reasonably necessary for the protection of the legitimate interests of the promisee and commensurate with the benefits secured to the promisor under the contract. For the purposes of this test, all the provisions of the contract must be taken into consideration' (at p 623H). Lord Diplock also made comments on the standard form of contract that the publishers used in this case. He described it as a 'take it or leave it' contract (at p 624D). The contract had not been the subject of negotiation between the parties or approved over the years by way of negotiation. A standard form contract or the usual terms of a publishing or record company will not stand the test of the courts' scrutiny unless they are considered in all the circumstances to be fair and reasonable.

RECORDING AGREEMENTS

Zang Tumb Tuum Records Ltd and Another v Holly Johnson [1993] EMLR 61

An action was brought by the claimants, Zang Tumb Tuum, a recording company, and Perfect Songs Limited, a music publishing company, against the defendant, Holly Johnson. The defendant was lead singer of the group Frankie Goes to Hollywood. He wanted to leave the group, and the claimants issued proceedings on the basis that the agreements the group had signed continued to be binding upon him both as an individual artist and as a composer.

The group had signed agreements in 1983 when they were young men with little business experience. The group were keen for Trevor Horn, the owner of the claimant companies, to produce their records. There was, however, no suggestion that the claimants exercised any undue influence over the group or the defendant or that they acted fraudulently or in bad faith. The group achieved some measure of success with a string of number 1 singles. Proceedings were bought by the claimant companies seeking to force Holly Johnson to record with them after he left the group. Holly Johnson resisted the proceedings on the basis that the contracts were so one-sided and unfair that they could not stand and could not be enforced. In addition, he counter-claimed for damages because the recording costs of the second album 'Liverpool' were excessive. Under the terms of the agreement, recording costs were recoupable from the royalties payable to the group.

Applying the principles laid down in *Schroeder Music Publishing* 'was the bargain fair?'. As part of the test, the court considered all the terms of the agreement.

In this case, the court found that the provisions of the recording contract which related to the duration of the agreement were grossly one-sided.

(1) Group members were bound collectively and individually for up to seven 'option periods', and the agreement, if the record company had chosen to exercise these options, could have lasted for up to 8 or 9 years.
(2) The claimants were free to terminate their obligations at any time, but the group was bound to record only for the claimants.
(3) The claimants had the last word on all matters, including the approval of compositions and expenditure on recording costs.
(4) The claimants also had an absolute discretion to refrain from releasing records and, even if records were not released, copyright in them would remain in the claimant companies.
(5) Further, even though the group and the individual members were bound exclusively to the record companies, the companies were not exclusively bound to them. The record companies could record and promote other artists at will.

The court found that the recording contract was not a fair bargain and was in restraint of trade. In respect of the excessive recording costs claimed by the defendant, the court stated there was an implied obligation on the part of the record companies to keep such costs within reasonable bounds.

Silvertone Records v Mountfield ('the *Stone Roses* case') [1993] EMLR 152

The defendants were in dispute with their record company and music publishers. The claimants brought an action seeking a declaration that the recording and publishing agreements entered into with the defendants were enforceable and valid. The defendants contended that the agreements amounted to an unreasonable restraint of trade. At the time the agreements were negotiated it was made clear to the defendants that the recording and the publishing agreements were a package and were not separately negotiable. The defendants were advised by a manager and a lawyer at the time when they signed the contract. However, the manager was inexperienced, and the lawyer appeared to have little or no experience of the music industry. The agreement gave the record company exclusive control of the defendants for up to 7 years. During that time, there was no obligation on the record company to release any records.

The court held that there was an immense inequality in bargaining power between the parties when the agreement was entered into. Considering all the terms of the agreement, if the defendants were prevented from reaching the public with their work over a prolonged period, then the agreement was a restraint of trade. The contract could lead to the sterilisation of the defendants' services. During the period of the contract, they could not work elsewhere. The lack of an experienced adviser will not always result in an unfair bargain. The court must always consider the contract itself to determine its fairness.

Panayiotou and Others v Sony Music Entertainment (UK) Ltd ('the *George Michael* case') [1994] EMLR 229

This case involved the singer George Michael, who sought to challenge an agreement entered into in 1988 with his recording company. This agreement was a renegotiation of an earlier agreement (signed in 1984) when George Michael was a member of the pop group Wham!. The 1984 agreement was renegotiated when George Michael became a successful solo artist. The main improvement of the terms was in the advances and royalties George Michael received. By 1991, the claimant had become dissatisfied with Sony and the 1988 agreement as he no longer regarded it as being in his interest. The claimant claimed that the 1988 agreement was unenforceable as an unreasonable restraint of trade or, alternatively, was rendered void by Article 81(2) EC.

The starting-point for the court was to determine whether the contract was one which attracted the doctrine of restraint of trade at all. The second stage was to determine whether the contract satisfied the test set out in *Nordenfelt* which involved reasonableness as between the parties and reasonableness in the public interest.

The court held that it could not regard the 1988 agreement as a new agreement, arising, as it did, out of the renegotiation of the 1984 agreement. The claimant failed on the basis that the compromise of the dispute relating to the 1984 agreement was genuine and bona fide and he had freely entered into it. Accordingly, he could not now seek to reopen issues which had been compromised at the time of the renegotiations for the 1988 agreement. There was, the court said, a public interest in upholding genuine and proper compromises. On this ground alone, the claimant failed in his action.

However, the court went on to consider whether the contract would have passed the reasonableness test as set out in *Nordenfelt*. The court held that the terms of the 1988 agreement were justified and the agreement was 'fair'. In reaching his decision, Parker J took account of the consideration received by the claimant, which was quite substantial. There was no risk, on the facts of this case, that the defendants would not exploit the claimant's works, although the claimant was exclusively bound to the defendants, who would own and be entitled to exploit all his master recordings during the term of the 1988 agreement. The court concluded that, taking into account all the terms of the 1988 agreement, the restrictions contained in that agreement were 'both reasonably necessary for the protection of the legitimate interests of Sony Music, and commensurate with the benefits secured to Mr Michael under it'.

Conclusions

These cases illustrate the doctrine of restraint of trade. Each case will turn on its own facts and, in particular, on the terms of the agreements entered into by the performers. The principles as set out in *Schroeder Publishing* will be applied by the court. It is important to contrast the cases.

The *Stone Roses* and *Holly Johnson* cases illustrate that where young, inexperienced and unknown artists enter agreements which are capable of operating in a one-sided or oppressive manner then the court will be willing to set aside the agreements. In contrast, George Michael was an experienced and successful performer able to renegotiate an agreement on favourable terms – which involved the payment of substantial advances – and, on the facts before the court, it was unlikely that the contract would be operated oppressively. The agreement was capable of being fair despite its exclusivity. The *George Michael* case was decided mainly on the question of public interest in upholding genuine and proper compromises, and the court's comments on the reasonableness of the contract were obiter.

In assessing whether a contract falls foul of the restraint of trade doctrine, the factors considered above must be taken into account. In the *Schroeder* and *Zang Tumb Tuum* cases, the important factor supporting the decision was the duration of the exclusive term of the agreements in question. In the *Stone Roses* case, there were no obligations for the release of any records, whereas, in the *George Michael* case, if Sony did not release George Michael's recordings, George Michael could terminate the contract.

The financial terms for the artists in the *Schroeder*, *Zang Tumb Tuum* and *Silvertone Records* cases were poor, particularly when compared to those received by George Michael.

When considering entertainment contracts, the alleged restraint of trade generally relates to a contract's exclusivity and duration. Whether a contract is reasonable between the parties and reasonable in the public interest depends on the particular facts of the case. Guidelines were set out in the *Esso Petroleum* case which are relevant to any examination of the reasonableness of the restraint of trade. For example, the consideration for the restraint, as well as any inequality of bargaining power must be considered. Also of relevance are any post-contractual restraints, whether standard forms of contract were used, and all the surrounding circumstances of the dispute.

Particular care must be taken where previous disputes have been settled and new contracts entered into, because it is in the public interest that settlements should not be challenged at a later date (*Colchester Borough Council v Smith and Others* [1992] Ch 421). George Michael attempted to raise so-called 'counter equities' to challenge this equitable defence put forward by Sony. He claimed that during the course of his relationship with Sony, the record company had behaved unfairly towards him. The court found on the evidence that George Michael's complaints were not sufficient to counter Sony's claim that the 1988 agreement had been affirmed by George Michael.

5.5 REMEDIES AND TERMINATION

5.5.1 Damages

Damages recovered are those which arise 'fairly and naturally ... from such breach of contract or such as may reasonably be supposed to be in the contemplation of the parties at the time of the contract' (*Hadley v Baxendale* (1854) 9 Exch 341). The general principle is that, where a contract has been breached and the damage is not too remote under the rule in *Hadley v Baxendale*, the innocent party should be awarded damages to place it in the same position as if the contract had been performed.

Loss of profits and wasted expenditure

A claim may be made for loss of profits or for wasted expenditure. Both heads cannot be claimed and an election must be made. In certain circumstances, a claim for wasted expenditure may be better than one for loss of profits, which, particularly in the entertainment business, may be very difficult to prove (see, further, *Anglia Television Ltd v Reed* [1972] 1 QB 60, and *CCC Films v Impact Quadrant Films Ltd* [1985] QB 16).

Loss of publicity

There is an exception to the normal rule that a breach of contract gives rise only to a claim for damages for the loss arising from the breach. An artist engaged to perform is promised both a salary and the opportunity to enhance his reputation (*Withers v General Theatre Corporation Ltd* [1933] 2 KB 536).

Accordingly, damages for breach of contract may be awarded to reflect both loss of earnings and loss of publicity. The damages in such cases are awarded on the basis of *Hadley v Baxendale*, so they must be in the contemplation of the parties at the time of the agreement. A court may consider the stage of the artist's career, as well as the prominence and popularity of the venue. The publicity right appears to extend to performers as well as to writers and directors. In addition, professional sportsmen may be able to claim for loss of publicity if they lose the chance to compete in particular competitions or on specific occasions.

Inducement to breach contract

A typical claim for inducement to breach a contract arises where a third party attempts to entice someone away from his contract, perhaps by offering better terms. Alternatively, a claim may occur where a party cancels a contract with the result that a third party is no longer required to perform a service ancillary to the first contract. For example, if a singer cancels a show and the promoter of that show no longer needs the orchestra he hired, the orchestra may be able to claim that the singer induced the promoter to terminate his contract with them so leaving them without their full income for that performance.

It is an actionable wrong to induce a party to a contract to breach the contract. There are four elements to the tort:

(1) a third party knows that a contract exists;
(2) he persuades or induces or in some way acts so as to cause a breach of contract by one party to the detriment of the other party;
(3) a breach of contract directly attributable to that interference results; and
(4) damage is caused to the other party.

5.5.2 Enforcement of negative covenants

A contract which contains express negative terms or covenants may be enforced by injunction. However, an injunction to enforce a negative covenant will not be granted where it indirectly requires specific performance of a contract for personal services (such as a recording contract or a footballer's contract) because, effectively, an individual then has no choice but to go back to work for the 'employer'.

A singer may be restrained from performing for an impresario if she has already agreed to sing for another and nobody else (see *Lumley v Wagner* (1852) 1 De GM & G 604). The court cannot compel her to sing under the original contract, but it can stop her singing elsewhere.

Where the terms of a contract are in restraint of trade, no injunction will be granted requiring performance of the contract. However, where the contract is a reasonable one, the court will grant an injunction unless in so doing it would amount to an order to perform the positive obligations in the contract (to work, record or play), as long as the employee or artist is left with some means of earning a living. This involves a careful evaluation of whether the employee or artist can actually work elsewhere or has to remain idle. In *Warren v Mendy and Another* [1989] 1 WLR 853, the court set out the appropriate principles:

(1) a court ought not to enforce the performance of negative obligations if that will compel performance of the contract;
(2) the longer the term of the injunction, the more readily that compulsion will be inferred;
(3) compulsion may be inferred where an injunction, is sought against a particular third party or may be sought against any third party who attempts to replace the employer; and
(4) an injunction will be less readily granted where there are obligations of mutual trust and confidence between the parties which have dissolved.

None the less, in appropriate cases, the court will grant an injunction enforcing negative terms even where the injunction lasts for a long time as happened in the *George Michael* case (see above). It is also important that a party seeking to rely on a negative covenant must not itself have acted in breach of contract.

5.5.3 Termination

A contract may end for a number of reasons. Its fixed term may simply expire or an option may not be renewed. If there is a breach of the terms of a contract which does not or would not ordinarily entitle a party to end the contract, specific contractual provisions may be included to entitle a party to end the agreement.

A contract may be terminated because of a frustrating event, ie an event which occurs without the default of either party which renders the contractual obligations incapable of performance, or only capable of performance in a manner radically different from the original obligation. In *Gamerco SA v ICM/Fair Warning (Agency) Ltd* [1995] 1 WLR 1126, where a contract for Guns 'n' Roses to perform at a rock concert was frustrated because the stadium in which they were to perform was unsafe. The claimants in the case were thus able to recover advances paid to the defendants on account of ticket sales. The ill health or death of an individual may also frustrate a contract. In *Condor v The Barron Knights Ltd* [1966] 1 WLR 87, the claimant drummer fell ill and was dismissed from the band. The drummer sued for wrongful dismissal, but it was held that because of his ill health it was impossible for him to perform the terms of his contract with the group and therefore the contract was frustrated.

Well-drafted contracts should contain terms dealing with both termination and frustration. Frustration of a contract may thus occur in a defined set of circumstances, lasting for a specific period of time, after which the contract ends if a given procedure is followed. These are known as 'force majeure' clauses.

Chapter 6

THE MUSIC BUSINESS

6.1 INTRODUCTION

The music business is based on the exploitation of copyright (in songs and sound recordings) and of performers' rights.

The copyright owners of the song and the recording expect to be paid for the exploitation of their rights. For performers, this payment usually takes the form of a percentage of the copyright owner's receipts from exploitation of the recording.

The traditional method of exploitation of songs and sound recordings is by sale, broadcast, cable diffusion and public performance. The copyright owners may also allow others to rerecord their songs and recordings for use in films and videos. Innovative technology presents new ways of exploiting copyright works. Songs and sound recordings are now included on computer games, in multimedia applications and in on-line on-demand services, such as the internet and WAP telephones, as well as being sold as sheet music and song books.

Most composers and performers enter a contract with a music publisher and a record company. The contractual relations between composers and performers and their managers, agents, publishers and record companies are examined in the chapters which follow. The most effective way of exploiting a song is by recording, performing and broadcasting it. The separate owners of copyright in the song and the recording try to maximise their return from the exploitation of the work. The performers on the recording seek to receive a fair return for their performances.

Chapter 6 contents
Introduction
Composers and publishers
The record industry
The Musicians' Union (MU)
Equitable remuneration

6.2 COMPOSERS AND PUBLISHERS

6.2.1 Introduction

The composer of a song is generally treated as the author and the first owner of copyright in the work. Composers have to exploit their works effectively to achieve any degree of success. Exploitation is usually effected by giving permission for the public performance, cable diffusion and broadcast of a work (dealt with by the Performing Rights Society (PRS)); by allowing people to record the song (dealt with by the Mechanical Copyright Protection Society (MCPS) and also by a music publisher); by allowing the song to be synchronised with film, TV shows and advertisements (usually dealt with by the MCPS or the music publisher) and through sales of sheet music (dealt with by the music publisher). There are other methods of exploiting songs, but these are the most important.

6.2.2 Publisher's function

Composers often assign or grant an exclusive licence of copyright to publishing companies of all the rights in a composition.

A music publisher does more than just arrange the printing, distribution and sale of sheet music. The publisher's main function is to promote the works of a composer, and collect income from doing so. This involves persuading people throughout the world to record the compositions and perform them live. It also includes procuring the use of the music on television, in films and in any appropriate media.

Much of the publisher's function relates to the 'mechanical rights' in a composition. The 'mechanical rights' in a work relate to the right to reproduce a recording of a work onto a mechanical device. This right may be granted both by the MCPS and the publisher in respect of different media. The MCPS usually deals with the mechanical rights for the administration and payment of royalties on record sales whilst the publisher sanctions the recording of the work on film and other media.

6.2.3 The Music Alliance

The Music Alliance brings together the PRS (see **6.2.4**) and the MCPS (see **6.2.5**) under one roof to share both office and administrative functions, as their membership consists of the same class of person – songwriters and publishers.

6.2.4 The Performing Rights Society (PRS)

The owner of the copyright in a work may control the public performance, cable diffusion and broadcast of the work. Collectively, these are known as 'the performing rights'. Controlling the performance and broadcast of a work would be difficult, if not impossible, for any individual composer and music publisher because of the number of organisations which make use of musical works.

The function of the PRS is to do collectively for its members something they cannot effectively do as individuals. The PRS was founded in 1914 as a non profit-making organisation. Its members consist of writers and publishers who assign the performing rights in their works to the PRS. There are membership requirements for individuals and publishers. An individual must have had three works either:

(a) commercially recorded; or
(b) broadcast within the last 2 years; or
(c) performed in public on at least 12 occasions within the past 2 years and commercially published.

Alternatively, an individual writer may have had just one work in the top 50 of a chart recognised by the PRS within the last 12 months. A publisher must have at least 15 works in its catalogue, of which at least 10 have been commercially published or commercially recorded and, in addition:

(a) the writers of those works must be members of PRS or one of its affiliates; and
(b) the publisher must have acquired rights of at least ten of the works for a territory within the EEA.

There are three grades of membership: full, associate and provisional. The various grades depend on the PRS earnings of the member.

The PRS administers the rights to perform a work in public, broadcast it or include it in a cable programme service. The PRS also administers film synchronisation rights, but only in works which have been specially commissioned for the purpose of being recorded onto the soundtrack of a film in contemplation at the time the work is commissioned.

Blanket licences

The PRS has the benefit of a full assignment of the performing rights, which rights are defined within its articles of association. The PRS then licenses the performing rights in its works in return for a royalty. Rights are licensed to broadcasters, cable operators and places where copyright works are performed. The PRS then collects revenues on behalf of its members.

Blanket licences with broadcasting organisations facilitate the collection of money for PRS members. The agreements with organisations such as the BBC, the independent television companies, and commercial radio, as well as satellite and cable broadcasters and operators, are separately negotiated by the PRS with the bodies concerned. The amount charged to such organisations is based upon a number of factors including the level of music usage and the revenue of the broadcaster. These broadcasters then provide returns to the PRS identifying the music used in films, television and radio programmes, and enabling the PRS to distribute the royalties it has collected to its members.

The PRS has various standard form agreements for public places such as bars and shops, with agreed tariffs for the use of its members' repertoire. The income from these licences is collected and distributed to members. Licences are granted to permit the playing of music, whether live or recorded (by means of juke-box or background music system) in premises including pubs, hotels, concert halls and discotheques. The PRS operates over 40 different tariffs which have been agreed with various organisations such as the brewers' associations.

PRS fees

In order to distribute income to its own members and to members of affiliated societies whose repertoires have been licensed in the UK by the PRS (see below), the PRS will distribute in proportion to the use made of a member's work. Detailed returns are made by TV and radio broadcasters and, where music is performed live, programme returns are obtained from so-called 'significant venues' in respect of every concert or festival. These returns enable the PRS to identify the composer and publisher of each work performed or broadcast during the period, and to pay each interested party his appropriate share of the royalties. Radio logs, background music returns and music charts are used to distribute the revenue from other public performance venues where it is not cost-effective to collect actual data.

The PRS also collects income from overseas use of British works. This currently accounts for approximately one-third of PRS income. Collection of income from overseas performance and broadcast venues is made possible because the PRS is affiliated to performing rights bodies in other countries and operates in the UK to collect fees on their behalf. Fees from UK performance and broadcast are then distributed to these foreign affiliates by the PRS. The PRS distributes income quarterly to its members. Distribution takes place after the deduction of administration costs which, on average, account for 19% of total income from the UK and overseas.

The PRS divides fees on the basis of fractions of 12 or multiples of 12, and not on a percentage basis. If a composer has not assigned rights in a composition to a publisher, then the whole of the fee collected by the PRS will pass to the composer. When a composer has assigned part of the rights to the publisher, then the fees are divided between the composer and the publisher in the proportion $^8/_{12}$ to $^4/_{12}$, unless the PRS has been sent an agreement which specifies a different ratio. The PRS does not distribute more than $^6/_{12}$ of a performing rights fee to a publisher. Where there is more than one person involved in a composition, the fees will be divided by the PRS according to the publishing agreements. For example, if there is a lyric writer and a composer, it is common for the publisher to take $^6/_{12}$ and for the composer and the lyric writer to take a share of $^3/_{12}$ each.

6.2.5 The Mechanical Copyright Protection Society (MCPS)

The right to record a work is a separate right from the performance right in a song. Permission to record a song is the subject of a separate agreement with the person wishing to record the work. The MCPS was formed in 1924 to regulate the payment of royalties to publishers and composers for sales of recordings of their works. MCPS deals only with rights in underlying works, not in the sound recordings themselves. Some of the larger publishing companies grant licences directly to record companies rather than appointing the MCPS as their agent. These publishers collect revenue on sales and exploitation of recordings using their works direct from the record companies.

Licences

The MCPS grants licences to record companies (the basic MCPS contracts are forms AP1 and AP2) and other bodies who wish to record works. It also issues licences to film companies and advertising producers to allow them to record members' works in films and commercials. The MCPS also licenses its members' work for use in broadcasting by means of blanket agreements in a similar manner to the PRS. In addition, the MCPS licenses work for re-recording as background music in lifts, shops, hotels, etc. The MCPS deals with the licensing of songs for inclusion on music videos, whether for retail sale or use on TV, satellite, cable or video juke-boxes. The MCPS also receives income from the use of its members' works abroad by means of various affiliations with over 50 foreign organisations.

MCPS and the British Phonographic Industry (BPI)

The most important of the MCPS contracts is its contract with the BPI. This agreement sets the royalty rate on sales of records. This is the amount the record companies (represented by BPI) have to pay songwriters and publishers (represented by MCPS) for sales of recordings of MCPS members' songs. The rate is currently set at 8.5% of the published price to dealers, ie the price at which dealers buy recordings from record companies and distributors.

6.2.6 The internet

The PRS/MCPS Music Alliance is, at the date of writing, not authorised to exploit its members' works in an online/internet environment. This category of exploitation is, as it stands, reserved to the music publishers who currently license their works directly in such environments if they are legitimately licensed at all.

6.3 THE RECORD INDUSTRY

6.3.1 Introduction

A separate copyright exists in recordings as opposed to the copyright in underlying material such as songs and compositions. The copyright in a sound recording is an important independent copyright which is exploited by producers and record companies.

A record company must obtain a licence or assignment of copyright before it can record a song. This licence may be obtained from the MCPS or directly from the music publisher concerned.

The exploitation of sound recordings, whether by sale of CDs and tapes or by way of broadcast, is as important to the record company and the performer as the recording and exploitation of the original song is to the composers and publishers. The record company pays a royalty (the mechanical royalty) to the composer and publishers of the song, and a royalty to the performers on the recording in consideration for their services. The agreement with the performers will be embodied in a record contract or a session musicians' agreement.

The record companies are members of their own organisations, Phonographic Performance Ltd (PPL), Video Performance Ltd (VPL), as well as the BPI.

Record companies take the recorded product and release it for sale and broadcast to the public. Various promotional and marketing activities are undertaken to try to gain as much exposure as possible for the work. Depending upon where the record company is based and its resources, it may conduct each stage of the manufacturing and distribution process itself. If a recording is to be exploited abroad, arrangements will be made to license a foreign company to undertake all the necessary commercial steps to manufacture, promote and distribute it.

6.3.2 PPL

PPL is a non profit-making organisation established by record companies and record producers to control broadcasting and public use of recordings. Members assign to PPL the usage rights in all their works. PPL negotiates and issues licences for the broadcasting and public performance of sound recordings in a similar way to the PRS. Fees are based upon the value to the user derived from the recordings.

Thus, radio and television broadcasters in the UK pay licence fees to PPL for the use of their members' recordings. In addition, PPL issues licences to performance venues such as discotheques, clubs, dance halls and juke-box operators to permit the public performance of sound recordings. PPL divides the licence fees between its members in proportion to the use made of its members' records. Detailed returns are made by broadcasters, and sample returns are taken from venues where sound recordings are performed publicly. PPL has set up the Performers Registration Centre (PRC) to distribute money to performers from the broadcast of sound recordings. The roles of AURA and PAMRA are also important in that respect (see **6.5**).

6.3.3 VPL

Another method of exploiting sound recordings and songs is to make a short video accompanying the release of the recording. VPL was established by record companies and producers of music videos to regulate the broadcasting and performance of music videos. In much the same way as those set up by PPL and the PRS, blanket agreements with television stations and other programme providers allow full use of the VPL repertoire in return for a fee.

6.3.4 BPI

The BPI is a non profit-making organisation whose members comprise record companies. Its current membership accounts for 90% of the sound recordings sold in the UK. The BPI administers the UK charts and organises the annual Brit Awards which are televised internationally. As part of its trade function, the BPI negotiates on behalf of the record industry agreements relating to the payment of session musicians and covering the rate of mechanical royalties paid to composers when their works are recorded. This contract is negotiated with the MCPS.

Principally, the BPI acts as a trade association for the record industry and represents the industry in negotiations with the Government, trade unions, retailers and other sections of the music industry. Another of its functions is to combat bootleg recordings (sales of unauthorised recordings) as well as counterfeit recordings (ie illegal copies of recordings) in the music industry. The BPI has an established anti-piracy unit set up to fight the counterfeiting and bootlegging of sound recordings belonging to its members. The BPI also works with PPL.

6.3.5 Sound recordings and performers

Apart from the copyright in a sound recording itself, there are also the performers' rights. These are the subject of a separate agreement between performers and producers or record companies.

Performers' rights must not be confused with the performance right in a copyright work. Agreements between performers and record companies or producers establish the royalty rates which the performer receives on sales and other exploitation of recordings of his performances, and these are commonly known as 'recording contracts'. Royalty rates vary and, in the past, there have been various legal problems associated with contracts between recording companies and performers. Recording contracts are discussed more fully in Chapter 8.

6.4 THE MUSICIANS' UNION (MU)

The MU is the only trade union in the UK which solely represents musicians. It has as its object the advancement and protection of musicians in a number of ways. Its functions include the setting of minimum rates of pay for its members, and the provision of standard terms of engagement. There are a number of standard contracts produced by the MU for its members. These cover various forms of engagement for members, including contracts for bands performing one-off 'gigs', contracts for musical acts for a club or cabaret, and contracts for solo musicians.

The MU also provides a comprehensive advice and representation service for its members.

6.5 EQUITABLE REMUNERATION

PAMRA (The Performing Artists' Media Rights Association) is a joint venture between Equity, the actors' union, and the MU. It was set up to collect income due to performers after the introduction of the Rental Rights Directive. Performers are now entitled to income whenever their performance is broadcast or communicated to the public. This right was previously available only to copyright owners. The effect on the music business is that PPL now shares performance income with performers. Performers can now register with the PPL direct (under the PRC scheme) and receive accountings as a songwriter does from the PRS. AURA (Artists United Recorded Association) was set up by the IMF (International Managers Forum) to collect such income on behalf of featured recording artists.

Chapter 7

GROUP MANAGEMENT

7.1 INTRODUCTION

This chapter considers the choice of business medium for an artist in the music business, as well as the need for and role of a manager in the development and representation of a group or individual artists. In particular, some of the more common terms of management agreements will be considered, together with the more usual pitfalls.

Chapter 7 contents
Introduction
Choice of business medium
Appointment of a manager
Terms of agreement
Manager's warranties and obligations
Artist's obligations
Other provisions

7.2 CHOICE OF BUSINESS MEDIUM

It is important that the business, as well as the artistic, side of a performer's career is managed professionally. All individuals involved in the music business must manage their affairs as well as possible, and, in particular, to the satisfaction of the Inland Revenue, to avoid any problems. All income should be accounted for, as should all items of expenditure. A group of musicians must also be aware of their responsibilities to each other. It is for this reason that, like all businesses, musicians should put a workable structure in place to help them manage their affairs. One of the initial considerations relates to the choice of business medium. The matters outlined in the LPC Resource Book *Business Law and Practice* (Jordans) are equally relevant in the entertainment industry.

The type of artist in question is important. An individual could consider running his affairs as a sole trader or a company. A group of musicians may consider running their business as sole traders, a partnership or a company.

Groups of performers may satisfy the definition in s 1 of the Partnership Act 1890 (PA 1890), namely they are carrying on a business in common with the intention of making a profit. Accordingly, the implied terms of the PA 1890 may apply when the group forms.

As with any trading partnership, it is usually more appropriate to draw up a written agreement to deal with the administration of partnership or group affairs. The usual terms of a partnership agreement are outlined in the LPC Resource Book *Business Law and Practice* (Jordans). An agreement for a group of performers must take account of all those factors. Until a formal agreement is reached, the implied terms are likely to prevail.

7.3 APPOINTMENT OF A MANAGER

7.3.1 Why appoint a manager?

A good manager has experience of management and good contacts within the music business. The manager can help the artist find venues to perform in, recording and publishing contracts. An artist rarely has the time, expertise and experience to manage himself. A manager can actively promote an artist's business interests. Depending upon the terms of appointment, the manager will be responsible for the artist's whole entertainment career, although it may be limited to his career in the music business. This commonly involves negotiating and agreeing terms for recording contracts, publishing deals and the live performance of the artist. An experienced manager with good contacts in the business can at least make the record and publishing companies aware of the artist through his contacts. The artist is left to concentrate on his music, while the manager concentrates on financial and contractual matters.

7.3.2 Role of a manager

In law, the manager acts as an agent for the artist. The relationship is one based on mutual trust and confidence and fidelity. This is all the more so in the music business because of the degree of responsibility most managers assume for the development of the artist's career. A manager performs a personal service for an artist and acts on his behalf in dealings with third parties.

A manager's main concern is to find work for an artist. Ideally, this will be lucrative work entailing the negotiation and signing of recording and publishing contracts, followed by the successful promotion and exploitation of recordings.

Prior to the appointment of a manager, both parties must be separately represented. There have been a number of cases where management contracts have been successfully challenged on the basis of undue influence being exercised by the manager over the artist or because arrangements have been in restraint of trade. If the artist obtains independent legal advice at this stage before signing an agreement with a manager, it should ensure both that the agreement is less open to challenge at a later stage by the artist, and also that the terms negotiated on the artist's behalf are not unduly restrictive or financially onerous.

If an artist is keen to sign an agreement contrary to advice, the legal adviser should record his advice in writing and, if necessary, particularly onerous clauses should be drawn to the attention of the artist to avoid any liability at a later stage. If a management agreement is subject to analysis by a court, the availability and experience of the artist's advice may be a major factor in the court's decision. A well-advised artist warned against an onerous contract may find it difficult to set the contract aside.

The manager should be responsible for a number of matters.

- He should plan the artist's career (in consultation with the artist).
- He should deal with all necessary administrative steps as appropriate for the touring and promotional arrangements. This may include the arranging of insurance, work permits and visas, as well as appointing touring agents and arranging meetings with third parties involved in the artist's career.
- He should agree to negotiate any necessary recording or appearance contracts on behalf of the artist. The artist must approve and sign such contracts.
- Whilst the provision of the manager's service is usually non-exclusive to the artist, it is important that the manager does not take on too much other work thus disabling him from carrying out his duties under this agreement effectively. An obligation should be included in an agreement ensuring that the manager does not create a conflict of interest between one managed artist and another and

possibly that the management services of a named 'key' individual are provided to the artist.
- There should be an all-inclusive obligation requiring the manager to provide any necessary advice and services which are customarily required or expected of a manager.

7.3.3 Manager's authority

The basis of the contract between artist and manager is usually an agency agreement. The artist gives the manager authority to act on his behalf. The usual agency rule applies in that the agent is not liable in any way under any contract negotiated with a third party, and cannot, in the normal course of business, be sued by a third party for the principal's default. It is important that most, if not all, obligations incurred by the manager on the artist's behalf are approved and signed by the artist. In particular, all performance, recording and publishing obligations should be understood, explained to and signed by the artist as well as the manager.

The artist should define carefully the nature and extent of the manager's authority, his duties and obligations. A valid contract will not arise between a principal, in this case the artist, and a third party, unless the manager has authority to bind the principal.

In the absence of actual or apparent authority, the artist, as principal, is not bound or liable to a third party for the acts of his manager acting as agent. It will be appropriate to consider whether the manager was acting in accordance with accepted practices of the music business, and also whether or not it is known or there has been any form of representation that a manager acts for a particular artist. A prudent third party would usually require some evidence that the artist is interested in the engagement or obligation before signing an agreement. If there is any dispute as to an agent's authority (whether actual or apparent), it is open to the principal to rectify an unauthorised act and thereby legitimise the contract with the third party.

7.3.4 Implied obligations of the manager

The management agreement should set out the specific obligations of the manager to the artist. In the absence of any express prohibitions to the contrary in the contract, there are a number of implied obligations which arise because in law the relationship is that of principal and agent. The most important of these implied duties are as follows.

- Where the manager agrees to act for the artist he must carry out the terms of the agreement as agreed and, unless the agreement states otherwise, carry out the artist's lawful instructions.
- The manager must exercise due care and skill in acting on behalf of the artist. A straightforward example of this is to negotiate and contract on the best terms available for the artist.
- Unless otherwise agreed, the manager must also act personally for his principal. Whether or not a manager is obliged to act personally or is permitted to delegate will depend upon the arrangements with the artist. Where the management services are provided by a company, then the artist should specify or agree who is responsible for management.
- The manager has a duty to act in good faith towards the principal. The relationship between manager and artist has a fiduciary nature. Accordingly, the

manager should not permit a conflict of interest between himself and the artist and, if any does arise, he must disclose that conflict to the artist. The manager must not make any secret profit or take a bribe from a third party. Any benefit that accrues to the manager for himself as a result of his agency will be a breach of this duty of good faith. If this trust breaks down, the artist may be able to terminate the management agreement (see *Denmark Productions Ltd v Boscobel Productions Ltd* [1969] 1 QB 699).

- The manager must not misuse confidential information for his own or a third party's benefit. This applies even after an agency ceases. 'What the butler saw' revelations by managers and employees of famous people are not uncommon and, in an appropriate case, the courts may prohibit such disclosure.
- The manager is under a duty to account to the artist. This involves a duty on the manager, as agent, to keep proper accounts of all transactions, and, in principle, the manager should keep the artist's money separate from his own. An artist should avoid the risk of trying to recover money from an insolvent manager. Any money the manager keeps on the artist's behalf should be placed in a separate trust account.

A number of implied terms affect the manager:

- The manager has the right to be indemnified by the artist for any expenses incurred acting on the artist's behalf. Once again, it is usual to include express terms in a management agreement detailing the amount and type of expenses that a manager can incur without having to seek express authorisation from the artist.
- Unless otherwise agreed, there is no right for an agent or manager to claim any remuneration from the artist as principal. Such a right must be expressly or impliedly agreed between the parties and, accordingly, extensive clauses are contained in management agreements which deal with payment of the manager by way of commission on an artist's gross or net earnings.
- Once a manager's contract is terminated, no further commission will be payable by the artist to the manager. It is very important that any continuing obligation to pay commission to a manager is carefully worded so that if one management agreement is terminated and replaced by another, there is no element of double payment. It is conceivable that the terms of the original management agreement provide for ongoing commission and that the new management agreement also provides for commission or remuneration on similar categories of earnings.

7.4 TERMS OF AGREEMENT

7.4.1 General

There are a number of areas which need to be covered in the terms of any management agreement. There is no industry standard, and there is inevitably a great difference in the terms that a manager would like to see in a finished agreement and the terms that the artist is well advised to insist upon. Although a good manager is important to an artist and may be able to influence his career path, terms should not be discussed on a 'take it or leave it' basis. The artist is using the manager's services and should retain some influence and control over his affairs.

The relationship between artist and manager is a business arrangement and, accordingly, the terms of the agreement should be reflected in writing. This is to ensure certainty as much as to avoid any later dispute as to the actual terms of the agreement. Whilst subsequent disputes may arise as to what those terms on their natural construction cover, the use of a written agreement is preferable to an oral arrangement. Before entering into a written agreement, both manager and artist need to consider the following questions.

- Are there any previous agreements which may affect the terms of this new agreement?
- Is the manager to provide an individual or corporate service? The distinction is that with the latter someone other than the person the artist has been dealing with may be responsible for the day-to-day management of his affairs. If this is to be the case, it should be ascertained at an early stage.
- For what territory and what activities is the manager appointed?
- Are there any problems with the solvency of either the manager or the artist?
- Is there a relationship of sufficient trust and confidence between the parties to the agreement to enable them to work together in a suitable way?

7.4.2 Appointment and exclusivity

The artist will appoint the manager to represent him in an agreed territory for an agreed period. In return, the manager receives a commission or percentage of the artist's receipts and provides the expertise to manage and administer his business affairs and career generally. The extent to which the manager has control over the artist and directs and advises him is very much a matter for negotiation. An inexperienced artist requires more guidance. An experienced manager with good contacts and business skills will be able to help the artist enormously. An inexperienced manager with few contacts may find it difficult to advance the artist.

It is usual for a group to appoint only one manager or management company to deal with their affairs. It is unusual for a manager to agree to manage only one artist. If the manager is free to manage other artists then it is important that the manager is able to fulfil his obligations under the agreement. A manager who fails to provide the necessary time and commitment may breach the terms of the agreement and, accordingly, entitle the artist to terminate the agreement. It is important that both parties consider this before signing the agreement. The artist wants to maximise the benefit from representation, and, equally, the manager wants to maximise his return by way of commission or royalties on the artist's earnings. A clause requiring the manager to use his best endeavours to further the artist's career is important.

7.4.3 Activities

The agreement should deal with the particular fields of the entertainment business in which the manager is appointed to represent the artist. This may depend upon the skill and experience of the manager, although consideration should be given to the future aspirations of the artist as well as any current activities. For example, the manager's representation may include an artist who later turns to acting, or one who decides to publish a novel or poetry collection. A catch-all appointment which deals with any activity or performance by the artist in the 'entertainment industry' should be avoided. Quite apart from the fact that such a clause may be too wide and (if ever challenged) could be void for uncertainty, the activities of a manager should be directed at particular sectors of the industry. In the case of a musical artist, this representation should include all aspects of the making of sound and promotional video recordings of musical works, live performances whether in concerts, on radio, on TV or other broadcasts, as well as the writing and composing of musical works. Some artists also become involved with the mixing and production of recordings, and this may also be covered by the management agreement. Many successful artists also engage in widespread commercial promotions, usually by way of merchandising and product endorsement. The income from such activities may also be included in the scope of the manager's representation.

The manager's role is a matter for negotiation and agreement. A manager will not accept a role which is so narrow and well-defined that his earning potential from the artist is severely limited and, likewise, an artist should not grant a manager rights over every aspect or potential aspect of his career at a stage when he does not know in what way his career may develop.

7.4.4 Territory

As well as the exclusivity of the appointment, it must also be ascertained to what extent the manager can effectively represent the artist throughout the world. It may be more practical for the manager's appointment to be limited to, say, Great Britain and Northern Ireland and the European Community. Separate representation might be obtained for the USA, Japan, etc. Again, this is a matter for consideration in the light of the manager's experience and expertise. A well-connected manager with representation abroad may well be able to fulfil the obligations in a very wide territory and, accordingly, all countries throughout the world might be appropriate territory. Most managers insist upon exclusive worldwide representation.

7.4.5 Duration of the agreement

The management agreement may be for a fixed term with options to renew or it may be indefinite, terminable upon notice by one or other party. There should be termination provisions in the agreement which deal with breaches of contract by the parties. There are two periods in the agreement to consider: the term of the agreement itself; and the term after the agreement has ended during which the manager is still entitled to receive some commission from the artist. This latter period is discussed at **7.4.7**.

The period of an agreement is open to negotiation. A manager will require a reasonable period of time – 3 years is acceptable – both to give him time to plan the affairs of the artist and to give him a substantial period over which to gain a return.

A management agreement may contain an option to renew the term for further periods exercisable by the manager. Ideally, the notice should be served some time before the end of the agreement enabling the artist to plan ahead. If the manager fails to exercise the option on time, the artist is not obliged to extend the agreement. An artist should avoid being tied to a manager indefinitely. The Musicians' Union recommends a term of no more than 3 years, although managers prefer up to 5 years.

The agreement should also impose some performance obligations on the manager. If the manager does not secure a certain amount of earnings or an acceptable major record deal to the artist's satisfaction within, say, one year, the artist may terminate the agreement.

7.4.6 Manager's commission

The manager provides his services in return for a commission which is usually based upon the artist's gross income from specified activities.

This is usually at a rate of between 15 and 25%. The usual sources of income are those which cover the representation of the manager. Thus, a manager appointed only in respect of musical recordings and performances can only claim a commission on receipts from those activities. It is possible to exclude certain categories of income from the manager's commission. During the agreement, commission should be paid only on income arising from contracts agreed or negotiated during the term of the agreement.

The first issue between the parties must be the agreed percentage of commission for the manager. This varies, although 20% is quite common, and depends upon the experience of the manager as well as the extent of his representation. Many artists, particularly in the early stages of their careers, are an unknown quantity and, accordingly, a manager will demand, and usually receive, a higher commission than for an established artist signing a new management agreement. Some agreements allow for an escalation of the commission percentage as income grows. The converse is also possible.

Net deals

An artist's expenses are not deductible from income before the calculation of commission unless it is a 'net' deal. In a net deal, if the artist makes a loss, the manager makes no money. The manager will want to control closely the categories of deductible expenditure for a net agreement.

The management agreement should set out the income and deductions for commission purposes.

Artist's income

An artist's income for commission purposes is all the money he receives from the defined management activities. This includes income from recording, publishing, performing, merchandising and any other professional entertainment activities. Artists sometimes receive gifts and payments in kind. It is usual for gifts to be excluded from the category of income on which commission can be charged. However, a payment in kind which is clearly meant as consideration for services would be included in the income of the artist and thus subject to commission.

Advances from most sources are subject to the manager's commission as long as they are income for the artist. An advance which is a payment on account of royalties is thus subject to the manager's commission and is a valuable source of income for both artist and manager.

Manager's business expenses

The manager should be primarily responsible for his own business expenses just as the artist is responsible for his own business expenses. There is certain expenditure the manager might seek to recover, namely expenditure which is directly referable to the management of the artist. This might include transportation, travel and accommodation, as well as associated office and professional fees.

If any such deductions are to be allowed, they should be within specified limits, and all such expenses incurred by the manager must relate directly to the management of the artist. The deduction or recovery of such expenses is something that an artist may normally seek to resist. Some expenditure will clearly be in an artist's best interests and not expenditure which a manager would otherwise be expected to incur on his own account. The agreement should provide that expenses incurred necessarily and wholly on behalf of an artist are recoverable by the manager from the artist.

Manager's authority

Wherever the manager has authority to incur expenses on the artist's behalf, there must be an upper limit on expenditure on any particular item. The manager should seek the prior approval of the artist for expenses exceeding this limit. It is important, however, that the agreement is workable. No manager will want to be continually answerable to an artist for every single item of expenditure. Essentially, any expenditure that the manager incurs should be directly attributable to the promotion of the artist. If that is the case, and the expenses are reasonable, then there is no reason why an artist should complain at a later stage that the manager has exceeded his authority or incurred unnecessary or excessive expenditure.

Recording and video costs

Advances made by record companies for recording costs or promotional video costs should not be subject to commission. Such sums are not income or earnings for the artist.

Tour income

A tour undertaken by a comparatively unknown or novice artist may produce little or no profit. Manager's commission on tours and personal appearances is based upon a net profit figure, the net profit being the money left over after the deduction of certain agreed categories of expenditure, such as lighting, staffing, travel and accommodation which are reasonably incurred and directly attributable to the tour.

A separate agent is usually appointed to book tours and venues, and that agent receives commission on gross fees for the tour. Such commission often amounts to 10% of gross receipts. Agent's commission should be excluded from the manager's commissionable figure.

Tour support is money provided by a third party, often a record company, to offset a touring loss. This money should be excluded from tour income in calculating a manager's commission.

Producers

Money paid to a producer by the artist should not be included in income. However, money an artist receives as a producer will be subject to commission.

Actual receipts

It is important that commission is payable to the manager only on the basis of moneys actually received. An artist should be concerned to ensure that the manager is only entitled to commission on moneys received and not moneys which are simply due to the artist, otherwise the manager may be entitled to his commission before income has finally been received from various sources.

Collection

If litigation is required to recover money, those costs should be deducted from income before commission.

7.4.7 Commission and termination of the agreement

Ideally, an artist will cease paying commission to a manager as soon as an agreement is terminated. In practice, the manager is entitled to commission on pipeline income. The delay between the receipt of income by a record or publishing company and that income being accounted for to the artist means that the manager will have to wait to take his commission on some income.

The simplest arrangement will entitle the manager to receive commission on income arising on records released or works published during the term of his agreement. This income may be short-term, long-term or indefinite. Future records and copyright are excluded. Under this type of arrangement, a new manager can be appointed with fewer complications.

However, many agreements contain provisions which entitle the manager to commission on income on deals negotiated by him during the term of the agreement. Thus, a manager could receive commission on each album under a three-album record deal negotiated by him even though the records are released after the management agreement has ended.

The artist may consider paying commission if an album has been recorded but not released, or a song written but not published or recorded at the date of termination. An indefinite obligation to pay commission once the agreement has ended, even on deals negotiated by the manager, should be avoided.

Commission can be limited as to amount (a reduced commission after the term) and time (commission for a specified number of years). Limitations should ensure that deals which did not exist at the end of the agreement are not commissionable. Attention must be paid to this subject so that a new manager can be appointed after the term with the prospect of some earnings for his commission.

7.5 MANAGER'S WARRANTIES AND OBLIGATIONS

7.5.1 Management of the artist

The purpose of a management agreement is that the manager agrees to the best of his ability to promote the artist. Failure by a manager to promote the artist using his best skill and endeavours may give the artist cause to terminate the agreement. Whilst the obligation to promote the artist underpins the manager's obligations, it is impossible for management to guarantee success. It is clearly in everyone's best interests for an artist to record, perform and generate income.

7.5.2 Receipt of income

A prudent artist will ensure that specified income is paid directly into a bank account controlled by himself or his accountant. Publishing and recording income should be treated this way. Commission is then paid with the artist's authority to the manager by an accountant or other third party.

The manager is then left to deal directly with all other income for which he should open a separate designated trust account. This includes performance and merchandise income from which the manager is authorised to deduct his commission. The manager must take appropriate steps to ensure that the artist receives all moneys due to him. If this involves legal action, the artist should be consulted prior to proceedings being issued.

Both the manager and the artist must be obliged to pay each other their dues. The manager must receive his commission promptly, and the manager must not retain that part of the artist's income within his control.

7.5.3 Accounting

In respect of the income which he controls the manager must provide full, accurate and regular statements of account to the artist. These statements must deal with all income received by the manager on behalf of the artist. Whilst it would not be usual to require the manager to provide audited accounts, the keeping of up-to-date accurate books is important. Without such information, the artist's accountant is unable to prepare tax returns. The manager should prepare cash-flow forecasts as well as estimates of expenditure. The manager must then provide brief but regular accounts and other financial information to keep the artist up to date with his financial situation. This may involve monthly accounting. The manager should also provide more detailed accounts on a half-yearly basis.

If the artist has appointed an accountant to receive some income, the accountant pays the manager's commission.

7.5.4 Miscellaneous

The manager must confirm that he has not entered into any conflicting agreements or arrangements which would in any way limit or hinder his ability to provide services as agreed under the terms of the agreement.

The manager should also undertake not to assign or attempt to assign the benefit of the agreement to any third party. An artist may consider agreeing to such an assignment; however, any assignment must be made with his prior written consent. Ideally, an artist should take independent advice in such a situation.

It is also customary for an acknowledgement to be placed in the agreement on the part of the manager stating that no copyright or performance rights are vested in the manager. Furthermore, no rights in the name or likenesses of the artist will vest in the manager. Accordingly, all intellectual property rights should, unless specifically assigned elsewhere (eg in publishing agreements), remain in the ownership of the artist. It is not usual for an artist to assign such rights to a manager, and he should resist such a requirement.

7.6 ARTIST'S OBLIGATIONS

The fundamental obligation for the artist is to provide his services as and when directed by the manager. A refusal to do so will prevent the manager from performing his obligations and, accordingly, there may be a breach of the terms of the agreement. That is not to say that an artist should do everything that a manager requests. However, to give efficacy to the agreement, the artist must provide services as reasonably required. The types of services the artist should perform relate only to the scope of the manager's appointment. Typically, for a musician this involves performing, recording, composing and promoting his work.

An artist will usually also agree not to provide services for any third party without the manager's permission. The artist is exclusively represented by the manager and, accordingly, performing or recording with someone else without the manager's knowledge or agreement could amount to a breach of the agreement.

The artist must disclose any prior or existing agreements which may hinder his ability to render his services. In particular, previous recording or management agreements may hinder the manager in effectively performing his tasks. Any such agreements should be disclosed. A diligent manager will usually seek to perform a full review of an artist's existing obligations before agreeing to represent him.

Frequently, agreements will be signed obliging new members of a group to sign a management agreement with the group's manager. Similarly, departing members will often be obliged under the terms of the agreement to use the manager in any new or solo career which they undertake.

It is usual for management agreements to be signed jointly and severally by the individual members of the group. In such a case, each member will be liable for the acts and defaults of the others. In principle, such joint and several liability also means that each individual is bound to the manager. An express clause dealing with the situation where one member of a group leaves to pursue a different career will normally be included in an agreement for the avoidance of doubt. In such a situation, a clause will specify what rights a manager has. Once again, this is a matter for agreement between the parties.

It is important for departing members of a band that they are fully indemnified against any risks or liabilities which might have arisen whilst they were part of the band. Usually, a group's partnership agreement will deal with this, often by way of an indemnity from the remaining members. If the group is a partnership then the usual steps upon departure or retirement of a partner should be taken, for example placing appropriate advertisements, and altering the group stationery and bank accounts.

A departing member may simply assume – despite a clause in the contract to the contrary – that the manager will have no interest in his new career. In such a case, the departing member cannot rely on the fact that a manager may have done nothing to assert his rights. If the rights are contained in the contract, then it will usually be some time before the manager is deemed to forego rights. It is possible that a failure by the manager to promote a departing member is a breach of his best endeavours obligation. However, this cannot be relied upon by the departing member and, if necessary, a specific release should be sought from the manager.

It is important to explain to the members of a group that the terms of the agreement may apply to them if they depart and seek a different career. There may also be other matters to be addressed upon departure of a member. These will relate particularly to the internal management of the group members as well as to the manner in which joint, but perhaps unrecorded, material will be dealt with. Regard should also be had to the terms of any recording agreements, which may similarly seek to bind the departing member to recording with the same company.

7.7 OTHER PROVISIONS

There are a number of provisions relating to termination which may be included in the agreement.

A force majeure clause will deal with unforeseen circumstances beyond the control of the parties which would otherwise frustrate the contract by preventing one or both of the parties to the agreement from fulfilling their obligations.

Failure by the manager to perform any of his obligations could also give a right to terminate the agreement, for example where:

(1) an allegation is made that the manager is not using best endeavours to promote the artist and, accordingly, is not performing his side of the bargain. In such a situation, the artist should keep careful records of evidence which, if necessary, could be produced before a court to help substantiate such allegations. Minor breaches should be remedied quickly. Persistent breaches, although minor in nature, should give the parties the right to terminate the agreement;

(2) there is a failure to account or render accounts as required by the agreement. This should be a specific breach of obligation on the part of the manager which could result in termination;

(3) automatic termination of the agreement if the manager becomes insolvent or is in any way unable to meet his debts as they fall due. In such a situation, the right to commission under the terms of the agreement should also cease.

A time-limit should be set within which the artist must complain or serve notice on the manager terminating the agreement. A distinction will usually be drawn between a breach of contract which brings or gives a right to terminate and minor breaches of contract which are more easily remedied. In any event, an artist may, by conduct, affirm the contract despite a breach by a manager. In such a case, an artist would not subsequently be entitled to terminate an agreement unless there was a new breach of agreement giving the right to termination.

Other boiler-plate clauses dealing with assignment of rights, confidentiality, choice of law and jurisdiction, service of notices and other relevant matters, for example arbitration, should be included as appropriate.

Chapter 8

ARTISTS' RECORDING AGREEMENTS

8.1 INTRODUCTION

8.1.1 Recording agreements

A recording agreement is the cornerstone of a successful career for successful 'popular' and 'classical' performers. Although live performances can create an enthusiastic following, the money and popularity created by recording and releasing work is the basis of wider popularity. The number, quality and popularity of artists signed on recording contracts to record labels is a basic asset for most successful record companies. This chapter considers some of the important clauses and considerations which must be borne in mind when drafting or reviewing recording contracts.

It is unusual for all but the most established artists to have a choice of record company and recording contracts. It is often the case that an unsigned band will accept any deals offered. This is despite the fact that in many cases the long-term effects of a bad deal may make it worse than no deal at all. The acceptability of a deal depends upon negotiation between the artist and the record company. The artist should always be advised by someone who is independent and experienced in the music industry (for the problems that can arise if this does not happen, see, eg, *Silvertone Records v Mountfield* [1993] EMLR 152). The absence of such advisers may, in the event of a subsequent dispute, prove fatal to the agreement. Whilst this may not be of immediate concern to the artist, record companies are best advised to ensure that the artist is aware of the need for and takes competent professional advice.

This book does not consider the international aspects of a record deal. One choice which an artist may have to make relates to the company with which he signs a contract. In circumstances where the artist has a choice, it may be between a direct signing with a record company, signing with a 'label' owned by a record company or signing with an independent production company. This book considers only the common terms of such deals.

8.1.2 Performers' rights

A recording agreement is based upon the ability of an artist to give a record or production company the exclusive rights to record and exploit performances. The statutory performers' rights contained in Part II of the CDPA 1988 and the consent necessary for the exploitation of performances are important aspects of a recording contract. The CDPA 1988 also recognises the existence of 'exclusive recording contracts' between performers and record companies. The performances in question usually take place in a recording studio with other musicians, a sound engineer and a record producer. Consent to record and exploit performances should be explicitly given in the contract.

Chapter 8 contents
Introduction
Sound recordings
Duration of the agreement
Artist's warranties and obligations
Company's warranties and obligations
Advances
Royalties
Other royalty rates
Calculating royalties
Accounting
Departing members
Termination provisions
Post-termination

In return for the grant of exclusive recording rights to a record company, an artist expects to receive payment. An artist's remuneration is paid as a royalty based on sales of recordings. In addition, it is common for an advance against royalties to be paid to the artist. The record company will also pay recording costs. Both sums are recouped from income. The artist's right to equitable remuneration is dealt with by receipt of a share of a recording's public performance income – the income collected by PPL.

8.2 SOUND RECORDINGS

8.2.1 What is a sound recording?

The CDPA 1988 defines a sound recording as a recording of sounds on any medium from which the sounds may be reproduced. For the purposes of a recording agreement, it is important to define exactly what sound recordings the company has the rights to and, in particular, what types of recording the artist gives his consent to the company to exploit. The agreement must define what is meant by a recording. A 'recording' may be defined in the agreement as:

> **an audio or audio-visual recording made for the Company by the Artist on any format known now or arising in the future under this agreement.**

The company will own and exploit the recordings. The agreement should stipulate exactly what medium the recordings can be exploited in, otherwise the artist may be able to argue at a later date that no consent was given for a particular form of exploitation. A record company should reserve the right to 'distribute and sell the recordings in any configuration and all media whether now known or known in the future'. Such a clause should include CDs, tapes, LPs and singles as well as audio-visual products. The definition should, from the record company's point of view, be wide enough to include methods of exploiting sound recordings which have not yet been invented but which may become popular. A good example of this is the development of the compact disc over the last 15 years, with the prospect of developments such as the mini disc and the DAT tape continuing in the future. Forms of multi-media exploitation such as CD-ROM and other computer formats may also be considered, as well as interactive products, webcasts and broadband exploitation. On-line distribution and exploitation of recordings is also developing and record companies now exploit these rights. The extent to which the artist will be able to negotiate royalties on unusual exploitation of the sound recording depends on the status of the artist and on the precise wording of the contract which may not have taken account of some technological advances and thus have no royalty rate in place for them. Although the definition of a 'recording' may cover a new technological advance, the contract may not provide a royalty rate for that new format. The company and the artist may then have to agree a rate for the format or the company may claim the artist is not entitled to further payment. Generally, a record contract provides a 'catch-all' royalty rate for all new technologies/formats.

8.2.2 Copyright

The copyright in a sound recording is distinct from the copyright in any underlying material such as the song itself. The exploitation of an underlying work, and the collection of income due from an artist's original compositions is a matter for the artist's music publisher, the PRS and the MCPS. In any sound recording, there will be a number of rights involved. The copyright in the song (music and lyrics) will either be with the original composer or authors of the work, or it may have been assigned to a music publishing company. The ownership of copyright in a sound recording is dealt with by s 9(2)(a) of the CDPA 1988, under which the author is the person by whom the arrangements necessary for the making of the recording are undertaken. This is often the producer of the sound recording or the record company itself. The performance right in this copyright is dealt with by PPL on behalf of individual record and production companies.

The recording contract will deal with ownership of copyright in sound recordings. It is usual for an express declaration that the record company owns copyright as well as for the artist to make an assignment of such copyright to the record or production company. Such an assignment will be included in the agreement so as to avoid any later arguments over copyright ownership in the recordings. This is quite distinct from copyright ownership in the underlying works, use of which requires permission from the songwriter or publisher.

8.2.3 Moral rights

Moral rights relate mainly to the underlying works in a sound recording (such as the song itself) and thus relate to the composer of works that are recorded. The scope of and need for any provisions in the recording contract dealing with moral rights must be carefully considered.

8.2.4 Rental rights

The contract must also deal with the artist's rights under the Rental Rights Directive. This means terms are included stating that rental rights are assigned or licensed to the record company. The record company must pay the performer or artist an 'equitable remuneration' for rental of the work. More importantly, the performer is entitled to 'equitable remuneration' for broadcasts and communication to the public of recordings. This income entitlement impinges upon the PPL income. Negotiations are currently taking place between the record companies and PAMRA, an organisation set up to collect and distribute performance income. On the one hand, record companies would like control of this income so as to use it to recoup advances and recording costs. On the other hand, the performers would like to receive such income directly. The matter is not yet resolved.

8.2.5 Contract considerations

Apart from matters dealt with expressly as a result of copyright, performers' rights, rental rights and moral rights, the recording agreement is mainly a matter of contract law. It is important that the terms of the agreement are all expressly included in writing in the document signed by the parties. Enforceability of a recording contract, together with the construction of its terms, is a matter for rules established under the common law. There have been particular problems with entertainment contracts over the years, which have resulted in extensive litigation. In particular, courts have been asked to look at contracts that are allegedly in restraint of trade or have been made as a result of undue influence. It is also important that where an artist is a minor, due regard is had to the common law governing contracts with minors.

The major terms of recording contracts are considered in this chapter. Matters that are purely contractual, and not particular to recording contracts, are considered in Chapter 1, which includes such considerations as undue influence and restraint of trade.

Before signing a recording contract an artist should be properly advised.

An independent, experienced manager can be appointed to help promote the artist and negotiate agreements on his behalf. It is important that the manager does not have any conflict of interest. For example, if the manager owned or had a holding in the production or record company with whom the artist was signing, he should not wear both those hats in any negotiation.

Independent legal advice explaining the terms and effects of any agreements should be obtained before such agreements are signed. Although such advice should be of assistance, there have been instances where, despite the provision of experienced legal advice at the outset, the courts have been willing to set aside or vary agreements. The fact is that many artists will sign with a record or production company despite adverse advice because of the difficulty in obtaining any contracts.

As far as possible, the terms of the agreement should be fair and reasonable and not unduly onerous. If possible, the obligations placed on both parties should contain the minimum restrictions necessary to give the contract business efficacy.

8.3 DURATION OF THE AGREEMENT

8.3.1 Term and minimum commitment

The duration of a recording contract should be as certain as possible. However, the term of the agreement, whether fixed or not, will be referable to a 'minimum recording commitment'. The agreement is also likely to be separated into a number of separate contractual periods. Each period may, especially for new artists, be tied to an option to renew the contract once the minimum recording commitment for the period has been satisfied. In contrast, an established artist may have a contract for a number of recordings with an option after two or three albums for the record company to extend the contract.

For example, an agreement may provide that it is to last one year during which time the artist has to make enough recordings to satisfy a minimum recording commitment. This commitment will almost certainly be for material previously unrecorded by the artist. It may also have to be for material written by the artist.

Alternatively, the term may be referable to the delivery of recordings. Thus, an initial period may last until 180 days after delivery of the recording for that period, but for not less than a year or 18 months in total. When considering the term of any contract, regard must be had to the potential length of the agreement including any options and other extensions (such as for late delivery) included in the agreement.

Late delivery of an album may allow the company to extend the term of the agreement by a certain number of days. Any extensions which are possible under the agreement should only be for reasons which are referable to the artist's default. If the term of the agreement can be extended, there should be a long stop beyond which the agreement cannot legitimately extend. As long as the artist satisfies his minimum recording commitment, there should be no extension or effective penalty for events that are out of the artist's control.

The contract may also require the artist to deliver the recordings within a certain period of time after which the record company may be able to terminate the agreement. This is to prevent long delays by previously successful artists subsequently wishing to resume a career. In addition, the artist is usually restricted to the delivery of one recording at a time. This prevents the total contractual commitment from being delivered by the artist at once in order to end the contract.

The duration of an agreement is one of the matters that the courts have considered in a number of the cases dealing with restraint of trade in music contracts. The contract should specify as clearly as possible when the term commences and the date on which it ends. Many record companies include in their agreements options to extend the term, exercisable by the record company on notice to the artist.

Despite the fact that an agreement may appear to be for a fixed term, if the minimum recording commitment is not satisfied during the term, there will be a clause allowing the record company to extend the term until the commitment is satisfied. The length of any such extension varies but there should be a long stop period beyond which any given period of the agreement cannot run.

If an artist fails to satisfy the minimum commitment during the agreement (and any extensions) it will amount to a breach of contract allowing the company to terminate its obligations under the agreement.

The minimum commitment should be for a definite number of master recordings. The number should be attainable, and the company should be obliged to provide the means for the artist to meet the commitment. This involves the allocation of a budget and the booking of studio time. Compositions must be chosen for the recording sessions. If necessary, a producer must be agreed. The terms upon which a producer is employed are usually a matter for the company to negotiate, although a producer royalty is often deducted from the artist's income. The minimum commitment may be for a certain number of singles or albums as defined in the agreement. The terms of the agreement should also deal with the obligation of the record company to promote, distribute and commercially exploit the master recordings.

8.3.2 Options

It is usual for a record company to include either an option to extend the length of the term or a number of break clauses at various points in the contract. Indeed, there may be an option to extend the term several times or a break clause exercisable on a different number of occasions. Each extension of the term of the agreement should be for a certain or defined period and for a certain recording commitment during that time. If the term of the contract, or the options granted under it, result in the artist being bound to the record company for a long period of time, this may be a factor in a subsequent challenge by an artist to the validity of the contract on the grounds of it being in restraint of trade.

There is no standard formula for the inclusion of an option or break clauses within an agreement. A new signing is unlikely to be given a long-term commitment from a record company until he has achieved some success. For the record company, the purpose of an option or break clauses is to enable it to retain successful artists and release those who are unsuccessful.

The option, or each successive period of the contract, should be accompanied by a payment, which may be an advance on royalties, and, as such, recoupable by the record company from the artist. Any option must clearly set out the conditions and terms of the extended contract (or not terminated). An artist who feels that the contract, if extended, does not reflect his status and success may seek to renegotiate terms. Any renegotiation inevitably centres on the amount of money (in terms of advance and royalties) the artist expects to receive and the duration of the agreement (in terms of the number of recordings the company may now commit itself to call on during each period of the agreement). Accordingly, the artist should negotiate increased advances and stepped royalties for each option or successive period of the agreement.

Record companies often cite the use of break clauses over options as preferable, because a company cannot 'inadvertently' neglect to exercise an option. The converse is also true – it may neglect to terminate.

8.4 ARTIST'S WARRANTIES AND OBLIGATIONS

8.4.1 Standard terms

Reference in this paragraph to 'standard' terms and conditions is to the common or usual terms normally found in a recording agreement. Although there is enormous variation from record company to record company, there are a number of matters that it is usual to find in an agreement.

8.4.2 Artist's obligations

Central to the recording contract is a promise by the artist to provide exclusive services (performances) to the record company in return for money. The exclusivity provisions are fundamental to the record company. An artist cannot record elsewhere without the record company's permission. Typically, there is also a re-recording restriction after the agreement has ended (this is discussed at **8.4.3**).

It is important that the artist – whether an individual or a member of a band – is not bound by any previous agreement which could affect the contract that is being offered. The artist is normally required to warrant that there are no existing obligations which would restrict his freedom to enter the contract. The record company will require a number of warranties from the artist relating to this point.

In particular, a record company usually requires the artist to state that:

(1) he is free to enter into the contract;
(2) he has the right to assign any rights granted to the company;
(3) he has not entered and will not enter into any other conflicting arrangements.

Alternatively, if an artist is still bound by a previous contract, this should be disclosed to the company. The new contract will almost certainly conflict with any previous exclusive recording agreement. The record company should not sign the artist unless and until the artist is released from the previous contract. All previous contracts should be disclosed to the record company to ensure that there are no existing obligations that conflict with the new agreement.

The record company will require a number of other obligations from the artist. For example, he may have to agree:

(1) that his performances will not be obscene, blasphemous or defamatory of anybody;
(2) to join and remain a member of the Musicians' Union or other similar organisation, if appropriate;
(3) not to do anything that would prejudice his standing or that of the record company or damage either party's reputation;
(4) to take reasonable practical steps to stay in good health and not put himself at any risk;
(5) to perform to the best of his abilities;
(6) not to grant any other person the right to record a live or other performance, including any one-off performance he may give which could, none the less, be exploited;
(7) to do what the record company reasonably requires to promote the recordings;
(8) to attend recording sessions and rehearsals. The artist should turn up on time and in a fit state to perform and rehearse;
(9) not to perform with any other artist without the record company's permission;
(10) that he is not a minor; and
(11) that he is a qualifying person for the purposes of the CDPA 1988.

The artist might also be obliged to use his own name or his stage name, as appropriate, and not to change it except with the company's permission. Part of the artist's goodwill is in his name. This is the easiest way for the buying public to identify the artist and buy his recordings. There may be an obligation on the artist to keep the company informed of his whereabouts at all times. Some of the more onerous terms might relate to the look or style the artist adopts. The company will be concerned that an artist does not abandon a successful image in favour of an untried one without proper consultation. An artist may warrant that he will not carry on any anti-social activity or be convicted of a crime, although such restrictions should be avoided as being unduly onerous. A mutual obligation may be imposed by the record company to ensure confidentiality so that the terms of its agreements are not disclosed.

The artist should avoid giving any warranty or entering into any obligation that is either unduly onerous or difficult to perform. Once again, this is a matter for considered advice and discussion.

The artist will usually allow the company to use his likeness and name for promotional purposes. It may be appropriate for the artist to be given the opportunity to approve any promotional or advertising material in advance of publication. This permission should be limited so that it covers only the right to use the artist's likeness for promoting records and not for any merchandising purposes. Merchandising rights should be the subject of separate agreements and negotiation.

Obligations to promote recordings and to tour may also be included in a recording contract, although the details of such obligations will be agreed between the management, the artist and the company.

8.4.3 Re-recording restrictions

The record company is likely to impose a restriction of a few (perhaps 5) years from the end of the agreement on the re-recording of any of the master recordings or any individual compositions contained on them. This restriction only binds the artist and does not stop third parties (who have the publisher's permission) from producing other versions of a previously recorded song. The restriction would apply to live as well as studio versions of recordings, but does not hinder an artist from performing his recordings live. This restriction should be tempered so that it only applies if the record company has released the composition in question either during the term of the agreement or within a specified period (of perhaps one or 2 years) after the end of the agreement.

Such a restriction exists to allow the company to exploit its catalogue of original recordings to its best ability. It is quite common for recordings to enjoy a resurgence of popularity some time after the original release because of an advertising campaign or a wave of nostalgia. It does not prohibit an artist from re-recording with the consent of the company although that consent may not be forthcoming. Such restrictions may be in restraint of trade.

8.5 COMPANY'S WARRANTIES AND OBLIGATIONS

8.5.1 Recording and release

It is important, if the artist is obliged to perform and record material, that there is some obligation on the company to fund, release and exploit those works. If the company is in no way obliged to do so, then the artist has no way of making a living. An agreement which places no obligation or no substantial obligation on a record company to release material may be challenged as being in restraint of trade. Whilst the artist is signed exclusively to the company, the company may effectively have no reciprocal obligations of its own. This obligation should include overseas release.

An artist should ensure that the record company is obliged to provide the money for him to record a specified number of master recordings, whether singles or albums. Without this commitment from the record company, the artist has no way of fulfilling the minimum recording commitment. On the other hand, record companies are concerned that they are not obliged to fund and release a large number of recordings where the artist in question is, as yet, unproven. In this case, the record company will usually be willing to commit itself to a certain minimum of product – perhaps two singles or one album – and then to have an option to extend the term of the agreement, as discussed at **8.3**, depending upon the success or otherwise of those recordings.

Acceptability of recordings

The artist will be concerned to ensure that the record company, having paid for and received master tapes of a recorded performance, is then obliged to manufacture and make those recordings commercially available to the public. The record company will be unwilling to undertake any minimum release commitment and will be allowed to use its own commercial judgement as to the date and manner of release. The record company will reserve the right to refuse recordings if they are not deemed to be suitable for its purposes. This suitability relates to technical matters (such as the quality of the equipment the performances have been recorded on) as well as the commercial suitability of the product. This latter requirement is likely to be the more controversial of the two as it involves the record company making an artistic judgement. If the artist and the record company have collaborated sufficiently in the making of the recordings, there should be no problem. The agreement should reflect this collaboration by requiring the company to consult the artist over the choice of material, approval of a budget, appointment of a producer and any other matters which are important to the parties.

Release

Some of the cases which have considered music industry agreements (such as *Silvertone Records v Mountfield* [1993] EMLR 61) have commented on the lack of obligation on the part of a record company to release or exploit recordings. If there is no such obligation, the contract may be challenged as being in restraint of trade. Such a challenge would usually only enable the artist to be released from the contract with an award of damages. Ideally, an artist would like to see a record company actively manufacturing, promoting and selling his work to the public.

Unfortunately, there is no guarantee that any works will be successful, however much money has been spent on making and promoting them. A record company cannot make the public buy a record, although there are certain steps that can be taken to ensure that recordings come to the attention of the public. Manufacturing recordings is the first step in this process, after which the work needs to be 'plugged' and marketed to receive as much broadcast coverage or 'air-time' and other publicity as possible. This involves giving copies of new releases out to disc jockeys, TV stations and the music press to encourage their broadcast and purchase. As a result of broadcasting, reviewing and appropriate promotional dissemination, public interest may arise sufficiently to stimulate sales of the work.

A record company must agree to release or procure the release of the master recordings delivered by the artist under the terms of the contract. It should do so within a reasonable time of delivery. A time should be stated in the contract. This time may vary, but must be at least long enough for the company to make all the necessary arrangements for the release of the recording. A provision requiring the company to use its best or reasonable endeavours to promote the recording should be considered. A company may not agree to the best endeavours clause, but, nevertheless, some commitment should be extracted. A period of between 4 and 6 months between recording and release is quite reasonable. The effects of the company's failure to release the recordings should also be dealt with in the agreement. If there is a legitimate reason (such as an event of force majeure), the artist may have no cause for complaint. If the company has simply been dilatory in fulfilling its obligations, the artist may consider serving a notice requiring it to fulfil its obligations within a specific time. If the company fails to do so, the termination provisions of the agreement could take effect. If the company never releases a recording, the artist may sue for breach of contract. In the event of no release, the artist should also ask for a reassignment of copyright in the recording.

8.5.2 Recording costs

An artist will generally be financed by the record company, which should provide the necessary means to fund studio time, payment for session musicians, studio engineers and, in certain circumstances, the producer. Recording costs are part of general advances which are recoupable from royalties. The recording costs are the record company's investment risk. If an album is not successful, it does not recover its investment. Although a record company is usually entitled under the terms of the recording contract to recover recording costs as a first charge on royalties in the same way as advances are recoverable, if an artist fails to break even in terms of recording costs alone after his first album, then the record company may not renew its options or release any further material by that artist.

The record company recovers recording costs (as it does advances) from all royalties payable to the artist on the sales of that artist's recordings. Effectively, the artist subsidises his unsuccessful recordings with his successful ones.

Recording costs can often be a bone of contention between an artist and a record company. Generally, it is in both parties' interests to control recording costs so that they do not escalate unduly. Excessive recording expenditure may be the difference between a recording being profitable and never recouping its costs. It is in both parties' interests to obtain the best results possible from the available budget. In *Zang Tumb Tuum Records Ltd and Another v Holly Johnson* [1993] EMLR 61, the court looked unfavourably upon the level of expenditure incurred in producing the second album by the group 'Frankie Goes to Hollywood', especially as the costs were largely spent in hiring the company's studios. In the circumstances, the court was prepared to state that there was a duty on the production company not to spend an excessive amount on production costs. This should be borne in mind by company and artist alike at the time of recording.

It is important that the artist limits the actual recording costs which can be recovered from royalties by ensuring that the way in which recording costs are defined is limited to actual direct costs incurred by the record company in producing the album. For example, an artist will not wish recording costs to include other productional packaging costs of the recording itself, such as the commissioning of artwork or sleeve design or the payment of royalties to third parties associated with the production of the recording. These are costs which should be borne by the record company, and not the artist.

The record company will recoup from the total of an artist's costs and expenses over the whole course of the agreement and sometimes from previous agreements. Thus, a successful back catalogue of recordings can subsidise an unsuccessful future recording. Cross-recoupment from music publishing deals and income from anything other than recordings should be avoided. The artist should police cross-recoupment from other contracts carefully, as terms allowing this can slip into deals.

8.5.3 Music publishing royalties

In addition to the payment of royalties to the artist for his performance, there are payments due from the record company to the owners of the underlying works. Underlying works in the case of popular music are usually the songs used and recorded by the performers. These songs may or may not be written and composed by the performers themselves and may include cover versions of previous songs, or songs specially written and submitted to the artist for recording.

The sale of records which contain copyright works attract a royalty, known as the 'mechanical royalty', which is due to the owner of the copyright in the song. The MCPS administers this right under an agreement reached with the BPI. These payments are unrelated to the royalty due to the artist as performer of a work.

It is important that the royalty rate and the retail selling price of the sound recordings do not include any deductions in respect of such royalties payable by the record company for use of the underlying copyright material. This is an expense properly borne by and accounted for by the record company.

8.5.4 Other obligations

Promotion

The promotion of the artist's recordings should primarily be undertaken by the company. The costs of the promotion should also be borne by the company. The company should undertake a certain basic level of promotion. This should ensure that the recording is promoted to the public. The cost of any higher or unusual promotion may be recoupable from the artist, although this must be agreed with the artist if not included in the agreement.

A typical method of promoting new recordings is the promotional video. The company may retain the right to request the artist to make a promotional video. The exploitation of the video is left in the hands of the company and VPL (the organisation that deals with block licensing of videos on behalf of the record companies). Record companies often release promotional videos in a similar way to tapes and CDs for sale to the public. The costs of such videos are usually treated as recording costs and deducted from royalties. The usual term is for 50% to be attributable to the artist's general recording costs and the remaining 50% to income from the exploitation of the video and recouped from such income. The exploitation of promotional videos by broadcast and sale should attract royalty payments. The agreement will enable the company to call upon the artist to make a video. The storyline, budget and all production matters of the video should be agreed with the artist before production.

It is part of the record company's function to promote the recordings which they eventually release. As part of this, they may institute advertising campaigns, perhaps by way of newsprint advertisements or sometimes by broadcast advertising. There are often provisions in recording agreements stating that where a recording is advertised by means of a broadcast medium – such as television or radio – then the royalty rates payable on sales of that sound recording may be reduced to one half or two-thirds of the normal royalties. The artist will be concerned to see that an excessive amount is not spent on any such broadcast campaign. The costs of such promotion should also be split between the artist and the record company. An artist may also contest the inclusion of such a clause in the first place. If a recording is to be advertised in such a way, then the budget for this should be pre-determined. Whilst both the artist and record company should recognise that promotion of the artist generally and of sound recordings particularly is an investment, restrictions should be maintained and budgets imposed on any such advertising or promotional campaign. Traditionally, artists have promoted recordings by touring and other live appearances as well as by the release of singles from albums.

Tour support

Touring is another effective method of promotion. Tours are usually undertaken to coincide with the release of recordings in order to maximise their impact and publicity. Whilst record companies are unlikely to underwrite the cost of a tour, they often provide support for tours. A record company may agree to contribute an unspecified amount of money to a loss-making tour (known as 'tour support'), as part of the recording's promotional expenses. The amount of tour support will be capped to a maximum figure, and the company will expect the artist and his management to manage the tour so as not to produce a loss if possible.

The artist and the company will agree which expenses are deductible from tour income in calculating any loss. Management and agent's commission is unlikely to be included as an expense of the tour. Any tour support should not be considered as commissionable income for the purposes of management or agent's commission. It is also important that tour support is not treated as a recoupable advance for royalty purposes.

8.6 ADVANCES

The record or production company normally provides all the money for an artist to record a work. Such an investment is almost entirely speculative on the part of the record or production company. It has been estimated by the BPI that the cost of launching a new pop single is in the region of £250,000, but it is further estimated that only one in ten of all new releases is ever actually profitable. Because of this, to a great extent, the record company's successful artists are indirectly funding the unsuccessful ones. Whilst every artist wants to get the best terms possible from a record company, it is unusual for a new signing to receive a large advance or to obtain a particularly advantageous royalty rate. At best, an artist may come to a company with a solid live following, but translating that into substantial record sales is a different matter. Such a risk is reduced where a company re-signs an existing artist, as the company already has a back catalogue from which it can continue to recoup advances and recording costs.

A record company should advance money to an artist. An advance is a payment made upon signing the contract on account of future royalties. The size of an advance is usually either based upon the success of an established band or reflects the record company's estimate of the artist's potential. A new signing is unlikely to attract a significant advance. In most cases, an advance is payment against future earnings from record sales. As such, it is recovered by the record company from future royalties; this is known as recoupment. Advances are usually recouped from all royalties received by the record company under the artist's contract. Thus, successful albums pay for unsuccessful albums. An artist's advance attracts manager's commission at the agreed rate.

Before an artist receives any royalties, the company will be able to recoup any advance paid on signing the recording agreement, as well as the actual costs of recording. The contract will contain detailed provisions dealing with these aspects.

Major recording artists may receive incentive payments to sign with a record company. This is known as a 'fee' and is not returnable or recoupable from royalties received by the artist in the future. Record companies only offer fees where the artist they are proposing to sign is already successful and well-established and has sufficient goodwill and reputation to ensure a certain minimum level of sales.

The majority of artists receive advances on a non-returnable, but recoupable basis. That is to say, they will be required (in the normal scheme of things) to repay the advance, but only from royalties due to sales. If an artist accepts an advance fraudulently or otherwise in breach of contract, the advance may become repayable after litigation.

In addition to an initial advance, there should be further advances if the record company exercises options to renew the contract.

The artist must appreciate that an advance is usually on account of royalties and is not to be thought of as a gift. In effect, the advance has to be earned at some point. The advance is deducted as a first charge from any royalties due if the recording sells. It is effectively a loan, although it is nearly always non-returnable and it does not bear interest.

8.7 ROYALTIES

8.7.1 Obligation to pay

The obligation to pay royalties is of considerable importance to the artist as it relates directly to his income earning capacity and livelihood. A record company must be obliged to pay a royalty to the performer. Royalties are based upon a percentage of income from sales and exploitation of the artist's recorded performance. Before any royalty income reaches an artist, payments on the artist's account made by the record company, including recording costs, recoupable advances and other agreed expenses must be paid back in full from this income. The amount of royalty payments and the method of calculation vary from record company to record company and from artist to artist. A new artist would not normally expect to receive as attractive a deal as an established artist negotiating a new contract.

An artist who is also a composer receives income from the PRS and the MCPS, which may be dealt with by a music publisher, for use of his compositions. The royalty from the recording contract is solely in respect of exploitation of performers' rights and is additional to these other payments. Publishing income is generated by use of songs embodied in sound recordings exploited by record companies. The record company has a payment obligation to the MCPS for use of the underlying works.

The record company is free to exploit the copyright in the sound recording itself, subject to its obligation to make payments to other people such as the artist and music publishers.

8.7.2 Royalty rates

The royalty rate offered by a record company varies. A previously successful artist renegotiating a contract or entering into a new contract may demand and receive a higher rate than an unknown artist. What the artist may regard as being fair in all the circumstances undoubtedly differs from the record company's perception. Although there is no 'standard' rate offered to artists, the norm is for a rate somewhere in the region of 8–18%. Such a rate is based on the dealer price of recordings. This is the price the MCPS uses to calculate royalties due from record companies for sales of recordings featuring MCPS members' songs. Some record companies base the artist's royalty on the shop price. Different rates apply to budget line labels, record clubs and compilations which include an artist's work. It appears to have been accepted by the courts in the *George Michael* case (*Panayiotou and Others v Sony Music Entertainment (UK) Ltd* [1994] EMLR 229) that the similarities between record companies in terms of royalty rates offered (as well as the similarities in other contractual terms they offer) are not due to any lack of competition between record companies. Instead, the royalty rate is a commercial rate which reflects the risk and investment the company makes. A record company may offer a higher percentage royalty rate – perhaps up to 50% – but any such royalty is likely to be based upon a share of net profits paid out to an artist after treating all income from exploiting a recording on a strict profit and loss basis.

8.7.3 Flat rates and sliding scales

The rate offered by a company may be a flat rate on all sales regardless of the success of the artist. Alternatively, the rate may be set at a comparatively modest level for a certain volume of sales and then operate on a sliding scale if and when sales escalate. An artist is thus effectively rewarded for success in a way which he would not have been under a flat rate arrangement. A sliding scale arrangement is a useful mechanism to represent the increasing popularity of an artist as reflected in increased sales. Increased royalty rates often apply on a recording achieving silver, gold and platinum sales.

The artist is usually concerned to establish whether any increased rate applies only to sales above a certain limit or to all sales once the limit has been reached. Obviously, this can have a major effect on the income of the artist, especially if there are a number of steps in the sliding scale as sales increase.

An artist and his advisers will be trying to obtain as high a rate as possible. It is very unlikely that a company will accept a retrospective rate. The rate varies only as the new level is reached. There may, however, be scope for agreeing that once an artist has achieved a given level of sales on recordings, the higher rate then applies to all subsequent sales. This ensures that each new recording does not have to climb the scale before the higher rate applies.

A royalty rate which appears to be very high must be approached with some scepticism, and all the provisions of the royalty clause carefully scrutinised. For example, although a high rate may be offered, it may be subject to various unacceptable deductions.

Other alternatives include an annual incremental increase in the rate, although this is unlikely to be offered by a recording company as it does not reflect the popularity of the artist and may reward nothing more than longevity.

As an alternative to a sliding scale royalty based on sales of any given record, the royalty could increase on subsequent releases if an earlier release attains a stated minimum in terms of sales. The most attractive arrangement for an artist is either an initially high rate or a sliding scale arrangement to reflect modest and exceptional levels of sales. Given the enormous unpredictability of the record-buying public, an artist is clearly best advised to seek a higher return on those records which are actually successful rather than on future records which may be successful.

8.8 OTHER ROYALTY RATES

8.8.1 Record clubs

Not all sales of a record are full-price sales. There are various mail order and record club organisations which advertise records variously at full price or reduced price, and often include introductory promotions as well as bonus offers once a minimum purchase level has been reached. Most artists would not expect to have their recordings offered immediately through such mail order facilities, although this may take place quite soon after release. However, mail order sales do provide a large source of income to recording artists and record companies.

An artist's royalties on records sold in this way are usually reduced. The reduction in royalties may be to one half or two-thirds of the full rates and, indeed, no royalty may be payable at all if an artist's recordings are offered as part of an introductory offer or a free or bonus record to the record club or mail order company. Reduced royalty rates are controversial on items such as this. The record companies argue that, since the purchase price is lower, there is effectively less to share between the record company and the artist, as other costs – such as the production costs and mechanical royalties for copyright owners in the underlying works – remain the same. This means that record companies take a bigger slice of the sale price of reduced price sales. In addition, record companies provide a large number of free goods to the clubs, often on a one-for-one basis.

8.8.2 Budget line labels

A number of record companies have introduced budget line labels. These are used as a means of selling records at a lower price. These are 'oldies but goldies' which may be part of a record company's back catalogue. These albums can then be rediscovered by purchasers or be released on new sound recording configurations, such as CD, and offered on slightly more competitive terms than new releases as a means of encouraging people to replace their old versions on vinyl or cassette.

Artists are usually concerned to prohibit the sale of their products on budget labels for a reasonable time after the first release of the recording.

Record companies insist on a lower royalty rate in respect of budget line recordings for the simple reason that the retail sale price is lower. Since many of these recordings are only released well after their original release and at a time when the company may have recovered all the initial costs associated with release, the reduced rate seems harsh. Once again, the reduced royalty rate will be in the region of one half or two-thirds of the full rate.

8.8.3 Compilations

There are two main categories of compilation albums. The first are compilations of an artist's old work – such as 'Greatest Hits' albums – and, secondly, there are compilation albums which may include hits from a given year or hits by particular types of artists, for example, the 'Now That's What I Call Music ...' compilations. Such compilation albums are often very popular with the public.

The royalties received by an artist on compilations of his own works, such as a 'Greatest Hits' album, should be at the full royalty rate. The release of a 'Greatest Hits' album will not count towards the minimum commitment under the artist's recording contract, nor will it usually attract an advance. Once tracks have been recorded, it is generally open to the record company to do with them as they wish, although the artist may limit the number of 'Greatest Hits' compilations released by the record company. There is unlikely to be any obligation to re-release a recording. Generally, the release of a 'Greatest Hits' or compilation album will be in addition to any other recording commitment as required by the recording contract. The royalty paid for the 'Greatest Hits' album may be calculated in a number of ways and varies from deal to deal.

If a single recording is included on a compilation album or film soundtrack, the rate offered should be pro rata to the other tracks on the album. This compilation may be of the record company's own artists, or it may be a compilation album produced by a wholly independent company which specialises in producing compilation albums containing hits of this year or yesteryear or particular styles of popular songs. On such an occasion, the artist may not be entitled to a royalty based on the full retail selling price of the compilation. Instead, the royalty is based on the artist's proportional contribution to the compilation. The artist will not usually receive more than a proportion of the total royalty based upon his contribution.

8.8.4 Overseas sales

Royalties offered on overseas sales are usually a percentage, perhaps 75–85% of the artist's full rate. Many record companies use licensees or subsidiaries in other countries to promote and distribute recordings. The company should be permitted in its discretion to do so. Full royalties on the sale of recordings overseas are unlikely unless an artist signs direct with an overseas label. In addition, the royalty rate for overseas sales may vary depending on whether the sales are in a major or minor territory. The exchange rate applied to payment should ideally be the same as that applied when the record company receives payments from abroad to ensure that the artist does not suffer as a result.

8.8.5 On-line exploitation and other categories

Record companies are generally offering royalty rates for sales and other online exploitation based on traditional royalty rates with deductions.

Income from any other use of the recording should also be shared between the record company and the artist. For example, PPL income used to be shared on an ex gratia basis by record companies with artists. This 'entitlement' is now collected and distributed to artists as an entitlement under performers' rights legislation to 'equitable remuneration' by PAMRA and AURA.

Other income arises from the synchronisation and use of recordings in advertisements, in films and in TV programmes, as well as in new technology applications. The artist should share in this income and must ensure that the recording agreement reflects this. On-line distribution may attract a standard royalty rate, a reduced royalty or a share of net profits. As such, exploitation increases and internet and other on-line sales increase, the payments will tend to 'standardise' and reductions should end, due to the fact that the technology is in its infancy.

An unsuccessful record may be deleted or scrapped by the record company. In such cases, the artist receives no royalty on the recordings in question.

8.8.6 Producer's royalties

Producer's agreements are not considered in this book except where they impinge upon an artist's recording agreement. The main consideration is whether the artist is responsible for the producer's royalty. If this is the case, the producer's royalty will be accounted for from the artist's royalty. A producer's royalty is usually in the region of 3–4%. The main difference with producers is that they do not have to bear any recording costs. This means that they are entitled to royalties from the first sales of recordings. The artist, however, is not entitled to any royalties until recording costs have been recouped. Both artist and producer may have received an advance against royalties from the record company. The artist's royalty is thus reduced by the amount of the producer's royalty.

The situation is complicated because the obligation to pay the producer is often placed on the artist, not the record company. The producer may be entitled to further royalties well before all recording costs have been recouped. This arises because the producer only has to recoup the producer advance and not the recording costs. Most agreements should provide that the producer is not entitled to any further royalty until recording costs have been recouped at the net royalty rate, ie the artist's royalty rate less the producer's royalty rate.

The question which then arises is who is obliged to pay the producer? The artist may have recouped recording costs, and the producer may have technically recouped his advance. This means the producer is entitled to his further royalty payments. However, although the artist may not have recouped his own royalty advance, he may none the less owe the producer money under the artist's agreement with the record company. This means the artist should pay the producer even though the artist has no income from the record company. In theory, the artist should retain money from his advance to pay the producer. However, artists rarely do this. The problem is exacerbated by the fact that the artist also has to recoup recording costs. If an artist has not recouped costs on a number of albums, he may have no additional income from the record company but still may owe the producer money. The solution is for the artist and the producer to ensure that the record company pays the producer direct once recording costs and the producer's royalty advance are recouped. These payments are then treated as additional advances to the artist by the record company. In this way, the artist can avoid having to pay the producer personally when he is unrecouped himself, and, once the artist is recouped, the record company pays the artist making the procedure administratively easier for the artist.

8.9 CALCULATING ROYALTIES

The royalty rate, once agreed, is then used to calculate the amount due to an artist by the record company. The royalty payment will be based upon the price and the number of recordings sold.

The rate an artist receives is based either upon a notional retail price or upon the price that the record company charges dealers. The basic price upon which an artist is paid a royalty is that agreed between the MCPS and the BPI as the royalty base price for the composer's and publisher's income. This figure is known as the Published Dealer Price. The MCPS defines this as the highest price published by the record company or its distributor. This is effectively the price shops pay before they sell the recordings at their retail price. The price with which the artist is concerned is the retail price of the recorded product as used by the record company.

The record company's dealer price is sometimes uplifted by a notional figure to give a retail price upon which the royalty is based. This figure is usually 131% for cassettes and 129% for CDs. A £5 dealer price for a cassette gives an uplifted figure of £6.55 retail.

However, the royalty is now usually based upon the record company's published dealer price. No uplift is applied to the price to create a notional dealer price. Because the figure for the royalty calculation is lower, the royalty paid by the record company should be proportionally higher. Thus, a 10% royalty under the 'old' system is replaced by a 13.1% royalty under the 'new' system.

The artist will want the same royalty rate whatever the product configuration – whether it is compact disc, pre-recorded tape or vinyl long-play or single record disc. Record companies reduce the royalty rate for certain types of recordings, particularly compact discs and pre-recorded tapes, on the basis that they are more expensive to produce. Any such reduction should be resisted by the artist. A solution to any problem over this is to attribute a slightly higher packaging cost to such sound recordings. This will reduce the retail selling price upon which royalties are payable (see **8.9.1**).

8.9.1 Deductions

Packaging costs

Packaging costs are the costs of the album sleeve, the tape cassette, the container for the compact disc or other medium in which the final retail product is packaged for sale. The two most popular forms of packaging are currently compact disc or pre-recorded cassette as the vinyl disc is being gradually phased out by many high street retailers. The packaging charge is expressed as a percentage amount of the retail price of the various configurations. The recording agreement may define packaging charges in respect of the various sound recording configurations, for example, pre-recorded cassette (20%) and compact disc (25%). The packaging charge is then deducted from the retail price prior to the royalties being calculated. The royalties are thus actually calculated on the retail price less the packaging costs of the format, giving a reduced figure.

For example, a £5 cassette less £1 packaging on a 13.1% royalty gives a payment of £0.524 per cassette sold.

VAT

Value Added Tax (VAT) and any other sales taxes are also deducted from the retail price. In allowing such deductions the artist must ensure that the taxes were included in the retail price in the first place. If this is not the case, then the record company is creating an extra level of profit for itself at the expense of the artist.

8.9.2 Net sales

The royalty rate is applied to the sale price of the recordings less deductions. This figure must then be applied to the number of recordings actually sold. However, the royalty figure obtained after applying the percentage royalty to the net retail sale price used only to be multiplied by between 90 and 95% of the actual sales figures. The figure of 90–95% was used by the record industry to take account of damaged or broken goods. Royalty payments should be based on 100% of sales. A company which seeks to pay on less than 100% should increase its royalty rate accordingly.

It is at this stage that the record company should be able to account to the artist for royalties actually due on sales.

8.9.3 Promotional and 'freebie' records

Whenever a sound recording is released, a certain number of promotional and 'freebie' records are given out to people in the music industry by the company in order to promote the album. In particular, copies of recordings will be given to the music press for review and to most radio and TV stations. Record companies promote their artists, and the provision of free records to people in the industry is one of the ways by which they do this. Royalties are not usually payable on free or promotional records, and the agreement may make specific provision for this. The agreement should limit the number of promotional or free records given out by the record company to ensure there is no abuse of the system resulting in a reduction in the artist's royalty income.

8.10 ACCOUNTING

8.10.1 Maintaining accounts

The company must undertake to maintain proper and accurate accounts. It should also account to the artist and pay royalties at regular intervals. This accounting may be twice yearly and within a certain number of days of a given date. A typical provision would oblige the company to account within 90 days of 30 June and 31 December each year. The accounting should include all UK and overseas receipts. The record company will be entitled to retain allowable deductions under the agreement and credit income against advances and recording costs. After deductions, the artist can expect to receive his royalties, although this may take some time.

The actual calculation of the royalties due to the artist will be performed by the record company itself. The agreement sets out standard accounting periods in which the company is obliged to account to the artist with a cheque and statement of account.

The artist may be given a period within which to challenge any account and may have the right to audit it. This represents a reduction of the limitation period and should be resisted. If there have been any mistakes in the calculations, then the agreement should require the company to make good any such payment. It may also be appropriate for the artist to direct the record company to pay royalties to the manager or into a particular bank account. The arrangements between the artist and the manager as to payment will be of no concern to the record company. The record company's only concern is that once money has been paid over at the direction of the artist, it incurs no liability if the recipient then acts improperly with that cash. That is a matter for the artist to safeguard himself against.

8.10.2 Reserves

Because records are sold on the basis that a retailer can return them if they do not sell, most agreements contain royalty reserve provisions. This is to ensure that record companies do not pay their artists more royalties than the artist has ultimately earned. The company retains a certain percentage of the total royalties payable to an artist on the basis that some of the records sold will be returned. Reserves for new artists are higher than for established ones and may amount to 25% of the royalties due. The company is entitled to keep the reserve for a certain amount of time after which it must be liquidated and paid to the artist. If the recordings are returned by the retailer, the artist will not have earned the royalty and it will not be paid to him.

8.11 DEPARTING MEMBERS

8.11.1 Group provisions

The recording agreement for a group (or a partnership) will contain provisions dealing with the position if one member of the group leaves. A group should have a partnership agreement or a company dealing with their collective arrangements, as well as a management agreement with their manager. All departing member provisions may be susceptible to challenge on the basis of a restraint of trade as they can tie up an individual's services with a company for a long period.

8.11.2 Services of departing member

The record company will include a clause in a group's agreement stating that any departing members must give notice of their intention to depart to the record company. This may be in addition to any notice to the band itself under their agreement. The record company may reserve itself a number of options.

(1) The company may be able to terminate the whole agreement (this should be resisted).
(2) The remaining members may be required to continue their services under the contract.
(3) The departing member may also be required (at the record company's option) to provide the same services as before, on his own for the company. If the record company is interested in the artist as an individual, it may require the departing member to produce a demonstration recording with one or two original compositions performed by the departing member. This helps the company to assess the potential of the departing individual. A time-limit should be placed upon the company requiring it to make its decision as soon as practically possible. If the company does not wish to use the departing member, a release should be obtained.

8.11.3 Departing member's income

The departing member is entitled to receive his share of income from recordings he appeared on during his time with the band. The income is subject to any charges attributable to the departing member. Thus, account will be taken of advances and other deductible costs before the departing member receives his share. The remaining members of a group have their income and expenses as a separate 'account' with the record company. Any provisions that enable the record company to apply income from both the departing member and the remaining group members to the group deficit or, alternatively, the individual's deficit from group income must be resisted. Only a pro rata share of the income should be charged to the group or to the individual's deficit with the company. Thus, the departing member takes his debt with him from which his share of the group income is then attributed to pay it off. The group retains the remainder of the debt, which their share of the income pays off.

Income and costs from future recordings should not affect the royalties of the departing member from previous recordings. The member's entitlement to income as an individual continues despite the fact that he is no longer part of the group, although the group may continue to record.

8.12 TERMINATION PROVISIONS

All recording agreements should contain termination provisions. If differences cannot be resolved, the agreement may then be terminated according to these provisions. It is important that the company cannot simply suspend the agreement indefinitely because of an alleged breach. In particular, the obligation to account for income should not cease.

During the course of the agreement, it is quite common for the artist to fall out with the company. This may result in litigation on a number of grounds. Many artists argue that the agreement they entered into was in restraint of trade. They also often argue that the record company has not fulfilled its side of the bargain and is in breach of contract. Record companies often drop an artist due to poor sales and do not exercise their option to extend the agreement.

8.13 POST-TERMINATION

Once an agreement has ended, the artist is free to move on or renegotiate an agreement. The copyright in the sound recordings is owned by the record company and these recordings may, in the course of time, be deleted from its active list, sold and licensed to others or become part of its back catalogue. This depends upon the success of the artist and the continued popularity of his recordings.

The company should continue to account for income due to the artist and the publishers on sales of recordings. The artist must also comply with any enforceable re-recording restrictions in the agreement. If the artist moves to another record company, the terms and conditions of that agreement should be considered in light of the matters raised in this chapter. In particular, a release should be obtained from the previous company confirming that the artist is no longer bound by the former agreement.

Chapter 9

DEFAMATION

9.1 INTRODUCTION

Of vital importance to all aspects of communication is the tort of defamation. The threat of a libel action is the single most inhibiting factor to media freedom in the UK. Solicitors with media clients are frequently called upon to 'clear' a potentially defamatory article or programme for publication. Individuals with claims of interference with privacy will need to be advised as to whether they have a potential action against the medium concerned.

Of increasing (although still limited) significance is malicious (or injurious) falsehood, which is an action which can be brought without the need for proof of loss of reputation. Public funding is available for an action in malicious falsehood (see Chapter 10), but not for defamation actions. It can thus be seen to complement the tort of defamation in some respects.

Chapter 9 contents
Introduction
What is defamation?
Libel or slander?
Publication
Words must be defamatory
Words must refer to the claimant
Defences
Remedies
Contentious considerations
Summary disposal of claim

9.2 WHAT IS DEFAMATION?

> 'A man commits the tort of defamation when he publishes to a third person words containing an untrue imputation against the reputation of another' (*Gatley on Libel and Slander* 8th edn (Sweet & Maxwell) at p 4).

This definition requires clarification:

- a defamatory imputation is an imputation in a form of words which tends to:
  (a) lower the claimant in the estimation of right-thinking members of society generally; or
  (b) expose him to hatred, contempt or ridicule; or
  (c) cause him to be shunned or avoided;
- an imputation may be defamatory (and thus lead to a successful action against the defendant) even where it is true;
- an imputation is not necessarily defamatory where it is untrue.

Defamation trials must take place in the High Court. The county court has no jurisdiction in respect of this tort. Either party has the right to claim trial by jury (subject to a limited exception – see **9.9.7**), thus making jury trials common in libel actions.

Public funding is not available to bringers or defenders of defamation actions. This, coupled with the fact that libel cases are notoriously expensive, leads to the justified criticism that defamation is a cause of action reserved for the rich. It has further been suggested that wealthy individuals may use the law of libel effectively to muzzle the printing of the truth (at the time of his death, Robert Maxwell had in excess of 20 libel cases running which had been started to prevent the publication of items concerning himself and his empire).

The tort of defamation is the product of both statute and case-law.

9.3 LIBEL OR SLANDER?

There are two forms of defamation in English law: libel and slander. Solicitors who advise media clients will be concerned principally with libel, ie defamation in a permanent form. Slander is defamation in a transient form such as the spoken word.

Uncertainties in the common law as to whether defamatory matter contained in television and radio broadcasts would be libel or slander have now been resolved by statute: they are libel (Broadcasting Act 1990, s 166(1)). Defamatory matter in theatre productions is defamation in a permanent form (Theatres Act 1968, s 4(1)). Films are subject to libel actions (*Youssoupoff v Metro-Goldwyn-Mayer Pictures Ltd* (1934) 50 TLR 581), and it is likely that the same principle will apply to video. Opinion is divided as to whether defamatory material contained in tape recordings or on compact discs would be libel or slander. Defamatory matter contained in printed matter such as books, newspapers and magazines will be subject to a libel action.

Libel is actionable per se and is a crime (although it will only be the subject of a prosecution when it is extremely serious and when the public interest requires the institution of criminal proceedings (*Gleaves v Deakin and Others* [1980] AC 477)) as well as a tort. Slander, subject to limited exceptions, requires proof of special damage, ie damage quantifiable in monetary terms. The exceptional cases where slander is actionable per se are those where the claimant:

- is imputed to have committed a criminal offence punishable with imprisonment;
- is imputed to have a contagious or infectious disease likely to prevent other persons from associating with the claimant;
- (being female) is imputed to be of adulterous or unchaste behaviour; or
- is imputed to be unfit, dishonest or incompetent in any office, profession, calling, trade or business held or carried on by the claimant at the time when the slander was published.

9.4 PUBLICATION

For either libel or slander to be actionable, it must be communicated to a third party, ie some person other than the claimant.

A person will be liable for any publication:

- which he intends;
- which he can reasonably anticipate; or
- where there is unintentional publication, which is published due to a want of care on his part.

    Example 1
    A person carrying a defamatory placard at a demonstration which he knew was being televised would be liable not only for his own publication, but also for the broadcast depicting the placard.

Example 2
A person sending a fax to X's place of business would be liable for any matter defamatory of X contained in it which was read by the fax operator or other employees at X's place of work.

The commercial publishing process will necessarily involve a series of publications; each repetition will be treated as a fresh publication creating a new cause of action in defamation. For example, a journalist who writes a newspaper article about a politician's speech may be sued in respect of any defamatory matter contained in the speech which he reproduces. Similarly, the editor, sub-editor, printer, distributor and retail seller of the newspaper (as well as the politician!) may be sued (the distributor and newsagent may, however, be able to avail themselves of the defence of innocent dissemination (see **9.7.5**)).

If you are advising a company, remember that it needs firm e-mail guidelines in place. Every e-mail sent by an employee containing a defamation is a fresh publication rendering the employee and his employer potentially liable.

This is a particular problem for internet service providers and operators of the information super-highway who will be prima facie liable for all defamatory material they pass on. The Defamation Act 1996 was intended to provide for the defence of innocent dissemination to cover such publications in certain defined circumstances. However, it is not certain that this defence will apply in these circumstances (see **9.7.5**).

If the publication is in the form of an article, the claimant must show that the statement is defamatory in the context of the article as a whole. In *Charleston and Another v News Group Newspapers Ltd and Another* [1995] 2 AC 65, the claimants were actors who played the parts of Harold and Madge in the Australian TV soap *Neighbours*. The article complained of appeared with a headline which read: 'Strewth! What's Harold up to with our Madge?'. Immediately beneath the headline was a large photograph of a naked man and woman engaged in a sexual act. The faces of the man and woman were those of the claimants. Beneath the photograph, the article went on to describe a new computer game in which the faces of soap stars were superimposed over the bodies of others. The claimants accepted that no defamatory meaning could be conveyed by the article as a whole, but contended that it was legitimate to identify a group of readers who read only part of a publication, ie the headline and photograph alone. The House of Lords held, with some regret, that it was not permitted to divide the readership of one publication into different groups. Thus, the article had to be looked at as a whole in deciding whether any part of it was defamatory.

9.5 WORDS MUST BE DEFAMATORY

The words used must be capable of defamatory meaning. Where no legal innuendo (see **9.5.1**) is alleged to arise from extrinsic circumstances known to some readers, the natural and ordinary meaning to be ascribed to the words of an allegedly defamatory publication is the meaning, including any inferential meaning, which the words would convey to the mind of the ordinary, reasonable and fair-minded reader (per Lord Bridge in *Charleston and Another v News Group Newspapers Ltd and Another* (above)). The jury will determine what the words mean to such a person.

In *Rubber Improvement Ltd and Another v Daily Telegraph Ltd; Lewis and Another v Daily Telegraph Ltd; Lewis and Another v Associated Newspapers Ltd* [1963] 2 All ER 151, the claimant claimed damages for libel as a result of an article appearing on the front page of the *Daily Telegraph*:

> 'INQUIRY ON FIRM BY CITY POLICE. Officers of the City of London Fraud Squad are inquiring into the affairs of Rubber Improvement Ltd and its subsidiary companies. The investigation was requested after criticisms of the Chairman's statement and the accounts by a shareholder at the recent company meeting. The Chairman of the Company, which has an authorised share capital of £1 million, is Mr John Lewis, a former Socialist MP for Bolton.'

The claimant argued that the words used meant that the firm was actually guilty of fraud. The House of Lords disagreed with this construction. Lord Reid gave the following general guidance as to the way in which the meaning of words is to be considered in a libel action:

> 'The ordinary man does not live in an ivory tower and he is not inhibited by a knowledge of the rules of construction. So he can and does read between the lines in the light of his general knowledge and his experience of worldly affairs. Ordinary men and women have different temperaments and outlooks. Some are unusually suspicious and some are unusually naive. One must try to envisage people between these two extremes and see what is the most damaging meaning that they would put on the words in question.'

The hypothetical reasonable reader is not naive but he is not unduly suspicious. He can read between the lines. He can read in an implication more readily than a lawyer, and may indulge in a certain amount of loose thinking. But he must be treated as a man who is not avid for scandal and someone who does not, and should not, select one bad meaning where other non-defamatory meanings are available (per Neill LJ in *Hartt v Newspaper Publishing Plc* (1989) *The Times*, November 9, CA).

It should be noted that what the ordinary, reasonable and fair-minded reader regards as defamatory may change from time to time. For example, it was at one time defamatory to call someone a 'German', ie in the context of wartime interest and the tendency to deride Germans.

9.5.1 Innuendo

In some cases, the claimant may plead that the words are defamatory in the light of certain additional facts. This is known as 'true' or 'legal' innuendo and is a separate cause of action for which separate damages should be awarded. It is, of course, possible that the words complained of are defamatory in their natural and ordinary meaning and *in addition* are defamatory in light of certain specified facts. Here, the claimant would plead defamation on the plain construction of the words as well as a separate defamation by way of innuendo.

In *Tolley v Fry & Sons Ltd* [1931] All ER Rep 131, the claimant, an amateur golfer, was depicted in an advertisement for the defendant's chocolate without his permission. He successfully pleaded that certain people familiar with the golfing world would draw the conclusion that he had prostituted his amateur status.

True innuendo must be specifically pleaded. RSC Ord 82, r 3 (as amended and reprinted in Civil Procedure Rules 1998, Sch 1) provides that:

'where in an action for libel or slander the claimant alleges that the words or matters complained of were used in a defamatory sense other than their ordinary meaning, he must give particulars of the facts and matters on which he relies in support of such sense.'

Such particulars should be set out in a separate paragraph of the statement of claim and will usually begin with the words, 'The said words meant and were understood to mean ...'.

The claimant must support his allegation of innuendo by pleading particulars of any extrinsic facts or oblique meanings to be attached to the words used which lead to such a conclusion. Thus, where the claimant alleges that certain people would understand a slang word or a technical word in a certain particular way, he must plead such specialised usage and the fact that some of the persons to whom the publication was made would have understood the word in that sense.

'False' innuendo arises where the claimant alleges that the words in themselves bear a particular meaning (usually in addition to their plain and ordinary meaning) which is discernible without the need for additional evidence.

The claimant does not need to give particulars of false innuendo but, except where the meanings of the words complained of are clear and explicit, the claimant should plead the meanings which he alleges. This should also be done where the words are obscure or have more than one possible meaning. Such pleadings should begin, 'The said words, in their natural and ordinary meaning, meant and were understood to mean ...'.

9.5.2 Function of judge and jury

In the High Court, the judge will decide whether the words are reasonably capable of bearing a meaning defamatory of the claimant. In doing so, and where legal innuendo is specifically pleaded, he will take into account any extrinsic evidence pleaded by the claimant. If the words are not capable of bearing a defamatory meaning, he will withdraw the matter from the jury. The jury will decide whether the words are defamatory or not, taking account of any admissible innuendo.

Delays at trial caused by this rule have been lessened to an extent by the introduction of a specific rule, which provides that the claimant must give particulars of any legal innuendo (see **9.5.1**).

In *Rubber Improvement Ltd and Another v Daily Telegraph Ltd; Lewis and Another v Daily Telegraph Ltd; Lewis and Another v Associated Newspapers Ltd* (above), the House of Lords considered that the headline was not capable of imputing guilt but only that the police had reasonable grounds for suspecting guilt. The first meaning should not have been left to the jury, so the jury's decision was quashed, and the case sent back for a new trial on the second meaning. The defence pleaded justification, and the case was settled out of court.

9.6 WORDS MUST REFER TO THE CLAIMANT

Clearly, the claimant must show that the words were published of and concerning him. It will be no defence that the claimant is not referred to by name if he would be capable of being identified by the reasonable person. Thus, it will be libel to broadcast a defamatory statement about 'the MP for York' or 'the President of The Law Society'.

The words used will be taken to refer to the claimant where he is mentioned by name, even if the defendant did not know the claimant. In *Hulton (E) & Co v Jones* [1910] All ER Rep 29, a newspaper carried a humorous account of the events at a motor festival in Dieppe, casting doubt on the moral standing of one Artemus Jones, a churchwarden from Peckham. A barrister by the name of Artemus Jones was successful in his action against the newspaper despite the fact that he was not a churchwarden, had not been in Dieppe and was not from Peckham.

The normal disclaimer at the beginning of books and at the end of films will not protect the publication if readers can sufficiently identify the claimant from the text. It is just one factor that the reasonable reader may take into account.

The defendant may also be liable where the statement is true of one person but defamatory of another with the same name. For this reason, great care must be taken by journalists when reporting proceedings in the criminal courts. In *Newstead v London Express Newspapers Ltd* [1940] 1 KB 377, the defendant published an article stating that Harold Newstead, a 30-year-old Camberwell man had been convicted of bigamy. The claimant, a different Harold Newstead, also of Camberwell and about 30 in appearance, was successful in his libel action.

However, in the recent case of *Kerry O'Shea v MGN Limited and Free 4 Internet Limited* (2001) unreported, 4 May, the court ruled that the strict liability rule would not apply to a 'lookalike' situation. In that case, a young woman claimed (and the court accepted) that she was a 'lookalike' of a glamour model used to advertise a pornographic internet service provider in a national tabloid newspaper. The court, not without sympathy for the claimant, considered that to apply a strict liability rule would impose an impossible burden on a publisher.

Defamation of a class is not actionable unless the claimant can be identified (per Lord Atkin in *Knupffer v London Express Newspapers Ltd* [1944] AC 116). This will largely depend upon the size of the relevant class and the nature of the allegation. The narrower the class and the more specific the allegation, the more likely it is that readers could reasonably take it to refer to each member of the group. For example, to say of the students at The College of Law that they cheat at exams is not defamatory as no individual student can be identified from the statement. To say it of the students in a particular 'small group' of 12 students at one of the branches of the College would be actionable. In this latter case, it would be likely that the right-minded reader would believe that the statement reflected on the integrity of the individual claimant, ie everyone in the group.

In *Aiken and Others v Police Review Publishing Co Ltd* (1995) unreported, 12 April, the Court of Appeal dismissed the application of the defendant to have the action struck out on the ground that 'the claimants would not have been identifiable to readers of the words complained of as the individuals to whom the said words were directed'. Hirst LJ found that it was not obvious that the words were incapable of referring to each or any of the individual claimants.

Aiken concerned an article in the *Police Review* magazine published under the headline 'Nazi "humour" forces Jewish PC to quit'. The text of the article, published next to a photograph of PC Nigel Brown, read as follows:

> 'The Metropolitan Police dog handler who recently won the right not to work on Saturdays because of his Jewish faith is quitting the force amid claims of anti-Semitism among colleagues. PC Nigel Brown, 34, said that despite his victory at last year's industrial tribunal, anti-Jewish feeling persisted. He alleged he was threatened,

if he returned to duty, he would be "fitted up". "The worst example of anti-Semitism I experienced was at a Christmas party. When I entered the room they started singing the Nazi party anthem and giving the Nazi salute. They thought it was funny but I was disgusted … It has been made clear to me that although I have won my case my career will not progress … It has been suggested that someone might try to plant drugs on me. We deal with them a lot in the dog section and I cannot risk 13 years' unblemished service".'

The ten claimants were the long-serving dog handlers in Area 8 Dog Section (located at Hyde Park Police Station) of the Metropolitan Police Force who had all served with PC Nigel Brown at the relevant time. The evidence was that there were 60 officers at Hyde Park Police Station, of whom up to 35 worked in the dog section.

9.7 DEFENCES

An understanding of the defences to a defamation action is crucial to those engaged in advising publishers and broadcasters. Despite the 'publish and be damned' philosophy which, though noble, can be very expensive, many defamatory statements would go unpublished were it not for the mind's eye view of a suitable defence to any potential action.

The principal defences used by media defendants are:

- justification (or truth);
- fair comment on a matter of public interest;
- privilege (absolute and qualified);
- innocent dissemination;
- offer of amends; and
- consent to publication.

In some circumstances, the proof by the claimant that the defendant acted maliciously will defeat the defence raised by the defendant.

9.7.1 Justification

Justification is a complete defence and it will not be defeated by a malicious motive on the part of the defendant. However, once the claimant has shown that a statement is defamatory, it is presumed that the statement is not true. The burden of proof therefore shifts to the defendant who must prove by evidence the truth (or substantial truth) of:

(a) each defamatory statement;
(b) any reasonable interpretation which may be understood of the words complained of; and
(c) any innuendoes (where, being 'true' innuendoes, they are pleaded by the claimant) lying behind them.

This may be no easy task and many defendants have backed down at some point in the litigation (or threatened litigation) process, even though they felt their statement to be true. It is thus possible to obtain substantial libel damages from a defendant where the statement published about the claimant is true. The message to journalists or other publishers is make sure you get your evidence *before* you publish!

When to plead justification

The decision to plead the defence of justification will not be an easy one. The defendant is not helped by the fact that the nature of jury trials makes their outcome impossible to predict. Further, an unsuccessful plea of justification will aggravate any damages awarded (due partly to the rigorous cross-examination to which the claimant will have been subject and partly to the necessary repetition of the libel by the defendant).

The harshness of the rule that each and every allegation must be proved to succeed in the defence of justification is mitigated somewhat by s 5 of the Defamation Act 1952:

> 'in an action for libel or slander in respect of words containing two or more distinct charges against the claimant, a defence of justification shall not fail by reason only that the truth of every charge is not proved, if the words not proved to be true do not materially injure the claimant's reputation, having regard to the truth of the remaining charges.'

Thus, it may well be worth pleading justification not only where the statement contains defamatory material of a comparatively minor nature, but also where there is defamatory matter present which, whilst incapable of proof, is of a less serious nature than that which can be justified.

What is important is to be able to prove the 'sting' of the allegation. So, for example, if you were to write an article saying that X robbed a bank on Tuesday, but you could not prove that it was Tuesday and in fact it turned out to be Thursday, it would not matter as long as you could prove the 'sting' that X robbed the bank.

Since *Lucas-Box v News Group Newspapers and Others* [1986] 1 WLR 147, defendants are obliged to state in the particulars of their defence of justification the precise meaning to be attributed to the words that they are seeking to justify ('*Lucas-Box* particulars'). => Can justify words by attributing a different meaning. Included now in Pre-Action Protocol

Evidence of justification

In *McDonald's Corporation v Steel* [1995] 3 All ER 615, the court considered the question of whether the defendant was required to have evidence of justification at the time of the service of the defence. The defendants had distributed leaflets, entitled 'What's wrong with McDonald's?', setting out details of, inter alia, health risks associated with the consumption of food purchased at McDonald's fast food restaurants. The claimant applied to have various particulars of justification in the defence struck out. The High Court judge granted the application to strike out various passages on the basis that there was no admissible evidence before the court supporting those passages. The Court of Appeal reversed this decision, stating that it was perfectly proper for a defendant to plead particulars of justification which he was in anticipation of being able to prove at the date of the trial. It was inappropriate to strike out such particulars at an interlocutory stage unless it was clear from disclosure that no other admissible evidence was ever going to be forthcoming.

Thus, before a plea of justification is included in a defence, the following criteria should normally be satisfied:

(1) the defendant should believe that the words complained of are true;
(2) the defendant should intend to support the defence of justification at trial; and
(3) the defendant should have:

   (a) reasonable evidence to support the plea; or

Defamation

(b) reasonable grounds for supposing that sufficient evidence to prove the allegations would be available at the trial.

Relevance of malice

There is one exception to the rule that malice is irrelevant to the defence of justification: the Rehabilitation of Offenders Act 1974. This statute provides that certain previous criminal convictions become 'spent' after the expiry of a certain number of years from the date of conviction. The number of years depends upon the punishment for the crime in question and is beyond the scope of this book. Section 8 states that malicious motive will defeat the defence of justification (and fair comment) in relation to such 'spent' convictions.

9.7.2 Fair comment

It is clearly one of the necessary elements of a free society that one should be able to comment freely on matters of public interest. The courts will give protection to such comment as long as it arises from an honestly held belief and is not made maliciously. It is often pleased by newspapers, however, that the complex nature of the defence makes it a potential minefield for journalists and their editors, and, consequently, for the solicitors who advise them.

The defence of fair comment will attach to:

- comment
- in the form of opinion
- which is based on true facts
- and which is made without malice
- on a matter of public interest.

Opinion based on fact

The comment must be one of opinion, not fact. It is not always easy to draw this distinction, and one must be aware that a set of words might be comment in one context, when the defence of fair comment may be available, and fact in another, when it will have to be justified. Gatley states (*Gatley on Libel & Slander* 8th edn (Sweet & Maxwell) at p 696):

> 'A comment is a statement of opinion on facts. It is comment to say that a certain act which a man has done is disgraceful or dishonourable; it is an allegation of fact to say that he did the act so criticised. A libellous statement of fact is not a comment or criticism on any thing. But while a comment is usually a statement of opinion as to the merits or demerits of conduct, an inference of fact may also be a comment. There are, in the cases, no clear definitions of what is comment. If a statement appears to be one of opinion or conclusion, it is capable of being comment.'

The comment, save for one exception, must be based on true facts. Thus, comment based on facts which are incorrect cannot be the subject of this defence, even where honestly made. For example, one can say of X that he is unfit to attend public houses if X has a record of causing fights in public places. One could not say it of Y whom X had provoked into fighting with him. The exception is where the comment made is based on facts which, although not true, are stated by a person on a privileged occasion, for example during Parliamentary proceedings (see **9.7.3** and **9.7.4**).

In *Telnikoff v Matusevitch* [1991] 4 All ER 817, the claimant, a Russian emigré employed by the BBC's Russian service, wrote an article for the *Daily Telegraph* attacking the BBC World Service for recruiting too many employees from members of the ethnic minorities of the Soviet Union and not enough from those people who 'associate themselves ethnically, spiritually or religiously with the Russian people'. The defendant wrote a letter to the editor of the *Daily Telegraph* in response to the claimant's letter. The letter, published in the paper, described the claimant's views as racist and anti-Semitic and said that the claimant was advocating a blood test for prospective BBC employees rather than a test of professionalism. The Court of Appeal held that the letter should be read in the context of the article in deciding whether it contained statements of opinion (in which case, the defence of fair comment would be available) or fact (in which case, the defendant would be liable as the statements were not true). The House of Lords disagreed, however, and held that only the contents of the letter itself could be considered. The reasoning behind this decision was that there would be many readers who saw the letter and not the article, and that therefore the letter should be judged on its own merits.

Where an article contains much factual material and selective comment, the defendant may be assisted by s 6 of the Defamation Act 1952:

> 'In an action for libel or slander in respect of words consisting partly of allegations of fact and partly of expression of opinion, a defence of fair comment shall not fail by reason only that the truth of every allegation of fact is not proved if the expression of opinion is fair comment having regard to such of the facts alleged or referred to in the words complained of as are proved.'

The effect of this section can be said to be that the defendant will be required to prove, in most cases, that the facts upon which the comment has been made are substantially true.

Fairness

For the comment to be fair, it must be judged, in the eyes of the jury, to be an opinion that could be honestly held. It is not necessary for the jury to find that the comment is one that could reasonably be held by a right-thinking person (thus, the word 'fair' is misleading and the Faulks Committee on Defamation recommended that the defence should be renamed 'Comment') nor is it necessary for the defendant to prove that the opinion was honestly held by him (see *Telnikoff v Matusevitch* (above)), although evidence that it was not may lead to a finding that the defendant was malicious.

The jury will be directed to ask themselves whether any honest man, however prejudiced he might be, or however exaggerated or obstinate his views, could have written the criticism in question.

All comments actuated by malice will be unfair (see below). Where the claimant makes such an allegation, he has the burden of proving it. It will be for the judge to decide whether there is enough evidence to find that the defendant acted maliciously, and he should do so before handing the case to the jury.

Public interest

A comment will be on a matter of public interest if it concerns a matter which affects people at large, so that they may be legitimately interested in, or concerned at what is going on or what may happen to them or to others. It will thus include opinions on the conduct of public figures, local and national government, and public and private companies insofar as it affects people and the administration of justice.

Court decisions concerning public interest show a tendency toward its expansion and development. In *Derbyshire County Council v Times Newspapers Ltd and Others* [1993] AC 534, the *Sunday Times* published an article which questioned the propriety of certain investments made by the council and its leader, Mr David Bookbinder. On the preliminary issue of the defendant's application to have the action struck out as disclosing no cause of action, the House of Lords held that a local authority does not have the right to maintain an action for damages for defamation as it is contrary to the public interest for organs of government to have such a right.

It remains to be seen whether a wholesale public interest defence becomes available in this country, as it is in the USA.

Malice

Where the defendant published the words complained of maliciously, the defence of fair comment will be unavailable (*Campbell v Spottiswoode* (1863) 3 B & S 769). A malicious statement is one which the defendant makes with some motive other than that of a pure expression of a critic's real opinion (*Merivale v Carson* (1887) 20 QBD 275).

Malice is spite or ill-will towards the claimant or any indirect or improper motive of the defendant at the time of publication which is his sole or dominant motive for publishing the words complained of (*Horrocks v Lowe* [1975] AC 135). With respect to fair comment, it is usually conclusive evidence of malice to show that the defendant did not honestly hold the opinion expressed.

In *Thomas v Bradbury, Agnew & Co Ltd and Another* [1906] 2 KB 627, it was held that evidence that the defendant was actuated by malice will always be admissible where the defence is one of fair comment even if the comment is prima facie fair. The case concerned a critical piece in *Punch*. The defendant contended that if the criticism does not of itself exceed the limits of fair comment then proof of malice in the writer does not destroy his immunity. This objective yardstick was rejected by Collins MR, who said (at p 638) that the right to make fair comment is a right which:

> '... though shared by the public, is the right of every individual who asserts it, and is, qua him, an individual right whatever it is called by, and comment by him which is coloured by malice cannot from his standpoint be deemed fair. He, and only he, is the person in whose motives the claimant in the libel action is concerned, and if he, the person sued, is proved to have allowed his view to be distorted by malice, it is quite immaterial that somebody else might without malice have written an equally damnatory criticism.'

The defence of fair comment will invariably be met by an allegation of malice. The disadvantage of this for media clients is that it widens the issues in the action, and that they will be required to produce, on disclosure, all relevant documentation including journalist's notes and internal memoranda concerning the article. Before running the defence of fair comment, it will thus be necessary to consider the type and content of relevant documentation in existence at that time.

9.7.3 Absolute privilege

Statements made on an absolutely privileged occasion are not actionable. This is the case even where the defendant is actuated by malice.

Parliamentary proceedings

Statements made during the course of Parliamentary proceedings, as well as the publication of official reports of those proceedings, are absolutely privileged. This does not extend to MPs' statements made other than in the course of a Parliamentary debate or proceeding. Work by a select committee is generally regarded as being included within the definition of Parliamentary proceedings.

The authority for such privilege is Article 9 of the Bill of Rights 1689 which precludes any court from impeaching or questioning proceedings in Parliament.

Reports of Parliamentary proceedings

Reports of Parliamentary proceedings in the media will not attract absolute privilege (although the defence of qualified privilege may be available). However, following a decision of the High Court, the media may be able to use Article 9 as a shield against a libel action. In *Allason v Haines* [1996] EMLR 143, Owen J held that a libel action brought by an MP will be stayed if Parliamentary privilege prevents the defendants from putting forward the defence which they wish to put forward. The defence in the case was justification, and the matter requiring proof was contained in Parliamentary debates.

Section 13 of the Defamation Act 1996 provides that where the conduct of any person in relation to Parliamentary proceedings is in issue in defamation proceedings, he may waive, for the purposes of those proceedings, the protection of privilege.

Judicial proceedings

Any statement made by any person in the course of proceedings before any court or tribunal is absolutely privileged. This does not apply to administrative proceedings, such as a local authority meeting to hear applications for music and dancing licences (*Royal Aquarium & Summer & Winter Garden Society Ltd v Parkinson* [1892] 1 QB 431).

It should be noted that the definition of judicial proceedings has been widened by the Defamation Act 1996 and includes official inquiries and proceedings of certain international organisations held anywhere in the world.

Reports of judicial proceedings

A fair, accurate and contemporaneous report of court proceedings is absolutely privileged (Defamation Act 1996, s 14).

Whether a report of court proceedings is published 'contemporaneously' will depend upon the nature of the publication. If it is a daily newspaper, for example, then the report should be contained in the edition published the day after the court decision is handed down. A magazine published monthly will have greater leeway and will not be deprived of the defence where it publishes the report in the next monthly edition.

9.7.4 Qualified privilege

Statements made on an occasion to which the defence of qualified privilege attaches will not be actionable unless it can be shown that the defendant was actuated by malice. Malice in the context of qualified privilege will usually be made out where the claimant can show that the defendant did not believe the truth of the statement he made.

Qualified privilege is best looked at as a collection of several defences, some common law and others statutory in origin.

Fair and accurate reports of Parliamentary and judicial proceedings

Fair and accurate reports of Parliamentary and judicial proceedings will attract the defence of qualified privilege, with the proviso in the case of judicial proceedings that the proceedings themselves must have been open to the public and the publication must not be forbidden (eg where an order of the court prevents publication).

Occasions where the person who makes a communication has an interest or a duty, legal, social, or moral, to make it to the person to whom it is made, and the person to whom it is so made has a corresponding duty or interest to receive it

The media here is under no different position from a member of the public. It should also be noted that for a defendant to take advantage of this common law defence by alleging 'duty' to publish, both the maker and the recipient must be acting under such a duty. It is difficult therefore to envisage a situation when a medium would be able to use the defence; a newspaper may be under a moral duty to publish a particular article, but its readership will not be under a similar duty to read it.

The important decision in *Reynolds v Times Newspapers Ltd and Others* [1999] 3 WLR 1010 re-stated and extended the law of qualified privilege. The House of Lords ruled that the appropriate test was the 'duty-interest test' as set out above, taking into account all the circumstances of the publication.

The Lords recognised that the press has a general duty to inform the public on matters with a real public interest element and the public has a right to be so informed. They also acknowledged the vital public watchdog role the media performed in conducting investigative journalism. The media is therefore entitled to some protection from libel laws when commenting on matters of public interest, but only if they act fairly and reasonably and can show that their research was careful and conscientious.

In considering whether a journalist had been suitably responsible, Lord Nicholls of Birkenhead set out a non-exhaustive list of ten principles:

(1) the seriousness of the allegation;
(2) the nature of the information and the extent to which the subject-matter was a matter of public concern;
(3) the source of the information;
(4) the steps taken to verify the information;
(5) the status of the information (the allegation might have already been the subject of an investigation which commanded respect);
(6) the urgency of the matter;
(7) whether comment was sought from the claimant;
(8) whether the article contained the gist of the claimant's side of the story;
(9) the tone of the article (a newspaper could call for investigation or raise queries – it need not adopt allegations as statements of fact);
(10) the circumstances of the publication, including the timing.

The Lords have therefore expanded the qualified privilege defence, protecting newspapers if they 'responsibly' publish false material in the public interest. The case has been seen as a real boon to journalists, given that, if they follow Lord

Nicholls' ten principles, they should be able to gain the protection of qualified privilege if what they have published turns out to be wrong.

In *Loutchansky v Times Newspapers Ltd and Others* [2001] 3 WLR 404, the Court of Appeal held that the duty to publish has to exist at the time of publication with the defendant having an adequate knowledge of the facts that give rise to that duty. It therefore refused permission for the defendants to amend their defence to add matters which were not known at the time of publication.

Following the House of Lords decision in *McCartan Turlington Breen v Times Newspapers Ltd* [2000] 4 All ER 913, press conferences are to be considered public meetings for the purposes of qualified privilege, so that fair and accurate reports of the proceedings can be protected by statutory qualified privilege.

Section 10 of the Defamation Act 1952 provides that a defamatory statement published by a candidate in a local government election shall not be deemed to be published on a privileged occasion on the ground that it is material to a question in issue in the election.

9.7.5 Innocent dissemination

The Defamation Act 1996, s 1, provides a defence for a person who can show that:

(a) he was not the author, editor or publisher of the statement complained of;
(b) he took reasonable care in relation to its publication; and
(c) he did not know, and had no reason to believe, that what he did caused or contributed to the publication of a defamatory statement.

The first hurdle for the innocent disseminator is thus to show that he was not the author, editor or publisher of the defamatory statement. 'Publisher' in this context has a more limited meaning than in the law of defamation generally and is defined in the Act as 'a commercial publisher, that is, a person whose business is issuing material to the public, or a section of the public'. 'Author' has its ordinary meaning save that it does not include a person who did not intend that his statement be published at all. 'Editor' means a 'person having editorial or equivalent responsibility for the content of the statement or the decision to publish it'.

A person shall not be considered to be the author, editor or publisher of a statement if he is only involved:

(a) in printing, producing, distributing or selling printed material containing the statement;
(b) in processing, making copies of, distributing, exhibiting or selling a film or sound recording containing the statement;
(c) in processing, making copies of, distributing or selling any electronic medium in or on which the statement is recorded, or in operating or providing any equipment, system or service by means of which the statement is retrieved, copied, distributed or made available in electronic form;
(d) as the broadcaster of a live programme containing the statement in circumstances in which he has no effective control over the maker of the statement;
(e) as the operator of or provider of access to a communications system by means of which the statement is transmitted, or made available, by a person over whom he has no effective control.

Secondly, the defendant must show that he took reasonable care in relation to the publication of the defamatory statement and that he did not know nor have reason to believe that what he did caused or contributed to the publication of a defamatory statement in general. The questions of what is reasonable care and whether the service provider had reason for such belief is left to the courts, albeit with some limited guidance from s 1(5) of the Defamation Act 1996:

> 'In determining ... whether a person took reasonable care, or had reason to believe that what he did caused or contributed to the publication of a defamatory statement, regard shall be had to –
>
> (a) the extent of his responsibility for the content of the statement or the decision to publish it,
> (b) the nature or circumstances of the publication, and
> (c) the previous conduct or character of the author, editor or publisher.'

It is clear from the case of *Lawrence Godfrey v Demon Internet* [2000] 3 WLR 1020 – the first case concerning defamation on the internet in the English jurisdiction – that a service provider is not an author, editor or publisher for the purposes of the 1996 Act. In that case, a posting to a newsgroup, which purported to have eminated from the claimant, was 'squalid, obscene and defamatory' of the claimant. On 17 January 1997 the claimant sent a letter by fax to the defendant's managing director, informing him that the posting was a forgery and that he was not responsible for it and requesting him to remove it from its Usenet news server. Although the defendant received the fax the item was not removed and remained on its news server until its expiry on 27 January. Upon proceedings being defended by the defendant, the claimant applied to strike out parts of the defence.

The argument of the service provider that it was not a common law publisher for the purposes of defamation law was rejected by the judge. However, on the meanings contained in the Defamation Act 1996 the court agreed with the defendant that the service provider was not a 'publisher' for the purposes of s 1. The requirements of s 1(1)(b) (reasonable care in respect of publication), and s 1(1)(c) (no knowledge or reason to believe that what it did caused or contributed to the publication of a defamatory statement) caused great difficulty for the defendant, as it knew of the defamatory posting after receipt of the claimant's fax but chose not to remove it. It was the opinion of the court, therefore, that the defendant could be liable for the defamatory comments contained within its newsgroups.

9.7.6 Offer of amends

An offer to make amends may be made by the defendant at any time up to the service by him of a defence to the proceedings, and may be made in relation to the allegedly defamatory statement generally or in relation to a specific defamatory meaning which the person making the offer accepts that the statement conveys (a 'qualified offer'). It must be in writing, must be expressed to be made pursuant to s 2 of the Defamation Act 1996 and must state whether it is a qualified offer.

An offer to make amends is an offer:

(a) to make a suitable correction of the statement complained of and a sufficient apology to the aggrieved party,
(b) to publish the correction and apology in a manner that is reasonable and practicable in the circumstances, and

(c) to pay to the aggrieved party such compensation (if any), and such costs, as may be agreed or determined to be payable.

Where an offer under the 1996 Act is not accepted by the aggrieved party it will be a defence to the proceedings (a qualified offer is a defence only in respect of the meaning to which the offer related) unless the offeror knew or had reason to believe that the statement complained of:

(a) referred to the aggrieved party or was likely to be understood as referring to him; and
(b) was both false and defamatory of that party.

There is a presumption, for the purposes of the defence, that the defendant did not know or have reason to believe these matters. Thus the burden of proving them rests with the claimant.

A defendant who makes an offer of amends under the 1996 Act need not later rely on it as a defence, but if he does so, cannot rely on any other defence in that action. The offer may, however, be relied on in mitigation of damages whether or not it was used as a defence.

If an offer to make amends under s 2 is accepted by the aggrieved party then the party accepting may not bring or continue defamation proceedings in respect of the publication concerned against the person making the offer. He is entitled to enforce the offer by applying to the court for an order requiring the offering party to take the steps that have been agreed to fulfil the offer. Where no such steps have been agreed by the parties, the party making the offer may take such steps by way of correction, apology and publication (including making a statement in open court) as he thinks appropriate. Where the amount of compensation is not agreed the court will determine the amount to be paid by reference to the principles of damages in defamation proceedings and shall take into account the steps that have been taken in fulfilment of the offer, including the suitability of the correction, the sufficiency of the apology and whether the manner of their publication was reasonable in the circumstances.

9.7.7 Consent

It is a complete defence to a defamation action to show that the claimant consented to publication of the matter complained of.

9.8 REMEDIES

9.8.1 Damages

The principal remedy for defamation is damages. The object of damages is to compensate the claimant for the lowering of his reputation that he has suffered as a result of the publication, and for any consequent loss that is recoverable (eg loss of earnings). An award of exemplary or punitive damages is also possible.

Awards often seem to go further than this, however. Newspaper headlines have been replete with examples of vast sums of money being awarded by libel juries. Amounts in the hundred thousands or even in excess of a million pounds have not been uncommon. Part of the reason for this is inherent in the nature of the jury system itself.

Juries typically find it irresistible to give someone else's money away and perceive media defendants to be 'able to afford it'.

Following criticism of excessive awards, s 8 of the Courts and Legal Services Act 1990 empowered the Court of Appeal to substitute its own award of damages for that made by the jury at trial. However, the general view of this section was that it did not alter the common law threshold for Court of Appeal intervention: that an award is so high that it is 'divorced from reality'.

The Elton John case

It has only been relatively recently that the court decided to take a greater control over damage awards. In *John v MGN Ltd* [1997] QB 586, Elton John had been awarded £350,000 by a jury following a report in the *Sunday Mirror* that he was on a diet which required that he chew food and then spit it out rather than swallow it. In reducing the award to £75,000, the court said that regard should be had to personal injury actions when considering libel damages. It was offensive to public opinion that a claimant should recover damages for injury to his reputation which were greater than the sum he might have been awarded for personal injuries rendering him helplessly crippled or insensate. Juries in future libel actions should be informed of awards made or approved by the Court of Appeal, and counsel and the trial judges should direct juries to decide upon an award within a certain bracket, always bearing in mind the maximum award currently available in personal injury cases.

Size of 'readership'

The actual or potential audience of the defamatory material will affect the size of the award. The statement of claim in a newspaper libel action will often state the circulation of the issue in question. Consequently, a successful claim against a newspaper with national circulation will result in a much higher damages award than that against a local paper with limited readership.

Malice

Proof of a malicious motive on the part of the defendant will aggravate a damages award, as will an unsuccessful plea of justification, particularly where it has been accompanied by rigorous cross-examination of the claimant.

Reduction of damages

Damages may be reduced where the claimant's name has been 'cleared' in public prior to the judgment, or where he has been successful in actions against other defendants in respect of similar defamatory statements.

9.8.2 Injunction

Interim injunctions will rarely be granted to prevent publication of defamatory matter (or to restrain malicious falsehood). In *William Coulson & Sons v James Coulson & Co* (1887) 3 TLR 46, the Court of Appeal held that, although the High Court has jurisdiction to grant an interim injunction in libel cases, such power should be used only sparingly. The Master of the Rolls said:

> 'Therefore to justify the court granting an interim injunction it must come to a decision upon the question of libel or no libel, before the jury decided whether it was a libel or not. Therefore the jurisdiction was of a delicate nature. It ought only to be

exercised in the clearest cases, where any jury would say that the matter complained of was libellous and where if the jury did not so find the court would set aside the verdict as unreasonable.'

Defamation provides a remedy for claimants who have been defamed and, therefore, the media have the freedom to publish defamatory statements, albeit at the risk of a later action. The principles in *American Cyanamid Co v Ethicon Ltd* [1975] AC 396 as they relate to injunctions (stated simply, that so long as the action is not frivolous or vexatious, the only substantial factor the court should take into account is the balance of convenience) do not apply to defamation actions.

Past decisions have shown an increasing tendency by the courts to refuse interlocutory injunctions on a different ground: that such prior restraint would go against the principles enunciated in Article 10 of the European Convention for the Protection of Human Rights and Fundamental Freedoms. See further *Re W (Wardship: Publication of Information)* [1992] 1 FLR 99 and *R v Central Independent Television plc* [1994] 3 WLR 20.

However, if the claimant is able to show that the defendant is intending to publish matter which is clearly untrue and that there is no arguable defence, an injunction could exceptionally be granted. Thus, the claimant will fail where the defendant intends to raise the defence of justification or privilege unless, in the case of qualified privilege, clear evidence of malice can be shown.

The unwillingness of the court to grant injunctions in defamation cases has led claimants to make their application for an injunction on the grounds of breach of confidence and breach of contract. Here, an interim injunction may be granted even though the defendant may have a strong defence. To establish breach of confidence, the claimant must show that the defendant has information which he is under a duty not to reveal (see Chapter 13).

9.9 CONTENTIOUS CONSIDERATIONS

9.9.1 Whether to litigate

The most difficult decision for any claimant is whether to commence an action. Counsel's advice will often be sought as to the chances of success, but in addition to the legal rights and wrongs of the action, the potential claimant should bear in mind the following factors.

Expense

Libel trials are expensive. This is in part due to the fact that it is not possible to commence a defamation action in the county court (thus usually requiring a barrister in addition to a solicitor). The fact that the mode of trial is by jury means that the trial will inevitably be lengthy. Public funding is not available in defamation cases.

Time

Libel actions may take some time to come to trial (although the delays of several months or even years seem to be disappearing thanks, at least in part, to the courts' active case management since the CPR 1998 came into force) and, once they do reach court, the enormous complexities of a defamation case can result in extensive legal argument and greatly protracted examination and cross-examination of witnesses.

Reputation

The object of proceedings is to redress the imbalance caused by the defamatory publication. It should be borne in mind, however, that a libel action can have the opposite effect. News reports of the trial will often lead to publication of the nature of the defamatory comments to a far greater audience than that of the original publication.

9.9.2 Forum

London has been described as 'the libel capital of the world'. The defamation laws of England and Wales coupled with the nature of trial by jury make it desirable for claimants to bring their action here.

Generally, an action can be commenced in the UK where there is publication within the jurisdiction. A complication arises as a result of the Convention on Jurisdiction and the Enforcement of Judgments in Civil and Commercial Matters (the Brussels Convention). States which are signatories (of which the UK is one) must enforce the primary rule of jurisdiction: that persons domiciled in a contracting State should be sued in the courts of that State (Article 2).

In *Shevill and Others v Presse Alliance SA* [1995] 2 AC 18, the defendant, a French newspaper, published an article defamatory of the claimants, one of whom was domiciled in England and the others in France. The paper had a circulation of 215,000, including 230 copies in England and Wales. The defendant applied to have the claim struck out on the basis that, under Article 2 of the Brussels Convention, English courts had no jurisdiction to hear it. The claimants argued that, under Article 5(3) of the Brussels Convention (which provides that a person domiciled in a contracting state may be sued in tort in the courts of the place where the harmful event occurred) the courts of England and Wales did have jurisdiction. The court held that 'the place where the harmful event occurred' under Article 5(3) was to be construed as referring both to the place where the publisher was established (the courts there having jurisdiction to award damages for all the harm caused by the defamation) and the place where the publication was distributed and where the victim claimed to have suffered injury to his reputation (the courts there having jurisdiction solely in respect of the harm suffered in that State). The question of whether a harmful event had occurred was not to be determined by the Brussels Convention but by the substantive law of the relevant State.

Thus, where there is an arguable case that there is publication of libel which carries with it the presumption of damage, then jurisdiction over the defendant may be assumed by the English court by virtue of Article 5(3).

In *Berezovsky v Forbes Inc and Another* (2000) *The Times*, May 16, a Russian businessman issued proceedings in England against the US publishers of *Forbes* magazine which had described him as 'a criminal on an outrageous scale'. 785,000 copies of the magazine were circulated in the USA, less than 2,000 in the UK and only 13 in Russia. The article only concerned the claimant's activities in Russia.

The House of Lords allowed the case to proceed, having accepted the argument that the claimant had sufficient personal and business connections in the UK to found a reputation there.

9.9.3 Apology

In the case of innocent publication, liability may be avoided by making an offer of amends under s 2 of the Defamation Act 1996 (see **9.7.6**).

Where the defence in s 2(4) is not available, it may still be advisable in certain circumstances to make a prompt correction and apology. Such action will have the effect of placating many would-be claimants. It will also satisfy the complainant's lawyers where the apology is accompanied by a payment of costs to date. A further advantage is that where the claimant is not dissuaded from litigation, publication of a prompt apology will mitigate any damages eventually awarded.

A potential media defendant who is considering making an apology would be well advised to seek an undertaking from the complainant that no further legal action will be brought.

9.9.4 Statements in open court

Statements in open court are often used as part of a negotiated settlement. Such a statement will often accompany an apology (see **9.9.3**), although its use is not limited to such occasions. Counsel for the claimant will read out a statement prepared and agreed by the parties and approved by the judge before whom it is made. It will usually contain an account of the circumstances in which the matter complained of was published, make it clear that the statement was untrue, and set out the terms of settlement. The press may, of course, be present.

Most statements are made as part of a settlement and are agreed between the parties, but it is possible for the defendant to make a unilateral statement. Where a party accepts money paid into court in full settlement of a libel action, either party may apply to a judge in chambers for leave to make a statement in open court. The judge will take into account all the circumstances of the libel and the amount of the payment in when deciding whether to approve any statement proposed.

9.9.5 Early ruling on defamatory meaning

It is possible for either party to apply to a judge in chambers for an order as to whether or not the words complained of are capable of bearing the meaning as pleaded. The judge may, where he feels that the defamatory meaning alleged by the claimant is not made out, dismiss the claim or make such other order as appropriate. An interlocutory ruling on a defamatory meaning suggested by a claimant may be sought at any time after the statement of claim has been served. However, each party may make only one such application. The advantage of such an application for the defendant is that no defence will have to be made out to any meaning pleaded by the claimant which is judged to be unsustainable.

The claimant is now able to obtain an interlocutory ruling that *Lucas-Box* particulars (see **9.7.1**) of a meaning pleaded by the defendant are inconceivable.

9.9.6 Payments into court

Judging the correct amount for a payment into court (CPR 1998, Part 36) will be especially difficult in a libel action, not least because of the unpredictability of jury damages awards. Counsel's advice must be sought as to the most effective sum.

There will be enormous pressure on the claimant to accept any reasonable sum, because failure to beat that sum at trial will result in a costs bill that, in a libel action, may run into hundreds of thousands of pounds.

Once the 21-day time-limit for acceptance of the payment in has expired, the claimant will not be granted leave for payment out nor for an extension of time for accepting if there has been 'a substantial change in the risks'. The introduction into an action for libel of a plea of justification instead of, or in addition to, a plea of fair comment will probably be such a change (*Proetta v Times Newspapers Ltd* [1991] 4 All ER 46).

The claimant in an action against two or more defendants sued jointly may accept a payment into court in respect of any of the defendants. The action is then stayed only in respect of the defendant who made the payment in. However, the claimant must be aware of two rules of court which make it considerably more risky to continue with the action against one defendant where he has accepted a payment in from another defendant:

(1) the sum recoverable under any judgment given in the claimant's favour against any other defendant in the action by way of damages shall not exceed the amount (if any) by which the amount of the damages exceeds the amount paid into court by the defendant as against whom the action has been stayed; and

(2) the claimant shall not be entitled to his costs of the action against the other defendant after the date of the payment into court unless either the amount of the damages awarded to him is greater than the amount paid into court and accepted by him, or the judge is of the opinion that there was reasonable ground for him to proceed with the action against the other defendant.

Example 1
The claimant accepts a payment in of £15,000 from defendant A but continues in his action against defendant B who has not made a payment in. At trial, the jury award £25,000 damages against defendant B. In this event, the claimant will be entitled to recover £10,000 from defendant B.

Example 2
The claimant accepts a payment in of £15,000 from defendant C but continues in his action against defendant D who has not made a payment in. At trial, the jury award £10,000 damages to be paid by defendant D. Here, the claimant is not entitled to any damages. Further, the claimant will not be entitled to any costs from defendant D unless the judge is of the opinion that it was reasonable for the claimant to proceed to trial against defendant D.

9.9.7 Jury trial

Section 69 of the Supreme Court Act 1969 provides that there is a right, subject to the exception discussed below, to trial by jury in claims for libel and slander. Despite a recommendation by the Faulks Committee on Defamation in 1975 that juries should be abolished in defamation cases, trial by jury remains the selected mode of trial in the vast majority of cases.

The right to jury trial is qualified in cases involving any prolonged examination of documents or accounts, or any scientific or local investigation which cannot conveniently be made with a jury (for further discussion, see *Goldsmith v Pressdram Ltd* [1987] 3 All ER 385 and *Viscount De L'Isle v Times Newspapers Ltd* [1987] 3 All ER 499). In these cases, the judge has a discretion to refuse to allow trial by jury.

In *Beta Construction Ltd v Channel Four TV Co Ltd* [1990] 2 All ER 1012, the defendants had admitted liability in a libel action, and the only issue that remained to be tried was that relating to quantum of damages. The claimant wanted damages to be assessed by a jury, while the defendant applied for trial by judge alone. The Court of Appeal, upholding the first instance decision that damages should be quantified by judge alone, stated that the question as to whether a libel action involving prolonged examination of documents or accounts should properly be tried by a jury depends upon a consideration of such factors as:

(1) the extent to which the presence of a jury might add to the length of the trial;
(2) the extent to which the presence of a jury might add to the cost of the trial by reason of its increased length and the necessity of photocopying a multitude of documents for use by the jury;
(3) any practical difficulties which a jury trial might cause, such as the physical problem of handling in the confines of a jury box large bundles of bulky documents;
(4) any special complexities in the documents or accounts which might lead a jury to misunderstand the issues in the case.

It should be noted that the parties may consent to trial by judge alone. As the Court of Appeal guidelines in the *Beta* case show, trial without jury will be more expedient and less costly. However, trial by jury in defamation cases remains the norm, possibly because large damages awards are perceived to be the habitual wont of juries. The parties are more likely to consent to trial without jury, therefore, in cases where a point of principle is at stake rather than a desire to obtain windfall damages.

9.10 SUMMARY DISPOSAL OF CLAIM

CPR 1998, Part 24 incorporates a procedure for dealing with the claimant's claim at an early stage. In addition to the power to dismiss the claimant's action, where it appears to the court that it has 'no realistic prospect of success and there is no reason why it should be tried', the court may give judgment for the claimant and grant him *summary relief* (s 8(3)).

The summary procedure may be invoked by the claimant, the defendant or the court of its own motion. A defendant may apply for summary disposal to avoid the obvious disadvantages of protracted litigation and to have the damages that he will be requested to pay limited to no more than £10,000 (see below).

Summary disposal may be attractive to a claimant who is more concerned with early vindication of his name than with a large damages award. The procedure may be invoked at any stage of the proceedings. Thus the claimant could, in appropriate circumstances, serve the summons for summary judgment with the writ.

Where the claimant applies for summary judgment he must show that:

- there is no defence with a realistic prospect of success; and
- there is no other reason why the claim should be tried.

The defendant may apply to dismiss the claimant's claim where:

- the claim has no realistic prospect of success; and
- there is no other reason why the claim should be tried.

Where the summary judgment process is invoked on the claimant against his will (due to an application by the defendant or to the court invoking the procedure of its own motion) there is an additional requirement:

- that the court is satisfied that summary relief will adequately compensate the claimant for the wrong he has suffered.

In considering whether a claim should be tried, the court (sitting without a jury) will take into account the following factors:

(a) whether all the persons who are or might be defendants in respect of the publication complained of are before the court;
(b) whether summary disposal of the claim against another defendant would be inappropriate;
(c) the extent to which there is a conflict of evidence;
(d) the seriousness of the alleged wrong (as regards the content of the statement and the extent of publication); and
(e) whether it is justifiable in the circumstances to proceed to a full trial.

Where the court decides to give the claimant summary relief under s 8 it shall have regard to the types of factors listed in s 9 as may be appropriate to the case before it. By virtue of that section, summary relief may consist of one or more of the following:

(a) a declaration that the statement was false and defamatory of the claimant;
(b) an order that the defendant publish or cause to be published a suitable correction and apology;
(c) damages not exceeding £10,000 or such other amount as may be prescribed by order of the Lord Chancellor;
(d) an order restraining the defendant from publishing or further publishing the matter complained of.

The parties should try to agree the content of any correction and apology, and the time, manner, form and place of publication. Where the correction and apology is to appear in a newspaper the parties should have regard to the page number, position, type of typeface, size of typeface, etc. The medium of television will raise issues of timing, type of voice and proximity to relevant programming. Where the parties are unable to agree on the *content* of the correction and apology, the court may direct the defendant to publish a summary of the court's judgment agreed by the parties or settled by the court. If the parties are unable to agree on the *time, manner, form or place* of publication, the court may direct the defendant to take such reasonable and practicable steps as the court considers appropriate.

The procedure for a summary judgment application will be determined by Rules of Court but it will probably be similar to the current summary judgment procedure, ie based on witness statements and without oral evidence or any form of disclosure. Media defendants often obtain their evidence of justification or fair comment at the disclosure stage and so the new procedure may be inappropriate in many cases.

Chapter 10

MALICIOUS FALSEHOOD

10.1 GENERAL

A false statement will be actionable in defamation only where it leads to a lowering of the claimant in the estimation of right-thinking members of society.

Statements may be made about the claimant which, whilst untrue, are not defamatory. In such cases, it may be possible for the claimant to bring an action in malicious (or injurious) falsehood.

An example is provided by the case of *Grapelli and Another v Derek Block (Holdings) Ltd and Another* [1981] 2 All ER 272. The claimant, Stephane Grapelli, employed the defendants as his managing agents. The defendants arranged, without the claimant's authority, for the claimant to give concerts at various venues in England. When the concerts had to be cancelled, the defendants stated that the reason for the cancellation was that Mr Grapelli was seriously ill and that it was doubtful if he would ever tour again. Such a statement was clearly damaging to Mr Grapelli's career but not defamatory, as it is not damaging to reputation to say that someone is ill. The claimant's action in slander was accordingly dismissed, but his alternative plea of malicious falsehood was successful.

10.2 DEFINITION

In order to succeed in an action in malicious falsehood the claimant must generally prove that the defendant:

(1) has published about the claimant words which are false;
(2) has published those words maliciously; and
(3) special damage has followed as the direct and natural result of their publication.

Malicious falsehood is therefore concerned with protecting the claimant's economic interests rather than his reputation. Past Court of Appeal cases (see below) have expanded the scope of malicious falsehood and demonstrate the above principles.

10.2.1 Untrue statement

In *Kaye v Robertson and Another* [1991] FSR 62, the claimant was a well-known actor and star of a television series called *Allo Allo*. He had undergone extensive surgery on his head after part of an advertisement hoarding had fallen through his car windscreen in a storm. The first defendant was the editor of the *Sunday Sport*, a tabloid newspaper renowned for its 'scoops', and was responsible for journalists who interviewed and photographed the claimant in his hospital bed. The claimant, through his next friend, sought an interlocutory injunction to prevent publication, alleging, inter alia, malicious falsehood. He claimed that he had not consented to the interview and had, in any event (to the defendants' knowledge), not been in a fit state

Chapter 10 contents
General
Definition
Defamation and malicious falsehood compared

to consent; shortly after the interview, he had no recollection of the incident. As to the requirement that the words complained of be false, Glidewell LJ said:

> 'I have no doubt that any jury which did not find that the clear implication from the words contained in the defendants' draft article were false would be making a totally unreasonable finding. Thus the test is satisfied in relation to this cause of action.'

10.2.2 Malice

In the context of malicious falsehood, 'malice' means to act without just cause or excuse and with some indirect, dishonest or improper motive. It is for the claimant to prove malice.

The requirement of malice in *Kaye* was made out because there was no doubt from the evidence that it was apparent to the reporter from the *Sunday Sport* that Mr Kaye was in no condition to give any informed consent to an interview. Even if there had been any doubt as to this, the defendant could not have been in any such doubt after he read the affidavit sworn by Mr Kaye in the proceedings. Any subsequent publication would therefore inevitably have been malicious.

The definition of malice in this context has arguably been broadened by *Joyce v Sengupta and Another* [1993] 1 All ER 897. The *Today* newspaper published an article on its front page headed 'ROYAL MAID STOLE LETTERS'. The article was based on police suspicions and went on to describe how Miss Linda Joyce had stolen the Princess Royal's intimate letters and handed them to a national newspaper. Instead of suing in defamation, for which public funding is unavailable (Legal Aid Act 1988, Sch 2, Part II, para 1), the claimant issued a writ against the defendants claiming damages for malicious falsehood and obtained public funding to pursue her claim. On appeal from a decision of the High Court striking out her claim, the Court of Appeal reversed the decision and held that the publication was capable of being malicious in that:

> 'the defendants went ahead and published the police suspicions as though they were fact and did so without taking any steps to check or verify them. This showed a calculated, reckless indifference to the truth or falsity of the allegations. Malice is to be inferred from the grossness and falsity of the assertions and the cavalier way they were published' (per Sir Donald Nicholls V-C).

10.2.3 Special damage

In most cases, special or actual damage must be proved for a successful action in malicious falsehood – see *Allason v Campbell and Others* (1996) *The Times*, May 8. Such special damage must have 'followed as the direct and natural result of [the] publication' (per Glidewell LJ in *Kaye v Robertson*).

Exceptionally, proof of special damage will not be required. This exception applies where:

(a) the words the subject of the action are calculated to cause pecuniary damage and are published in writing or other permanent form; or
(b) the words are calculated to cause pecuniary damage to the claimant in respect of any office, profession, calling, trade or business held or carried on by him at the time of the publication (s 3(1) of the Defamation Act 1952).

10.3 DEFAMATION AND MALICIOUS FALSEHOOD COMPARED

The following chart highlights the main differences between an action in defamation, and its counterpart in malicious falsehood.

	Libel	Malicious falsehood
Proof of damage required	✗	✓
Right to jury	✓	✗
Proof of loss of reputation required	✓	✗
Presumption of falsity of statement	✓	✗
Proof of malice required	✗	✓
Public funding available	✗	✓
PR's action after death	✗	✓

Chapter 11

OBSCENITY

11.1 INTRODUCTION

The matters dealt with in this chapter and the next are largely criminal in nature. The powers of the court to punish individuals and companies following a successful prosecution are tempered by the fact that the court may also order forfeiture of the offending material.

It should be borne in mind that there is a close relationship between the law of obscenity and both the self-regulatory notion of 'indecency' and the concept of 'censorship'. This chapter should therefore be mentally cross-referred with other aspects of this resource book.

11.2 DEFINITION OF 'OBSCENE'

The well-known test for obscenity as enunciated by Cockburn CJ in *R v Hicklin* (1868) LR 3 QB 360, namely 'whether the tendency of the matter charged as obscenity is to deprave and corrupt those whose minds are open to such immoral influences and into whose hands such a publication might fall', was closely followed by the draftsmen of the Obscene Publications Act 1959 (OPA 1959) (to which Act all section numbers in this chapter refer unless otherwise stated). Section 1 provides that:

> 'an article shall be deemed to be obscene if its effect or (where the article comprises two or more distinct items) the effect of any one of its items is, if taken as a whole, such as to tend to deprave and corrupt persons who are likely, having regard to all relevant circumstances, to read, see or hear the matter contained or embodied in it.'

The publisher of an obscene article will be liable to criminal prosecution. The offence of publishing obscene material is one of strict liability.

11.2.1 'Article'

An 'article' is defined widely to include anything containing or embodying matter to be read or looked at, as well as records and films. The Broadcasting Act 1990 adds matter recorded in television programmes to the list of 'articles'.

11.2.2 'Taken as a whole'

It is clear from s 1 that a work should be taken as a whole in considering whether it is obscene. The only exception seems to be magazines which should be taken item by item and not as a whole. Such was the decision in *R v Anderson and Others* [1972] 1 QB 304. The appellants published 'Oz No 28 School Kids Issue', a 48-page magazine printed in bright and attractive colours and containing a great assortment of items. In addition to the array of innocent and innocuous articles, dealing with

Chapter 11 contents
Introduction
Definition of 'obscene'
The offences
Defences
Human rights
Television
Cinema exhibition
Video recordings
Obscenity and children

such matters as school affairs and the system of education in the UK, other articles dealt with matter which was the subject of the prosecution. One such article was an advertisement for a magazine called 'Suck' which described the joys from the female aspect of an act of oral sexual intercourse. A further article showed a picture of children dressed in school clothes engaging in various sexual activities.

The reasoning behind the exception seems to be that a magazine comprises a number of distinct items and, therefore, the fact that a number of such items are of an innocent character should not detract from the objectionable nature of only one.

11.2.3 Deprave and corrupt

The prosecution must prove beyond reasonable doubt that the article is obscene. To be obscene, the article must 'deprave and corrupt' its audience. It appears from case-law that to deprave and corrupt means to make morally bad or to pervert or corrupt morally. An article is not necessarily obscene under the Act merely because it is 'repulsive, filthy, loathsome or lewd' (*R v Anderson* (above)).

The question of whether an article does have the effect of perverting or corrupting morally is entirely a matter for the jury, and expert evidence is not admissible on this point.

11.2.4 'Persons ... likely ... to read ...'

Section 1 deems an article obscene only where it tends to deprave and corrupt persons who are likely to read, see or hear it. This test is thus more subjective than the test for defamatory material (where one has to consider the reasonable fair-minded reader). Both the reasonable reader and the particularly sensitive reader are excluded from consideration where they are not likely readers.

R v Calder and Boyars Ltd [1969] 1 QB 151 concerned the publication in the UK of a book entitled *Last Exit to Brooklyn*. The book gave a graphic description of the depths of depravity and degradation of life in Brooklyn, including homosexual acts and drug-taking, but it was a serious work genuinely believed by its publishers to be in the interests of literature. The appeal against conviction was allowed because, inter alia, the trial judge gave no guidance to the jury on the question of what the Act meant by persons who were likely to read the book. Salmon LJ said that the jury should have been directed to consider whether the effect of the book was to tend to deprave and corrupt a significant proportion of those persons who were likely to read it.

What is a significant proportion is a matter for the jury to decide but it is clear from the case-law that it is not appropriate to consider only the largest category of likely readers. Other categories of persons may be likely readers and should not be disregarded unless they are numerically negligible – see *DPP v Whyte* [1972] AC 849 and *Goldstar Publications v DPP* [1981] 2 All ER 257.

11.3 THE OFFENCES

Two offences may be committed in respect of obscene publications.

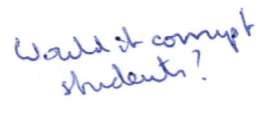

The first (which is now a 'serious arrestable offence' for the purposes of the Police and Criminal Evidence Act 1984 (s 85(3) of the Criminal Justice and Public Order Act 1994)) is under s 2 of the 1959 Act, which provides that any person who, whether for gain or not, publishes an obscene article shall be liable to prosecution. A person publishes an article where he:

'(a) distributes, circulates, sells, lets on hire, gives, or lends it, or who offers it for sale or for letting on hire; or
(b) in the case of an article containing or embodying matter to be looked at or a record, shows, plays or projects it' (s 1(3)).

The definition of publication under s 1(3) has been construed widely enough to include the development and printing and return to the customer of a photographic film (*R v Alan Taylor* (1994) 158 JP 317, CA).

The Broadcasting Act 1990 provides that publication extends to matter included in a television programme.

The second offence, introduced by the Obscene Publications Act 1964, provides that a prosecution may be brought in respect of the possession, ownership or control of an obscene article for publication for gain and was intended to fill a gap in the 1959 Act effectively opened up by the case of *Fisher v Bell* [1960] 3 WLR 919.

The offence under the OPA 1964 does not require proof of publication, but the prosecution will have to prove that the obscene article was owned, possessed or controlled for gain. A person is deemed to have an article for publication for gain if, with a view to such publication, he has the article in his ownership, possession or control. Such gain can be in relation to another, in addition to or instead of, the person charged. Both offences are triable either way and, in addition to the normal criminal sanctions, an order for forfeiture of the offending material may be made.

11.4 DEFENCES

11.4.1 Public good

Section 4 provides that a person shall not be convicted of the offence in s 2 and an order for forfeiture shall not be made where it is proved that publication of the article was justified as being for the public good.

Publication will be for the public good in the case of books and magazines where it is in the interests of science, literature, art or learning, or of other objects of general concern. 'Learning' in this context means the product of some scholarly activity (*Attorney-General's Reference (No 3 of 1977)* [1978] 3 All ER 1166). The phrase 'other objects of general concern' does not widen the defence as much as it would at first sight appear. It is to be construed in the light of the words coming immediately before it and thus any object of general concern must fall within the same range of factors as science, literature, art or learning. Expert evidence is admissible on the question of whether an article has any of the merits listed in the defence.

In *R v Calder and Boyars Ltd* [1969] 1 QB 151 (see **11.2.4**), Salmon LJ stated that the proper direction to be given in cases where the defence is raised is that the jury must consider on the one hand:

- the number of readers they believed would tend to be depraved and corrupted by the article;

- the strength of the tendency to deprave and corrupt; and
- the nature of the depravity or corruption.

On the other hand, they should assess:

- the strength of the literary, sociological or ethical merit which they considered the article to possess.

The jury should then weigh up these factors and decide whether, on balance, the publication was proved to be justified as being for the public good.

Where the medium in question is television, the definition of 'public good' is somewhat wider (see **11.6**).

11.4.2 'Aversion'

Although not actually a defence, the practical result of the decision in *R v Anderson* (see **11.2.3**) that merely repulsive, loathsome or lewd articles are not obscene means that material that is shocking or disgusting may not be obscene because it has the effect of discouraging readers or viewers from engaging in the activity in question. Per Lord Widgery:

> '… many of the illustrations in "Oz" were so grossly lewd and unpleasant that they would shock in the first instance and then they would tend to repel. In other words, it was said that they had an aversive effect and that far from tempting those who had not experienced the acts to take part in them they would put off those who might be tempted so to conduct themselves.'

This 'defence', if successfully pleaded, would result in a finding that the article was not obscene because it did not tend to deprave or corrupt.

11.4.3 Innocent publication or possession

A person may not be convicted of publishing an obscene article under the 1959 Act or of having an obscene article for publication for gain under the 1964 Act if he proves that he had not examined the article in respect of which he is charged and had no reasonable cause to suspect that it was such that his publication of it or his having it would make him liable to be convicted of such an offence.

11.5 HUMAN RIGHTS

The argument that the national obscenity laws interfere with a person's right to free expression (European Convention on Human Rights, Article 10) is unlikely to meet with much favour. In *Handyside v United Kingdom* [1976] 1 EHRR 737, the European Court of Human Rights was asked to overturn a conviction which resulted from the publication of a reference book for children aged 12–18, entitled *The Little Red School Book*. Chapters in the book included material on sex (both heterosexual and homosexual), pornography and drug-taking. The court concluded that the prosecution and conviction of the publishers and seizure of the offending books was 'necessary in a democratic society' and within the State's margin of appreciation and competency.

11.6 TELEVISION

The Broadcasting Act 1990, s 162(1)(a), removed the exemption of television in relation to the OPA 1959. A person now publishes an article where it is included by him in a broadcast or cable programme. It should be remembered that the offence is one of strict liability, and so the broadcaster may be liable where any obscene matter is provided by any person during the broadcast of a live programme.

The definition of 'public good' (see **11.4.1**) is somewhat wider in the case of broadcasts. A publication will be for the public good where it is in the interests of drama, opera, ballet or any other art, science, literature or learning or any other objects of general concern.

The ITC has drawn up a Code for its licence holders (see **20.2.1** for a discussion of ITC broadcast licences) to observe in their broadcasting business. The Programme Code lists a number of types of viewing material to be regulated. It does not refer specifically to obscenity, but provides that the ITC must do all it can to:

> 'secure that every licensed service includes nothing in its programmes which offends against good taste or decency ... or be offensive to public feeling.'

Further:

> '[the] portrayal of sexual behaviour, and of nudity, needs to be defensible in context and presented with tact and discretion.'

The ITC 'Family Viewing Policy' (details of which appear in the Programme Code) dictates that nothing must be shown prior to 9 pm which is unsuitable for children.

Each licence holder (ie each broadcaster) must employ staff to check programming for breaches of the Code. The ITC has the power to fine broadcasters up to 5% of their annual revenue and, ultimately, to revoke the licence for any breach.

Similar provisions apply in respect of BBC programming (enforced by the Broadcasting Standards Commission).

In respect of non-terrestrial broadcasters, the position is less clear. The ITC Code will apply only to its licence holders. Satellite services are required to hold an ITC licence where they are either a 'domestic satellite service' or a 'non-domestic satellite service'.

A domestic satellite service is:

> 'a television broadcasting service where the television programmes included in the service are transmitted by satellite from a place in the United Kingdom:
>
> (a) on an allocated frequency; and
> (b) for general reception in the United Kingdom' (s 43(1)).

There are currently no domestic satellite services in operation.

A non-domestic satellite service is:

> '(a) a service which consists in the transmission of television programmes by satellite:
>
> (i) otherwise than on an allocated frequency; and
> (ii) for general reception in the United Kingdom or in any prescribed country (or both),
>
> where the programmes are transmitted from a place in the United Kingdom; or

(b) a service which consists in the transmission of television programmes by satellite:

  (i) from a place which is neither in the United Kingdom nor in any prescribed country; but
  (ii) for such reception as is mentioned in paragraph (a)(ii),

  if and to the extent that the programmes included in it consist of material provided by a person in the United Kingdom who is in a position to determine what is to be included in the service.'

In 1992, Red Hot Dutch, a hard-core pornographic satellite service, was transmitted to the UK. It was neither a domestic satellite service nor a non-domestic satellite service; it was broadcast from The Netherlands and it used a frequency not allocated to satellite transmissions to the UK. Red Hot Television (the owner of Red Hot Dutch) was therefore able to broadcast obscene material to viewers in the UK without needing to apply for a licence.

Red Hot Television argued that the UK was unable to bring a prosecution under the OPA 1959 because it was prevented from doing so by the EC Directive on Transfrontier Television (89/552/EEC). The general purpose of the Directive is to ensure that television programmes licensed in one Member State enjoy freedom of reception in other Member States. A reference to the European Court of Justice on the point was never heard because Red Hot Television ran into financial difficulties and ceased broadcasting. This important point has thus not been resolved.

11.7 CINEMA EXHIBITION

The Director of Public Prosecutions may bring a prosecution for obscenity in a film exhibited in a cinema. Such prosecutions are rare due to the local authority's jurisdiction over cinemas. A local authority must license the showing of each film in cinemas in its area of control. It will often do so by relying on the classification produced by the British Board of Film Classification (BBFC).

No film containing scenes which breached the test for obscenity in the 1959 Act would be classified by the BBFC. It would be highly unlikely for a local authority to allow the screening of films without a BBFC classification.

11.8 VIDEO RECORDINGS

Video is subject to the same restrictions in relation to obscenity as other media. In *Attorney-General's Reference (No 5 of 1980)* [1980] 3 All ER 816, the Court of Appeal held that the video cassette was subject to the OPA 1959.

In practice, the BBFC ensures compliance with the law. No video which deals in any respect with sex or violence may be distributed to the public unless it has BBFC approval. No video which breaches the OPA 1959 would be certified as suitable for viewing in the home.

The Director of Public Prosecutions has indicated that any videos approved for showing by the BBFC will not be prosecuted as being obscene. A distributor of video cassettes (as well as laser discs and electronic publications) can thus feel safe in his reliance on the decision of the BBFC.

11.9 OBSCENITY AND CHILDREN

The above offences apply equally to a child readership as to an adult one. The test of likely audience may result in articles being obscene where available for children to consume, even if the same article would not result in the commission of an offence in respect of an adult audience.

In addition, it may be an offence to use children in material for publication. Section 1(1) of the Indecency with Children Act 1960 provides that:

> 'Any person who commits an act of gross indecency with or towards a child under the age of fourteen, or who incites a child under that age to commit such an act with him or another shall [commit an offence].'

Section 1 of the Protection of Children Act 1978, which covers children under the age of 16, makes it an offence for an individual:

> '(a) to take, or permit to be taken, any indecent photograph of a child; or
> (b) to distribute or show such indecent photographs; or
> (c) to have in his possession such indecent photographs, with a view to their being distributed or shown by himself or others; or
> (d) to publish or cause to be published any advertisement likely to be understood as conveying that the advertiser distributes or shows such indecent photographs, or intends to do so.'

Photographs in the context of the 1978 Act include material comprised in a film. It should be noted that there is no definition of what is 'indecent'. It would appear from case-law that what would be shocking, disgusting and revolting to ordinary people would be indecent.

Chapter 12

RACIAL HATRED AND BLASPHEMY

12.1 INCITING RACIAL HATRED

12.1.1 Definition

'Racial hatred' is defined by the Public Order Act 1986, s 17 as 'hatred against a group of persons in Great Britain defined by reference to colour, race, nationality (including citizenship) or ethnic or national origins'. All section numbers in this chapter refer to this statute unless otherwise stated.

In *Mandla and Another v Dowell Lee and Another* [1983] 1 All ER 1062, the House of Lords found that the word 'ethnic' was to be construed in a broad cultural and historic sense. For a group of persons to be ethnic, the members had to regard themselves, and be regarded by others, as a distinct community by virtue of certain characteristics, two of which are essential:

(1) the community has to have a long shared history, of which the group was conscious as distinguishing it from other groups, and the memory of which it kept alive;
(2) it has to have a cultural tradition of its own.

It should be noted that the House was looking at the word 'ethnic' in the context of s 3 of the Race Relations Act 1976. However, there is no reason to believe that the definition would differ for the purposes of the 1986 Act.

12.1.2 The offences

(1) Non-broadcast material

Section 18 makes it an offence for a person to use threatening, abusive or insulting words or behaviour, or to display any written material which is threatening, abusive or insulting if:

(a) he intends thereby to stir up racial hatred; or
(b) having regard to all the circumstances, racial hatred is likely to be stirred up thereby.

Section 19 provides that it will be an offence for a person to publish or distribute written material which is threatening, abusive or insulting if:

(a) he intends thereby to stir up racial hatred; or
(b) having regard to all the circumstances, racial hatred is likely to be stirred up thereby.

Under s 21, a person who distributes, or shows or plays, a recording of visual images or sounds which are threatening, abusive or insulting is guilty of an offence if:

(a) he intends thereby to stir up racial hatred; or
(b) having regard to all the circumstances, racial hatred is likely to be stirred up thereby.

Chapter 12 contents
Inciting racial hatred
Blasphemy

Under s 25, the court can make an order for the forfeiture of any written material or recording to which the offence relates.

(2) Broadcast material

By virtue of s 22 (as amended by the Broadcasting Act 1990, s 164), the offence can be committed as a result of the broadcast of television or radio programmes if it was intended that racial hatred be stirred up or, having regard to all the circumstances, racial hatred was likely to be stirred up by the programme. Those liable to prosecution are the person providing the programme service, the producer or director of the programme and the person who uses the offending words.

Producers, directors and broadcasters of programmes about racism should note, therefore, that they can be liable to prosecution irrespective of their intention.

Section 25 applies to broadcast material as well as non-broadcast material (see *(1)* above).

12.1.3 Defences

(1) Non-broadcast material

A defence is provided to the offence in s 18 where the accused is not shown to have intended to stir up racial hatred, and where he did not intend his words or behaviour to be, and was not aware that it might be, threatening, abusive or insulting. A similar defence exists in s 19 where the accused proves that he was not aware of the content of the material and had no reason to believe that it was threatening, abusive or insulting.

It is a defence under s 21 for the accused, who is not shown to have intended to stir up racial hatred, to prove that:

(a) he was not aware of the content of the recording; and
(b) he did not suspect, and had no reason to suspect, that it was threatening, abusive or insulting.

Section 21 does not apply to the showing or playing of a recording solely for the purpose of enabling the recording to be included in a programme service.

(2) Broadcast material

Where the broadcaster, producer or director is not shown to have intended to stir up racial hatred, it is a defence for him to prove that:

(a) he did not know and had no reason to suspect that the programme would involve offending material; and
(b) having regard to the circumstances in which the programme was included in a programme service, it was not reasonably practical for him to secure the removal of the material.

The producer and director have a further defence where it is not shown that there was intention to stir up racial hatred, and where it is proved that the accused had no reason to suspect that:

(a) the programme would be included in a programme service; or
(b) the circumstances in which the programme would be so included would be such that racial hatred would be likely to be stirred up.

12.1.4 Human rights

It is unlikely that the coming into force of the Human Rights Act 1998 will significantly impact on court decisions in the arena of racial hatred.

Freedom of expression (European Convention on Human Rights, Article 10) prevailed in the important case of *Jersild v Denmark* [1994] 19 EHRR 1, which concerned a television documentary about the views of openly racist youths in Copenhagen. The broadcast had included short extracts from interviews with the youths who had made derogatory and racist comments about 'niggers'. Black people and all 'foreign workers' were said to be 'animals'. The youths were convicted of making racist statements and the documentary-maker of assisting in such dissemination. The latter's argument that his conviction interfered with his Article 10 rights found favour with the European Court – the programme had not sought to propagate racist views, but to inform the public of the existence of such views. Such a distinction is of considerable benefit to the media.

12.2 BLASPHEMY

There have been very few prosecutions for blasphemy this century, the most recent being a private prosecution in 1977. The subject has recently become topical following an application by a British national to the European Court of Human Rights (see the *Wingrove* case below) following the censorship of a video by the British Board of Film Classification.

The offence relates to indecency or ridicule concerning the Anglican faith. Other religions, where they depart from the fundamental tenets of the Church of England, are unprotected. This was affirmed by a decision of the Divisional Court in 1991, in relation to Salman Rushdie's *The Satanic Verses*, which stated that Bow Street magistrates had been correct in refusing to issue a summons on the ground that the offence of blasphemy protected only the Christian religion (*R v Bow Street Magistrates' Court ex parte Choudhury* [1991] 1 All ER 306).

Once publication of alleged blasphemous material has been proved, it is for the jury to decide whether the material crosses the dividing line between 'moderate and reasoned criticism of Christianity' on the one hand, and immoderate or offensive treatment of Christianity or sacred subjects on the other hand.

In *R v Lemon; R v Gay News Ltd* [1979] QB 10, the appellants, the editor and publisher of a newspaper for homosexuals, published in the newspaper a poem with a drawing beside it which described, in explicit detail, acts of sodomy and fellatio with the body of Christ immediately following the moment of death. The Court of Appeal upheld the appeal (though quashed the sentences of imprisonment remarking that it did not consider this an appropriate case for a prison sentence) and stated that proof that the publication amounted to an attack on Christianity, or that it was published with the subjective intention of attacking Christianity, was not required to establish the offence.

Where a prosecution is to be brought against a newspaper or its editor, leave of a High Court judge must first be obtained (s 8 of the Law of Libel Amendment Act 1888). In exercising his discretion, the judge is required to consider all the circumstances and will make no order unless he is satisfied that the case will not be met by a civil action.

The *Wingrove* case (*Nigel Wingrove v United Kingdom*, (1997) EHRR 1) referred to above concerned an 18-minute video which was refused a classification certificate by the British Board of Film Classification. The film was entitled *Visions of Ecstasy* and portrayed ecstatic visions of Jesus Christ by St Theresa de Avila, a 16th-century Carmelite nun. The refusal of a classification certificate (on the ground that it would 'outrage' the feelings of believing Christians as a result of unacceptable treatment of a sacred subject) meant that it would be an offence for Mr Wingrove to supply or offer to supply his video to members of the public (Video Recordings Act 1984).

Mr Wingrove's application under Art 10 of the European Convention on Human Rights was initially rewarded with some degree of success. The European Commission of Human Rights concluded that:

> 'The fact that certain Christians, who have heard of the existence of the video, might be outraged by the thought that such a film was on public sale and available to those who wished to see it, cannot, in the view of the Commission, amount to a sufficiently compelling reason to prohibit its lawful supply.'

However, in November 1996 the European Court of Human Rights upheld the BBFC's decision to censor the video. Such censorship was justified as being necessary in a democratic society within the meaning of Art 10(2) of the Convention. The BBFC has therefore placed itself in the position of ruling on the question of whether material is or is not blasphemous; the practical result of this power is that the public will not get to view such material, whether or not it could be the subject of a criminal prosecution.

Parliament has resisted calls for the laws of blasphemy to be extended to all religions. It has similarly not taken up invitations to abolish the blasphemy law.

Chapter 13

PRIVACY

13.1 BREACH OF CONFIDENCE

13.1.1 Introduction

As with any commercial enterprise, the media and entertainment industry relies for its existence on creativity and new ideas. Whilst the law of copyright will protect the written form and expression of many ideas, at an early stage of development, no formal intellectual property rights may be created or will exist to protect an idea.

In *Coco v AN Clarke (Engineers) Limited* [1968] FSR 415, McGarry J stated that three elements must be established if a case of breach of confidence is to succeed:

(1) the information itself must have the necessary quality of confidence about it;
(2) that information must have been imparted in circumstances importing an obligation of confidence;
(3) there must have been an unauthorised use of that information to the detriment of the party communicating it.

The jurisdiction of the court is an equitable one and does not always depend upon the existence of a contractual relationship between the parties to an action.

13.1.2 Protecting ideas

In *Fraser and Others v Thames Television and Others* [1983] 2 All ER 101, three actresses formed a rock group and developed an idea for a television series. The series was to be known as *Rock Follies*. The actresses discussed the idea at a meeting with Thames Television, and it was agreed that if the television company proceeded with the idea they would give the actresses first refusal for the parts of the rock group. In this case, one of the actresses was not used in the television show and successfully sued Thames Television for breach of confidence. Despite the fact that the idea had been communicated orally, an express obligation of confidence attached to it, and the actress was able to obtain substantial damages.

The court stated that a person would be prevented from disclosing an idea until it became public knowledge if:

(1) the circumstances imputed an obligation of confidence; and
(2) the content was clearly identifiable, potentially attractive in a commercial sense and capable of being brought to fruition.

In this case, the idea had not been produced to a sufficiently material form to attract copyright protection. Indeed, it is doubtful whether the idea for a story involving a rock group could on its own attract copyright protection until, at the very least, story outlines and characters had been conceived in writing or otherwise recorded.

As well as protecting ideas in their formative stages, the law of confidence is also useful in the governing of contractual relations between parties in the media industry.

Chapter 13 contents
Breach of confidence
Data protection
Human rights

Clauses can be included in contracts requiring the parties to an agreement not to disclose or otherwise reveal information which is not already in the public domain.

13.1.3 Personal life

The law of confidence might also be used to restrain employees of well-known personalities from publishing 'kiss and tell' type stories in the press or otherwise. An unsuccessful example of such an attempt to restrain the publication of such confidential information occurred in the case of *Woodward and Others v Hutchins and Others* [1977] 2 All ER 751, where the defendant had performed various public relations duties for the claimants, a number of pop singers including Tom Jones and Gilbert O'Sullivan. After his services to the claimants ceased, the defendant published an account of the claimants' activities whilst on tour. The claimants attempted to restrain publication of articles on the grounds that they were both defamatory and had been written in breach of confidence. In this case, they were unsuccessful. The court said that 'if a group of this kind seek publicity which is to their advantage ... they cannot complain if ... an employee of theirs discloses the truth about them. If the image they offered was not a true image, it is in the public interest that it should be corrected'.

13.1.4 News items

There are provisions in s 10 of the Contempt of Court Act 1981 for the protection of journalists' sources.

13.2 DATA PROTECTION

13.2.1 Introduction

Data protection is an area of law that creates privacy rights for individuals and is as important to media clients as it is to any commercial client. The UK data protection laws, which are based on EC Directive 95/46/EC, provide for various rights to be conferred on individuals about whom personal data are held. Perhaps more importantly, from the point of view of media clients, the law imposes various obligations on those who hold such data. This would apply, for example, to a cable company's list of subscribers, a television company's employee records and a journalist's notes of his investigations into the conduct of an individual.

The Data Protection Act 1998 substantially altered the law of data protection in the UK, and it entered into force on 1 March 2000. The new Act repeals the Data Protection Act 1984 and establishes a new regime for the processing of personal data (which will include certain manual records). It gives enhanced subject access rights and creates a new category of 'sensitive personal data'. It prohibits the transfer of personal data to countries which do not have an 'adequate level of protection for the rights and freedoms of data subjects' (ie most non-EEA countries).

This chapter gives an overview of the data protection law of the UK. Essentially, a person about whom data is held (the data subject) is entitled to be informed by the person who holds the data (the data controller) of the nature of the data held and to a copy of that data in an intelligible form. The data subject has the right to request the rectification of any inaccuracies in the data held and to prevent the processing of any data for the purposes of direct marketing. A data subject can request that no decision concerning him be taken solely by automated means.

13.2.2 Manual records

One of the most significant changes from the 'old' law is that manually processed information is now included in the definition of 'data'. Whereas the 1984 Act regulated the handling of electronic data only, the new statute relates not only to automatically processed information but also to information which forms part of a 'relevant filing system'. Such a system is any method of filing information which is structured by reference to individuals so that specific information relating to individuals is readily accessible.

Examples of a relevant filing system include an employer's personnel files, a journalist's written and filed notes about particular individuals and a written customer or subscriber list.

13.2.3 Data protection principles

There are eight data protection principles which govern the processing of personal data. It is essential for businesses to comply with all eight principles in respect of each and every activity undertaken concerning personal data. The eighth principle in the new Act did not appear in the 1984 Act, and relates to the prohibition on transferring personal data to countries that do not have an adequate level of protection for 'rights and freedoms' of data subjects. Each of the principles concerns 'personal data', defined in the Act as:

> 'data which relate to a living individual who can be identified –
>
> (a) from those data, or
> (b) from those data and other information which is in the possession of, or is likely to come into the possession of, the data controller.'

The eight principles are as follows.

(1) Personal data shall be processed fairly and lawfully and such processing must comply with at least one of a set of specified conditions. Additional conditions apply to sensitive personal data.
(2) Personal data shall be obtained only for one or more specified and lawful purposes, and shall not be processed in any manner incompatible with that purpose or those purposes.
(3) Personal data shall be adequate, relevant and not excessive in relation to the purpose or purposes for which they are processed.
(4) Personal data shall be accurate and, where necessary, kept up to date;
(5) Personal data processed for any purpose or purposes shall not be kept for longer than is necessary for that purpose or those purposes.
(6) Personal data shall be processed in accordance with the rights of data subjects under the Act.
(7) Appropriate technical and organisational measures shall be taken against unauthorised or unlawful processing of personal data and against accidental loss or destruction of, or damage to, personal data.
(8) Personal data shall not be transferred to a country or territory outside the European Economic Area unless that country or territory ensures an adequate

level of protection for the rights and freedoms of data subjects in relation to the processing of personal data.

The definition of 'processing' in the Act is so wide that it includes anything that can be done with personal data.

13.2.4 Conditions for processing

Under the new law, personal data cannot be processed by any business unless the business can show that it meets one of the six conditions for processing contained in Sch 2 to the Act. The six threshold conditions are as follows:

'1. The data subject has given his consent to the processing.
2. The processing is necessary–

(a) for the performance of a contract to which the data subject is a party, or
(b) for the taking of steps at the request of the data subject with a view to entering into a contract.

3. The processing is necessary for compliance with any legal obligation to which the data controller is subject, other than an obligation imposed by contract.
4. The processing is necessary in order to protect the vital interests of the data subject.
5. The processing is necessary–

(a) for the administration of justice,
(b) for the exercise of any functions conferred on any person by or under any enactment,
(c) for the exercise of any other functions of the Crown, a Minister of the Crown or a government department, or
(d) for the exercise of any other functions of a public nature exercised in the public interest by any person.

6. The processing is necessary for the purposes of legitimate interests pursued by the data controller or by the third party or parties to whom the data are disclosed, except where the processing is unwarranted in any particular case by reason of prejudice to the rights and freedoms or legitimate interests of the data subject.'

13.2.5 Sensitive data

A data controller who processes sensitive personal data must comply with one of the threshold sensitive personal data processing conditions listed in Sch 3 to the Act. It is thus vital for data controllers to check all sensitive processing to see that it complies with one of the provisions listed. Sensitive personal data are personal data consisting of information as to:

- the racial or ethnic origin of the data subject;
- his political opinions;
- his religious or other beliefs;
- whether he is a member of a trade union;
- his physical or mental health or condition;
- his sexual life;
- the commission or alleged commission by him of any offence; or

- any proceedings for any offence committed or alleged to have been committed by him, the disposal of such proceedings or the sentence of any court in such proceedings.

There is likely to be considerable argument as to precisely what is meant by each of the above types of information. Some will cause greater difficulties than others. Could the racial or ethnic origin of a data subject, for example, be gleaned from their surname or family name (eg Jones, Patel, McGregor, Abdullah)? If so, this would seem to result in a data subject's name being sensitive personal data. This is unlikely to be the intention of the statute or the directive but may have to be resolved by the data protection tribunal or a court for certainty.

The Sch 3 threshold processing conditions include 'explicit consent' of the data subject and processing to comply with 'employment law obligations'.

13.2.6 Rights of data subjects

A person about whom information is held is entitled to be informed by any data controller ('a person who determines the purposes for which and the manner in which any personal data are processed') whether he holds data on him and to:

- a description of the data; and
- a copy of the information in an intelligible form.

The data subject is also entitled to request and receive information pertaining to:

- the purposes for which the data is being held;
- the recipients or classes of recipients to whom it may be disclosed; and
- the source of the data.

If the data has been processed by a computer in order to arrive at a decision and the outcome of such processing significantly affects the data subject then the individual concerned is entitled to be informed of the *logic* behind the decision-making process.

Where the processing of a data subject's personal data causes unwarranted and substantial damage or distress he is entitled to send a notice (the 'data subject notice') to the data controller requiring him to cease such processing. The data controller must, within 21 days, send the data subject a written notice stating that he has complied with the request or the reasons why he feels the data subject notice to be unjustified. Inadequate compliance with a data subject notice may be remedied by court order. Similar provisions exist in respect of direct marketing personal data, in that a data subject can request a data controller to cease processing such data. Direct marketing is advertising or marketing material directed at individuals and therefore includes 'junk mail'.

13.2.7 The media exemption

Various exemptions exist to benefit certain types of processing. For example, the new law will not apply to data processed for the purposes of safeguarding national security or for purely recreational or domestic purposes (a Christmas card list is therefore excluded). Similar exemptions exist for data held for the prevention or detection of crime and for the assessment or collection of taxes, as well as certain 'regulatory activities'.

Section 31 of the Act, the 'media exemption', gives exemption to certain journalistic, literary or artistic material (known as 'special purposes' material). Processing only for the special purposes will be exempt from any provision relating to data subject rights of access if:

(a) the processing is undertaken with a view to the publication by any person of any journalistic, literary or artistic material;
(b) the data controller reasonably believes that, having regard in particular to the special importance of the public interest in freedom of expression, publication would be in the public interest; and
(c) the data controller reasonably believes that, in all the circumstances, compliance with that provision is incompatible with the special purposes.

In determining whether the data controller's belief that publication is in the public interest is a reasonable one, the Data Protection Act 1998 states that regard shall be had to the provision of the relevant codes of practice as in the box below.

Medium	Code
Newspapers and magazines	Press Complaints Commission's Code of Practice
BBC Television	The Producer's Guidelines
Other Television	Broadcasting Standards Commission's Fairness, Privacy and Standards Codes Independent Television Commission's Programme Code
Radio	Radio Authority's Radio Code

13.2.8 Penalties

Contravention of the Act may constitute a criminal offence punishable with a fine. Directors and other corporate officers may be held personally liable. In addition, the court and the Information Commissioners (the body responsible for enforcing data protection law) have the power to award compensation to data subjects who suffer damage and distress as a result of any contravention by a data controller of any of the requirements of the Act.

13.3 HUMAN RIGHTS

The right to privacy is enshrined in Article 8 of the European Convention on Human Rights, as follows:

> '1. Everyone has the right to respect for his private and family life, his home and his correspondence.
> 2. There shall be no interference by a public authority with the exercise of this right except such as is in accordance with the law and is necessary in a democratic society in the interests of national security, public safety or the economic well-being of the country, for the prevention of disorder or crime, for the protection of health and morals or for the protection of the rights and freedoms of others.'

Note should be taken of the words 'by a public authority' in Article 8(2) – this would indicate that the media, the constituent parts of which do not usually comprise 'public bodies', should be unaffected by the privacy right. However, two things should be borne in mind. The first is that it is possible to argue that media bodies which are in public ownership (such as the BBC and Channel 4) are, in fact, 'public authorities' within the meaning of the Convention. The second is that there has been an increasing tendency by the European Court of Human Rights to impose a positive obligation to provide a remedy to a person who suffers as a result of the breach of privacy 'right' (see, for example, *Fuentes Bobo v Spain* (Application No 39293/98) (2000) unreported, 29 February).

The latter argument was considered in *Douglas, Zeta-Jones and Northern & Shell plc v Hello! Ltd* [2001] 1 FLR 982, [2001] UKHRR 223, CA. Following *OK!* magazine's successful £1 million bid for exclusive rights to publish photos of the highly publicised wedding of Catherine Zeta-Jones and Michael Douglas, both *OK!* and the couple were unhappy when *Hello!* sought to publish, in advance of the *OK!* 'exclusive', its five photographs of the event. The High Court granted the couple and Norther & Shell (publishers of *OK!*) an injunction to prevent *Hello!* from publishing its weekly edition that featured the disputed photographs. However, after 3 days of heated legal debate in the Court of Appeal, the injunction was overturned and *Hello!* was free to publish, albeit 3 days late. In having obtained a set of photographs from an independent third party, the court of appeal found that *Hello!* was not in breach of any copyright that *OK!* may have had in its photographs of the wedding; neither was it found to be acting maliciously by proclaiming its pictures to be 'exclusive'. However, the court left the door open for considerable argument at trial as to the privacy rights of the couple.

The claimants included 'privacy', as well as confidence and data protection, as a cause of action due to the possibility that the person who had taken the disputed photographs had not been a guest at the wedding (the relationship of confidence would therefore have been impossible to show). Two members of the court felt that confidence would be the claimants' best chance for a successful outcome at trial. Sedley LJ went further in stating that English law could now recognise and protect a general right to privacy. He said:

> 'The law no longer needs to construct an artificial relationship of confidentiality between intruder and victim: it can recognise privacy itself as a legal principle drawn from the fundamental value of personal autonomy.'

Chapter 14

CONTEMPT AND COURT REPORTING

14.1 INTRODUCTION

This chapter analyses those aspects of the law which interfere with the two fundamental freedoms of free speech and a free press. The subject is approached from the point of view of the solicitor advising journalists and editors (whether of broadcast or non-broadcast media) and a consideration of contempt of court is followed by an examination of the restrictions on court, parliamentary and current affairs reporting.

The greatest risk for a journalist in reporting current affairs is to be found to be in contempt of court by, for example, publishing material which is likely to prejudice a fair trial. Actions for contempt of court are the means by which the legal system can ensure that information likely to affect the outcome of litigation is not circulated. The Contempt of Court Act 1981 amended and clarified the law of contempt, bringing it into line with the European Convention on Human Rights and the decision of the European Court of Human Rights in *Sunday Times v United Kingdom Government* (1979–80) 2 EHRR 245. All references to section numbers in this chapter are to the 1981 Act unless otherwise indicated.

Contempt under the 1981 Act operates within a narrower field than the offence at common law. The statute has created an offence of strict liability in the sense that the prosecution does not have to prove that the publisher intended to prejudice legal proceedings. The residual common law offence requires proof of intent.

Chapter 14 contents
Introduction
Strict liability contempt
Intentional contempt
Contempt by publishing jury deliberations

14.2 STRICT LIABILITY CONTEMPT

Conduct, regardless of intent, will be contempt as tending to interfere with the course of justice where there is a publication (in writing, by broadcast or in any other form of communication) addressed to the public or a section of the public and where:

(1) it creates a substantial risk that the course of justice in particular legal proceedings will be seriously impeded or prejudiced; and
(2) the proceedings are active.

14.2.1 Substantial risk of serious prejudice

There must be a substantial risk that the course of justice in particular court proceedings will be seriously impeded or prejudiced. This will depend, in part, on the type of court which is hearing the proceedings. A jury will be at a greater risk of being affected by media publications to which they have been exposed than will a judge. It is for this reason that a Crown Court trial is at greater risk of prejudice than many other courts. Guilt or innocence of a defendant in a Crown Court will be decided by a jury. Magistrates' courts may also be prejudiced by media publication, particularly where the case is to be heard by lay justices. A stipendiary magistrate is not likely to be affected by media publication. Civil cases, where the decision rests with the judge alone, should not be the subject of contempt proceedings.

The risk itself must be a practical and not merely a theoretical risk. Thus, each case will have to be looked at on its own facts. In *Attorney-General v Guardian Newspapers Ltd* [1992] 3 All ER 38, the *Guardian* newspaper published an article criticising judges for their propensity to impose reporting restrictions in major fraud trials. The article, written by the city editor, mentioned in particular a trial of six defendants in Manchester in relation to which reporting restrictions had been imposed due to the fact that one of the defendants faced a pending trial in the Isle of Man. The Court of Appeal pointed out that the publication of a statement that a defendant in criminal proceedings was awaiting trial on other charges did not necessarily create a substantial risk that the course of justice would be seriously impeded. The question in each case was whether at the time of publication the statement created a substantial risk that the course of justice would be seriously impeded, and not whether it was the type of publication which was inherently liable to create such risk.

No need for actual prejudice

The offence may be committed even though there is no actual prejudice, provided that the risk is substantial. Whether the risk is substantial is measured at the time of publication and thus it does not matter what actually happens subsequent to publication. As to the meaning of 'substantial', Lindsay J, in *MGN Pension Trustees Ltd v Bank of America National Trust and Saving Association and Credit Suisse* [1995] EMLR 99, found that it did not have the meaning of 'weighty' but rather meant 'not insubstantial' or 'not minimal'. The courts seem prepared, therefore, to allow the press more latitude than the words of the statute would at first sight suggest. In *R v Horsham Justices ex parte Farquharson and West Sussex County Times* [1982] QB 762, Lord Denning MR, speaking of juries, said that they are generally not influenced by what they have read in newspapers:

> 'They are good sensible people. They go by the evidence that is adduced before them not by what they may have read in the newspapers. The risk of their being influenced is so slight it can usually be regarded as insubstantial.'

Serious prejudice

Where there is a substantial risk, it does not necessarily follow that it is a risk of serious prejudice. Where proceedings are to be heard by a judge alone (as opposed to trial by jury), for example, there is little likelihood of the course of justice being seriously prejudiced. A newspaper article will not be treated as a contempt of court if the risk of prejudice is merely incidental (see *Attorney-General v English* [1983] 1 AC 116, where it was held that the test of whether the risk of prejudice is merely incidental to the discussion is not whether an article could have been written as effectively without the relevant passages, but whether the risk created by the words actually chosen is no more than an incidental consequence of expanding its main theme).

14.2.2 Active proceedings

A substantial risk of serious impairment or prejudice is not of itself enough to constitute strict liability contempt. The proceedings which are the subject of the contempt (which includes those taking place in any court or tribunal including the

Industrial Tribunal (*Peach Grey & Co (a firm) v Sommers* [1995] 2 All ER 513)) must be sub judice, or 'active' at the time of publication. Similarly, articles about active proceedings will not constitute contempt without a substantial risk that justice will be seriously prejudiced.

Times at which proceedings become active are listed in Sch 2 to the Act and depend upon the type of proceedings in question.

Criminal proceedings

Criminal proceedings in this context means all criminal proceedings other than appellate proceedings. They become active from the point of one of the following:

(1) arrest without warrant;
(2) issue of a warrant for arrest;
(3) issue of a summons to appear;
(4) service of an indictment or other document specifying the charge.

Criminal proceedings are concluded:

(1) by acquittal or sentence;
(2) by any other verdict, finding, order or decision which puts an end to the proceedings;
(3) by discontinuance or by operation of law.

Conclusion of criminal proceedings by discontinuance or operation of law occurs when:

- the charge or summons is withdrawn;
- in the case of proceedings commenced by arrest without warrant, the person arrested is released, otherwise than on bail, without having been charged;
- in the case of proceedings commenced by arrest warrant, the end of the period of 12 months beginning with the date of the warrant unless the accused has been arrested within that period;
- the accused is found to be unfit to be tried or unfit to plead.

Civil proceedings

Civil proceedings, other than appellate proceedings, become active from the time when arrangements for the hearing are made or, if no such arrangements are previously made, from the time the hearing begins. They cease to be active when the proceedings are disposed of, or discontinued, or withdrawn.

Appellate proceedings

Appellate proceedings are active from the time when they are commenced:

(1) by application for leave to appeal or apply for review, or by notice of such an application;
(2) by notice of appeal or of application for review;
(3) by other originating process,

until disposed of, abandoned, discontinued or withdrawn.

14.2.3 Fair and accurate reports

A person will not be guilty of contempt of court under the 1981 Act (see **14.2.1**) in respect of a fair and accurate report of legal proceedings held in public, published contemporaneously and in good faith (s 4(1)). However, the court may, where it appears to be necessary to avoid a substantial risk of prejudice to the administration of justice in those proceedings, or in any other proceedings pending or imminent, order that the publication of any report of the proceedings be postponed for whatever period is necessary (s 4(2)). In *MGN Pension Trustees Ltd v Bank of America National Trust and Saving Association and Credit Suisse* (above), there was an application by the Serious Fraud Office to postpone the reporting of civil actions brought by the trustees of Maxwell pension funds until after the criminal trial of those involved. The application was opposed by six newspapers. Lindsay J in refusing the application held that there were three questions to be answered as the preconditions of making an order under s 4(2):

(1) was there a substantial risk of prejudice to the administration of justice in the criminal trials? If so –
(2) did it appear necessary for avoiding that risk that there should be some order postponing publication of reports of the civil actions? If so –
(3) ought the court in its discretion to make any, and if so what, order?

For further consideration of 'substantial risk' see *Re Central Television plc* [1991] 1 WLR 4 and *R v Horsham Justices ex parte Farquharson and West Sussex County Times* [1982] QB 762.

14.2.4 Innocent publication or distribution

A publisher of matter to which the strict liability rule applies will not be guilty of strict liability contempt where, at the time of publication, he did not know and had no reason to suspect that the relevant proceedings were active (s 3(1)).

The defence is wider for a distributor of material (to whom the strict liability rule applies) who must merely show that at the time of distribution he did not know that it contained such matter and had no reason to suspect that it was likely to do so.

14.2.5 Discussion of public affairs

Where a publication is made by way of discussion in good faith of a matter of public affairs or general public interest, it will not be a contempt of court where the risk of impairment or prejudice to particular legal proceedings is merely incidental to the discussion (s 5).

In contempt proceedings, the prosecution must prove first that the publication creates a substantial risk of prejudice to the course of justice, and secondly that, if the publication is part of a wider discussion on a matter of general public interest, the risk of prejudice is not merely incidental to the discussion.

An example of a successful plea of the s 5 defence can be seen in *Attorney-General v English* [1983] 1 AC 116. The *Daily Mail* published an article in support of a pro-life candidate for parliamentary election criticising the practice of allowing deformed babies to die of starvation. The article was published in the same week that the trial began of a doctor accused of the murder of a handicapped baby by starvation. The Attorney-General applied for an order for committal against the editor and owners of the paper for strict liability contempt. The House of Lords held that the test of whether the risk of prejudice was merely incidental to the discussion was not whether an article could have been written as effectively without those passages or whether some other phraseology might have been substituted for them that could have reduced the risk of prejudicing the trial, but whether the risk created by the words actually chosen by the author was no more than an incidental consequence of expounding its main theme.

14.3 INTENTIONAL CONTEMPT

The provisions of the Contempt of Court Act 1981 overlap the common law in relation to strict liability. However, it remains possible for a person to be convicted of contempt outside the provisions of the Act where he intended to create prejudice. This residual offence of contempt at common law does not require the proceedings to be active, but it must be shown that the defendant intended to prejudice a fair trial.

> *Example*
> A television news broadcast shows pictures of a bank's employees and customers being held hostage by X and then goes on to list X's previous convictions.
>
> Common law contempt, where proceedings are not active, requires intent. In the above example, there are no proceedings currently active against X, but common law contempt is committed because it must be obvious to the producer of the news programme that the future trial of X will be prejudiced. In *Attorney-General v News Group Newspapers Ltd* [1988] 2 All ER 906, the *Sun* newspaper was fined £75,000 as a result of publishing articles entitled 'Rape Case Doc: *Sun* Acts' and 'Doc groped me, says girl'. The articles referred to the alleged rape of an 8-year-old girl by a 'Dr B'. The *Sun* made an offer to the girl's mother to fund a private prosecution of the doctor when the Director of Public Prosecutions decided, in the absence of any evidence corroborating the girl's story, not to proceed with the case. After the doctor was acquitted, the Attorney-General made an application to the court in contempt at common law. The *Sun* argued that common law contempt could not be committed unless the proceedings were 'pending or imminent' (there had been a 9-month delay between the publication and the acquittal) and that, in any case, there was no intention to prejudice the proceedings.
>
> The case demonstrates the following principles:
>
> (1) there is no absolute requirement at common law that the proceedings in question be either pending or imminent (although where they are not, they should be reasonably likely to occur);
>
> (2) the requirement of intention will be fulfilled where it is obvious that the publisher must have foreseen that his article would create a real risk of prejudice to a fair trial.

14.4 CONTEMPT BY PUBLISHING JURY DELIBERATIONS

A person will be in contempt where he publishes or solicits any particulars of communication between jurors in the jury room (s 8). This provision applies only to the deliberations of jurors, and so a newspaper will not be in contempt where it publishes a journalist's interview with a juror in respect of the juror's opinion of the trial.

Chapter 15

FILM AND TELEVISION: PRE-PRODUCTION

15.1 INTRODUCTION

Chapter 15 contents
Introduction
UK television production
Development
Personnel

The production of feature-length films and television programmes in the UK is largely based around the major terrestrial, satellite and cable broadcasters (BBC, ITV, Channel 4, Channel 5, and BSkyB) who produce, commission and broadcast TV programmes and films. Cable and satellite channels have also created opportunities to exploit older programmes, as well as showing more sport and the first run of feature films on subscription channels before terrestrial broadcasts. Since the Broadcasting Act 1990, the BBC and ITV have a statutory duty to commission at least 25% of their programmes from independent producers. In order to maintain the independent status of a production company, the Broadcasting (Independent Productions) Order 1991, SI 1991/1408, states that a broadcaster must not own more than a 15% shareholding in a production company, and a production company must not own more than a 15% shareholding in a broadcaster.

There are a large number of independent production companies providing programmes for broadcasters. A few are large companies which were previously broadcasters themselves who lost their licences in the last round of ITC franchise bids. Others are small companies reliant on the larger production companies and broadcasters for their development and production finance to develop their own ideas into programmes.

This chapter concentrates on the main stages in a TV production, and the steps and common agreements used by a producer who does not have the necessary finance to exploit a production itself. The basic concepts of TV production are the same as for feature film production, except the sums of money and number of different parties involved with film are often greater than for television production.

There are three main stages to film and TV production: the development and hiring stage (pre-production); the production stage; and, finally, exploitation (or distribution) of the finished product. The contents of the finished programme must also be legally safe. A lawyer's contribution to TV production usually relates to the contracts necessary to set out the rights and obligations of the parties involved in the financing and production of the programme as well as ensuring that the content of the programme complies with the ITC or BBC Programme Codes and is not defamatory or in breach of third party rights.

Some contracts are in a standard form negotiated between representative bodies, such as Equity (the actors' union), and the major broadcasters' and producers' trade association. Other contracts, such as the production contract, contain similar terms depending upon the commissioner or broadcaster in question. These terms vary according to the practices of the commissioner or broadcaster involved. For example, Channel 4 and the BBC have a set of working practices which are used whenever a work is being commissioned by the broadcaster.

The main TV agreement is the production agreement. If a producer is being fully financed by a single broadcaster, then primary broadcast and secondary exploitation of the programme is likely to be undertaken by the financing broadcaster. However, production companies often have to raise finance from more than one source. Each source of finance may require repayment, a proportion of the copyright or a licence of particular rights and/or a share of profits. Few production companies have the financial resources to produce a programme without external finance. Raising finance for productions is always difficult. In the UK, broadcasters provide the major source of finance for producers. Other finance comes in the form of advances from distributors and pre-sales to foreign broadcasters, the use of which inevitably involves splitting up rights in the completed programme by territory or language.

There are various ways in which productions are financed. An investment may be made in the production company itself, in the production itself or by way of a licence of rights in the finished programme. The exploitation of a completed programme is the means of recouping the investment made by all parties in the production. This is done in a number of ways. It may be by broadcast on the commercial channels which attract advertising revenue and sponsors which help the broadcaster (rarely the producer) to recoup its investment. Video sales and foreign broadcasts also generate income for the broadcaster and the producer. A share of this income may also be due to the various contributors in the programme such as writers, actors, the director and musicians, either as a use fee or as a share of the profits.

15.2 UK TELEVISION PRODUCTION

There are a number of bodies involved in UK TV production and broadcasting. First of all, there are the broadcasters themselves. The main broadcasting and commissioning bodies in the UK are the British Broadcasting Corporation (BBC), the ITV channels, Channel 4 and, from January 1997, Channel 5. Each of these organisations is under an obligation to commission at least 25% of its programme output across each of the main genres of programming from independent producers. The Producers Alliance for Cinema and Television (PACT) is the main representative body for independent film and TV producers within the UK.

15.2.1 The broadcasters

The BBC

The BBC is a programme maker, it controls its schedules and then broadcasts its programmes. Its income is derived from the TV licence fee and the commercial exploitation of its catalogue of programmes by way of overseas broadcast, video sales, licence to UK cable networks such as UK Gold and from secondary rights such as publishing and merchandising. Through its separate company, BBC Worldwide, it also acts as a distributor of programmes throughout the world. The BBC acts either by commissioning programmes from independent producers or producing programmes itself in-house. In addition, the BBC licenses programmes from third parties, mainly US producers, but also, increasingly, independent UK producers. Where programmes are commissioned from independent producers, the BBC will generally require a complete assignment of copyright in the completed programme. The producer will receive a production fee based on the programme budget and a share of net profits. The whole cost of the programme is usually met by the BBC which also cash flows the production. The production cost is then treated as a fee for the UK broadcast rights and effectively written off; accordingly, any further income from the programme is treated as profit. Sometimes, the BBC's distribution arm, BBC Worldwide, will supplement the BBC's resources by making an advance to provide the balance of the production budget. In such cases, the advance must be recouped from distribution income before the BBC or the producer can share in the profits.

This means the BBC usually appoints its own distributor, BBC Worldwide, for the programme, which licenses video rights and overseas broadcast as it sees fit. Alternatively, the producer or a third party may be appointed as one of these distributors.

ITV

Programmes for broadcast on the ITV network may be for regional use only or for broadcast over the entire ITV network. The ITV licensees finance productions and commission and license programmes through the sale of advertising during programme breaks and a certain amount of sponsorship. Further income arises from overseas sales and other exploitation. To deal with programmes for broadcast over the entire network, the regional ITV companies set up the Network Centre. The Network Centre licenses limited UK broadcast rights in programmes produced by the regional companies and by independent producers, and schedules and broadcasts programmes over the entire ITV network. The regional companies also produce their own programmes, some of which are used by the Network Centre but others are only used locally.

Where the ITV Network Centre enters into a licence with an independent production company, a regional company monitors those independent productions for broadcast by the Network Centre. The obligations imposed on ITV companies under their licences and by the Broadcasting Act 1990 require programmes to meet certain standards of quality as policed by the Independent Television Commission. The Network Centre pays the licence fee upon completion of the production. Because of the problems of funding programme development and arranging cash-flow for the production, most independent production companies use a regional company to finance their production. The regional company enters a production and finance agreement with the producer. This agreement is additional to the supply agreement dealing with the UK broadcast rights which is entered into between the regional company and the Network Centre. The regional company will take an assignment of the remaining rights in the programme in return for providing finance. Alternatively, a producer may take the direct access route and go straight to the Network Centre. The Network Centre then enters an agreement directly with the producer in the form of its standard tripartite agreement.

Channel 4, Channel 5 and Sky

Channel 4 commissions programmes from independent producers for broadcast. Channel 4's income arises from the sale of advertising, as well as the exercise of distribution rights in commissioned programmes. In addition to its investment in programmes for broadcast, Channel 4 also invests in film projects, some of which have cinema release before video and broadcast exploitation.

Channel 5 and Sky operate in a similar manner, with a mixture of commissioned and acquired programming.

15.2.2 Professional bodies involved in television production

TV and film productions rely on creative and technical personnel such as writers, actors and directors, as well as financiers. Many people and professional bodies are involved in UK TV production and broadcasting. Independent producers have their own professional body. Actors and technical staff are represented by different professional bodies which agree minimum terms and conditions of service.

PACT

The Producers Alliance for Cinema and Television (PACT) represents independent producers operating in film and TV. PACT negotiates standard minimum terms with Equity, the Writers Guild and the Musicians' Union. PACT also provides an industrial relations service to its members including supplying suggested forms of documentation for its members to use when dealing with producers and directors, for development agreements, when interviewing people for inclusion in TV programmes, and such like.

Writers Guild of Great Britain (WGGB)

The WGGB represents writers. It has agreements with the BBC, the independent television companies and PACT which set out the minimum terms upon which a writer is commissioned to write by a producer.

Equity

Equity is the performers' union, representing actors, singers and variety artists throughout the UK. There are equivalent organisations throughout the world. Equity negotiates minimum terms on behalf of its members with the BBC, ITV companies, and PACT and other organisations which use its members' services. Whenever these companies employ an Equity member, they are obliged to use the minimum terms as a starting-point for negotiations. As well as negotiating in traditional TV and film works, Equity negotiates individual agreements for the use of its members' services in developing other media such as interactive CD-ROM games.

Musicians' Union (MU)

The function of the MU is to represent and advise musicians. The MU agrees terms of engagement for musicians which producers use when engaging musicians in recording sessions for productions.

Broadcasting, Entertainment, Cinematographic and Theatre Union (BECTU)

BECTU represents the technical staff used in productions. There are similar union agreements negotiated with broadcasters and PACT, the terms of which allow producers to engage behind-the-camera personnel for productions and to buy out any rights they may have (perhaps in the nature of copyright in set or costume design).

Directors' Guild of Great Britain

The Directors' Guild of Great Britain represents directors in TV and film productions. Although the CDPA 1988 does not recognise the contribution of directors in film productions (other than their right to be identified as director (s 77(1)), European legislation has changed this position. Directors will have more bargaining power with producers to share in the profits from productions following the introduction of the EC Copyright Harmonisation Directive 93/98 (under which they are now treated as co-authors of the film or television programme for copyright purposes) and EC Directive 92/100 on Rental and Lending Rights. At the date of writing, there is no standard agreement in force between directors and broadcasters or PACT.

15.3 DEVELOPMENT

15.3.1 Underlying works

The producer must deal with a number of development matters before filming begins. Whether the production is a drama, a game show or a documentary, the concept and idea should have been developed sufficiently to warrant copyright protection. Basic ideas should be kept confidential by the producer, and circulation of any documents detailing such ideas restricted accordingly to ensure that competitors cannot use them. The risk of disclosing an idea which is not protected by copyright may mean a competitor can develop the idea with impunity. Smaller production companies have to approach larger companies and broadcasters for production and development finance. These larger companies and broadcasters also develop and produce their own programmes, and may receive suggestions for programmes, which are very similar in content to ones which they are developing. The originator of an idea must take appropriate steps to protect his idea.

Protecting an idea

Ideally, no ideas, characters or storylines are ever disclosed until production finance is secured. This is to prevent the use of the idea by other producers or broadcasters unless and until the work is commissioned and produced. However, this is not commercially practicable. It is very important for a writer or producer with programme ideas to keep accurate records and dates of the inception of those ideas. It is useful to send a copy of any script or treatment by registered post to a bank, lawyer or accountant for safe keeping. Some authors send scripts to themselves by registered post to prove the date of inception for copyright purposes, although an independent recipient is better. Copyright and the law of confidence should be used to the utmost to protect an idea or project. This may mean asking a producer, broadcaster or other backer to sign a confidentiality agreement acknowledging that the discussions are confidential and that no use can be made of an idea without the permission of the originator of the idea in question. However, the courts have recognised the protection of confidential information even without the existence of a confidentiality agreement (see *Fraser and Others v Thames Television and Others* [1983] 2 All ER 101).

15.3.2 Developing an idea

If a producer finds a backer willing to finance the development of a production idea, the producer should take other development steps. This usually means:
- finding and taking an option over the services of suitable technical and artistic personnel;

- considering appropriate rights clearances from technical and creative personnel; as a starting-point, one of the minimum terms agreements (such as the Equity agreements) may be used;
- scouting and agreeing locations;
- obtaining professional advice;
- setting a budget and production timetable;
- acquiring the right or an option to use any necessary underlying rights, eg an existing novel or play, or commissioning a script.

15.3.3 Development agreements

A broadcaster, distributor or a larger production company may fund the producer to take these development steps. The backer may require the producer to enter a development agreement. There is a suggested form of agreement for PACT members. The agreement should deal with the matters set out below.

The project

The project should be defined by the backer and the producer so that they both know exactly what they are developing. The name of the programme may need to be specified.

Finance

The backer will provide a specified amount of money (a development budget) to develop the project. This money may be provided piecemeal or all at once. The producer may have to open a separate joint bank account in which money from the backer is placed and held on trust for the backer and used in the agreed way. The backer will then wish to see receipts and bank statements establishing that the money has been spent accordingly. On rare occasions, a fee may be paid to the individual producer responsible for the development steps. This may be separate from the development finance.

Development steps

The agreement should set out exactly what the backer requires the producer to do and how the budget can be used. The development steps will vary according to the project, but will normally include those set out in **15.3.2**. The development steps, once completed, should place the producer in the position to offer the backer a complete package if the backer chooses to take the project further.

Rights

At this stage, the backer will almost certainly require the producer to assign all the rights in the project to itself. Although the producer will want to resist this step, there is very little else a backer can do to take security for the money it is providing. The producer effectively loses control of the rights in the project and inevitably puts the producer at a disadvantage in any subsequent negotiations for the funding of the production itself. The producer will usually be able to negotiate a turnaround clause allowing the repurchase of rights if the backer does not finance the production within specified time periods. A number of issues arise from the assignment of rights to the backer by way of security.

- The producer must ensure that the backer only uses the producer's services to produce the programme.
- The backer should make a decision on production within a reasonable time, after which the producer can exercise the turnaround provisions and take the project elsewhere and continue to develop or film it. If the backer does not wish to commission the programme, the producer should be able to go elsewhere.
- The backer will want an obligation that the development budget should be repaid if the production goes ahead with another backer. Alternatively, the development budget will form part of the budget for the final programme where the backer funds the programme.
- Development finance is included in the amount of money the producer has to raise for production. If the backer does not want to pursue the production, the full repayment of this money by the producer to the backer should secure the release or reassignment of any interest the backer has in the project. This repayment may take place when filming starts. The producer may then deal with rights in the programme to raise money for the production. The producer must take care not to conclude any agreements with third parties which grant or deal with rights it does not have.

15.3.4 Underlying rights

The producer needs to acquire the right to use underlying material in the production. There are three categories of underlying material: existing works, commissioned works, and public domain material.

(1) Existing works

A copyright work such as a novel cannot be 'adapted' or dramatised without the copyright owner's permission (see s 22 of the CDPA 1988). It is common for a producer, before acquiring all rights in a work for a full fee, to take an option over an existing work. The option agreement will contain all the rights the producer requires for the production (such as an assignment of copyright), but it will be contingent upon the exercise of the option for the agreed fee. An option entitles a producer to acquire exclusive rights over a work if he makes the programme in question.

The option should deal with a number of matters:

- the length of the option (usually one or two years), any option extensions and the rights that can be exercised during that time (such as to prepare a screenplay or synopsis);
- the cost of the option (and any extensions) and the cost of exercising it. The option price is often a percentage of the final price (normally 10%), and deductible from it. The final fee for the acquisition of rights may be a fixed sum or an advance against a share of net profits;
- the method of exercising the option and the terms of the acquisition once exercised (the producer will normally require a partial assignment);
- warranties from the author;
- screen credits and moral rights issues;
- exactly what rights are being obtained. Such rights may be strictly limited to TV, or film and TV; in addition, the number of films or programmes which can be made may be limited;
- any reserved rights (or 'holdback'), such as radio, theatre or book rights retained by the writer, as well as merchandising rights; and

- any share of profits the writer is entitled to. The producer must be careful to define exactly what profits the writer can claim, as any 'net profit' shares must correspond with other agreements.

The acquisition of underlying rights is fundamental to the production. If an option is taken over an existing work, a treatment or draft script (an adaptation or dramatisation of the work for copyright purposes) will be commissioned. Whether or not an existing work is used, an additional agreement will be entered into with the author of the screenplay in similar terms to those set out below.

Full rights and content clearance procedures (as discussed in Chapter 17) should be taken with the acquired work to ensure that there are no legal problems with title or otherwise with the copyright.

(2) Commissioned works – scriptwriters

A producer may commission an original script, a script based on a format provided by the producer, or a script based on another work. The WGGB have agreed minimum terms for works commissioned by broadcasters (such as the BBC and ITV) and independent producers, represented by PACT. The terms of these agreements vary according to the organisation that the WGGB is dealing with. The PACT agreement covers various types of production classified according to budget. No such distinction is made in the BBC and ITV agreements. The agreements have similar elements.

The terms deal with payments to the author (minimum rates are set out); use fees entitlement (such as for repeats, foreign distribution and video release); assignment of copyright (this may be the whole copyright or just film or TV rights, depending on the author); time for delivery of the script (this covers the time for commissioning and delivery of the various drafts of the script), as well as screen credits (covered by the Screenwriting Credits Agreement 1974) and the author's moral rights.

The WGGB/PACT agreement has a model form of agreement for the writer to sign which incorporates the terms of the main agreement. The agreement operates by taking an assignment of copyright from the author. The title of the production, together with delivery dates for each draft of the script and the fee payable for each draft is set out. Additional use fees are detailed in line with the minimum terms agreed. The other agreements also use the agreed terms as their basis.

(3) Public domain material

The producer need not acquire rights in material which does not have copyright protection. It is important that a work in which copyright previously existed is out of copyright in all the countries where the finished programme will be exploited.

True public domain material (such as facts or information) which is not usually the subject matter of copyright protection may require no rights clearance or acquisition. However, great care must be taken when using a work that relates facts in the public domain (such as a history or biography) as the basis for a programme. The work itself may still have copyright protection. In such a case, the producer should either acquire rights in the work itself or commission a script or treatment based solely on original source material and not the copyright work. *Harman Pictures NV v Osborne and Others* [1967] 1 WLR 723 illustrates the problem where a film producer was unable to agree terms with the rights owner of a book concerning the events leading up to and culminating in the Charge of the Light Brigade. The producer commissioned a script which was similar to the claimant's work in its choice of incidents. An injunction was granted to the claimant because the similarities in aspects of the works were not explained or accounted for by the defendants.

15.4 PERSONNEL

Film and TV productions require a mixture of specialist and creative personnel. Some of these personnel will be employees of a production company or broadcaster. Other contributors may be self-employed for tax purposes. Employees will be allocated to productions by their employer and, generally, no separate agreement will be required. For personnel who are not employed by the production company or broadcaster, separate agreements should be entered into specifying their obligations, assigning their rights (such as copyright, moral and rental rights) and agreeing terms for payment. (See also Chapter 17, Rights and Content Clearance.)

15.4.1 Actors

Actors are generally employed on the basis of the terms agreed between Equity and the relevant production organisation. The terms have different provisions depending upon the type of performer (eg there are different provisions for actors, dancers, singers, puppeteers, quiz masters, presenters, etc) in the main BBC and ITC agreements.

The agreements contain terms relating to two important factors: first, the actual obligations during filming; and, secondly, the rights obligations, consents and fees payable for initial and subsequent uses of the programme. The actor will also be required to prioritise his commitments to the production. The producer will specify a guaranteed period when the actor will be needed for filming and also periods once filming is complete when the actor may also be required. These periods are known as 'first call' (priority to the production) and 'second call' (can finish other work).

Filming obligations

The agreement contains terms relating to the conditions of the actor's engagement such as nudity and simulated sex acts, billing and credits, transport, clothing and make-up, and rehearsals. The agreements themselves set out these matters and many more in detail.

An artist is then engaged using a form of engagement which incorporates the terms of the main agreement. The form of engagement should set out the name of the programme the artist is appearing in, the period of engagement, the agreed fee and time for payment, and the artist's billing (ie screen credit), and should be signed by both parties.

Rights and payments

Rights and payments to the actors are dealt with in Chapter 17.

15.4.2 Producer and director

An individual producer and director are usually appointed for filming. The individual producer is distinct from the production company and has responsibility for the day-to-day running of the production with overall responsibility for completing a programme within budget and with minimum deviation from the production schedule. Individual producers may be engaged on separate contract terms setting out their responsibilities and functions, or they may be employees of the production company. The producer may technically be the author of the film for copyright purposes (even though he acts as agent for a production company), so an assignment of copyright will be taken by the production company. The producer also has a rental right in the film.

A director has overall artistic and creative responsibility for the production. His role is to liaise with scriptwriters, technical crew and actors to film and create a final edited version of the programme. The producer will appoint a director to work on the programme. A separate agreement will often be drawn up for this depending upon whether the director is already employed by any of the bodies responsible for filming (such as the production company). The director of a programme has moral rights and rental rights in the completed programme (since for rental rights purposes a director is considered as one of the authors of the completed work).

PACT provides sample agreements for its members to use which contain typical terms of service for both producers and directors.

15.4.3 Technical staff

There are standard terms in force between the technical union BECTU and each of the BBC, ITV and PACT.

15.4.4 Composers and musicians

If original music is required for a production, a composer may be contracted to compose suitable music. An agreement with a composer may have to take account of any previous publishing and recording contracts the composer has entered into as they will invariably be exclusive in nature. The producer must agree suitable terms with the composer for the writing of music. This will have to take account of the composer's music publishing agreement. If the composer performs, produces and records his work, an agreement similar to a recording contract must be agreed. The producer must also obtain permission to synchronise the music and recording with the filmed programme.

Musicians used in the programme should be engaged on the appropriate minimum terms agreed with the Musicians' Union. Where a musician is already subject to an exclusive recording contract, a release should be sought from the person with the benefit of that contract (usually the record company) permitting the use and exploitation of the musician's services.

Chapter 16

FILM AND TELEVISION: FINANCE AND PRODUCTION

16.1 INTRODUCTION

If a project is fully developed and financed, it may proceed to production. This is the point at which filming schedules, locations, personnel and the technical paraphenalia of a production come together. If a producer is going to make the commitment of time and resources to filming, there must be money available to cash-flow the production. Cash-flow is important because all productions incur costs which cannot be deferred until after the production is complete and are thus due for payment during production. If the length of time it takes to film even the shortest programme is also taken into account, the need for cash during the production becomes clear. Before any filming takes place, finance and cash-flow must be in place. If a producer has the means to finance and cash-flow a production itself, the financial arrangements discussed below are not relevant. The producer may instead move straight on to consider the most effective methods of exploitation and attempt to recoup production costs by concluding distribution or pre-sales agreements.

This chapter discusses some of the common methods of financing a television production in the UK, as well as common terms in a production agreement. Every deal is different, and some or all of the terms considered may be varied or excluded altogether from an agreement. A lawyer's contribution to the production process relates to the negotiation and preparation of documentation and the content and rights clearance issues arising during production.

The production, finance and distribution agreements may be separate agreements, although they are often dealt with in one document, especially where a broadcaster fully commissions a production and acquires all the rights in it. For the sake of convenience, production and finance are dealt with together in this chapter, and distribution separately in Chapter 18.

16.2 METHODS OF FINANCE

The producer has a number of ways of raising money to finance a production. For in-house productions with a broadcaster or production company, raising finance is not an issue. An independent producer may have obtained development funding from a broadcaster or won a tender to produce a programme. In these cases, the commissioner will generally finance and cash-flow the production. An independent producer selling a production idea may not be able to convince one entity to provide all the finance, in which case the funding alternatives discussed below are likely to be directly relevant. Each method of funding is flexible, and it is common for a producer (out of necessity) to acquire finance from a number of different sources. Each source may provide finance on a different basis and have differing requirements as to repayment and the eventual rights it owns in the production.

Chapter 16 contents
Introduction
Methods of finance
Production agreements

In order to obtain finance for a production, the producer will have to convince distributors and equity investors that there is a profit to be made from the production. Profit is typically made from broadcasts at home and abroad (for which broadcasters pay), as well as other forms of exploitation such as video release.

16.2.1 Full commission with cash-flow

A full commission from a UK broadcaster where the broadcaster provides all necessary money for the production is (in terms of finance) a relatively straightforward way of funding a production. The production is cash-flowed and, as long as the production is run on schedule and within budget, the producer has fewer financial concerns. The commissioner will impose strict terms on the producer. These terms will cover approval of the script, personnel and budget, as well as the right for the commissioner to take over or abandon the production in certain circumstances. In return for finance and cash-flow, the commissioner will be assigned the rights in the production. The producer will receive a production fee and a share of any eventual profits (usually known as 'net profits'). The commissioner may then exploit and distribute the completed production as it sees fit.

The terms of a full commission vary between the major UK broadcasters. Each of the BBC, ITV and Channel 4 have their own preferred terms which they use in most commissions. Although major broadcasters do not always insist on a full assignment of copyright they always insist on a period of exclusivity for their rights. Even if rights are assigned to the broadcaster, the producer may be able to retain some rights in the production itself, in addition to a right to income from the exploitation of the production.

16.2.2 Equity investment

Investment in a TV production is risky because the success of a production cannot be guaranteed. Equity investors take great care to protect their position and ensure a return on their investment. The investment of cash in a production may be achieved in a number of ways. There are a number of ways of investing.

Company

It is possible to provide capital for a production company. This form of investment may be in return for shares in a company or may take the form of a loan to a company. Investment may be by private individuals, banks, venture capitalists or other production companies. Such investments are generally for the setting up and running of a production company and not a particular production. Production companies should be careful to maintain their independent status for Broadcasting Act purposes if they are providing programmes for UK broadcasters.

Production

An investment in the production itself rather than in the production company is a common way of financing a film. The investment is made based on the budgeted cost of the film. A proportion of the cost is provided on terms as to repayment set out in the production and finance agreement and cash-flowed by the investor. In return, the investor is repaid the amount of the loan, together with interest, and usually also receives a share of profits. The repayment of the loan is from the first receipts of the production. These receipts will often be sums paid by a distributor on delivery of the completed film; however, such sums are often 'discounted' by a bank (see **16.2.3**) and so are due in priority to the bank. Where there are a number of equity financiers, they may need to agree the priority in which they are repaid. The various financiers should negotiate a separate 'collection agreement' using a collection account with a bank. This agreement may state that all moneys from the exploitation of the production are paid into the collection account. Each financier is then repaid 'pari passu and pro rata' (ie without preference and in proportion to) their contribution as moneys are received in the account until they are each repaid. In this way, the financiers are all repaid at the same time and in proportion to the amount they have lent to the producer.

16.2.3 Distribution advance

The pre-sale of rights to a distributor is also known as a 'negative pick-up' agreement. A distributor agrees to take certain rights in a completed production. However, unlike the equity investor, a distributor often only pays the producer once the production is complete and delivered to the distributor in accordance with the agreed programme 'specification'. Rights may be granted for certain territories and certain types of exploitation (see further Chapter 17). Until satisfactory completion of the production, no money is exchanged unless the distributor is owned by a broadcaster, in which case the advance is paid during production. Once the production is completed on the terms agreed, the distributor pays over the agreed sum. This is an advance against distribution income from the production. The distributor usually retains all income from the exploitation of the rights it was granted until the advance is recouped, after which income is divided between the rights owners and distributor. Once paid, the advance may be used to repay equity investors. The advance will often be recouped from the rights owner's share of profits, not all income received by the distribution. Effectively, the distribution advance is an advance on profit share/royalties.

Discounting distribution advances

Accordingly, unless distributors' advances are due before satisfactory delivery of the production to the distributor, pre-sales may not help the producer to cash-flow the production itself. Accordingly, producers often 'discount' distribution advances by assigning the right to receive advances from the distributor to a lender. This is known as discounting because lenders do not lend or provide the full amount of the advance as cash to the producer. The full amount of the advance is lent, but the producer only receives, for example, 75% of the advance, because the lender takes the other 25% of the advance as its fee, including interest and costs, for taking the risk of lending to the producer.

The terms of these loan agreements are generally beyond the scope of this book; however, discounting advances is an important method of cash-flowing finance for producers. Banks which provide this service are keen to ensure that the distribution advances payable on completion of the production are guaranteed. The bank may also be a party to any collection agreement. The bank will require an assurance that the production will be completed and delivered to the distributors. To this end, banks require 'completion guarantors'. A completion guarantee is a contract from a third party to complete the production if certain events delay, disrupt or prevent completion of the film. A fee is paid for this service.

16.2.4 Sponsorship, merchandising and product placement

The ITC Sponsorship Code prohibits product placement in the UK and places strict requirements on producers and broadcasters raising money for productions from sponsors. A sponsor providing finance enters an agreement for certain credits at the beginning and end of the broadcast programme. Broadcast sponsorship is discussed in more detail in Chapter 22.

Merchandising arrangements may also be used to part finance a programme. Many companies granted merchandising rights pay an advance on royalties payable under the agreement, which can then be used to finance the production. The ITC Sponsorship Code must also be complied with where merchandising arrangements are made.

16.2.5 Sale of rights after production

The rights in a completed production can be licensed or assigned by the rights holder before or after production is complete. Typically, rights are licensed. Any dealings with the production, even once it has been completed, will be subject to any obligations to contributors, such as writers and performers, as well as other agreements that are already in place relating to the production. Usual terms of distribution agreements are considered in Chapter 18.

The rights owner in the production may deal with rights that have not been dealt with under any other agreement. For example, although the rights owner may have appointed distributors for various European territories, further distributors could be appointed for North and South America. Video rights together with on-line and CD-ROM rights may also have been retained by the rights owner. Such rights can generate substantial income of their own.

16.2.6 Sales agents

A sales agent is given the right to find and appoint distributors for the finished programme in territories where distributors have not been appointed by the producer. The agent usually pays the producer an advance against future income in return for the right to seek and appoint distributors and generally exploit the production. The agent first recoups its advance from all income it receives, and then deducts a percentage commission from proceeds of sales to other distributors before accounting to the producer. In the same way as distributors, sales agents recoup their advances before equity investors are repaid. The appointment of a sales agent takes the problem of exploitation out of the producer's hands but, especially if the agent then appoints distributors, introduces a further element of commission into the financial equation. This reduces the programme's net profits.

16.2.7 Net profits

An important term in any finance agreement relating to programme production and finance is the definition of 'net profits'. Typically, 'net profits' are the income sums received from exploitation of a programme after deduction of commission, expenses (for sales agents and distributors) and the costs of production. 'Distribution expenses' must be defined in the distribution agreement and will usually include advertising costs and the cost of manufacturing prints of the programme (this concept is dealt with further in **18.2.2(3)**).

A producer who is entitled to a share of net profits will be careful to ensure that the definition of net profits does not contain any unusual items of expenditure. A producer also often offers a share of net profits to other participators (such as writers and directors) in the production. These parties must clarify whether they are to receive a share of the producer's net profits or the net profits of the actual production itself. Obviously, a share of the producer's net is a small proportion of the production net. The definition of producer's net will also take account of any share of net profits due to equity investors.

Some production agreements also take account of 'deferments'. A deferment is a sum paid to an actor or other participator in a production after it has recouped its other finance expenses. The other backers of a production have to agree a deferment as it usually involves delaying their share of net profits. Because of the number of participators in some productions, many production and finance agreements contain a 'recoupment schedule'. This is a list of the order and priority of repayment for investors and distributors.

16.2.8 Example

An independent producer seeking finance for a short made-for-television film has a number of alternatives.

A full commission with cash flow from an organisation such as the BBC is the easiest way to finance the film. The financier would take an outright assignment of copyright in the completed film. The producer may take a production fee based on a percentage of the production budget, perhaps 10% or 15%, and a share of net profits, which may be some 30%. The commissioning organisation will deal with all exploitation of the film.

If the producer cannot raise finance in one place he will have to raise the money as best he can from a number of sources. A broadcaster may be prepared to make an equity investment. The equity will be advanced during production and recouped from the film's income. The investor will also take a share of net production profits.

The producer may raise money from a pre-sale of rights in the film. The money for the pre-sale may be advanced during production or payable on completion of the film.

The producer may appoint distributors for particular territories, such as Europe or the USA. The distributors will agree to make advances, on account of the producer's profit share, either during production or on delivery of the film.

For territories where the producer is unable to find a distributor, the producer may appoint a sales agent who will pay an advance against distribution income.

In the case of distributors and sales agents, the money they advance will be recouped from income derived from exploitation of the completed film.

Where moneys are only payable on completion of the film the producer may approach a bank to discount the advances so that he has money to finance cash flow during production.

Assuming a bank can be found to do this, the producer must:

- enter a loan agreement with the bank (this agreement will take a charge over the producer's rights in the film and assign the producer's right to receive the distribution advances to the bank); and
- find a suitable completion guarantor; and
- send notice to each distributor stating that the producer has assigned the right to receive the advances to the bank; and
- obtain a laboratory pledgeholder's agreement. This agreement is further security for the bank, as it will state that the finished programme is held to its order, although the distributors will also be allowed to order prints of the programme for their own distribution purposes.

Repayment

Once the film is completed and delivered to the distributors, the distribution advances will be paid to the bank. Assuming the production was brought in on budget, this should cover the bank's loan, including interest and costs. The bank will then release its security and rights in the programme.

The equity investor is then entitled to be repaid its equity investment together with interest. As there is only one equity investor, there is no need to enter a collection agreement. As moneys are received, they are applied to repay the investor's equity. However, the investor will not receive anything until the distributors have recouped their advances. At the point where the distributors are recouped, they will pay income (less their expenses and percentage) to the producer. Once repaid, the broadcaster will release any security it obtained over the programme.

At this stage, the producer should have repaid all its borrowings and its investors. The remaining income is then applied as 'net profits'. The investor is entitled to a share of this net profit. The remaining 'net profit' belongs to the producer. The producer may offer a share of net profits to other investors and participators in the production.

16.3 PRODUCTION AGREEMENTS

16.3.1 Purpose

A production agreement is a contract entered into between the financier or financiers of a film and a producer to carry out all the work necessary to create the programme and deliver it in final form to the financiers and distributors. In this respect, it is simply an order for a product, namely a specified film programme. A wholly funded in-house production by a broadcaster or other production company will not usually require such an agreement. For independent producers, the production agreement provides the specification for the final programme, and also usually sets out the rights which the parties to the agreement will retain once the programme is completed, together with the right of the parties to the agreement to share in any profits from exploitation.

The terms included in a production agreement vary enormously depending upon the way in which finance has been raised. There is a direct relationship between the terms of the finance deal and the production and distribution aspects of the agreement.

16.3.2 Finance and production

The type and variety of finance raised by the producer tends to dictate the terms of the production aspects of the agreement. An independent producer wishing to make a programme is first of all faced with the hurdle of getting a work commissioned and raising finance for the production. Producers may be specially commissioned to produce programmes. Individual producers may also be full-time employees of larger production organisations. A producer will wish to see some profit and retain some rights in the enterprise through successful distribution of the programme. The way in which the financing of a film affects a production agreement is considered below.

Full commission with cash-flow

A production agreement based on commission with cash-flow will contain greater rights for the commissioner than if the money was being paid as a licence once the film was complete. A full commission will cover most, if not all, of the items dealt with below. The commissioner will, in particular, retain the right to take over the production in certain circumstances and to oversee the whole production.

Equity investment

An investor in a film usually acquires no rights other than the right to repayment and a share of the production's net profits. Such an investor may be a party to the production agreement. Where there is an equity investment, the investor will take rights in the production (such as an assignment of copyright and security over the physical property of the film, usually the negatives) in return for repayment. Once repaid, it may be entitled to a share of profits, but will not deal with rights in the film.

Pre-purchase

The pre-purchase of rights by a distributor, involving the provision of finance by the distributor upon completion or during production, may contain similar terms to a full production agreement. This gives the distributor greater protection and enables it to specify the exact product expected by the distributor from the producer and thus to take rights by prospective assignment of copyright if the programme is satisfactorily completed. If a programme is not cash-flowed by its investors and distributors, the producer must take steps, as outlined in **16.2.3**, to borrow money from a bank and discount the finance.

Licence and distribution agreements

An agreement dealing with the rights to broadcast an existing programme usually takes the form of a licence of copyright. Distributors, under the terms of their distribution agreement, often have the right to enter into such licences. The terms of a straightforward distribution and licence agreement are considered in Chapter 18.

Co-production

Co-production agreements contain some, but not all, of the stipulations of a full production agreement. Co-production agreements take a number of forms; they are often arrangements used to take advantage of tax reliefs available in particular jurisdictions. They are also used where the parties jointly develop and finance a project, and sometimes are simply used to pre-purchase rights in the final programme. Depending upon the type of arrangement, the co-production agreements may contain clauses dealing with budgeting, the spending of the budget and distribution rights.

16.3.3 Parties

The parties to a production agreement vary according to the type of finance available and the contractual requirements. An equity investor or a party commissioning a production will be parties to the agreement. A distributor who has agreed to take specified rights in a finished product will usually only be concerned to see that the programme matches its specification and, accordingly, will not be a party to the production agreement itself unless the agreement combines both production and distribution. A separate distribution agreement will be concluded.

16.3.4 Rights

The production agreement should specify exactly how copyright is apportioned between the parties. Specific rights may be retained according to the financial role of the parties. An equity investor will take an assignment of copyright as security for its investment. A distributor under a pre-sale agreement takes no rights until the production is completed and the money is due, at which point an exclusive licence or assignment of certain rights is granted. A co-producer will provide an agreed amount of finance and other services in return for an agreed share of rights. Each co-producer may split ownership as tenants in common, and rights according to their agreement and respective investment. A commissioning broadcaster may require a full assignment of copyright in the programme, in return for which the producer receives a production fee and a share of net profits.

16.3.5 Take-over, abandonment, force majeure and termination

If the producer does not fulfil its side of the bargain, the financier or other investment partner may require the right to take over or abandon the production. The events which trigger this right should be specified in the agreement. Typical terms governing this right include:

- producer's insolvency;
- a material breach of the agreement which is not remedied within a certain time;
- exceeding budget;
- failing to comply with the production schedule or departing from the agreed specification of the programme.

Take-over is usually optional rather than compulsory, and a well-advised producer will seek to limit the circumstances in which the right is exercisable. The role of a completion guarantor may also be important in this regard. If the producer has discounted distribution advances, a lender may have entered arrangements to allow for this contingency and will have appointed a completion guarantor. A guarantor is appointed to ensure that the production is completed. Wherever the possibility of take-over by a third party exists, the contracts with the producer and the cast and technical crew must be assignable. The producer will require an indemnity from the third party if the production is taken over, as the producer remains liable for the obligations in those contracts.

A pre-sale agreement should not include take-over rights, as money normally only becomes due upon delivery of the completed programme. Co-producers do not usually include take-over terms, although there will be default and termination provisions in the agreement providing for insolvency and breach of agreement by the parties.

An event of force majeure (such as war breaking out) may give the commissioner the right to take over or abandon the production. An event of force majeure may give rise to suspension of the contract or, in the case of a contract which stipulates a delivery date for the production, an extension of the contractual term by the length of the delay.

16.3.6 Budget and banking

The agreement should set out the budget and related arrangements such as the keeping of accurate accounts and opening, maintaining and paying moneys into a production bank account. This account will be held on trust for the financier to protect it from insolvency; there should also be joint signatories to the account. The bank should confirm that it will not exercise any right of set off against any other debts not relating to the production which the producer may have with that bank. If the budget is apportioned between, for example, the acquisition of rights and equity investment, this should be set out.

Limits may be placed upon the amounts the producer can spend during each week of production. All expenditure should be in line with the budget and cash-flow forecast contained in it. In the case of film production, the producer should provide regular reports detailing the total minutes of film taken during the period and the budget position. A provision for any spending over the amount of the budget should be made in the agreement and allowances for the producer to allocate money from one part of the budget to another if expenses vary. If possible, the financiers may want the producer to bring the production in under budget so that any savings cannot be applied elsewhere in the budget but will reduce the amount the company has to pay once production is completed. If there are savings (underspend), the producer will want that money to be shared between itself and the financier. The consequences of any overspend vary depending upon the amount and the cause of the overspend. A serious overspend due to the fault of the producer can have severe consequences and may lead to the take-over of the production by the financier.

16.3.7 Programme specification and delivery

The exact specification of the programme will be set out in the agreement. Some financiers require a right of approval over all elements of the production such as the cast, script and key personnel. The agreement should also set out the exact technical specification of the programme, ensuring that the producer delivers the completed programme in such form. These specifications establish matters known as the essential elements (such as casting, director and script) as well as the length, pictorial and technical quality of the programme. If the programme does not fit this specification exactly, the producer may find that it has breached its agreement, and the commissioner or distributor will refuse to pay until the programme matches its specification.

The producer will have to deliver the programme in final form to the commissioner by a specified date. Time is usually of the essence for delivery. The commissioner then has to approve the delivery materials within a certain time. If changes are required, the producer must generally make them if the programme as delivered was not in accordance with the specification. The cost is borne by the producer. If changes are not because of such a breach, the commissioner must bear the cost of the alterations.

16.3.8 Warranties and obligations

Producer

Other obligations which the producer should accept vary. It is important that the producer agrees to complete the production and deliver the programme in final form in accordance with the programme specification. Other terms typical of any copyright agreement will be included, such as: the right of the producer to enter the agreement; assurances that the programme does not breach any third party rights, is not defamatory, obscene, etc, and complies with appropriate laws and regulations; an indemnity for any breach of the producer's obligations; an agreement not to charge or create any lien over the programme (this may not be done except where a bank is used to discount finance, or in cases where the commissioner is one of a number of financiers who are repaid pro rata pari passu).

Commissioner

The commissioner should agree to pay money over as agreed either in appropriate tranches or upon satisfactory delivery of the programme.

Distributors and licensees

The producer warrants that it has all the rights necessary to permit the distributor or licensee to exploit the programme in its territory for the period of the agreement. The producer or rights owner will also indemnify the licensee or distributor against any breach of its warranties.

The licensee or distributor will further warrant as set out in **18.2.2(4)**.

16.3.9 Clearances

The producer must obtain all necessary rights and content clearances under the agreement. The extent to which rights are cleared and prepaid, rather than fees agreed in advance, depends upon the extent and method of exploitation immediately envisaged by the parties. If it is certain that the programme is only going to be shown once on, for example, UK terrestrial TV, then fees for other uses will be agreed at the production stage but not paid until such time as further exploitation occurs. Any further use fees or residual payments required will be treated as expenses for distribution purposes. The producer must notify the other relevant parties as to exactly what rights have been cleared and paid for at the time of production and what rights require further payment. Ideally, the rights for all territories and methods of exploitation immediately envisaged will be paid for at the time of production although this will usually not be the case with talent (eg performers, writers, etc) and with library clips.

16.3.10 Insurance

The producer should maintain a number of insurance policies. All usual public and employer's liability insurance should be taken out and maintained by the producer. Insurance should be maintained for all property used in the production, including sets and technical equipment. The film negatives and the raw film stock should also be insured. The commissioner or financier may require an interest to be noted on the policy.

In addition, the producer may take out and maintain errors and omissions (E&O) insurance. This insures against matters arising from the broadcast or other exploitation of the film. It usually covers the producer and distributors against claims arising for infringement of intellectual property rights by the production, such as copyright, defamation and breach of confidence or, in some jurisdictions, rights of privacy. Before E&O insurance is granted, the content of the programme must be checked (usually by a lawyer) to the satisfaction of the insurer. If a claim is made under the E&O policy, the producer may also be in breach of its obligations under the production agreement. This may result in liability to the commissioner or financier.

The producer should also have the interest of the financiers and commissioners noted on all the policies. This enables them to claim their share of proceeds of insurance moneys.

In the case of major UK broadcasters, an E&O policy may not be necessary as they will effectively insure the programme themselves against such problems.

16.3.11 Editing

The editing of a programme once it has been completed should also be dealt with in the agreement. The editing provisions and the reasons for editing a programme vary. If the programme delivered at the end of filming does not match the technical specification set out in the agreement, a commissioner will require the programme to be edited to bring it up to specification. If the programme needs editing to comply with any rule of law or regulation, then that should be permitted. Any legal advice taken on the content of a programme may require programme editing. In addition, the ITC Programme and Sponsorship Codes, as well as the British Board of Film Classification, may have an effect on the final edit.

A commissioner will invariably require the right to final approval over any editing of the programme. Editing may be carried out by the producer or even by the commissioner itself. Co-producers should usually consult each other over editing, although in their capacity as distributors they may be able to edit the programme to make it suitable for broadcast in their distribution territory or in a particular medium. A distribution agreement or licence of rights in the completed programme may not permit any editing without prior written consent from the copyright owner or distributor. The editing requirements of some distributors vary, for example, a distributor may need to edit for the purposes of local regulations or because commercial breaks are being inserted during the programme. The distributor may try to insist on the right to do this without the approval of the producer. However, the producer must not grant rights which breach any other obligations such as to the authors of a work.

Editing of a work may constitute an infringement of copyright as well as a breach of an author's or director's moral rights. The producer should normally obtain appropriate clearances to permit editing.

16.3.12 Titles and credits

The producer will have credit obligations to all personnel involved in production of the completed programme. The commissioner, distributors and licensees must agree to honour all the producer's credit obligations. In certain circumstances, a commissioner or distributor may wish to approve screen credits, particularly where programme sponsors are concerned. In addition, the commissioners, financiers and distributors may require an agreed credit in the programme titles. Where a production is advertised, there should be credit obligations, although the obligations will be more limited and generally only for major paid advertising.

The producer will have tried to exclude its liability to contributors for inadvertent failures to give proper credit in the production. The commissioner or distributor may seek to do the same for such inadvertent failures. However, any failure to give proper credits should be rectified by the commissioner or distributor in all future exploitation.

Chapter 17

FILM AND TELEVISION: RIGHTS AND CONTENT CLEARANCE

17.1 INTRODUCTION

This chapter considers the steps necessary to ensure that a programme – whether it is a film, TV series, documentary or radio programme – is, legally speaking, safe from challenge. There are a number of steps a producer and legal advisers can take to minimise any potential third party liability. Rights clearance relates particularly to the various contributions and contributors to a completed work. Rights clearances involve the rights of performers (such as actors and musicians) who appear in a programme, as well as copyright, moral rights and rental rights issues. Content clearance relates more particularly to the vetting of the script and finished programme itself for legal problems. This means looking at additional legal rights such as defamation, trade marks and relevant regulations. There are common considerations in both processes, in particular where the use or potential abuse of copyright material is being considered.

Wherever problems arise or are spotted in advance, it is important that the lawyer and producer concerned take steps to avoid any form of legal action. However, some producers may refuse simply to give in to the demands of third parties and, in certain circumstances, will risk the threat of legal action being taken. Occasionally, a programme is broadcast despite a serious legal problem because the producer and broadcaster concerned consider the commercial or public interest in broadcasting to be greater than the risk of legal action.

17.2 RIGHTS CLEARANCE: COPYRIGHT

There are various matters that the production team must consider before a work can be broadcast or published in any way. The producer must decide whether he wishes to acquire rights outright or simply 'clear' rights.

A producer may have the choice between an outright acquisition of copyright or a licence to use material. An unconditional assignment of copyright in a work is always preferable. In all cases, a producer should attempt to make a licence of rights irrevocable.

Whether an assignment or a licence has been agreed, a producer will often pay for only certain uses or methods of exploitation of a work. If a different type of exploitation occurs, the producer will have to pay another fee to the original copyright holder concerned. In this way, a producer may either acquire all the rights in question or simply clear rights for specific uses.

A producer may only be able (or willing) to acquire certain rights because there is no money available to pre-purchase all the rights or because only certain types of exploitation are envisaged. Other uses are 'cleared' and paid for as and when they

Chapter 17 contents
Introduction
Rights clearance: copyright
Moral rights clearance
Performers' rights consents
Copyright and Related Rights Regulations 1996: rights considerations
Content clearance

occur. The producer effectively obtains permission in principle for other uses or exploitation and agrees to pay a specified amount for that use if and when it occurs. If permission has not been obtained for a specific use or a full buy-out of rights has taken place, there may be an infringement of copyright and a breach of contract. The copyright owner and the producer must consider the extent of the rights granted which may then ultimately be a question of contractual construction for a court.

If a producer fails to 'clear' certain uses at the outset, he will subsequently need to enter separate negotiations, because no specific contractual provision has been made for these uses. The extent to which a producer is able to acquire permission for various uses depends upon the money available in the production budget or the share of profits he is prepared to offer to participants in the production. The requirements of the broadcaster and distributor of the finished work are also important in this regard. If certain uses are immediately foreseen, the producer should obtain permission for them. The distributor will specify this in the distribution agreement. The producer need not always pay up front for a particular use but it is important to agree a fee in advance for a use which may occur at a later date. It will also be more expensive to agree terms for subsequent uses once the programme or film has been completed.

There are various union agreements in force in the TV industry which make specific provision for this situation. The producer under the PACT/WGGB agreement takes an assignment of copyright from the scriptwriter for a basic fee which includes certain uses, and the agreement goes on to provide for further use fees to be payable for future exploitation abroad or in different media than those paid for by the producer. This was discussed further in **15.3.4**.

The producer must take care to ensure that the agreements for use of copyright do not contain termination provisions that would make future exploitation of the finished work impossible. The producer or his advisers must pay particular attention to the extent of the rights granted, as well as the duration and territory of the agreement.

The right to terminate an agreement should be restricted by the producer so that a copyright owner only has a right to compensation. The risk that the producer's right to use underlying copyright material could terminate is unacceptable.

17.2.1 Underlying works

As well as using an underlying work such as a book or script, a producer may use parts or the whole of other copyright works. A TV drama may use extracts from songs, sound recordings, films, literary, dramatic and artistic works. The use of any other copyright work is likely to attract the attention of the copyright owner. The owner will invariably require a fee for the use as well as a credit or other acknowledgement for inclusion. The producer should obtain this permission before using the copyright work.

Literary works

The producer may be basing a work on an existing book or play, or commissioning a screenplay from an author. In the case of existing works, the permission of the copyright owner should be obtained before any pre-production steps are taken or filming starts. The acquisition of copyright for films and TV programmes is discussed in Chapter 18. Initially, a producer may take an option on a work to allow pre-production steps to be taken until sufficient finance has been raised to make the project viable. If a producer commissions a work for the production, it is more likely that a full agreement has been reached between author and producer. Once finance or the promise of finance is in place, the producer can exercise an option over the existing underlying work and acquire the full rights to film and exploit it.

Commissioned music

If a producer commissions a piece of music for the programme, appropriate copyright agreements must be reached. A composer may have existing agreements with a publishing company and a recording company which restrict his ability to compose and record for third parties. The PRS, MCPS and PPL may also control certain rights in his compositions and recordings. The producer and the composer should check the contractual position. In the case of a composer and/or performer with publishing and recording agreements, those agreements will inevitably require the composer:

- to assign or license copyright in the compositions to the publisher; and
- not to record for anyone other than the recording company without the recording company's permission.

The producer must reach agreement with these parties to use the composer and his recording services on the soundtrack. Synchronisation licences will be required from the music publisher for the compositions. If the composer also records the compositions the producer will usually own the master recordings.

If the composer has no existing publishing or recording agreements, the producer can reach a more flexible arrangement with him. An assignment or licence of the compositions may be agreed, although the composer will be concerned to establish that the producer has the ability to exploit his works. A form of recording agreement may also be reached so that the producer pays recording costs and takes an assignment of the copyright in return for a royalty or other payment to the performer. This agreement will be similar to the traditional recording contract, although it is unlikely that the composer/performer will want to sign a long-term deal with a film and TV producer. The recorded compositions may then be included on the soundtrack and sold separately to the public on CD, on tape and on the video of the programme. If the compositions and recordings are used elsewhere, the producer and the composer will be entitled to income from those sales, other recordings, performances and broadcasts.

Whether or not the composer and performer have existing agreements in place, the producer must acquire all the rights necessary in the compositions and recordings to exploit them in conjunction with the programme. The cost of acquiring such extensive rights depends upon the fame of the composer and performer in question. A producer may have to be content with acquiring limited rights for foreseeable exploitation of the programme and agreeing the fees or royalties which will become payable for further future exploitation of the programme.

Songs and recordings

Incorporating existing songs and sound recordings into films and television programmes requires the permission of the copyright owners. The various collecting societies such as PRS, MCPS, PPL and VPL administer certain rights on behalf of their members. In addition, music publishers and record companies deal with rights in some or all of their copyright works. Identifying the rights owner is the first step before including a work in the film. If the rights owner is not known, the PRS, MCPS or PPL are a useful starting point for identifying the owner.

The form of agreement required for including a song in a film is a synchronisation licence. This is the permission of the copyright owner to use a specified copyright work (permission is required to use the song and to make or use the recording) in synchronisation with the film soundtrack and to exploit the film (perhaps by broadcasting it or selling videos of it) with that music. A separate agreement is required for the song and the recording of the song. A fee is usually payable for this use. If the film is to be broadcast, the broadcaster's PRS and PPL agreement should cover broadcast use. If the film is to be sold on video, the licence should also specify that use and any other uses included in the agreement. The performer's consent to any use of the sound recordings has usually been obtained by the record company which signed the performer or which has acquired rights in the recordings.

There are various situations in which it is not necessary for the producer to obtain permission from a copyright owner before using extracts from copyright material. The producer must take professional advice in these situations. Chapter 1 deals with these situations in detail, although they are briefly discussed below.

Excerpts from films

Incorporating excerpts from other films and television programmes in a work usually requires permission. This avoids the risk of an infringement action against the producer and any distributors.

The producer should agree a copyright licence with the appropriate rights owners. In the case of film excerpts, the underlying rights owners in the extract may also need to be consulted.

Use without permission

If a producer uses material without obtaining the necessary clearances, he may seek to depend on the copyright defences.

The fair dealing exception is available where extracts of a work are being used for criticism or review, or reporting current events. The extent to which use is 'fair' is a matter for judgement, although a competing commercial use may not be 'fair' within the meaning of the CDPA 1988 as interpreted by the courts. The fair dealing exception does not apply to photographs; permission for their use must be obtained from the copyright owner.

The incidental inclusion exception is available in limited circumstances. Whenever the producer has control or choice over the filmed environment, care should be taken that copyright works are not included without the owner's permission (CDPA 1988, s 31).

Buildings, sculptures, models for buildings and works of artistic craftsmanship permanently situated in public places or in premises open to the public may be included in films, photographs or broadcast or included in a cable service (CDPA 1988, s 62).

17.3 MORAL RIGHTS CLEARANCE

It is important when producers acquire rights in underlying authors' works, that the moral rights of the author are not ignored and are dealt with in the agreement. This is the case even where the copyright in question existed before commencement of the CDPA 1988. Schedule 1 to and ss 22–23 of the CDPA 1988 provide detailed rules dealing with moral rights and existing copyright works. Broadly speaking, the producer should obtain an irrevocable and unconditional waiver of the author's moral rights.

A number of issues may be raised by an author or director and should be dealt with to avoid any later problems.

The author may want to be identified with the work (his paternity right). The moral right may be waived in favour of a title credit in an agreed form which binds not only the producer but also other parties such as a subsequent rights owner or distributor. Although notice of assertion of moral rights is probably sufficient to bind a third party, this should, from the author's point of view, be guaranteed in the contract. The producer should also consult the distributor or broadcaster before agreeing credits. A screen credit should be sufficient recognition of the author's right of paternity.

The paternity right (unless waived) also applies to directors, and similar consideration should be given to dealings with them as with authors. The director's agreement will contain provisions for a screen credit which should satisfy the paternity right.

The integrity right of authors and directors must be dealt with by the producer. It is possible that any changes made by a producer to an author's work or to the director's edit of the film may amount to 'derogatory treatment' as defined in the CDPA 1988. The producer should obtain an unconditional and irrevocable waiver from both the author and director giving the producer flexibility in editing a work. Broadcast and distributors' requirements should also be taken into account so that, where relevant, foreign language versions and broadcasts with commercial breaks or sponsorship are permissible.

It is also worth noting that there may be many copyright works used in a film, not just those of a writer. The paternity and integrity rights apply to all authors of copyright works. This potentially includes set designers, special effects personnel, composers and choreographers. Some of these authors may require an agreed credit. The producer should therefore obtain waivers of their moral rights.

17.4 PERFORMERS' RIGHTS CONSENTS

The essence of clearing a performer's right is that the producer obtains the performer's written consent to the recording and exploitation of his performance by the producer. It is common to require all contributors to a programme to sign a consent covering not only performance but also giving a complete assignment of copyright. A copyright work may be created once a contributor gives an interview or ad libs on film. Although the producer may own the physical recording of the work, the speaker still has copyright in his spoken words. The producer should also obtain consent and release from any company with which a performer has an exclusive recording contract.

The type of consent to be obtained from an actor depends upon the extent of the contribution. A producer working for the BBC or ITV or a producer who is a member of PACT who engages an actor who belongs to Equity is bound to use the agreed terms between the relevant organisation and Equity. Even a casual contributor to a documentary or news programme should sign an interview release form permitting the recording and use of the interview. This allows use of the copyright and the performance.

An actor is engaged on terms requiring payment at agreed minimum levels for agreed exploitation. The producer may have to make additional payments for future uses. Such future uses are often only 'cleared' at this stage because it is uncertain whether they will occur. Thus, if a further use occurs (perhaps a video release or foreign sale), the producer must pay a further amount to each actor. These are known as 'use fees'.

17.5 COPYRIGHT AND RELATED RIGHTS REGULATIONS 1996: RIGHTS CONSIDERATIONS

The Copyright and Related Rights Regulations 1996 implemented the EC Rental Rights Directive, which created additional rights for the producer and directors of films and sound recordings, and for the authors of original works as well as performers. Essentially, the right is to 'equitable remuneration' for the rental and broadcast of works in which these persons were involved.

The producer's concern, and the concern of those bodies exploiting works caught by the Regulations, is that the rental right is transferred along with any other rights (such as copyright and performers' rights) and that the agreed remuneration is an equitable one for the purposes of the Regulations. The director, performer or author cannot waive their right to equitable remuneration, although the right to object to rental of a work can be waived. Rental rights are deemed to be assigned (unless the contrary is shown) in relation to films and TV programmes. A producer must ensure that any assignment or consents taken are wide enough to contain a consent for rental rights purposes, and that the author or person concerned agrees that they are receiving an equitable remuneration for their services. Until a Member State or the EC gives further guidance on the scope of this term the possibility exists that contributors may come back and ask for more money.

17.6 CONTENT CLEARANCE

The substance of the matters relevant to content clearance has already been considered in detail. The essence of content and script clearance is to avoid any possible civil or criminal liability for the producer and other parties such as the broadcaster or distributor. The producer will always be obliged under its production agreement to warrant and indemnify that it has abided by all applicable laws and regulations. In certain cases, the producer and broadcaster may assess the risk of action by a third party inherent in broadcast or exploitation and take an informed view to publish. This is the type of situation which occurred with the *Clockwork Orange* case (*Time Warner Entertainment Co v Channel Four Television Corp plc*

[1994] EMLR 1) where the broadcast of excerpts from the film *A Clockwork Orange* was ultimately justified by the courts.

However, it is important that the producer and distributor are aware of any risks. The role of a legal adviser in this situation is to outline all the potential risks with the client and then to discuss the available alternatives. This involves an assessment of the risk as well as the implications of any action decided upon. The production's E&O insurers should be notified of any problems and be involved in the discussions. Producers obtain errors and omissions insurance to cover against precisely this sort of problem. Depending upon the degree of risk involved, the insurer will set a premium and an excess and may exclude certain claims from the cover.

The E&O insurer should be informed of all clearance and rights matters by the lawyer together with the producer. Essentially, since so much of the production is outside the lawyer's remit, any guarantee by the lawyer that the film is clear for insurance purposes should be limited to matters that the producer has asked him to advise upon and expressly subject to any problems and risks identified by the lawyer.

The producer and lawyer should consider the content of the production in the light of copyright, moral rights, defamation, obscenity and indecency, official secrets, breach of confidence, contempt of court and any relevant regulatory guide-lines. Care should also be taken with the use of trade marks and the application of the tort of passing off, as well as with product placement in programmes and films.

The British Board of Film Classification (BBFC) has official status in relation to videos by virtue of the Video Recordings Act 1984 (VRA), although it has no official status in relation to films. In return for a fee, the Board will classify films and videos. The BBFC's categories of video classification are considered at **18.4.4**.

The VRA creates various offences for breach of its terms.

A broadcaster who fails to abide by the statutory guide-lines (for commercial broadcasters) imposed under the Broadcasting Act 1990 or (in the case of the BBC) the terms of its charter may find the Broadcasting Complaints Commission (BCC) considering a complaint. The BCC considers complaints which involve an allegation of unfair treatment or infringement of privacy in a programme.

Chapter 18

FILM AND TELEVISION: DISTRIBUTION AND EXPLOITATION

18.1 INTRODUCTION

The preceding chapters covered the pre-production and production considerations applicable to the process of making films and television programmes. This chapter provides a brief introduction to the commercial exploitation of the finished product. It begins with a general overview of distribution agreements, and then looks at relevant aspects of the more important media.

Chapter 18 contents
Introduction
Distribution
Cinema
Video
Television

18.2 DISTRIBUTION

18.2.1 The need for distribution

Makers of feature films and television programmes will rarely be in a position to arrange distribution of their product. The production industry generally passes the task of distribution to specialist companies. This will especially be the case where there is to be distribution outside the territory of the producer.

The distributor will need to acquire rights from the producer necessary to enable him to distribute the product. In preparing the distribution agreement, the anticipated distribution medium will need to be uppermost in the mind of the draftsman. The agreement may relate to the cinema, to cable or satellite television or to the video market. However, the commercially less profitable markets should not be forgotten: hotels, aircraft, ships, etc. It will often be necessary to produce an agreement which deals with distribution in any medium (an 'all media distribution agreement').

18.2.2 Distribution agreements

A distribution agreement will often be a lengthy document dealing with many aspects of the relationship between the producer and the distributor. In addition to the usual terms found in commercial contracts (see LPC Resource Book *Commercial Law and Practice* (Jordans)), the following aspects of a film or television programme distribution agreement require consideration.

(1) Copyright

The owner of the copyright in the film or television programme will transfer such rights as are necessary to enable the distributor to exploit the product. The agreement will commonly contain a list of media in relation to which the rights are granted, for example:

> **In consideration of the proper carrying out of his duties and responsibilities under the terms of this Agreement the Producer grants to the Distributor the following exclusive rights:**

> (a) Cable Television Rights;
> (b) Satellite Television Rights;
> (c) Videogram Rental Rights;
> (d) Videogram Sale Rights.

This list may be supplemented with additional forms of exploitation, such as online exploitation, mobile rights and interactive rights.

The rights may be granted to the distributor in the form of a licence or an assignment. The latter is permanent (unless subject to a grant-back), but has the advantage of allowing the distributor to bring infringement actions in those territories which require the claimant to own the copyright as a pre-requisite to infringement litigation. The most common way of dealing with copyright is to grant a licence.

The owner of copyright (where granted to the distributor in the form of a licence) should retain the right to terminate the licence prior to the expiry of the term of the agreement. This will ensure that the producer does not suffer loss in the event of the liquidation or bankruptcy of the distributor.

The copyright licence should contain a provision allowing the distributor:

- to edit or cut the film (in the event, for example, that the territory in question has laws relating to content which would not allow the uncut version to be shown, this provision would allow those cuts to be made);
- to make copies (the original may not be in the correct format for the relevant medium);
- to sub-license its rights (the distributor may need to grant rights to a distributor in a different territory or to allow a broadcaster to make its own cuts).

The legal title in the film or programme will remain the property of the licensor.

(2) Payment and accounts

The distributor will receive gross income as a result of distribution. Before remitting payment to the rights owner, the distributor will seek to make deductions, principally any expenses of distribution (see (3) below) and his commission. The income and expenditure relating to the distribution of the product will be detailed in a set of accounts.

Payment should be stated to be payable to the rights owner within a specified time of receipt of income by the distributor. This allows the distributor time to prepare its accounts in accordance with the agreement.

The rights owner should have a contractual right to inspect the accounts prepared by the distributor, which should relate purely to the income and expenses of distribution of the film or programme in question. The rights owner must have a right to any shortfall between the amount payable under the accounts and the amount actually paid by the distributor to him. It is common to require the distributor to meet the cost of accounts inspection if the amount of the shortfall is above a specified percentage of the whole amount payable.

(3) Distribution expenses

Distribution expenses should be clearly defined in the agreement. This is commonly done by reference to a schedule which lists the expenses that the distributor is entitled to deduct from the gross receipts, for example:

The Distributor shall be entitled to deduct from Gross Receipts any Distribution Expense (defined in Schedule 2) properly incurred in connection with the exploitation of the Rights pursuant to this Agreement on production of vouchers, receipts or other evidence satisfactory to the Producer.

The list of distribution expenses will commonly include payments made for the following:

- advertising and publicity;
- censorship fees;
- any editing costs incurred as a result of meeting censorship requirements;
- any cutting, editing or printing costs required for any other reasonable purpose (eg to produce film or television programme trailers);
- freight and carriage costs, customs duties and permit fees incurred as a result of importing the film into any other country;
- insurance (of the physical property of the film);
- commission charged by any licensees of the distributor (unless the licensee is an associated company of the distributor);
- any sums of money which become payable to actors, writers, etc, as a result of broadcasting the programme (commonly called 'use fees' or 'residuals');
- legal expenses incurred as a result of distribution;
- legal expenses of bringing infringement actions (where the distributor is obliged to bring such proceedings by the terms of the agreement);
- taxes imposed on the distributor in connection with the distribution of the film or programme.

(4) Distributor's obligations

Distribution agreements will commonly incorporate the following obligations of a distributor:

- to submit the film or programme for censorship or certification in respect of each of the types of release envisaged;
- to ensure:
    (i) the theatrical (cinema) release of the film by a specified release date;
    (ii) the videogram release of the film [6 months] after the release date;
    (iii) the television exploitation of the film within a specified time from the [theatrical] release date;
- to pay the revenue to the rights owner;
- to produce accounts at specified intervals;
- to advertise the film or programme (it is common to specify a figure representing the minimum amount to be spent on advertising);
- to pay use fees and residuals which become payable as a result of the exploitation of the film or programme;
- to accord proper on-screen credit to persons to whom the rights owner has incurred such obligations;
- at regular intervals, to audit and check all sub-distributors and sub-licensees and ensure prompt and proper payment by them to the distributor.

(5) Payment and taxation

The distributor will agree to pay the net income (gross receipts less distribution expenses, commission and tax) to the rights owner within a specified period of its receipt by him. During the period between receipt of income by the distributor and payment to the rights owner, the money should be paid into a separate bank account in the joint names of the distributor and the rights owner and expressed to be held in trust for the rights owner. This will facilitate access to the money by the rights owner in the event of bankruptcy or liquidation of the distributor.

Where the rights owner and distributor are in separate countries, the tax on the income must often be deducted by the distributor before making payment to the rights owner. Withholding tax of 25% is generally applicable to payments abroad from the UK. However, many countries have double taxation treaties with many other countries (there is one between the USA and the UK) which provide a reduced rate of tax (often 10%) for payments by distributors to copyright owners between those countries.

Certain countries do not permit income earned there to be remitted to another country. The agreement must therefore contain a provision for the rights owner to make an appropriate direction in such circumstances – usually that the income will be paid into a bank account in that country opened by the distributor in the name of the rights owner (thus giving the rights owner access to the money when he is present in that country).

(6) Infringement actions

The rights owner should not force the distributor to bring infringement proceedings on every occasion when copyright is breached. It will be necessary in the case of each infringement to assess the commercial reality of litigation. The contract should therefore incorporate a provision which obliges the distributor to notify the rights owner of any infringement as soon as it comes to the distributor's attention. Where the distributor is required to bring proceedings, there should be a provision for deducting the cost as a distribution expense or, where the cost exceeds gross receipts, for payment by the rights owner.

18.3 CINEMA

18.3.1 General

A cinema (or theatrical exhibitor) must have a licence, commonly issued by the local authority responsible for the area in which the cinema is situated, to show films to the public (Cinemas Act 1985, s 1(1)). The local authority is required to impose conditions restricting the access of children to certain types of film. In most cases, local authorities rely on the classification of the British Board of Film Classification (BBFC). For further detail on the BBFC, see **11.6** and **11.7**.

18.3.2 BBFC classification

The BBFC will, upon payment of a small fee, produce a classification for a film submitted to it. The current categories of film classification which may be applied in respect of cinema exhibition are as follows:

U   Universal: suitable for all.
PG   Parental guidance: some scenes may be unsuitable for young children.
12   Suitable for persons of 12 years and over.
15   Suitable only for persons of 15 years and over.
18   Suitable only for persons of 18 years and over.
18R   Suitable only for restricted distribution through segregated premises to which no one under 18 is admitted.

The classification applied by the Board may have enormous commercial significance – a 15 certificate instead of 18 can mean a far larger audience potential – and so it will be essential for the distributor to have authority to edit and cut the work to meet BBFC requirements and to be able to sub-license such rights in respect of distribution in other countries.

18.4 VIDEO

18.4.1 General

It will be common for a distributor of a film for cinema release also to acquire the rights for video (and television) release.

Consumers obtain video products in one of two ways: by rental from a video rental outlet, and by purchase from a retail outlet.

Rental outlets will take supply of videogram material between 6 and 9 months after its cinema release date. The distributor will usually agree that there will be no free television distribution in the territory within a specified period, often 2 to 4 years (although cable or satellite distribution may be much sooner). Distribution to outlets for resale will usually commence some months after distribution for rental.

18.4.2 Release dates

The television, particularly free television (see **18.5**), release of a film will have a significant detrimental effect on the video rental market. It is thus vitally important for a distributor who has not acquired the television rights to negotiate for a period of time to elapse between the video and the television release dates (a 'hold back'). Such a clause will, of course, not be necessary where a distributor takes both video and television rights as he will then be in control of the release dates.

18.4.3 Payment

Payment to the rights owner will generally be on the basis of a lump sum (usually an 'advance' or 'minimum guarantee'), together with a royalty based on the price charged by the distributor to its customers. The royalty in the case of the sale of video for resale will be smaller than in the case of the sale of video for rental to reflect the fact that the price the distributor can charge for the former is considerably less than for the latter and hence the profit margin is smaller.

18.4.4 Illegal supply

It is generally an offence to supply or offer to supply a video recording which has not received a classification certificate (Video Recordings Act 1984 (VRA 1984), s 9).

(It is a further offence to supply such material without specific labelling of the certificate obtained.) The British Board of Film Classification currently applies five classifications to videogram material:

18	Suitable only for persons of 18 years and over.
15	Suitable for persons of 15 years and over.
12	Suitable only for persons of 12 years and over.
PG	Parental Guidance: some scenes may be unsuitable for young children.
U	Suitable for all.
UC	Universal: particularly suitable for children.

A further category, E, is available for videograms which are exempt from the provisions of the Act.

A video work is an exempted work if, taken as a whole:

- it is designed to inform, educate or instruct;
- it is concerned with sport, religion or music; or
- it is a video game.

A video work will, however, not be exempted under these provisions if, to any significant extent, it depicts:

- a human sexual activity or acts of force or restraint associated with such activity;
- mutilation or torture of, or other acts of gross violence towards, humans or animals;
- human genital organs or human urinary or excretory functions;
- techniques likely to be used in the commission of offences.

A video work will not be exempted if, to any significant extent, it depicts criminal activity which is likely, to any significant extent, to stimulate or encourage the commission of offences (VRA 1984, s 2(3)).

Certain types of supply of video recordings will be exempted from the provisions of the VRA 1984:

- supplies which are neither for reward nor which are in the course of a business;
- supplies of material which is designed to form a record of an event or occasion (where such material does not, to any significant extent, offend the above provisions) to a person who took part in such event (eg a wedding video);
- supply to the BBFC for classification;
- supply to the BBC, ITC or any other broadcaster with a view only to its being broadcast.

For further details, see the Video Recordings Act 1984 (as amended by the Criminal Justice and Public Order Act 1994) and the Video Recordings (Labelling) (Amendment) Regulations 1995, SI 1995/2550.

18.5 TELEVISION

There are two principal types of television transmission. The distinction will be relevant when negotiating distribution agreements, particularly in relation to release dates (see **18.4.2**).

The first, 'free television', is generally used in distribution agreements to describe those television transmissions which are capable of being received by an ordinary aerial without the need for decoding or decrypting equipment. Free television in the UK is provided by the BBC, the 15 regional television companies, GMTV, Channel 4 (S4C in Wales) and Channel 5.

The second category is all other television transmissions and usually refers to cable and satellite television. The definition of the term 'free television' must be carefully drafted as it could be taken to refer to a cable or satellite channel for which there is no extra charge made.

Chapter 19

ADVERTISING: THE INDUSTRY

19.1 INTRODUCTION

Advertising is prevalent in our society and confronts us in all media at every turn. Each new medium gives rise to new advertising opportunities, and new technology finds novel advertising methods. This multi-million pound industry is not subject to a separate body of 'advertising law' as such, but, rather, as with many of the media industries, to a hotch-potch of common law, statute and industry self-regulation.

This chapter looks at the nature of the advertising industry. Chapters 20 and 21 examine the law and other regulatory frameworks which govern the form and content of advertising.

19.2 WHAT IS ADVERTISING?

An advertisement is a message containing information about products or services which emanates from an advertiser to a particular target audience. The message will be carried by one or more of the advertising media, which include newspapers, magazines, cinema, television and radio.

Advertising is extremely big business. In 1998, over £10 billion was spent on advertising in the UK, a figure equivalent to nearly 2% of gross domestic product.

19.3 THE ADVERTISING MEDIA

Advertising is possible in any medium from posters on advertising hoardings to the internet 'home pages' or 'web sites' of companies and firms.

Crucial to an advertiser in getting his message to his target audience will be the choice of medium. Size of 'readership' must be weighed against the cost of the advertisement. A preliminary decision will be whether the advertisement is to be published or broadcast. This will largely depend upon the nature of the product and the advertising budget. Where the decision is taken to publish the advertisement, the advertiser must consider the wealth of publications open to him, from national daily newspapers giving blanket coverage to a wide variety of persons, to a specialist magazine or professional journal with a limited readership having a common interest.

Often such decisions will be taken by advertising agencies, who will have a wealth of useful information, such as the type of people who watch ITV at 8 pm on a Sunday evening, and the number of people who could be expected to read a half-page advertisement on p 8 of the *Daily Telegraph*.

Chapter 19 contents
Introduction
What is advertising?
The advertising media
The advertising agency
Advertising on television

19.4 THE ADVERTISING AGENCY

19.4.1 Introduction

The production of an advertisement will usually involve the expert skills of writers, artists, photographers, designers, television production crews and lawyers. The advertiser will rarely have these skills and so will draw on the expertise of an advertising agency.

The agency will require detailed statistics of the product to be advertised:

- How much does it cost?
- How does the price compare with alternative similar products?
- How many are currently sold?
- How does this figure compare with the total sales of similar products?
- What sort of people buy the product?
- What do those people think of the product?

Where this information is not available from the advertiser, the agency will conduct market research. A campaign plan will be formulated based on the information obtained by the market research and existing knowledge of the media industry. The appropriate medium or media will be selected and advertising space booked.

Often an advertiser will invite tenders from several advertising agencies. The agency will want to ensure that its idea is protected; much would be lost by having a 'pitch' rejected, only to find that a similar idea was later used by the advertiser. It is advisable therefore for the agency to enter into a contractual arrangement for the tender so that it can protect its ideas for advertising the product in the event that its tender is not selected. Where this is not possible, the agency will have to rely on the laws of copyright (see Chapter 2) and confidentiality (see Chapter 13) to deter such poaching.

19.4.2 The agency/client contract

Once it has been established that an advertiser wishes to employ the services of a particular agency, a contract will be required. Terms of such contracts vary widely, but should deal with the following matters:

- terms of appointment;
- services to be provided by the agency;
- remuneration;
- approvals;
- tax;
- ownership of copyright in advertising materials produced;
- ownership and custody of advertising materials produced;
- liability;
- advertising standards;
- insurance;
- confidential information;
- duration of agreement;
- termination.

19.5 ADVERTISING ON TELEVISION

19.5.1 General

Television advertising is a special category of advertising and is subject to particular rules. Television is an extremely powerful and persuasive medium and therefore warrants close regulation of its output.

19.5.2 The Independent Television Commission

The Independent Television Commission (ITC), compelled to do so by the Broadcasting Act 1990, publishes a Code of Advertising Standards and Practice to which all advertisements must adhere (see Chapter 20). In addition, there are legal controls on the format of television advertising.

The ITC is responsible for regulating all television programme services other than those provided by the BBC and the Welsh Authority.

The ITC grants a licence to 15 regional television companies (eg Granada Television), three national television companies (Channel 4, Channel 5 and GMTV) and cable and satellite companies to provide a programme service for the UK. In return for a licence fee and a percentage of gross revenues, the ITC allows the television companies to sell advertising air-time.

The ITC must ensure that its licensees have in place an effective method of screening all advertisements which will be broadcast.

19.5.3 Restricted advertising

The ITC must ensure that a licensed service does not include:

- any advertisement which is inserted by or on behalf of any body whose objects are wholly or mainly of a political nature;
- any advertisement which is directed towards any political end; or
- any advertisement which has any relation to any industrial dispute (other than an advertisement of a public service nature inserted by, or on behalf of, a government department).

A licensed service must not discriminate between advertisers and must not allow sponsorship of a television programme by any person whose business is engaged wholly or mainly in the manufacture of a product which the licence holder would otherwise be prohibited from advertising (s 8(2)).

Section 6(1)(e) effectively prevents the technique known as subliminal advertising by requiring the ITC to ensure that no programmes of a licensed service include 'any technical device which, by using images of very brief duration … exploits the possibility of conveying a message to, or otherwise influencing the minds of persons watching the programmes without their being aware, or fully aware, of what has occurred'.

Chapter 20

ADVERTISING: SELF-REGULATION

20.1 INTRODUCTION

There exists an extensive body of industry self-regulation in respect of both print and broadcast advertising.

This chapter gives an introduction to the self-regulatory controls. Chapter 21 considers legal constraints on the advertising industry. These controls can be conveniently divided into those which deal with broadcast and those which deal with non-broadcast media.

20.2 BROADCAST ADVERTISING

20.2.1 ITC Code of Advertising Standards and Practice

The ITC was required, by the provisions of the Broadcasting Act 1990, to draw up and enforce a code governing standards and practice in television advertising and the sponsoring of programmes.

The ITC Code of Advertising Standards and Practice (set out in part at **20.4**) applies to all television services regulated by the ITC. At present, these comprise Channel 3 (ITV), Channel 4, Channel 5, GMTV, non-domestic satellite services which operate from the UK but do not use broadcasting frequencies allocated to the UK (eg BSkyB), licensable programme services (which include those cable channels which are not also in any of the above categories, eg Nynex, Bell Cable Media) and public teletext services.

The ITC Code applies to 'any item of publicity inserted in breaks in or between programmes, whether in return for payment or not, including publicity by licensees themselves'. Such items must be clearly distinguishable and recognisably separated from the programmes themselves. Television companies usually achieve this by displaying their logo immediately before and after the commercial break.

All ITC licence holders (the 15 regional television companies, the national breakfast-time service, Channel 4, Channel 5 and various cable companies) must ensure that any advertising they transmit complies with the Code and must satisfy the ITC that they have adequate procedures in place to fulfil this requirement. There is no pre-vetting by the ITC of broadcast advertisements, but the ITC monitors licensees' output closely and can impose substantial penalties on television companies who fail to comply with the Code.

The general principles running through the Code are that advertising should be 'legal, decent, honest and truthful' and that the detailed rules of the Code should be applied in the spirit as well as the letter.

The Radio Authority (RA) performs a similar function to the ITC with respect to advertisements on radio.

Chapter 20 contents
Introduction
Broadcast advertising
Non-broadcast advertising
The ITC Code of Advertising Standards and Practice

The ITC ensures compliance with the Code by requiring all service providers to employ trained staff to check all advertising before transmission. Any claims made in relation to products should be checked and documentary evidence inspected. In practice, advertising agencies will submit all television advertising in script form for clearance by the television companies. Where there is any doubt about the interpretation of the Code, the television company will seek guidance from the ITC. In addition, the ITC monitors the output of all television companies within its remit and will intervene to forbid the broadcast of any advertisement found to breach the Code.

The Broadcast Advertising Clearance Centre (BACC) is a body funded by the broadcasters which assists them to fulfil their legal and code-derived obligations and responsibilities. The BACC is a general advisory service to the broadcasters and will scrutinise scripts at the pre-production stage to ensure that they comply with the ITC codes.

20.2.2 Complaints procedure

The ITC has a statutory duty to investigate all complaints it receives and will make a personal reply to each complainant. A monthly report describes all 'complaints of substance' with details of the complaint, assessment, decision and the advertising agency responsible for the advertisement (see examples below). All other complaints received are listed.

20.2.3 Advertising breaks

In addition to detailed rules on the content of television advertising, the ITC has established a code on the amount, distribution and presentation of advertising.

The ITC Rules on Advertising Breaks give effect to an EC Broadcasting Directive (85/552/EEC) and the European Convention on Transfrontier Television.

Advertising slots, which must be readily recognisable as such, must be separated from general programming by optical and/or acoustic means. This is generally done by the display of the licence holder's logo. Where an advertising break occurs within a programme (as opposed to immediately preceding or succeeding it), it must be taken only at a point of natural break in continuity of the programme.

ITV (the regional television companies and GMTV), Channel 4 and Channel 5 must not have, in any one day, more than an average of 7 minutes of advertising per hour. In the periods 7 am to 9 am and 6 pm to 11 pm, the total amount of advertising must not exceed an average of 8 minutes per hour on any one day.

Advertising on cable and satellite channels must not exceed an average of 9 minutes per hour in any one day nor more than 12 minutes in any one clock hour.

For the purposes of calculation of advertising time, the following will be deemed to be advertising items:

(1) all items of publicity broadcast on behalf of someone other than the licensee in breaks in or between programmes, apart from public service announcements and charity appeals broadcast free of charge;
(2) publicity by the licensees themselves, except information to viewers about or in connection with programmes.

The following types of products must not be advertised in any break in a children's programme or in an advertising slot before or after such a programme:

- alcoholic drinks;
- low or no alcohol drinks presented as such;
- liqueur chocolates;
- pipe tobacco and cigars;
- matches;
- cinema trailers and videos where the film in question has a 15 or 18 certificate;
- vitamin supplements for children;
- religious advertising;
- merchandise based on children's programmes (nor must they be advertised in the 2 hours immediately preceding or succeeding editions of the relevant programme).

Children's medicine and condoms cannot be advertised before 9 pm. Advertisements for female sanitary products must not be broadcast on ITV between 4 pm and 9 pm on weekdays and before 9 pm on weekends and on major public holidays.

20.3 NON-BROADCAST ADVERTISING

The non-broadcast media, including newspapers and magazines, posters, brochures, leaflets, cinema and video cassettes, must comply with the requirements of the British Codes of Advertising and Sales Promotion (BCASP).

20.3.1 Advertising Standards Authority

The Advertising Standards Authority (ASA) was established in 1962 to supervise compliance with the then British Code of Advertising Practice. It is a limited company which is independent of both the government and the advertising industry. It is financed by a compulsory levy of 0.1% of the cost of all advertising which comes within its remit. The advertising industry therefore pays for its own policing.

The ASA does not provide a pre-vetting service but monitors a random selection of advertisements to check compliance with the Code. Each year, the ASA scrutinises approximately 150,000 of the 15 million advertisements published annually in the UK. In addition, the ASA investigates complaints made to it by individuals and companies. Approximately one-quarter of the 12,000 or so complaints the ASA receives each year are upheld.

Complaints to the ASA must be in writing and will be dealt with more speedily if accompanied by a copy of the advertisement complained of. Complainants may choose to be anonymous. Upon receipt of a complaint, the ASA will evaluate it. Complaints tend to fall into three broad categories:

- those which fall outside the scope of the ASA's work (for example, complaints about broadcast advertisements, which the ASA will forward to the ITC or the RA);
- those which arise from some misunderstanding of the advertisement;
- those which seem, prima facie, to provide a case for investigation.

Those complaints falling in the latter category will be investigated by the secretariat and will appear in the 'ASA Monthly Report', a newsletter describing all investigated cases and their outcome (examples of some specific cases appear below). The ASA does not, however, have the power to force an advertiser to comply with its requests to withdraw or amend an offending advertisement. This 'lack of teeth' has been a reason for substantial criticism of the ASA. It can, however, refer a case to the Director-General of the Office of Fair Trading, who may take action under the Control of Misleading Advertisement Regulations 1988 (see **21.2.3**). In addition, an advertiser who continually flouts ASA rulings may find the media unwilling to accept its advertising. Advertising agencies involved in producing offending advertisements may find their recognition withdrawn from the relevant media association.

20.3.2 The Committee of Advertising Practice and the British Codes of Advertising and Sales Promotion

The BCASP, which are an amalgamation of the former British Code of Advertising Practice and the British Code of Sales Promotion Practice (BCSPP), are published and reviewed by the Committee of Advertising Practice (CAP).

The CAP is composed of representatives of the major trade and professional organisations of the advertising business, each of which must require their own members to observe the Codes, actively promote the Codes and sanction their members for non-compliance with the Codes. The CAP responsibilities include:

- reviewing and amending the Codes;
- administering the mandatory pre-clearance of cigarette advertising;
- pre-publication advice to advertisers, agencies and media;
- co-ordinating the sanctions operated by members to secure compliance with the Codes;
- giving advice, information and support to the ASA on all matters relating to self-regulation.

For more information on the CAP, see the booklet 'The Committee of Advertising Practice' and other publications available from the Advertising Standards Authority.

The general principles of the BCASP are similar to the ITC Code in that advertisements should be legal, decent, honest and truthful. In addition, advertisements should be prepared with a sense of responsibility to the consumer and society generally, should be in line with the principles of fair competition generally accepted in business, and should not bring advertising into disrepute.

General rules

The Advertising Code contains the following general rules to be applied to all advertisements within its scope.

> **'Substantiation**
>
> Before submitting an advertisement for publication, advertisers must hold documentary evidence to prove all claims, whether direct or implied, that are capable of objective substantiation.
>
> Relevant evidence should be sent without delay if requested by the ASA. The adequacy of evidence will be judged on whether it supports both the detailed claims and the overall impression created by the advertisement.
>
> If there is a significant division of informed opinion about any claims made in an advertisement they should not be portrayed as universally agreed.

If the contents of non-fiction books, tapes, videos and the like have not been independently substantiated, advertisements should not exaggerate the value or practical usefulness of their contents.

Obvious untruths or exaggerations that are unlikely to mislead and incidental minor errors and unorthodox spellings are all allowed provided they do not affect the accuracy or perception of the advertisement in any material way.

Legality

Advertisers have primary responsibility for ensuring that their advertisements are legal. Advertisements should contain nothing that breaks the law or incites anyone to break it, and should omit nothing that the law requires.

Decency

Advertisements should contain nothing that is likely to cause serious or widespread offence. Particular care should be taken to avoid causing offence on the grounds of race, religion, sex, sexual orientation or disability. Compliance with the Codes will be judged on the context, medium, audience, product and prevailing standards of decency.

Honesty

Advertisers should not exploit the credulity, lack of knowledge or inexperience of consumers.

Truthfulness

No advertisement should mislead by inaccuracy, ambiguity, exaggeration, omission or otherwise.

Matters of opinion

Advertisers may give a view about any matter, including the qualities or desirability of their products, provided that it is clear that they are expressing their own opinion rather than stating a fact.

Fear and distress

No advertisement should cause fear or distress without good reason. Advertisers should not use shocking claims or images merely to attract attention.

Advertisers may use an appeal to fear to encourage prudent behaviour or to discourage dangerous or ill-advised actions; the fear likely to be aroused should not be disproportionate to the risk.

Safety

Advertisements should not show or encourage unsafe practices except in the context of promoting safety. Particular care should be taken with advertisements addressed to or depicting children and young people.

Consumers should not be encouraged to drink and drive. Advertisements, including those for breath testing devices, should not suggest that the effects of drinking alcohol can be masked and should include a prominent warning on the dangers of drinking and driving.

Violence and anti-social behaviour

Advertisements should contain nothing that condones or is likely to provoke violence or anti-social behaviour.

Protection of privacy

Advertisers who have not obtained prior permission from entertainers, politicians, sportsmen and others whose work gives them a high public profile should ensure that they are not portrayed in an offensive or adverse way. Advertisements should not claim or imply an endorsement where none exists.

Prior permission may not be needed when the advertisement contains nothing that is inconsistent with the position or views of the person featured. Advertisers should be aware that individuals who do not wish to be associated with the advertised product may have a legal claim.

Testimonials and endorsements

Advertisers should hold signed and dated proof, including a contact address, for any testimonial they use. Testimonials should be used only with the written permission of those giving them.

Testimonials should relate to the product being advertised.

Testimonials alone do not constitute substantiation and the opinions expressed in them must be supported, where necessary, with independent evidence of their accuracy. Any claims based on a testimonial must conform with the Codes.

Fictitious endorsements should not be presented as though they were genuine testimonials.

Reference to tests, trials, professional endorsements, research facilities and professional journals should be used only with the permission of those concerned. They should originate from within the European Union unless otherwise stated in the advertisement. Any establishment referred to should be under the direct supervision of an appropriately qualified professional.

Prices

Any stated price should be clear and should relate to the product advertised. Advertisers should ensure that prices match the products illustrated.

Unless addressed exclusively to the trade, prices quoted should include any VAT payable. It should be apparent immediately whether any prices quoted exclude other taxes, duties or compulsory charges and these should, wherever possible, be given in the advertisement.

If the price of one product is dependent on the purchase of another, the extent of any commitment by consumers should be made clear.

Price claims such as "up to" and "from" should not exaggerate the availability of benefits likely to be obtained by consumers.

Free offers

There is no objection to making a free offer conditional on the purchase of other items. Consumers' liability for any costs should be made clear in all material featuring the offer. An offer should only be described as "free" if consumers pay no more than:

  (a) the current public rates of postage
  (b) the actual cost of freight and delivery
  (c) the cost, including incidental expenses, of any travel involved if consumers collect the offer.

Advertisers should make no additional charges for packing and handling.

Advertisers must not attempt to recover their costs by reducing the quality or composition or by inflating the price of any product that must be purchased as a pre-condition of obtaining another product free.

Availability of products

Advertisers must make it clear if stocks are limited. Products must not be advertised unless advertisers can demonstrate that they have reasonable grounds for believing that they can satisfy demand. If a product becomes unavailable, advertisers will be required to show evidence of stock monitoring, communications with outlets and the swift withdrawal of advertisements whenever possible.

Products which cannot be supplied should not normally be advertised as a way of assessing potential demand.

Advertisers must not use the technique of switch-selling, where their sales staff criticise the advertised product or suggest that it is not available and recommend the purchase of a more expensive alternative. They should not place obstacles in the way of purchasing the product or delivering it promptly.

Guarantees

The full terms of any guarantee should be available for consumers to inspect before they are committed to purchase. Any substantial limitations should be spelled out in the advertisement.

Advertisers should inform consumers about the nature and extent of any additional rights provided by the guarantee, over and above those given to them by law, and should make clear how to obtain redress.

"Guarantee" when used simply as a figure of speech should not cause confusion about consumers' legal rights.

Comparisons

Comparisons can be explicit or implied and can relate to advertisers' own products or to those of their competitors; they are permitted in the interests of vigorous competition.

Comparisons should be clear and fair. The elements of any comparison should not be selected in a way that gives the advertisers an artificial advantage.

Denigration

Advertisers should not unfairly attack or discredit other businesses or their products.

The only acceptable use of another business's broken or defaced products in advertisements is in the illustration of comparative tests, and the source, nature and results of these should be clear.

Exploitation of goodwill

Advertisers should not make unfair use of the goodwill attached to the trade mark, name, brand, or the advertising campaign of any other business.

Imitation

No advertisement should so closely resemble any other that it misleads or causes confusion.

Identifying advertisers and recognising advertisements

Advertisers, publishers and owners of other media should ensure that advertisements are designed and presented in such a way that they can be easily distinguished from editorial.

Features, announcements or promotions that are disseminated in exchange for a payment or other reciprocal arrangement should comply with the Codes if their content is controlled by the advertisers. They should also be clearly identified and distinguished from editorial.

Mail order and direct response advertisements and those for one day sales, homework schemes, business opportunities and the like should contain the name and address of the advertisers. Advertisements with a political content should clearly identify their source. Unless required by law, other advertisers are not obliged to identify themselves.'

The Codes go on to list specific rules, common to both the Advertising Code and the Sales Promotion Code, in relation to the following categories of advertisement: alcoholic drinks; children; motoring; environmental claims; health and beauty products and therapies; slimming; distance selling; list and database practice; employment and business opportunities; and financial services and products.

Alcoholic Drinks Code

By way of example, the Alcoholic Drinks Code is reproduced below.

'ALCOHOLIC DRINKS CODE

(1) For the purposes of the Codes, alcoholic drinks are those that exceed 1.2% alcohol by volume.

(2) The drinks industry and the advertising business accept a responsibility for ensuring that advertisements contain nothing that is likely to lead people to adopt styles of drinking that are unwise. The consumption of alcohol may be portrayed as social and thirst-quenching. Advertisements may be humorous, but must still conform with the intention of the rules.

(3) Advertisements should be socially responsible and should not encourage excessive drinking. Advertisements should not suggest that regular solitary drinking is advisable. Care should be taken not to exploit the young, the immature or those who are mentally or socially vulnerable.

(4) Advertisements should not be directed at people under eighteen through the selection of media, style of presentation, content or context in which they appear. No medium should be used to advertise alcoholic drinks if more than 25% of its audience is under eighteen years of age.

(5) People shown drinking should not be, nor should they look, under twenty-five. Younger models may be shown in advertisements, for example in the context of family celebrations, but it should be obvious that they are not drinking.

(6) Advertisements should not feature real or fictitious characters who are likely to appeal particularly to people under eighteen in a way that would encourage them to drink.

(7) Advertisements should not suggest that any alcoholic drink can enhance mental, physical or sexual capabilities, popularity, attractiveness, masculinity, femininity or sporting achievements.

(8) Advertisements may give factual information about the alcoholic strength of a drink or its relatively high alcohol content but this should not be the dominant theme of any advertisement. Alcoholic drinks should not be presented as preferable because of their high alcohol content or intoxicating effect.

(9) Advertisements should not portray drinking alcohol as the main reason for the success of any personal relationship or social event. A brand preference may be promoted as a mark of a drinker's good taste and discernment.

(10) Drinking alcohol should not be portrayed as a challenge, nor should it be suggested that people who drink are brave, tough or daring for doing so.

(11) Particular care should be taken to ensure that advertisements for sales promotions requiring multiple purchases do not actively encourage excessive consumption.

(12) Advertisements should not depict activities or locations where drinking alcohol would be unsafe or unwise. In particular, advertisements should not associate the consumption of alcohol with operating machinery, driving, any activity relating to water or heights, or any other occupation that requires concentration in order to be done safely.

(13) Low alcohol drinks are those that contain 1.2% alcohol by volume or less. Advertisers should ensure that low alcohol drinks are not promoted in a way that encourages their inappropriate consumption and should not depict activities that require complete sobriety.'

20.3.3 The ASA Monthly Report

The Monthly Report produced by the ASA is distributed free of charge to all interested parties, including all those engaged in the business of advertising. It may thus be a deterrent against breaching the Code in that knowledge of offending advertisements will be circulated generally. Each complaint is detailed, together with the section of Code it is alleged to contravene, the name and address of the advertiser, the name of the advertising agency responsible for production of the advertisement and the type of publication in which the advertisement appeared.

20.4 THE ITC CODE OF ADVERTISING STANDARDS AND PRACTICE

The ITC was obliged, under the provisions of the Broadcasting Act 1990, to draw up and from time to time review, a Code of Practice governing advertising on the channels which are subject to its regulation. The following are significant extracts from the Code.

'**General principles**

(1) Television advertising should be legal, decent, honest and truthful.

(2) Advertisements must comply in every respect with the law, common or statute, and licensees must make it a condition of acceptance that advertisements do so comply.

(3) The detailed rules set out below are intended to be applied in the spirit as well as the letter.

(4) The standards in this Code apply to any item of publicity inserted in breaks in or between programmes, whether in return for payment or not, including publicity by licensees themselves, and the term "advertisement" is to be so construed for the purposes of this Code.

Standards

(5) Separation of advertisements and programmes

(a) Advertisements must be clearly distinguishable as such and recognisably separate from the programmes.

(b) Situations, performances and styles reminiscent of programmes must not be used in such a way as to risk confusing viewers as to whether they are watching a programme or an advertisement. In marginal cases the acceptability of such an advertisement may depend on positive indication that it is an advertisement.

(c) Direct imitations of specific programmes (ie treatments so close to the original as to be virtually indistinguishable) are not permissible in any circumstances.

(d) Advertisements parodying programmes are acceptable provided:

   (i) different performers are used from those who appear in the programme itself;
   (ii) it is readily apparent that the advertisement is no more than a parody.

NOTE:
Such advertisements must not be scheduled in breaks in or adjacent to the programme which inspired the parody.

(e) Advertisements must not include extracts from recent or current programme material except in the case of advertisements for products or services having a direct connection with the programme concerned (eg books, videos, sound recordings). In this case the advertisement must not appear in breaks within or immediately before episodes or editions of the programme concerned but may appear in the break immediately following, provided it is not first in the break. Different restrictions apply to the scheduling of advertisements for products or services related to children's programmes.

NOTES:

(i) The Commission will normally regard as "recent" any programme or series last transmitted in the previous two years and "current" as including material from series which are still running or likely to be resumed.

(ii) The fact that an advertiser sponsors a programme does not constitute a direct connection for the purpose of this rule.

(iii) The prohibition on use of recent or current programme material does not apply to news footage or brief extracts from interviews where the interviewer is not identified or in the case of programme material not readily identifiable as such.

(f) Extracts of footage from broadcasts of Parliamentary proceedings are not acceptable.

(g) Advertisements must not refer to themselves as "programmes".

(h) Expressions such as "News Flash" are reserved for important news and public service announcements; their use in advertisements is not acceptable.

(i) Advertisements must not refer to the use or appearance of any product or service in any programme.

NOTES:

(i) More detailed rules relating to the scheduling and presentation of advertisements are set out in Sections 4 and 7 of ITC Rules on Advertising Breaks. Section 7 of the rules contains particular guidance on the identification of advertisements lasting longer than one minute.

(ii) Advertisements referring to a television programme in any of the ways described in (a) to (e) above are acceptable only with the permission of the copyright holder.

(iii) No part of this rule applies to programme promotions.

...

(26) Comparisons

Advertisements containing comparisons with other advertisers, or other products or services, are permissible in the interest of vigorous competition and public information provided they comply with the terms of this rule and rule 27.

(a) All comparative advertisements must respect the principles of fair competition and must be so designed that there is no likelihood of the consumer being misled as a result of the comparison, either about the product or service advertised or that with which it is compared.

(b) The subject matter of a comparison must not be chosen in such a way as to confer an artificial advantage upon the advertiser.

(c) Points of comparison must be based on facts which can be substantiated and must not be unfairly selected.

   In particular:

   (i) the basis of comparison must be the same for all the products or services being compared and must be clearly established in the advertisement so that it can be seen that like is being compared with like;
   (ii) generalised superiority claims must not be made on the basis of selective comparisons.

(27) Denigration

Advertisements must not unfairly attack or discredit other products or services, advertisers or advertisements expressly or by implication.

(28) Reproduction techniques

It is accepted that on television the technical limitations of photography can lead to difficulties in securing a faithful portrayal of a subject, and that the use of special techniques or substitute materials may be necessary to overcome these difficulties. These techniques must not be abused; no advertisement in which they have been used will be acceptable unless the resultant picture presents a fair and reasonable impression of the product or its effects and is not such as to mislead. Unacceptable devices, include, for example, the use of glass or plastic sheeting to simulate the effects of floor or furniture polishes.

(29) Testimonials

Testimonials must be genuine and must not be used in a manner likely to mislead. Licensees must seek and obtain satisfactory documentary evidence in support of any testimonial and any claims therein before accepting advertisements.

...

(40) Alcoholic drink

(a) Advertising for alcoholic drinks must not be directed at people under 18 or use treatments likely to be of particular appeal to them. Children must not be seen or heard in an advertisement for alcoholic drink. In advertisements for drinks containing 1.2% alcohol by volume or less, anyone associated with drinking must be, and appear to be, at least 18 years old. In all other advertisements for alcoholic drinks they must be, and appear to be, at least 25 years old.

(b) No advertisement for alcoholic drink may feature any personality whose example people under 18 are likely to follow or who has a particular appeal to people under 18.

(c) Advertisements must not imply that drinking is essential to social success or acceptance or that refusal is a sign of weakness. Nor may it be implied that the successful outcome of a social occasion is dependent on the consumption of alcohol.

(d) Advertisements must not claim that alcohol has therapeutic qualities nor offer it as a stimulant, sedative or tranquilliser. While advertisements may refer to refreshment after a physical performance they must not give any impression that performance can be improved by drink.

(e) Advertisements must not suggest that a drink is to be preferred because of higher alcohol content or intoxicating effect and must not place undue emphasis on alcoholic strength.

(f) Nothing in an advertisement may link drinking with driving or with the use of potentially dangerous machinery.

(g) Advertisements must neither claim nor suggest that any drink can contribute towards sexual success or that drinking can enhance sexual attractiveness.

(h) Advertisements must not suggest that regular solitary drinking is acceptable or that drinking is a means of solving personal problems.

(i) No advertisement may suggest that drinking is an essential attribute of masculinity. Treatments featuring daring, toughness or bravado in association with drinking must not be used, and alcoholic drinks must not be advertised in a context of aggressive or antisocial behaviour.

(j) Alcoholic drinks must not be seen to be consumed in a working environment unless it is clearly established that the working day has ended.

(k) Advertisements for alcoholic drinks must not publicise competitions, nor may they publicise other sales promotions which entail or encourage multiple purchase.

(l) Advertisements must not foster, depict or imply immoderate drinking. This applies to the quality of drink consumed and to the act of drinking portrayed. References to buying rounds of drinks are not acceptable.

(m) Advertisements may employ humour but not so as to circumvent the intention of these rules.

NOTES:

(i) These rules apply principally to advertisements for alcoholic drinks but the incidental portrayal of alcohol consumption in other advertisements must always be carefully considered to ensure that it does not contradict the spirit of these rules.

(ii) Provided they comply with the generality of the Code and reflect responsible consumption or behaviour, advertisements for drinks containing 1.2% alcohol by volume or less will not normally be subject to rules (j), (k) or (l) above. However, where it appears to the Commission that a significant purpose of the advertising for them is to promote a brand of higher alcoholic strength or where their low alcohol content is not apparent from the copy, this exemption will not apply. Licensees are strongly advised to consult the Commission in advance where there is any doubt about the applicability of this exemption.

(41) Advertising and children

Particular care should be taken over advertising that is likely to be seen by large numbers of children and advertisements in which children are to be employed. More detailed guidance is given in Appendix 1.

(42) Financial advertising

Subject to the generality of the Code, financial advertising is governed by the rules in Appendix 2.

(43) Medicines, treatments, health claims, nutrition and dietary supplements

Subject to the generality of the Code, health claims and the advertising of medicines, treatments and dietary supplements are subject to the detailed rules in Appendix 3.

(44) Advertising on ancillary services

Advertising on Ancillary Services on Channel 3, Channel 4 and Channel 5 is acceptable only if directly related to advertising on the main television service. It will therefore be considered by the Commission as is it had been transmitted as part of that main service advertising.

NOTE:
More detailed guidance is available on request.

(45) Pan-European or non-UK advertising

(a) This rule applies to advertisements which are addressed exclusively to audiences outside the UK. In deciding whether advertising is deemed to fall into this category the Commission will take account of the following factors:

  (i) the distribution of the programme service concerned;
  (ii) the language of the advertisement;
  (iii) whether or not the product or service being advertised is available to viewers in the UK.

(b) In relation to an advertisement to which this rule applies the Commission may, if it considers it to be appropriate and consistent with the requirements of the EC Directive on Television Broadcasting and the Council of European Convention on Transfrontier Television to do so, disapply any other rule of this Code to the extent that the rule requires an advertisement or advertiser to comply with legislation or voluntary codes in force in the UK which do not apply:

  (i) to the advertisement in question because it is directed exclusively to audiences outside the UK; or
  (ii) to the advertiser, because he does not carry on business in the UK.

(c) An advertisement which is directed specifically and with some frequency to audiences in the territory of a single party to the Council of Europe Convention other than the UK must comply with the television advertising rules of that particular party.

NOTE: the requirement in (c) does not apply:

(i) where the party concerned is a Member State of the European Community;

(ii) where the television advertising rules in the party concerned discriminate between advertising broadcast on services within its jurisdiction and that on services outside its jurisdiction;

(iii) where the UK Government has concluded a relevant bilateral or multilateral agreement with the party concerned.'

Chapter 21

ADVERTISING LAW

21.1 INTRODUCTION

This chapter examines those areas of law that are relevant to the advertising industry. Both the law of passing off and the law of trade marks will be considered although these topics are not exclusively relevant to advertising law.

There is much detailed regulation on advertising in relation to investment and financial services. This chapter, as it is of an introductory nature only, does not consider this field. For detail, see the Financial Services Act 1986, the Banking Act 1987, the Personal Pension Scheme (Advertisements) Regulations 1990 and the Consumer Credit Act 1974.

Chapter 21 contents
Introduction
Descriptions and prices
Passing off
Trade marks
Copyright and moral rights
Comparative advertising
The law of contract
Summary

21.2 DESCRIPTIONS AND PRICES

21.2.1 General

An advertiser must be aware that he is not free to describe the goods or services that he wishes to promote in any manner he sees fit. Any descriptions or price indications attached to the goods or services will be subject to legal control. This section looks at the main restrictions on freedom of description and pricing.

21.2.2 Trade descriptions

The Trade Descriptions Act 1968 contains provisions prohibiting misdescriptions of goods and services provided in the course of trade or business. An offence is committed by any person who applies such a false trade description. Prosecutions are usually undertaken at a local level by the trading standards officers of a local authority but a private prosecution is also possible. Where the person convicted of the offence is a corporate body, any director, manager or secretary found to have consented to or to have been negligent in relation to the offence will also be convicted. It is an either way offence and punishable, on indictment, to a maximum of 2 years' imprisonment (s 18).

(1) Goods
A trade description is a direct or indirect indication of any of the following matters with respect to goods:

- quantity, size or gauge;
- method of manufacture, production, processing or reconditioning;
- composition;
- fitness for purpose, strength, performance, behaviour or accuracy;
- any other physical characteristics;
- testing by any person and the results of such tests;
- approval by any person or conformity with a type approved by any person;

- place or date of manufacture, production, processing or reconditioning;
- person by whom manufactured, produced, processed or reconditioned;
- other history, including previous ownership or use.

A person applies a trade description to goods if he:

(a) affixes or annexes it to or in any manner marks it on or incorporates it with:

(1) the goods themselves; or
(2) anything in, on or with which the goods are supplied;

(b) places the goods in, on or with anything which the trade description has been affixed or annexed to, marked on or incorporated with, or places any such thing with the goods; or

(c) uses the trade description in any manner likely to be taken as referring to the goods.

Thus, the provisions of the Act apply not only to descriptions of the goods on the goods themselves but also to any markings placed on packaging or anything in which the goods are supplied or displayed, for example vending machines, display stands and point-of-sale advertising material. It will also apply to oral statements about the goods as well as any other statement likely to be taken as referring to the goods. This latter provision will include all advertising material which relates to the goods.

(2) Services

It is an offence for any person in the course of a trade or business to make a false statement as to any of the following matters:

- the provision in the course of any trade or business of any services, accommodation or facilities;
- the nature of any services, accommodation or facilities provided in the course of any trade or business;
- the time at which, manner in which, or persons by whom any services, accommodation or facilities are so provided;
- the examination, approval or evaluation by any person of any services, accommodation or facilities so provided;
- the location or amenities of any accommodation so provided.

Unlike a false trade description in relation to goods, the offence of making a false statement in relation to services is not one of strict liability. It can only be committed intentionally (where the individual knows the description to be false) or recklessly.

(3) Meaning of 'false'

A false trade description is a trade description which is false to a material degree (Trade Descriptions Act 1968, s 3(1)). As to the meaning of 'to a material degree', see, for example, *Donnelly v Rowlands* [1971] 1 All ER 9, where a milk retailer supplied milk in bottles with foil caps bearing the words 'Untreated milk produced from TT cows' followed by his name and address, although the bottles themselves were embossed with names, other than the retailer's, of milk suppliers to whom they belonged. It was held that the words on the foil caps were an accurate trade description of the milk and that, in their context, the words on the bottles did not refer to the milk but merely conveyed that they were bottles belonging to the persons whose names were embossed on them, and, accordingly, it was held that such trade description was not false in any material degree.

In relation to trade descriptions which, while not false, are misleading, the 1968 Act deems such descriptions to be false where they are likely to be taken as an indication of any of the matters in the list above as would be false to a material degree.

(4) Class of goods

Where a trade description is used in relation to a class of goods, the trade description shall be taken as referring to all goods in the class whether or not in existence at the time the advertisement is published (s 5(2)).

(5) Defences

It is a defence for a person charged with the offence of applying a false trade description to goods or services to prove that:

(a) the commission of the offence was due to a mistake or to reliance on information supplied to him or to the act or default of another person, an accident or some other cause beyond his control; and

(b) he took all reasonable precautions and exercised all due diligence to avoid the commission of such an offence by himself or any person under his control (s 24(1)).

This defence is not available to a person who deliberately applied the false trade description himself.

In addition, the defence of innocent publication is available to a person who can prove that his business is to publish or arrange for the publication of advertisements and that he received the advertisement for publication in the ordinary course of business and did not know and had no reason to suspect that its publication would amount to an offence under the 1968 Act (s 25). Publishers of magazines, for example, would usually be able use this defence to a charge under the 1968 Act.

21.2.3 Misleading advertisements

The Control of Misleading Advertisements Regulations 1988 were made to give effect to EC Directive 84/450 (OJ 1984 L 250/17) relating to misleading advertising. The regulations impose a duty on the Director General of Fair Trading (DGFT) and the Independent Television Commission to consider complaints and confer powers upon them to take appropriate steps to deal with such advertisements.

It is the duty of the DGFT to consider any complaint made to him that an advertisement within his remit (all advertisements except those which are broadcast and those which relate to investment or financial services) is misleading except where the complaint appears to him to be frivolous or vexatious. The DGFT will usually require some evidence from the complainant that all established means of dealing with such complaints in relation to the advertisement have been exhausted before he will consider the complaint.

If the DGFT considers the advertisement to be misleading, he may apply to the court (under Control of Misleading Advertisement Regulations 1988, reg 6) for an injunction or interlocutory injunction (see *Director General of Fair Trading v Tobyward Ltd and Another* [1989] 2 All ER 266 considered below) or, where he does not make such an application, he must give his reasons for not doing so. The court will grant an injunction where it considers the advertisement to be misleading, but only after taking into account all the interests involved and, in particular, the public interest.

In *Director General of Fair Trading v Tobyward Ltd and Another* (above), the respondent advertised a product called 'Speedslim', claiming that its use could result in permanent weight loss, that success was guaranteed, that the product contained an ingredient that was a medical and scientific breakthrough, and that the product was 100% safe in all cases. A complaint was made to the Advertising Standards Authority who found the advertisement to be misleading and consequently in breach of the British Code of Advertising Practice. Despite advice on how to comply with the Code given to the respondent by the Authority, the respondent continued to publish the advertisement. The Authority referred the matter to the DGFT who applied to the court for an interlocutory injunction. The court granted the interlocutory injunction because there was a strong prima facie case that the respondent's advertisement was likely to deceive the persons to whom it was addressed by making false claims for the product and was likely to induce those persons to buy the product.

The Independent Television Commission has similar powers to the DGFT except that where it considers an advertisement to be misleading it does not need to make an application to the court; it will simply refuse to broadcast the advertisement.

21.2.4 Prices

A person will be guilty of an offence under Part III of the Consumer Protection Act 1987 where, in the course of a business of his, he gives to a consumer a misleading price indication as to goods, services, accommodation or facilities (s 20).

Even if the price indication was not misleading at the time it was given but later becomes misleading, the person who gave the indication will be guilty of an offence if:

(a) consumers might reasonably be expected to rely on the indication at a time after it has become misleading; and
(b) he fails to take all such steps as are reasonable to prevent those consumers from relying on the indication (s 20(2)).

Misleading

As far as this offence is concerned, a price indication will be a misleading price indication where consumers might reasonably be expected to infer from it, or from any omission by it, any of the following:

(a) that the price is less than in fact it is;
(b) that the applicability of the price does not depend on facts or circumstances on which its applicability does in fact depend;
(c) that the price covers matters in respect of which an additional charge is in fact made;
(d) that a person who in fact has no such expectation:
    (i) expects the price to be increased or reduced (whether or not at a particular time or by a particular amount); or
    (ii) expects the price, or the price as increased or reduced, to be maintained (whether or not for a particular period); or

(e) that the facts or circumstances by reference to which the consumers might reasonably be expected to judge the validity of any relevant comparison made or implied by the indication are not what in fact they are.

Consumer

The offence will be committed where a misleading price indication is given to a consumer. The definition of 'consumer' appears in s 20(6) of the Act where it is provided that a consumer:

(a) in relation to any goods, means any person who might wish to be supplied with the goods for his own private use or consumption;
(b) in relation to any services or facilities, means any person who might wish to be provided with the services or facilities, otherwise than for the purposes of any business of his; and
(c) in relation to any accommodation, means any person who might wish to occupy the accommodation otherwise than for the purposes of any business of his.

Defences

The defence of innocent publication exists (s 24(3)) in respect of a price indication published in an advertisement. The person charged must show that:

(a) he is a person who carries on a business of publishing or arranging for the publication of advertisements;
(b) he received the advertisement for publication in the ordinary course of that business; and
(c) at the time of publication, he did not know and had no grounds for suspecting that the publication would involve the commission of the offence.

There are various other provisions of some relevance to this area which do not warrant detailed analysis here. For further detail, see the Price Indications (Method of Payment) Regulations 1991, SI 1991/199, which apply where a price indication is given but this indication is not applicable to all methods of payment, and the Price Marking Order 1991, SI 1991/1382, which deals with mandatory rules for unit prices of goods and provides, inter alia, that they must state the VAT inclusive price where the goods are sold retail.

21.3 PASSING OFF

21.3.1 The nature of a passing off action

In *Warninck Erven BV and Another v J. Townend and Sons (Hull) Ltd and Another* [1979] AC 731, Lord Diplock set out five characteristics necessary to launch a valid passing off action:

(1) a misrepresentation,
(2) made by a trader in the course of trade,
(3) to prospective customers of his or ultimate customers of goods or services supplied by him,
(4) which is calculated to injure the business or goodwill of another trader (in the sense that this is a reasonably foreseeable consequence), and
(5) which causes actual damage to the business or goodwill of the trader by whom the action is brought or (in a quia timet action) will probably do so.

In *Consorzio del Prosciutto di Parma v Marks & Spencer plc and Others* [1991] RPC 351, Nourse LJ reduced these characteristics to:

'the classical trinity of:

(1) a reputation (or goodwill) acquired by the claimant in his goods, name, mark etc;
(2) a misrepresentation by the defendant leading to confusion (or deception); causing
(3) damage to the claimant.'

Interpretation of the essential characteristics has been wide-ranging and sometimes confusing, not least because there is inevitably some overlap between them.

Examples of misrepresentation

Examples of misrepresentation could include the following:

- a misdescription, provided there is a class of products or services to which the description can validly be applied (Champagne, for example, in relation to sparkling wine produced in the Champagne region of France) and provided the association of that description and the reputation of the claimant (Bollinger, for example) is established so that the customer expects such products and services to meet certain standards;
- claiming without reason a connection with some well-established business;
- using the claimant's advertising to give the impression that the defendant's goods or services are those advertised by the claimant or even that low quality goods of the claimant are the claimant's normal quality goods (eg where the defendant collects used razor blades manufactured by the claimant and resells them as new, having repackaged them in the claimant's distinctive containers);
- use of a mark similar to the claimant's mark;
- use of a name or trading name similar to that of the claimant. Distinctions here can be especially fine. Normally, no one can be stopped from using his own name (or one which has by association become his own: for example, in the way that Harry Webb has become known as Cliff Richard), but they must do so 'honestly' and 'not go beyond that' (see *Wright, Layman & Umney Ltd v Wright* [1949] 66 RPC 149). However, it seems that if a person uses his natural or assumed name with the intention of taking business from another, then there can be a misrepresentation and such action may be restrained. Where the defendant's name is his own, the burden of proof on the claimant is usually heavy, but when it is an assumed name, the burden is lighter. Use by a company of its registered name may still amount to a misrepresentation. It should be remembered that all this assumes some misrepresentation on the defendant's part. If there is no such intent, then use of one's own name, or one to which a right has been established independent of the claimant, is usually not actionable – it is a normal commercial hazard;
- alteration of or addition to the claimant's product;
- imputing the authority or consent of the holder of the goodwill. This has a variety of guises, for example claiming membership of The Law Society or the British Medical Association. An interesting and novel example is *Associated Newspapers plc v Insert Media Ltd and Others* [1991] 1 WLR 571. The claimant published various magazines and wished to prevent retailers and distributors inserting advertising material between the pages of the magazines, which the publisher had not authorised or arranging with third parties to make such

insertions. It was held that insertion of advertising leaflets into newspapers would be a misrepresentation that the inserts were made or authorised by the publishers if there was also evidence that a substantial number of readers would believe the inserts were so made or authorised;
- substitution of rival goods.

21.3.2 Remedies for passing off

Remedies for passing off include:

(1) damages;
(2) an inquiry to establish loss;
(3) an account of the defendant's profits;
(4) an order for delivery up or destruction of infringing articles; and
(5) injunctive relief (final and interlocutory).

21.3.3 Defences

As well as denial of the existence of the necessary characteristics, there are a number of defences or bars to a passing off action. These include:

(1) proof that the claimant's mark is not distinctive;
(2) proof that the claimant's mark is merely descriptive and has not acquired a secondary meaning;
(3) proof that the mark has ceased to be distinctive and has become generic;
(4) proof that the claimant and defendant have concurrent rights;
(5) proof that the defendant is merely using his own (genuine or assumed) name;
(6) the claimant's consent or acquiescence;
(7) the claimant's delay in instituting proceedings;
(8) the claimant's abandonment of the mark.

21.4 TRADE MARKS

21.4.1 What is a trade mark?

A trade mark has been defined as 'any sign capable of being represented graphically which is capable of distinguishing goods or services of one undertaking from those of other undertakings' (Trade Marks Act 1994).

By s 1(2), this includes, but is not limited to:

- words, including personal names;
- designs;
- letters;
- numerals;
- the shape of goods or their packaging, except (under s 3(2)) those which consist exclusively of the shape which results from the nature of the goods themselves or which is necessary to obtain a technical result or which gives substantial value to the goods.

It seems that registration may also extend to:

- colours and/or colour combinations; and
- sounds,

so long as they otherwise fall within the definition.

For example, this could cover advertising jingles, toothpaste stripes or the 'snap crackle and pop' of a breakfast cereal. The previously unsuccessful Coca-Cola application ([1986] 2 All ER 274) for registration of the shape of the Coca-Cola bottle has now succeeded under the 1994 Act.

21.4.2 Infringement (ss 9 and 10)

A mark registered under the 1994 Act is a property right, and the proprietor has the rights and remedies given by the Act (s 2(1)). That right is an exclusive right and is infringed by use of the mark in the UK without the proprietor's consent (s 9(1)).

Infringing acts (specified in s 10) are, in the course of a trade:

- using a mark which is identical to a registered mark in relation to identical goods or services; or
- using a mark which is identical to a registered mark in relation to similar goods or services provided there is a likelihood of confusion on the part of the public, which includes the likelihood of association with the trade mark;
- using a mark which is similar to a registered mark in relation to similar goods or services or to identical goods or services provided (in each case) there is a likelihood of confusion on the part of the public, which includes the likelihood of association with the trade mark;
- using a mark which is identical or similar to a registered mark in respect of non-similar goods or services where the proprietor of the registered mark has established a reputation and the later mark, being without due cause would take unfair advantage of or be detrimental to that reputation. Examples would be marks such as KODAK, LEGO or CHAMPAGNE, which have such a high reputation that applying them to any type of goods would be likely to amount to a statutory 'passing off' if there were unfair advantage or detriment.

The meaning of 'likelihood of association' (a new concept introduced by the 1994 Act) was considered in *Wagamama Ltd v City Centre Restaurants plc (UK) Ltd* [1995] FSR 713, ChD. The claimant registered the name WAGAMAMA under which it operated a Japanese-style noodle bar. The defendant opened a restaurant selling Indian food under the name RAJA MAMA'S. The claimant argued that the words 'likelihood of association' would result in infringement arising where the registered mark would be caused to come into the minds of customers, even though no confusion as to origin arose. The judge rejected that argument and held that there must still be likelihood of confusion (but went on to say that there was, in fact, confusion due to substantial similarity of marks) under the 1994 Act.

By s 10(4), 'use' of a mark includes:

- putting it on goods or packaging; or
- offering, marketing or stocking goods, or offering or supplying goods under the mark; or
- importing or exporting goods under the mark; or
- putting it on business papers or advertising material.

Section 10(5) extends liability to anyone who applies a registered mark to labelling, packaging or advertising material or business papers if, at the time of application, he knew or had reason to believe that such application was not duly authorised.

Section 10(6), however, allows use of trade marks in comparative advertising in certain circumstances (see **21.6.3**).

Further, s 92(1) of the Act makes it a criminal offence for a person:

(a) with a view to gain for himself or another, or with intent to cause loss to another; and
(b) without the consent of the proprietor, to
(c) apply to goods or their packaging a sign identical to or likely to be mistaken for a registered trade mark.

Section 92(2) provides a further offence where a person:

(a) with a view to gain for himself or another, or with intent to cause loss to another; and
(b) without the consent of the proprietor;
(c) applies a sign identical to or likely to be mistaken for a registered trade mark to material intended to be used for advertising goods.

21.4.3 Remedies

The right to bring proceedings vests in the proprietor from the date of filing of the application. However, no proceedings may be brought before the mark is actually registered (s 9(3)).

An infringement is actionable by the registered proprietor who has the right to such relief as would be appropriate in relation to infringement of any other property right, including damages, injunctions and accounts (s 14).

Specific remedies include:

- an order for erasure of the mark or destruction of the infringing goods, materials or articles (s 15(1)); or
- an order for the delivery up of infringing goods, materials or articles (s 16(1)), but subject to a 6-year limitation period as described in s 18.

There is even a right, under s 56, for the owner of a 'well-known' (but unregistered) trade mark to apply for injunctive relief (but not damages) preventing use in the UK of a mark which is similar or identical to his mark in relation to similar or identical goods or services. Well-known marks are those protected as such under the Paris Convention for the protection of intellectual property. The owner of the well-known mark must be based in a country which is a signatory to the Paris Convention (which covers most of the industrialised nations). The owner is barred from relief if he has acquiesced for a continuous period of 5 years or more, ie if, with knowledge, he has allowed the action about which he now complains.

The 'well-known' provisions may mean that if they had applied under the provisions of the 1994 Act, the original US brewers of 'Budweiser' beer who failed to protect the name of their beer using common law passing off (*Anheuser-Busch Inc v Budejovicky Budvar Narodi Podnik* [1984] FSR 413) would have been more successful.

21.4.4 Non-infringement

The practice known as comparative advertising, formerly outlawed by s 24(1)(b) of the Trade Marks Act 1938 is permitted under s 10(6) of the 1994 Act (for a definition of comparative advertising, see **21.6.2**).

A trade mark may now be used to identify goods or services as being those of the proprietor so long as the use:

- is in accordance with honest practices in industrial or commercial matters (eg use of a person's own name and address or an indication of quality or geographic origin); and
- is not such as to take unfair advantage of or cause damage to the distinctive character or reputation of the trade mark (see **21.6.3**).

On the other hand, this must be seen in context. The wildest dreams of those who write 'knocking copy' have not come true. There is still the possibility in the case of untrue claims of an action for trade libel or breach of the British Codes of Advertising and Sales Promotion (see **20.3.2**). It should be noted that s 10(6) may have to be interpreted in the light of the EC Directive on Comparative Advertising (see **21.6.3**).

Similarly, under s 11, there is no infringement by use in accordance with honest practices where the use is:

- by a person of his own name or address; or
- to indicate the kind, quality, quantity, intended purpose, value, geographical origin, time of production of goods or of rendering of services, or other characteristics of goods or services; or
- necessary to indicate the intended purpose of goods and services, provided there is compliance with honest practices, for example, in the sale of spare parts or accessories for third party products, like clothes for Barbie dolls.

Finally, under s 11, there is no infringement by use in a particular locality of an earlier right applying only in that locality which would have enough goodwill to protect it by any rule of law, for example a passing off action.

According to s 12, there will be no infringement by use of a mark in relation to goods put on the market in the European Community under the mark by the owner or with his consent, because by doing so the rights are exhausted. There is an exception if there are legitimate reasons for the proprietor to oppose further dealings with the marked goods, for example if the condition of them has been changed or impaired after they were put on the market.

21.5 COPYRIGHT AND MORAL RIGHTS

21.5.1 Copyright

Copyright is discussed above in Chapter 1.

Copyright in original work produced by an employee of an advertising agency will belong to the agency (s 11(2)). Wherever there is any doubt, the agency should include an assignment clause in its contract with the employee or contractor. Whether the copyright will transfer to the client of the agency will depend on the terms of the agreement between them. Commonly, the agency retains the copyright in all artwork, storyboards, copy and other material until the contract is terminated, at which time the agency assigns the copyright to the client.

An infringement of copyright will occur where there is a copying in material form of the 'whole or substantial part' of a copyright work. Advertisers will often use copyright works as part of their advertisement, for example, a sound recording in a television commercial, and must obtain permission to use such works. The exception where the use is only incidental (s 31) will not apply to advertisements.

21.5.2 Moral rights

In appropriate circumstances, the moral rights of authors of underlying works must be considered. The position regarding the moral rights of employees is discussed in Chapter 3.

21.6 COMPARATIVE ADVERTISING

21.6.1 General

Comparative advertising, sometimes known as 'knocking copy', is advertising which, explicitly or by implication, identifies a competitor or the goods or services of a competitor.

Advertisers use the device of comparative advertising to increase their profits by achieving higher sales figures for their products. A secondary effect could be said to be that the consumer is provided with information enabling him to make a more informed purchasing decision. However, comparisons are often made only on a single attribute of a product, leading to the criticism that comparative advertising is often unfair and misleading and even that it distorts competition and restricts consumer choice.

21.6.2 Definition

Comparative advertising can be subdivided into, on the one hand, that which describes only one product or its attributes and compares it generally and indirectly to competing products ('indirect comparative advertising'), and, on the other hand, that which describes one product and specifically compares it (or certain of its attributes) to the product (or attributes of such a product) of another ('direct comparative advertising').

> *Example 1 – direct comparative advertising*
> In its television advertising campaign, the manufacturer of X car shows a picture of it alongside Y car (the car of a rival manufacturer), stating that X car gives more miles per gallon than Y car.

> *Example 2 – indirect comparative advertising*
> X plc publishes an advertisement in a national newspaper stating that its widget is significantly more productive than any other widget on the market.

Further, comparative advertising may be either positive or negative. Positive comparative advertising is advertising which seeks to associate the advertiser's product with the product of another, and is based in the premise that the competing product has a good reputation and that, therefore, the advertiser's product will benefit from being associated with it. Negative comparative advertising seeks to draw the attention of the consumer to the differences between the products. It is possible for a single advertisement to incorporate both techniques.

Example 3 – positive comparative advertising
'In tests it was shown that X cola tastes exactly like Y cola.'

Example 4 – negative comparative advertising
'X car is better than Y car in several important respects: it gives more miles to each litre of petrol, has more comfortable seats and comes with a 3-year anti-rust warranty.'

Example 5
'X brand dishwasher is just as good as Y brand but will cost you £67 less.' (Hybrid)

The remainder of this chapter deals with the areas to be looked at when considering comparative advertising.

21.6.3 Registered trade marks

A trade mark is any mark used for the purpose of indicating a connection in the course of trade between the goods and some person having the right either as proprietor or as registered user to use the mark, whether with or without any indication of the identity of that person. A trade mark holder should always identify the registered mark by use of the 'R' symbol enclosed by a circle. Examples of trade marks include 'Kelloggs' and 'Weetabix'. For further detail on trade marks, see **21.4**.

Comparative advertising, whether using broadcast or printed media, will commonly use the trade mark of a competitor. For example, a cola manufacturer may display its product next to the famous bottle of the Coca Cola Company (now registered under the 1994 Act) with a price comparison.

Section 10(6) of the Trade Marks Act 1994 (implementing the EU Trade Marks Harmonisation Directive (89/104/EC)) provides:

'Nothing in the preceding provisions of this section should be construed as preventing the use of a registered trade mark by any person for the purpose of identifying goods or services of those of the proprietor or a licensee.'

The only saving grace for the registered trade mark holder is the qualification to s 10(6):

'But any such use otherwise than in accordance with honest practices in industrial or commercial matters shall be treated as infringing the registered trade mark if the use without due cause takes unfair advantage of or is detrimental to the distinctive character or repute of the trade mark.'

This qualification effectively outlaws comparative advertisements which are dishonest and which take unfair advantage of or are detrimental to the trade mark.

Confusion as to the correct interpretation of s 10(6) was dispelled somewhat in the first case to be decided under that section: *Barclays Bank plc v RBS Advanta* [1996]

RPC 307. In the promotion of its new credit card, RBS Advanta, a joint venture between the Royal Bank of Scotland and the Advanta Corporation of America, provided a table of 15 reasons why its card was 'better'. Various features of the card, including its Annual Percentage Rate, were set out alongside the corresponding information in relation to other cards, including Barclaycard. Barclays Bank applied for an interlocutory injunction restraining RBS Advanta's use of its trade mark, BARCLAYCARD.

Laddie J in the High Court provided a 4-stage test to determine whether a comparative advertisement would be an infringement of another's trade mark.

(1) The proprietor of the trade mark in question has the burden of proving that the factors in the qualification to s 10(6) are made out.
(2) The test for infringement is an objective one and would not be satisfied unless a reasonable audience considered the use to be otherwise than in accordance with an honest practice.
(3) Honesty is to be gauged against what is reasonably to be expected by the target audience of the advertisement for the goods or services concerned.
(4) The use of the trade mark must either give some advantage to the defendant or inflict some harm on the character or repute of the mark which is more than simply de minimis.

The use of Barclays' trade mark by RBS Advanta was not restrained by the judge as he felt that Barclays were unlikely to win the case at trial: it was unlikely that any reasonable reader would perceive RBS Advanta's advertisement as dishonest.

Laddie J's interlocutory decision in *Barclays Bank* was considered by Jacob J in the Chancery Division in *Vodafone Group plc and Another v Orange Personal Communications Services Ltd* [1997] EMLR 84. The defendants ran an advertising campaign which used as its slogan, 'On average, Orange users save £20 every month'. The saving was expressly stated to be in comparison with the claimant's 'equivalent tariffs'. The claimants sued for infringement of their registered trade mark VODAFONE. Both parties accepted that, in order to succeed in its action, Vodafone had to establish that the comparison in the Orange advertisement was significantly misleading, on an objective basis, to a substantial proportion of a reasonable audience of the advertisement. The judge found that the statement made by Orange was true and not misleading and, hence, the claim for trade mark infringement failed. He went on to say that he agreed with Laddie J in *Barclays Bank* that the words 'takes unfair advantage of or is detrimental to' in most cases add nothing of significance to the words 'honest practices in industrial or commercial matters' since if a defendant is not honest he will almost invariably also be taking unfair advantage of or causing detriment to the claimant's work.

Thus, a comparative advertisement will constitute trade mark infringement where the claimant can show that it is objectively dishonest as viewed from the perspective of the informed reasonable reader of the advertisement.

The EU Directive on Comparative Advertising (implemented by the Control of Misleading Advertisements (Amendment) Regulations 2000, SI 2000/914) provides that comparative advertisements will be permitted only where a number of conditions are met. Some of the conditions are directly relevant to the use of trade marks in comparative advertisements. (For an analysis of the Directive see **21.6.8** below.)

It may be that the Directive will have little effect on s 10(6) itself, but it is clear that the section will have to be construed in order to give effect to the Directive.

21.6.4 Passing off

In publishing a comparative advertisement, the advertiser runs the risk that his product will be identified with the product of a competitor. Where this happens as a result of a misrepresentation leading to confusion in the market place and eventual damage, there can be an action in the tort of passing off. See **21.3** for a general discussion of passing off.

The relevance to comparative advertising of a passing off action is demonstrated by the case of *McDonald's Hamburgers Ltd (McDonald's Golden Arches Restaurants Ltd) v Burger King (UK) Ltd* [1986] FSR 45. The defendants placed advertisements on various underground tube trains in London depicting a bun stuffed with meat and salad products. In prominent letters across the top were the words: 'It's Not Just Big, Mac'. In the bottom right corner was the Burger King logo, and to its left were the words: 'You know when you've got a Whopper'. In smaller type were the words: 'Like some burgers, a Whopper is big. Too big to hold in one hand. Unlike some burgers, it's 100% pure beef, flame grilled never fried, with a unique choice of toppings. And, unlike some burgers, it comes any way you want it. With extra ketchup or no pickle, or any other way. So it's big, but there's more to it than that'. The claimants, whose main product was the Big Mac, sought an injunction to restrain alleged passing off. Their case was that a substantial number of people, seeing the advertisement, would notice the words 'Big Mac' and 'Burger King' and would, as a result, expect to obtain Big Macs at Burger King establishments. The judge agreed with the claimants that it was likely that the advertisement would be construed as being for a Big Mac and granted an injunction.

The evidence from Burger King was that the words 'It's not just' in the advertisement had meant that what was being displayed was not the Big Mac, but was an improved version of it. Had this view been accepted by the judge, the defendants would have successfully resisted the passing off action.

In *Ciba-Geigy plc v Parke Davis & Co Ltd* [1994] FSR 8, the defendants successfully contended that consumers would not have been confused by their advertisement. The claimant produced medical products under the registered trade mark VOLTAROL, using a picture of a green apple as its brand symbol. One of the products of the VOLTAROL range was Voltarol Retard, a successful slow-release tablet. The defendant launched a slow-release product under the trade mark Diclomax Retard and placed an advertisement in a medical journal showing a picture of an apple with a bite taken out of it, accompanied by the words, 'Diclomax Retard takes a chunk out of your prescribing costs'. The advertisement was comparative in that it impliedly referred to the claimant's product by use of the green apple symbol (which was unregistered, thus preventing a trade mark infringement action). Aldous J refused an injunction on the basis that the claimant had not established that the defendant's advertisement represented that its product was the claimant's product or a product connected or associated with the claimant's business. Any reasonable doctor would realise that what was being advertised was a Voltarol substitute at a cheaper price.

Thus, where the reasonable consumer would not be confused as to the origin of each product in a comparative advertisement, there will be no action for passing off.

21.6.5 Copyright

Producers of comparative advertisements (as of advertisements generally) must be aware that there may be copyright in the material which is being used. For example, there may be some artistic work depicted on the container of the competitor's product, thus effectively preventing an advertiser from using it without the consent of the copyright owner. For further detail on copyright, see **21.5.1** and Chapter 1.

21.6.6 Trade libel/malicious falsehood

Defamation has been discussed generally in Chapter 9.

An action in trade libel or malicious falsehood may arise in the context of comparative advertising where there has been a false statement in relation to the goods of a competitor which has been made maliciously and which has caused damage.

In *Compaq Computer Corporation v Dell Computer Corporation Ltd* [1992] FSR 93, the Chancery Court issued an interlocutory injunction to stop Dell Computers running advertisements which compared the price and quality of the two makes of computers. The advertisement in question, headed 'It doesn't compute', appeared in the national press in the UK at the end of 1990 and in early 1991. Down the left side of the advertisement were depicted the defendant's computer systems with a price and description. On the right side were pictures of the claimant's systems with similar descriptions. Comparisons were made between the systems, a typical example being a comparison between a 'Dell System 33D, 33MHz 386' and a 'Compaq DeskPro 386/33L 33MHz 386'. Words adjacent to the pictures read as follows: 'Now here's a little conundrum for you. Dell's new 386 desktop systems are basically the same as Compaq's. Yet Compaq's prices are, quite literally, thousands of pounds higher'. Various other comparisons were then made between the two companies' performance, reputation and servicing guarantees, followed by the words, 'Dell computers are essentially the same as Compaq's. Both are US quality-designed, developed and built in-house. Yet Dell give superior service and support. So are Compaq's computers worth thousands of pounds more? If you don't think so, fill in the coupon below or pick up the telephone now'. The basis of the trade libel claim was that the computers being compared were different not only in price but also in essential characteristics. By way of example, the Dell 325D, priced at £2,999, had a 100MB hard disk, whereas the Compaq 386/25e at £5,340, had a 120MB hard disk. The judge agreed with Compaq that such material differences meant that the statement that the computers were 'essentially the same' could constitute trade libel.

In granting an interlocutory injunction, Aldous J was mindful of the necessity of protecting the right to free speech but said that:

> 'if an injunction can be framed which will prevent the alleged injurious falsehoods, but will not prevent the defendants using advertisements which make the statements they believe can be justified, there can be no reason why the right to freedom of speech will be materially affected.'

For an example of a case where a claim in malicious falsehood failed, see *Emaco & Electrolux v Dyson Appliances Ltd* (1999) *The Times*, February 8.

21.6.7 The Codes of Practice

The ITC Code of Advertising Standards and Practice

The Independent Television Commission Code applies to all advertisements broadcast by ITC licence holders (see **20.2**).

The provisions of the Code which apply to comparative advertising prohibit advertising which, directly or by implication, unfairly attacks or discredits other products, advertisers or advertisements.

However, comparative advertising is permissible 'in the interests of vigorous competition', provided it complies with the above rule and:

- there is no likelihood of the consumer being misled;
- the principles of fair competition are complied with;
- the subject matter of the comparison is not chosen in such a way as to confer an artificial advantage upon the advertiser;
- points of comparison are based on facts which can be substantiated and must be clearly stated in the advertisement so that it can be seen that like is being compared with like;
- there are no generalised superiority claims made on the basis of selective comparisons.

The British Code of Advertising and Sales Promotion Practice

In relation to non-broadcast advertising, the Advertising Code section of the British Codes of Advertising and Sales Promotion provides the following:

> **'Comparisons**
>
> Comparisons can be explicit or implied and can relate to advertisers' own products or to those of their competitors; they are permitted in the interests of vigorous competition and public information.
>
> Comparisons should be clear and fair. The elements of any comparison should not be selected in a way that gives the advertisers an artificial advantage.
>
> **Denigration**
>
> Advertisers should not unfairly attack or discredit other businesses or their products.
>
> The only acceptable use of another business's broken or defaced products in advertisements is in the illustration of comparative tests, and the source, nature and results of these should be clear.
>
> **Exploitation of goodwill**
>
> Advertisers should not make unfair use of the goodwill attached to the trade mark, name, brand, or the advertising campaign of any other business.
>
> **Imitation**
>
> No advertisement should so closely resemble any other that it misleads or causes confusion.'

21.6.8 The EU Directive

The practice of comparative advertising is to be changed by the implementation of Directive 97/55/EC. The Control of Misleading Advertisements (Amendment) Regulations 2000 come into force in April 2000.

In its introductory paragraphs, the amended proposal Directive states that the completion of the internal market will result in an ever wider range of choice and that the use of comparative advertising must therefore be authorised (under stringent conditions) to help demonstrate the merits of the various products available. It acknowledges that comparative advertisements can be 'unfair and therefore may distort competition, cause damage to competitors and have an adverse effect on consumer choice' but goes on to state that they can 'stimulate competition between suppliers of goods and services to the consumer's advantage'.

The body of the text of the new law provides that:

'(1) A comparative advertisement shall, as far as the comparison is concerned, be permitted only when the following conditions are met:

(a) it is not misleading;
(b) it compares goods or services meeting the same needs or intended for the same purpose;
(c) it objectively compares one or more material, relevant, verifiable and representative features of those goods and services, which may include price;
(d) it does not create confusion in the market place between the advertiser and a competitor or between the advertiser's trade marks, trade names, other distinguishing marks, goods or services and those of a competitor;
(e) it does not discredit or denigrate the trade marks, trade names, other distinguishing marks, goods, services, activities, or circumstances of a competitor;
(f) for products with designation of origin, it relates in each case to products with the same designation,
(g) it does not take unfair advantage of the reputation of a trade mark, trade name or other distinguishing marks of a competitor or the designation of origin of competing products;
(h) it does not present goods or services as imitations or replicas of goods or services bearing a protected trade mark or trade name.

(2) Any comparison referring to a special offer shall indicate in a clear and unequivocal way the date on which the offer ends or, where appropriate, that the special offer is subject to the availability of the goods and services, and, where the special has not yet begun, the date of the start of the period during which the special price or other specific conditions shall apply.'

The aim of the Directive is to harmonise the laws of Member States on comparative advertising, and one effect of this is that both indirect and direct comparative advertising will be allowed in all Member States.

21.6.9 Summary – comparative advertising

Comparative advertising can be used in the UK provided that it does not fall foul of any tort, statutory provision, regulation or Code provision. It should be noted that numerous statutes seek to regulate use of comparative advertising in specific contexts which is it is not possible to deal with in a book of this generality.

When acting for an advertiser or an advertising agent, the solicitor should have regard to the following areas (in addition to the various statutory provisions):

- trademarks;
- passing off;
- copyright;
- defamation;
- malicious falsehood;
- the ASA and ITC Codes of Practice;
- the Control of Misleadings Advertisements (Amendment) Regulations 2000.

21.7 THE LAW OF CONTRACT

21.7.1 General

The law of contract needs consideration when defining the relationship between the advertiser and the advertising agency, and between the advertiser (or agency) and the medium.

This section considers contract law as it affects the relationship between the advertiser of products or services and his target audience.

21.7.2 Offers or invitations to treat?

When can an advertisement be treated as an offer rather than an invitation to treat? The answer will be crucial to the advertiser and must be taken into account when designing advertisements. An offer is capable of acceptance and thus, in the presence of consideration, of becoming a binding contract.

> 'An offer by way of advertisement, of a reward for the rendering of certain services addressed to the public at large, prima facie creates a power of acceptance in every person to whom it is made. But a contractual obligation to pay the reward only comes into existence when an individual person performs the stipulated services and not before.' (*Anson's Law of Contract* (Oxford University Press)

An invitation to treat, however, is an invitation to make offers and therefore is not capable of acceptance. It is unlikely that an advertiser of products would want contracts to be created without his knowledge or consent. How can the problem be avoided?

It is established law that the display of goods in a shop window or on shelves in a self-service store are invitations to treat (*Pharmaceutical Society of Great Britain v Boots Cash Chemists (Southern) Ltd* [1952] 2 QB 795). A careless shopkeeper who displays a lower price than he intended will thus not be bound by it unless he chooses to be. Lord Parker in *Partridge v Crittenden* [1968] 2 All ER 421 said, 'when one is dealing with advertisements, unless indeed they come from manufacturers, there is business sense in their being construed as invitations to treat'.

21.7.3 Acceptance

It is not necessary for an offer in the form of an advertisement to be addressed to a specific individual or class of persons. It can be capable of acceptance if it is addressed to the world generally. In *Carlill v The Carbolic Smoke Ball Co* [1893] 1 QB 256, the defendant company issued an advertisement claiming that their 'smoke ball' would prevent influenza provided that it was used according to instructions. The company further stated in the advertisement that they would pay £100 to anyone who used the product but subsequently contracted the disease. The claimant, after suffering from influenza despite inhaling smoke from the ball, sued for the stated sum. She was successful. The company's argument that they had never heard of Mrs Carlill and thus could not be held to be making her an offer failed.

A further argument put forward by The Carbolic Smoke Ball Company was that, even if an offer could be made to the whole world, Mrs Carlill had not communicated acceptance of the offer to the company. The court dismissed this argument, saying that this particular advertisement was an exception to the general rule that acceptance must be communicated to the offeror.

21.7.4 Misrepresentation or 'puff'?

The vast majority of advertisements will of course be 'mere puffs' and not offers. The defendant company in the above case had made the mistake of saying that '£1,000 is deposited with Alliance Bank, Regent Street, showing our sincerity in the matter'. The reasonable man, felt the court, would take this as a representation demonstrating a clear intention by the company to abide by its promise. The advertiser's skill lies in making positive statements about a product or service without showing to the reasonable man an intention to be bound by them.

The line between a representation and a puff can be a difficult one to draw. In *Dimmock v Hallett* (1866) 2 Ch App 21, useless land was described as 'very fertile and improvable'. The court held this to be a 'flourishing description by an auctioneer' and, as such, merely a puff. But in *Smith v Land and House Property Corporation* (1884) 28 Ch D 7, a tenant persistently in arrears with his rent was described as 'most desirable'. This was held to be a credible statement of fact and thus a binding representation.

It is fair to say that the twentieth century has seen a relaxation in the perception of the reasonable man. It would seem that he now has enough common sense to realise that 'reaches the parts that other beers cannot reach' is unlikely to be a justifiable claim.

Further, an opinion cannot be legally binding. 'Probably the best lager in the world' can thus be subject to no legal comeback. As Treitel says, 'Some statements of opinion are mere puffs. Others, while more specific, yet have no legal effect as they are not positive assertions of fact but only statements of opinion or belief' (*The Law of Contract* (Sweet & Maxwell, 1999)).

It may not always be clear whether a statement is one of opinion or one of fact. If the maker of the statement has some particular qualification or experience relevant to the representation, then it is more likely to be upheld by the courts as a statement of fact. In *Esso Petroleum v Mardon* [1976] QB 801, the company leased a petrol filling station to the defendant after estimating the annual turnover to be 200,000 gallons. The defendant found that he was only able to pump 60,000 gallons. In an action by the company for loss of revenue, the Court of Appeal held that the statement amounted to a collateral warranty that the forecast had been prepared with reasonable care and skill. The statement was one of fact, and the company was liable in damages because the statement was incorrect.

21.8 SUMMARY

Contract law should always be considered when producing an advertisement so as to avoid the advertiser inadvertently being bound by a provision which he did not intend to have legal effect. In addition, contract law will be central to the relationship between an advertiser and his agent and between the agent and the media.

It will be necessary to 'clear' the advertisement for possible actions in:

- defamation;
- malicious falsehood;
- passing off;
- trade mark infringement;
- copyright or moral rights infringement.

Further, an advertiser must consider whether his advertisement:

- breaches a provision of one of the advertising Codes of Practice;
- is comparative.

Chapter 22

COMMERCIAL ASPECTS OF SPORT

22.1 INTRODUCTION

This chapter considers some aspects of the subject often referred to as 'sports law'. In reality, there is no separate legal topic of sports law, although there are particular applications of established legal principles applied in a sporting context. This chapter is concerned only with the following: the basic elements of commercial sponsorship contracts and the ITC Code of Programme Sponsorship.

22.2 THE SPONSORSHIP AGREEMENT

A sponsorship agreement is a marketing tool for the sponsor and an important method of raising finance for sport. The first consideration for both the sponsor and the organiser is that they both have power to contract. A particular problem may arise with event organisers that are representative federations and bodies. A sponsor should always ensure that this body can grant the rights it is purporting to grant. It is important to establish that a sports federation can bind its members so that the sponsorship package is binding upon those members.

Usually, the governing body's powers are delegated by its members who may go on to ratify the deal. Such a power may be found in the rules of the relevant association or else a vote of the membership may grant such a right. It is preferable for a federation or organiser to contract on its members' behalf. Representative bodies should also take care that its players and clubs are bound to it and will take part in the sponsored event. This may involve a single contract between player and club or an additional contract between the player and the federation. If the player has a club contract, the club may have to release the player from that contract to allow the player's participation in a national tournament. The agreement or rules of the federation and its members may well provide for this.

22.3 THE SPONSOR'S RIGHTS

The agreement should set out the sponsor's rights in some detail. The rights represent part of the sponsor's return on its investment. The sponsor is concerned to include clauses guaranteeing rights of control and approval over products. Similarly, use of the event name and the organiser's name or likeness to promote the event will be strictly controlled.

22.3.1 The sponsor's description

Event titles

At the top end of its shopping list of rights, a sponsor typically obtains either title rights or official supplier rights. A title sponsor will usually also be granted official

Chapter 22 contents
Introduction
The sponsorship agreement
The sponsor's rights
The sponsor's obligations
The organiser's obligations
Commercial conflicts and ambush marketing
Merchandising and endorsement agreements
Broadcast sponsorship

status as part of its overall package. However, conversely, official status may not warrant any title identification. The agreement should describe exactly how the sponsor is to be identified with the event.

A title right allows the sponsor to have the event renamed to reflect its involvement. The Worthington Cup and the Barclaycard Premiership are good examples of such arrangements.

A sponsorship agreement should grant the sponsor the right to use the organiser's logo. The right to use of the event name and logo should be non-exclusive to allow the organiser to use it and to grant others the right to use it. Any degree of exclusivity over use of the name and logo should relate only to a particular product category or the agreed designation of the sponsor.

Designations

Sponsors publicise their involvement with an event using their own manufactured products. The categories of products that the sponsor is granted rights over should be stated. A sponsor may wish to promote its involvement with one particular brand, a range of products or services or the company as a whole. The agreement typically grants the sponsor an exclusive right to use a 'designation' or 'official status' in a specified way on certain products. Where the rights are not title rights, the designations are more important to the sponsor. The agreement will contain the right for the sponsor to describe itself as 'official sponsor of' a stated product or service or 'official supplier to' a certain competition or event.

Many agreements only envisage the sponsor using the event logo and designation for their own products. Thus, a drinks manufacturer can use the logo and the 'official status' on its drinks but not on any other products. If the sponsor also makes other products then either these should be included in the definition of the sponsor's products or else a separate merchandising agreement should be entered into.

Event logo

The event logo is often the symbol used to promote the event. Such a logo may be a combination of the organiser's logo and the sponsor's logo, both of which may be set out in a schedule. If appropriate, a trade mark application should be lodged for greater protection of the event logo and mark. This is particularly important where the event is ongoing and involves related merchandising. Where the event establishes sufficient trading goodwill, it may be protected using the tort of passing off. All products and merchandise using the event name and sponsor's logo should be marketed and protected. The parties must set out the agreed ownership of rights in the combined logo.

Sponsor's marks

The sponsor should control use of its logo and marks by the organiser and the agreement should set out exactly what use is allowed and how the sponsor's mark can be exhibited and reproduced. Some agreements contain a schedule setting out exactly how the sponsor's logo can be reproduced and the colours, type set and location the organiser can place it in.

The sponsor will also be concerned to ensure that any third parties that make use of the event logo and the sponsor's logo do so in an appropriate way. This might involve an approved form of agreement or licence to would-be merchandisers.

Ideally, the sponsor will enter agreements direct with these parties to ensure the sponsor's marks are used properly. Where other official suppliers are appointed, the comments made above apply.

Exclusivity

Organisers and individuals may grant sponsorship rights to a number of different companies who provide different products or services. Sponsors should ensure that organisers cannot do so without any restraint. It is unlikely that the agreement will give the organiser complete freedom to appoint other sponsors. A major sponsor will not usually accept this as it raises the possibility of any category of sponsor – not just competing sponsors – achieving equal prominence at an event. If the organisers wish to retain the right to grant sponsorship rights to others then this should be stated in the agreement. Exclusivity in any product category should be defined and included in the agreement. If the event is the 'Hamburger Games' the sponsor could appoint a number of official suppliers in different product categories as well. An official sports drinks supplier could be appointed with no danger of breaching the agreement. The question of exclusivity and the division of rights is simply one for contract.

Although ambush marketing (referred to at **22.6.2**) of an event is an extreme problem, sponsors are often concerned to ensure that the overall image and benefit they are attempting to build is not spoilt or denigrated by other incompatible or undesirable sponsors and advertisers. Accordingly, major sponsors might wish to approve any other sponsors before the organisers sign them. This could involve an absolute bar on the appointment of any other sponsors without prior written approval of the main sponsor. An agreement may outline categories of sponsor and product that are unacceptable although this may relate only to competitors. An agreement may define categories of competing products which are unacceptable to the incumbent sponsors, and these competing sponsors will be excluded from sponsorship activities.

The sponsor and the governing body must strike a balance between the organiser's legitimate desire to maximise its sponsorship income and apportion rights in respect of certain categories of products, and the sponsor's desire for exclusivity.

Where the products and categories of sponsorship are wide because of the popularity of an event or the individuals involved in the event, rights could be granted to other sponsors with little conflict of interest or prospect of any breach of contract. Once an official drinks supplier has been appointed, the governing body could appoint official clothing manufacturers, official transport and official financial services suppliers.

The availability of broadcast coverage has a great effect on both the cost of sponsorship and the exclusivity offered to potential sponsors. Broadcast coverage may further complicate event sponsorship agreements as this can introduce a separate category of broadcast sponsorship (and associated revenue) which can dilute an event sponsor's rights. A sponsor should establish at an early stage in negotiations the existence of coverage contracts, and whether these rights have been sold, and consider what (if any) restrictions it should place on the organiser and, where possible, the broadcaster.

If broadcast rights are particularly important to the sponsor, then the sponsorship contract should state that the fee is based on so many hours of TV coverage and will be reduced pro rata if this coverage is reduced.

22.3.2 Secondary or ancillary rights

The sponsors of an event, whatever their title or other status, require further rights. The further rights granted to a sponsor may include some or all of the following:

(1) a right to use the designation on any advertising, promotional or publicity material produced by the sponsor in connection with the event;
(2) the exclusive right to manufacture and sell products bearing the designation for the period of this agreement;
(3) a non-exclusive right allowing the sponsor to reproduce the event logo on all promotional materials and in any promotional activities associated with the event. This would include media advertising although the organiser may want to approve any promotional or advertising activities prior to their taking place;
(4) the non-exclusive right to occupy and use hospitality facilities at the event. Such a right may or may not be at the expense of the sponsor. An organiser may not be able to contract on behalf of a site caterer which may mean that hospitality is at the expense of the sponsor and subject to the usual terms of the caterer or the management of the venue. A separate agreement for these facilities may be necessary;
(5) in addition to the use of hospitality facilities, the sponsor may have a specified number of seats for the event. There may be a certain number of free seats in specified positions for corporate entertainment, and others which will be paid for if the sponsor requires them. It would be usual to forbid the resale of these tickets although use in promotions – such as for prizes in competitions – would be permitted. Any additional rights such as tickets for post-event celebrations, refreshments or additional facilities as required should also be dealt with in this way;
(6) the sponsor may require event advertising. This may include advertising at the event itself such as a specified number of advertising hoardings in agreed positions at the event. The siting of such hoardings will be influenced by importance of the sponsor and whether or not a broadcast agreement is in place. Advertising on or adjacent to the score board or timing equipment should be agreed and must be placed with restrictions in the ITC Code in mind;
(7) the sponsor may agree that the event logo and the sponsor's designation will appear in the event programme. This may be on the cover; on the title page; and on a page in the programme listing the cast, teams or timing of heats in a competition;
(8) placement of the logo and designation should also be agreed in all press releases and other promotional or advertising material released by the organiser as well as at all event press conferences held by the organisers;
(9) the organiser and sponsor may also agree the right to a full-page colour or black and white advertisement in the official programme for the event;
(10) any agreed merchandising rights must also be dealt with in the agreement. This may involve the manufacture of products by the sponsor and/or the manufacture of official merchandise by licensees. Any rights to manufacture, purchase and use event merchandise (other than the sponsor's own products) must be consistent with the sponsorship rights.

22.3.3 Duration

The duration of a sponsorship agreement can be agreed in a number of ways. It is quite common for an agreement to cover a fixed term such as a club's season or an annual cup competition.

A fixed-term arrangement expires on an agreed date subject to any options to renew or any other extensions to the agreement. The termination date of such an agreement should take account of all the opportunities the sponsor wants to exploit the relationship. If the sponsor wishes to advertise before and after an event and not just on the day there may be a run-on period for the rights. If merchandise is involved then the seasonal nature of many sports and shopping habits should also be taken into account and sale of rights provided in the agreement.

Where a contract relates directly to the holding of a number of events scheduled to take place during a given period, the agreement may specify both a contractual duration and a minimum number of events covered by the agreement. The minimum number of events should take place within the contract period; if they do not then the sponsor may require the agreement to be prolonged. If the events are cancelled or postponed, the sponsor may be able to terminate the agreement. Some sponsors are tied to particular competitions which take place within a season or a year. Because the event is part of the sports calendar it is extremely unlikely that it will be postponed or cancelled for anything but the most drastic of circumstances which would amount to frustration of the contract.

The sponsors and the organiser may want to extend or continue a successful agreement. There are two popular methods of extending an agreement. The first is the use of an option clause which specifies when and how the option to renew the agreement should be exercised. The other is a matching rights clause. The sponsor and organiser start negotiations for a fixed period before expiry of the term. If they cannot agree terms, the organiser goes away to negotiate a deal but before the new deal is signed the original sponsor has the right to match any other offer made.

Both types of clause should state they are subject to the performance by both parties of their obligations under the agreement.

22.4 THE SPONSOR'S OBLIGATIONS

The sponsor's primary obligation is to pay the agreed fee and provide any agreed extras, such as services and products to the organiser. The agreed fee for the sponsorship rights will reflect the popularity of the event and the extent of the rights granted. Terms for payment vary but agreements are often concluded using staged payments over a period of time. A lump sum payment in advance provides fewer safeguards for sponsors if there is any subsequent default in the organiser's obligations.

The benefit of staged payments for the sponsor is the ability to terminate the contract if certain specified events do not occur without having paid over the full fee. The payments can be conditional on the organiser achieving certain goals in the preparation of the event.

The sponsor may provide a supply of its products as well as prizes or trophies. Where products are concerned, the agreement will contain various obligations on the organiser as to the use and visibility of the products. For instance, after races and events at sporting meets, track officials may be required to hand out products to the competitors.

There will be various other obligations on the sponsor which may include the following:

(1) to comply with all applicable national and international media and domestic rules and regulations. As the sponsor is being given the right to advertise and promote the event and the association with the organiser, it is important that this assurance is given. A failure to do so may give rise to third party claims and/or complaints against the sponsor and the organiser. The organiser may also require an indemnity from the sponsor in case of any such problems;

(2) as well as external regulations, the sport or the event may have its own rules and regulations that the sponsors should agree to comply with – these will usually be set out by a governing body such as the Rugby Football Union or the Football Association. If these rules apply to the event or its competitors, the sponsor should be aware of them and obey them. A good example was the former amateur status of players in rugby union – sponsors used to agree to abide by those regulations and any dealings with players had to be in accordance with them;

(3) use of the event logo and the sponsor's designation should be only as authorised by the agreement. A sponsor that exceeded the agreed usage might find that there had been a breach of the organiser's rights as well as a potential breach of third party rights;

(4) in the event that the sponsor becomes aware of any breach or suspected breach of any of the event rights, such as unauthorised merchandising activities, the sponsor should immediately notify the organisers;

(5) if the sponsor's logo has available IP protection, ownership or at least an entitlement to use the logo should be maintained. A failure to do so could result in liability for the organiser;

(6) a general prohibition on acting in any manner which would prejudice the image or the running of the event may also be included. This might include running a tasteless advertising campaign;

(7) the sponsor must agree not to exercise the rights except as specifically set out in the agreement. Such a clause could be more extensive. For instance, it could provide for prior submission of all promotional material to the organiser for approval. It could also specify the submission of any proposed packaging or design for any of the products that incorporate the event name or logo. An express obligation not to adapt the event logo now or at all and an obligation not to adopt or use any logo that is similar to the event logo or the organiser's logo once the agreement has ended could also be included.

22.5 THE ORGANISER'S OBLIGATIONS

The organiser's primary obligation is to hold the event and to make all the necessary arrangements for it to take place. Coupled with this, the sponsor might want to be kept up to date with how preparations are progressing. Some sponsors require specified organisational targets to be met by certain dates. This might mean that tickets are on sale by a given date, or that advertising and promotional campaigns locally and nationally are instituted at a certain time, perhaps to co-ordinate with a branded product launch. Such targets might be reflected in the staging of payments.

Additional obligations may require the organiser:

(1) to maintain all necessary insurance and other cover. This may include insurance covering the cancellation or postponement of the event and any ensuing third party liability;
(2) to comply with all relevant rules and regulations in the organisation, running and promotion of the event. This should include any internal and relevant external regulations. The sponsor will be concerned that the organiser does nothing to tarnish its image or reputation;
(3) not to grant any third party the right to use the designation and not to grant any sponsorship rights, any right to use the event logo, the sponsor's logo or the designation to any third party who manufactures, distributes or sells any competing product;
(4) not to use the sponsor's logo except as permitted by the agreement;
(5) to use its best endeavours to obtain wide media exposure for the event and to keep the sponsor advised of such exposure and any promotional opportunities;
(6) not knowingly to do anything to prejudice the image or reputation of the sponsor;
(7) not to enter any merchandise agreements involving the use of the event logo or the sponsor's logo with a third party except on the terms of an agreed licence and to require any such third parties to enter an agreement direct with the sponsor;
(8) to an indemnity for breach of any warranty.

The agreement should also contain terms dealing with the postponement and cancellation of the event.

22.6 COMMERCIAL CONFLICTS AND AMBUSH MARKETING

22.6.1 Commercial conflicts

Each participant in the commercial aspect of the event wishes to maximise its own revenue. A balance must be struck between these competing interests. For example, an event organiser will appoint its own commercial partners and will undoubtedly promise them exclusive rights – a soft drink manufacturer will usually only sponsor a tournament in return for a degree of exclusivity. A participating team will want to appoint its own sponsors who may want to see the name of their product on (for example) the players' shirts. A player may want to endorse a product of his own.

Thus, a sportsman may be wearing his sponsor's kit whilst playing in his club's sponsored shirt in a tournament which is sponsored in a stadium full of advertising in a broadcast game for which the broadcast is sponsored. The organiser, the team and the players have to find an accommodation that suits their respective commercial interests. The potential for conflicts is enormous.

22.6.2 Ambush marketing

Sponsors and rights owners are concerned with ambush marketing, which involves an attempt by a third party to take advantage of the goodwill of an event. The 'ambush marketeer' may attempt to do this by taking advantage of the name and reputation of an event without the approval of the organisers or participants. Ambush marketing may occur in a number of ways.

Unauthorised merchandising

This involves the marketing and sale of merchandised products bearing the name and logo of the event. An event organiser may appoint various official suppliers in product categories. An unauthorised supplier effectively passes his goods off as being official ones and thereby obtains a commercial advantage.

Advertising

The bulk purchase of advertising in all media in and around an event and in any media associated with an event by a company – often a competitor to an authorised sponsor – interferes with the rights of official sponsors and suppliers. Major events will also have broadcast advertising which if bought up by a competitor can saturate the official sponsors. In such a situation, there is unlikely to be any legal remedy – except perhaps in passing off or defamation, which are both costly and time-consuming remedies. The best action is preventative. Appropriate contractual obligations should be obtained to limit the sale of advertising space to competitors in and around events. In these circumstances, great care must be taken to avoid competition law problems intrinsic in such exclusive arrangements.

Broadcast sponsorship

Where an event is broadcast on commercial television, a competitor may be able to buy broadcast advertising time during commercial breaks or even sponsor the transmission of the event itself. Such an arrangement can diminish and even negate the value of the event sponsorship. One solution to avoid this is to ensure that all the rights in broadcast events are dealt with together, at least giving an event sponsor the opportunity to cover the transmission as well if that is appropriate. Conversely, a transmission sponsor may want first 'bite' at the event rights as well.

As far as possible, all sponsorship rights should be controlled in agreements between governing bodies, broadcasters and event sponsors.

Independent sponsorship deals with teams and players

These deals can represent a threat to the exclusivity of an event sponsor's rights. As far as possible, a governing body may require teams and participants to be free of sponsorship when they enter their competitions.

Interference with the broadcast

There is a broadcasting production technique commonly known as Electronic Broadcast Substitution which can be used to alter images in and around events to impose alternative brands and logos. Such technology and techniques have to be closely monitored and controlled by organisers, sponsors and broadcasters in their agreements.

Protection from ambush marketing

Organisers and sponsors can take certain steps to avoid problems.

(1) All contractual arrangements relating to an event must prohibit unapproved third party advertising or sponsorship. An organiser should clear an event of advertising prior to a new event, thus enabling him to go to the market with no existing obligations. All the rights to the advertising and sponsorship at the event can then be sold afresh. All commercial activities within a stadium should be controlled or approved by the organiser.

(2) The principal protectable elements of an event – and the rights which are licensed to sponsors – relate to use of the event name and logo and associated goodwill. All available intellectual property protection should be maintained and policed. Appropriate copyright and trade mark notices and warnings should be placed on all official merchandise. All official products should be well advertised and of good quality to establish strong protectable goodwill. All counterfeiting activities should be stamped out using available civil and criminal remedies. Where appropriate, the ASA and ITC Codes should also be used.

(3) Individuals and teams competing or performing at an event may have their own sponsorship arrangements. This can cause problems for event organisers and sponsors. The rules of entry of the competition should limit the commercial activities of competitors whilst in competition. This should not amount to a restraint of trade as long as such rules do not also attempt to prohibit a competitor's or performer's commercial activities outside of competition or performance. Competitors and performers are protected from unauthorised use of their image or reputation by third parties.

22.7 MERCHANDISING AND ENDORSEMENT AGREEMENTS

These agreements are commonly encountered in sports practice. Merchandising and endorsement provide a useful way of exploiting the names and goodwill associated with sport. An endorsement agreement usually relates to an individual sportsman's use and approbation of a particular company's product, whereas a merchandising agreement permits a company to manufacture and sell products using a particular brand name. The brand name may be that of an event or a team or individual participant in that event.

The terms of these agreements are beyond the scope of this work.

22.8 BROADCAST SPONSORSHIP

22.8.1 An introduction to television sponsorship – the Broadcasting Act 1990

The Broadcasting Act 1990 introduced a new regime allowing sponsorship of television broadcasts. The Act required the ITC to draw up (and, from time to time, to review) a code which sets standards and guidelines for the sponsorship of television programmes. This is the ITC Code of Programme Sponsorship ('the Code'). At the time of writing, the Code is under review, but a new code has not been adapted.

Whilst the Code does not provide for any particular form of agreement, it does dictate the rights which can be granted by broadcasters and producers. Television companies, sponsors, event organisers and programme producers must have regard to its provisions. The Code applies to all television services licensed by the ITC under the Act and thus covers the commercial stations – ITV, Channel 4, Channel 5, GMTV, and satellite services. It is not possible to sponsor any BBC programming. Compliance with the Code is a requirement of an ITC licence. This makes it important for licensees to ensure compliance not just by their own employees and producers but also by outside producers, and production companies.

A failure to comply with the Code may result in the imposition of a fine or, in extreme circumstances, the revocation of a company's licence. Thus, sponsors and producers should consult the relevant licensee before entering any agreements. At the very least, this should ensure that sponsorship which does not comply with the Code has to be withdrawn.

BIBLIOGRAPHY

This book is designed to provide an introduction to the areas of law commonly dealt with by solicitors working for the media and entertainment industry. Inevitably, in a work of this size, many important areas are considered merely in outline. The following books and periodicals should be consulted for further detail as relevant:

Robertson and Nicol *Media Law* (Sweet & Maxwell, 1999)
R. Baker *Media Law* (Routledge, 1995)
P. Carey *Media Law* 2nd edn (Sweet & Maxwell, 1999)
P. Carey and R. Verow *Media and Entertainment: The Law and Business* (Jordans, 1998)
Gately on Libel & Slander (Sweet & Maxwell, loose-leaf)
R. Bagehot *Sales Promotion and Advertising* (Sweet & Maxwell, 1993)
M. Henry *Publishing and Multimedia Law* (Butterworths, 1994)
V. Nelson *The Law of Entertainment and Broadcasting* (Sweet & Maxwell, 1997)
M. Flint *A User's Guide to Copyright* 5th edn (Butterworths, 2000)
Holyoak and Torremans *Intellectual Property Law* 3rd edn (Butterworths, 2001)
R. Verow, C. Laurence and P. McCormick *Sport, Business and the Law* (Jordans, 1999)
Entertainment Law Review (Sweet & Maxwell)
Entertainment & Media Law Reports (Sweet & Maxwell)
British Code of Advertising Practice
British Code of Sales Promotion Practice
ITC Code of Advertising Standards & Practice
ITC Sponsorship Code

INDEX

References are to paragraph numbers.

Abroad
   see also EC
   advertising   20.4
   copyright protection   1.2.1
   distribution of TV programmes   15.2.1, 18.2.2
   use of music   6.2.4
Account of profits   21.3.2, 21.4.3
Accounts
   distribution agreement, provision in   18.2.2
   management agreement, provision in   7.3.4, 7.5.3
   recording contract, provision in   8.10.1
Acquiescence   5.4.4
Actor   15.4.1
   see also Performance, rights in
   Equity, and   15.2.2, 15.4.1
   film   15.4.1
   'first call' periods   15.4.1
   representative bodies for   15.2.2
   television programme, in, *see* Programme production (film and TV)
   terms of engagement   15.4.1
   use fees   17.4, *see also* Performance, rights in
Adaptation, *see* Copyright; Copyright infringement
Advance
   distributor, by   16.2.3, 16.2.8
   management agreement, provision in   7.4.6
   recording contract, *see* Recording contract
Advertising   19.1 *et seq*, 20.1 *et seq*, 21.1 *et seq*
   see also Promotion
   alcoholic drinks   20.3.2
   Advertising Standards Authority   20.3.1, 21.6.9
   agency   19.4
      contract with client   19.4.2
      employee and copyright   21.5.1
      use of   19.4.1
   British Codes of Advertising and Sales Promotion   20.3.1, 20.3.2, 21.6.7
   broadcast   19.5.2, 19.5.3, 20.2
      breaks, rules on number, length   20.2.3
      children's programmes, during   20.2.3
      Code   19.5.2, 20.2.1, 20.4, 21.6.7
      complaints to ITC   20.2.2
      music, performer's income for use   8.8.5
      refusal, where misleading   21.2.2
      separation from programmes   20.2.1, 20.2.3
   children, and   20.2.3, 20.3.2
   'clearing'   21.8
   Committee of Advertising Practice   20.3.2
   comparative   21.4.4, 21.6
      copyright, and   21.6.5
      defamation   21.6.6
      definition   21.6.2
      EC draft Directive   21.6.1, 21.6.3, 21.6.8
      indirect or direct   21.6.2
      passing off, and   21.6.4
      representation or puff   21.7.4
      trade marks, and   21.6.3
      when permitted   21.4.4
   complaints   21.2.2, 21.3.1, 21.2.3
   contract law, and   21.7
      acceptance   21.7.3
      invitation to treat, when advert is   21.7.2
      offer, when advert is   21.7.2
   copyright work, use of   21.5.1
   descriptions   21.2.2, 21.2.3
   distribution agreement, in   18.2.2
   'knocking copy'   21.6.1
   'legal, decent, honest and truthful'   20.2.1, 20.3.2
   meaning   19.2
   medium, choice of   19.3
   misleading   21.2.3
   misrepresentation   21.7.4
   moral rights   21.5.2, 21.8
   newspaper, poster, leaflets etc   20.3
      complaints   20.3.1
      general rules in Code   20.3.2
   prices   20.4, 21.2.4
   'puff'   21.7.4
   radio   20.2.1
   self-regulation   20.1 *et seq*
   subliminal   19.5.3
   television   19.5
      ITC Code   19.5.2, 20.2.1, 20.4, 21.6.7
      ITC control   19.5.2, 19.5.3, *see also* 'broadcast' above
   trade descriptions, and   21.2
   trade mark, use of identical an offence   21.4.2, *see also* Trade mark
   video   20.3
Advice (professional)
   contract, on   5.4.3
      recording contract   8.1.1
   manager's agreement, on   7.3.2
Agent
   advertising, *see* Advertising
   manager as   7.3.2, 7.6
      authority, nature and extent   7.3.3
      implied duties   7.3.4
      see also Musician(s)
   musician, for   7.4.6
   television programme, for sale of   16.2.6

Agent *cont*
    tour and venue booking, for   7.4.6
Agreement, *see* Contract
Aircraft
    distribution agreement covering   18.2.1
Album, *see* CD; Record; Recording contract; Tape
Alcohol
    Code for advertisers   20.3.2
Architecture   1.4.5, 17.2.1, *see also* Copyright
Artistic craftsmanship, work of
    copyright in   1.4.5
        incidental inclusion   17.2.1
Artistic work
    copyright in   1.3, 1.4.5, *see also* Copyright
Assignment
    copyright of, *see* Copyright
Audio recording, *see* Sound recording
Audio-visual product
    see also Multi-media; Video recording
    recording contract, in   8.2.1
Author
    see Book; Copyright; Moral rights

Band, *see* Musician(s); Recording contract
Blasphemy   12.2
    restricted to Anglican faith   12.2
Book
    copyright in   1.4, 1.4.2, *see also* Copyright
        manuscript ownership compared   1.3
    dramatisation
        copyright, and   15.3.4, 17.2.1
British Board of Film Classification   11.7, 11.8, 17.6
    categories   18.3.2
British Broadcasting Corporation   15.2, 15.2.1
    complaints to   17.6
    income   15.2.1
    Worldwide   15.2.1
British Phonographic Industry Ltd   6.2.5, 6.3.1, 6.3.4
    cost of launching new single   8.6
    MCPS contract with   6.2.5
Broadcast
    see also Cable transmission; Contempt of court; Film; Radio; Satellite television; Television
    advertising   19.5.2, 19.5.3, 20.2, 20.4
    bodies involved in   15.2
    content clearance   17.6
    copyright in   1.3, 1.5, *see also* Copyright
        'author'   1.9.3
        definition for   1.5.3
    obscenity offences, and   11.6, 11.8
    performance, of, rights of performer   4.3, *see also* Performance, rights in
    performing rights, and, *see* Musical work

programme production, *see* Programme production (film and TV)
racial hatred offence, and   12.1.2
rights clearance, *see* Rights clearance
song, use on   6.1, 6.2.2, *see also* Musical work
sponsorship
    ITC Code   22.8
    see also Sponsorship: television Code
sports event, coverage of   22.1, 22.3.1, 22.6.2
Broadcasting, Entertainment, Cinematographic and Theatre Union   15.2.2, 15.4.3
Building   1.4.5, 17.2.1, *see also* Copyright

CD
    dealer price and uplift   8.9
    defamation on   9.3
    packaging costs   8.9.1
    recording contract, in   8.2.1, *see also* Recording contract
    royalty on   8.9–8.9.2, 8.8
CD-ROM   1.5.2, 1.12, 1.12.5, 8.2.1
Cable transmission
    see also Broadcast; Programme production (film and TV)
    advertising breaks   20.2.3
    copyright, and   1.5
        'cable programme'   1.5.4
    distribution agreement for   18.2
    obscenity offences, and   11.6, 11.8
Charity
    appeal, not counted as advert time   20.2.3
Child
    cinema licensing, and   18.3.1
    film classification   18.3.2
    indecent photo of   11.9
    obscenity, and   11.9
    television, and   11.6
        advertising breaks   20.2.3
    video classification   18.4.4
Choreographer   17.3
Cinema, *see* Film
Colour
    trade mark, as   21.4.1
Company, limited
    musician's use of, *see* Musician(s)
    production (film/TV)   16.2.2
Comparative advertising   21.4.4, 21.6
    infringing trade mark, test for   21.6.3
Compilations   8.8.3
Complaints   20.2.2
Composer   6.2.1–6.2.4
    see also Music publishing contract; Musician(s)
    assignment of rights   6.2.2
    commissioned work   17.2.1
    musician, also is, royalties for   8.7.1

Composer *cont*
    publishing agreement, *see* Music publishing contract
    recording contract for   15.4.4, *see also* Recording contract
    television programme or film, music, of   15.4.4
Computer
    copyright of games, programmes etc   1.5.2, 1.12, 1.12.5
        no integrity right   3.3.2
        no paternity right   3.2.2
        rental of copy   2.4
    data protection   13.2.1, 13.2.3
    songs and music in games   6.1
    sound recording contract, and   8.2.1
Computer-generated works   3.2.2, 3.3.2
Confidence, breach of, *see* Privacy
    alternative to defamation injunction application, as   9.8.2
Confidentiality agreement
    programme idea, for   15.3.1
Consumer
    misleading price information to   21.2.4
Contempt of court   14.1–14.4
    appellate proceedings   14.2.2
    civil proceedings, and   14.2.2
    common law   14.3
    criminal proceedings, and   14.2.2
    fair and accurate report of legal proceedings   14.2.1
    interference with course of justice   14.2
        'active proceedings'   14.2.2
        discussion of public affairs   14.2.5
    innocent publication   14.2.4
        'substantial risk' of serious prejudice   14.2.1
    journalists' sources, protection of, and   13.1.4
    jury deliberations, publication of   14.4
    postponement orders   14.2.3
    strict liability offence   14.2
        defences   14.2.4, 14.2.5
    use of law of   14.1
Contents clearance   17.1, 17.6
    producer's warranty and indemnity   17.6
Contract (commercial)   5.1 *et seq*
    advertising agency, and   19.4.2, 21.7, *see also* Advertising
    assignment
        copyright, of, *see* Copyright
    breach   5.5.1
        inducement to   5.5.1
        remedies   5.4.4
    capacity   5.4.2
    composer entering   6.1, *see also* Music publishing contract
    copyright licence or assignment, *see* Copyright
    damages   5.5.1
    duration   5.2.5
    exclusivity   5.2.4, 5.4.4
    force majeure clause   5.5.3
    form of   5.2.1
    formation   5.3.1
    frustration   5.5.3
    independent advice on   5.3.5
    legal restraints   5.2.4, 5.2.5
    licence, *see* Copyright
    lock-in/lock-out agreements   5.3.2
    merchandising   22.7
    minors   5.4.2
    moral rights, dealing with   3.5
    multi-media, for   5.3.1
    negative covenants   5.5.2
    negotiation   5.2.1, 5.3.1
    option clause   5.2.5
    parties   5.2.2
    payment   5.2.7
    performer entering   6.1
    personal services, for   5.2.4, 5.2.5
    pre-emption right   5.2.1
    production (TV programme)   16.3, *see also* Programme production (film and TV)
    programme production, for   15.1
    recording, *see* Recording contract
    renegotiation of terms   5.3.3
    restraint of trade clause, *see* Restraint of trade
    rights clause   5.3.1
    sponsorship   22.2, *see also* Sponsorship
    termination   5.5.3
    terms   5.2, 5.3.1
        minimum terms agreements   5.3.5
    territory   5.2.5
    undue influence   5.3.5, 5.4.3, 7.3.2
Copyright   1.1 *et seq*
    adaptation   2.8, 3.3.1
    advertisements   1.4.2, 21.5, 21.6.5
    artistic work   1.4, 1.4.5, *see also* 'literary etc works' below
    assignment   1.11.3, 1.12
        backer of TV programme, to   15.3.3
        construction   1.12.5
        drafting   1.12.3, 1.12.4
        form of   1.12.2, 1.12.3
        future copyright, of   1.12.1
        limits to   1.12.1
        meaning   1.12.1
        partial   1.12.1
        property right, as   1.12.3
        termination   17.2
        title guarantee   1.12.4
        warranties   1.12.4
    author   1.7, 1.7.1
        definition   1.9, 1.9.1
        first owner of copyright, as   1.9, 1.10, 1.11.1
        joint   1.9.1, 1.10

Copyright *cont*
    author *cont*
        paternity and integrity rights, *see* Moral rights
        'qualifying person'   1.7.1
        unknown   1.8.1
    author's work   1.5
    Berne Convention   1.2.1
    breach, *see* Copyright infringement
    broadcast and cable transmission   1.3, 1.5
        'author'   1.9.3
        broadcasting as infringement   2.7
        copying as infringement   2.3.2
        definitions for   1.5.3, 1.5.4
        ownership   1.11.4
        period of protection   1.8.3
    cable programme   1.5, 1.5.4
    clearance   17.2, 18.3, *see also* Rights clearance
    compilation   1.4.1, 1.4.2
        skill, discrimination and judgement, use of   1.4.2
        TV listing   1.4.2
    conditions for protection   1.7
    country of first publication   1.7.2
    databases   1.5
        copyright protection   1.5.4
        Database Right, the   1.5.5
        definition   1.5.3
        regulations   1.5.2
    deletion or mutilation   3.3.1
    derivative work   1.1, 1.5
    dictionary, encyclopedia etc, exception to moral rights   3.2.2, 3.3.2
    dramatic work   1.4, 1.4.3, *see also* 'literary etc works' below
    dress design pattern   1.4.5
    duration   1.8, 1.10
    employee, position of   1.11.2, 3.2.2
        advertising agency, and   21.5.1
        competing work in spare time   1.11.2
        'in course of employment'   1.11.2
    engineering drawing   1.4.5
    exclusive rights of owner   2.2.1, *see also* Copyright infringement
        list of   2.2.1
    exploitation   1.1, 1.12, *see also* 'assignment' above, 'licensing' below
        insolvency, and   1.12.5
        producer, by   17.2.1
        see also Programme production (film and TV)
    film   1.3, 1.5.2
        'author'   1.9.2
        copying   2.3.2
        false attribution   3.4
        ownership   1.11.4
        period of protection   1.8.2
        privacy of person commissioning   3.7

    infringement, *see* Copyright infringement
    international element   1.2.1
    legislation   1.2
    licensing   1.4.3, 1.11.3, 1.12
        bare licence   1.12.3
        construction   1.12.5
        distinguished from assignment   1.12.3
        drafting   1.12.4
        employee, and   1.11.2
        exclusive or non-exclusive   1.12.3
        implied   1.12.3
        limits to   1.12.1
        meaning   1.12.1
        partial   1.12.1
        royalty payments   1.12.3, 1.12.5
        sole licence   1.12.3
        termination   17.2
        title guarantee   1.12.4
        types of   1.12.3
        use of licence   1.12.3
        warranties   1.12.4
        written agreement   1.11.3
    literary etc works   1.3, 1.4
        adaptations   2.8, 17.2.1
        anonymous   1.8.1
        'artistic work'   1.4.5
        author   1.9.1, *see also* 'author' above
        characters   1.4.2
        commissioned   17.2.1, *see also* Programme production (film and TV)
        compilations, *see* 'compilation' above
        copying or performing, *see* Copyright infringement
        current events reporting   1.4.2, 2.10.2
        'dramatic work'   1.4.3
        expression of ideas protected   1.4.1, 1.4.2
        false attribution   3.4
        integrity right   2.3
        'literary work'   1.4.2
        'musical work'   1.4.4
        'originality'   1.4.1
        paternity right   3.2
        period of protection   1.8.1
        same story or information   1.4.2
        skill and effort   1.4.1
        titles   1.4.2
        two and three dimensional shift   1.4.5, 2.3.1
        writing, record in   1.4
    meaning   1.1
    moral rights, *see* Moral rights
    musical work   1.4, 1.4.4, *see also* 'literary etc works' above
    names   1.4.2
    newspaper publication   1.4.2, 2.10.2
        moral rights exceptions   3.2.2, 3.3.2
        photograph, use private   3.7

Copyright *cont*
  overlap with other intellectual property rights 1.1
  ownership 1.3, 1.11
    author as first owner 1.9, 1.10, 1.11.1
    authorship distinguished 1.9
    commissioned work 1.11.3
    employment, work made during 1.11.2
    joint 1.10
    rights of owner 1.5, 2.2.1, *see also* Copyright infringement
  performance
    infringement, as, *see* Copyright infringement
    rights of performers, *see* Performance, rights in
  personal property, form of 1.12
  photograph 1.4.5, 1.4.6
    author 1.9.2
    definition 1.4.6
  'publication' 1.7.2
  published editions, typographical arrangements of 1.3, 1.6
    'author' 1.9.4
    copying 2.3.3
    definition 1.6
    ownership 1.11.4
    period of protection 1.8.4
  registration not required 1.3
  revisions 1.4.2
  revived 1.8.5
  Rome Convention 1.2.1
  royalties 1.12.3, 1.12.3
  slogans 1.4.2
  sound recording 1.5, 1.5.1, 8.2.2
    'author' 1.9.2
    ownership 1.11.4
    period of protection 1.8.2
  subject matter 1.3, *see also* 'literary etc works' above
  subsistence 1.3, 1.7
  television 1.4.1, 1.4.2, 1.4.3
    adaptation for 1.12.1
    news presenter, *see* Performance, rights in
    news reporting 1.4.2, 2.10.2
    programme listings 1.4.2
    programme production, and 15.3.1, 15.3.3, 15.3.4, 18.3, *see also* 'broadcast and cable transmission' above
  underlying rights 1.5, 15.3.4, 17.2.1
  Universal Copyright Convention 1.2.1
Copyright infringement 2.1 *et seq*
  adaptation 2.8
    methods 2.8
    'writing' 2.8
  authorship, presumption of, and proceedings for 2.9.6
  broadcast or cable programme
    broadcasting or inclusion in cable service 2.7
    copying or performing 2.3.2, 2.6
  civil remedies 2.11
  copying 2.2.1–2.3.3
  criminal 2.1, 2.9, 2.12
  criticism, use of material in 2.10.2
  defences 2.10
  distributing copies 2.9.2
  distributor to notify rights owner 18.2.2
  educational establishments 2.10.2
  electronic storage 2.3.1
  exhaustion of rights 2.9.6
  extracts 2.2.2
  fair dealing 2.10.2, 17.2.1
  film 2.3.2, 2.4, 2.6, 2.9.5, 2.9.6
    authorship 1.9.2
    director's and author's right to be identified 3.2
    privacy, right to 3.1, 3.7
  guidelines 2.2.2
  importing copies 2.9.1, 2.9.6
  incidental inclusion 2.2.2, 2.10.3, 17.2.1
  'infringing copy' 2.9.6
  issuing copies to public 2.4
  librarians 2.10.2
  limited rights granted, where 17.2.1
  literary, artistic, dramatic and musical works 2.2.1, 2.3.1, 2.10.4
    two-dimensional/three dimensional copying 3.3.1
  means for making copies, providing 2.9.3, 2.9.6
  music 2.6, 2.8, 2.10.3
    authorship 1.9.2
  news reporting 2.10.2
  parody 2.2.2
  performance 2.6
    apparatus for, providing 2.9.5, 2.9.6
    permitting use of premises for 2.9.4, 2.9.6
    'public' 2.6
  permitted acts 2.10
  possessing or dealing with copies 2.9.2, 2.9.6
  primary 2.1–2.8
  public interest 2.10.5
  published work, typographical arrangement 2.3.3
  rental or lending of copies to the public 2.5
  research and private study 2.10.2
  restricted acts, list 2.2.1
  reviews, use of material in 2.10.2
  sampling 2.2.2
  secondary 2.1, 2.9
    EC, and 2.9.6
  sound recording 2.4, 2.6, 2.9.5, 2.9.6
  'substantial' part of whole 2.2.1, 2.2.2

Copyright infringement *cont*
   television programme   2.3.2
   translation   2.8
   transmitting work by telecommunication system   2.9.3
   twin deck recorders   2.9.3
Court proceedings
   see also Contempt of court; Reporting restrictions, judicial reports, and absolute privilege   9.7.3

DAT disc   8.2.1
Damages
   contract breach, for   5.5.1
   defamation, for   9.8.1
   passing off, for   21.3.2
   performers' rights, for breach of   4.6.1
   trade mark infringement, for   21.4.3
Dance   1.4.3, *see also* Copyright
Data protection, *see* Privacy
Defamation   9.1 *et seq*
   apology   9.7.6, 9.9.3
      qualified offer of amends   9.7.6
   audience, relevance of size of   9.8.1
   author or editor, showing that not   9.7.5
   broadcaster of live programme, defence for   9.7.5
   class, of, not possible   9.6
   comparative advertising, and   21.6.6
   complexity, length and delay of actions   9.9.1
   context   9.4
   correction and compensation offer   9.7.6
   court for action   9.2, 9.5.2
   crime, as   9.3
   damages   9.7.6, 9.8.1, 9.9.7
      mitigation   9.9.4
      reduction in   9.8.1
   defamatory meaning
      early ruling on   9.9.5
      HL guidance   9.5
      jury decision on   9.5.2
      reasonable reader   9.5
      words capable of   9.5
   defences   9.7
      absolute privilege   9.7.3
      consent   9.7.7
      fair comment   9.7.2
      innocent dissemination, new law   9.7.5
      justification   9.7.1
      offer of amends, new law   9.7.6, 9.9.3
      qualified privilege   9.7.4
   definition   9.2
   dismissal of claim   9.9.5
   distributors   9.7.5
   duty, statement made under, where receiver duty to read   9.7.4
   European Convention for the Protection of Human Rights, and   9.8.2
   freedom of expression   9.7.2
   fresh publication   9.4
   injunction, use to prevent   9.8.2, 21.6.6
   innuendo   9.5.1, 9.7.1
      additional to plain meaning defamation   9.5.1
      pleadings in support   9.5.1
   judge alone trying case   9.9.7
   judicial proceedings, statements made in and reports of   9.7.3
   jurisdiction   9.9.2
   jury
      function of   9.5.2
      right to   9.2, 9.9.7
   libel   9.3
   litigation
      adverse effects of   9.9.1
      expense of   9.9.1, 9.9.7
      forum for   9.9.2
   local government election candidate, statement by   9.7.4
   Lucas-Box particulars   9.7.1, 9.9.5
   malicious falsehood distinguished   10.1, 10.3
   malicious motive, relevance   9.7.1, 9.7.2, 9.8.1
      'malice', and 'fair comment'   9.7.2
      qualified privilege, and   9.7.4
   named person   9.6
   opinion   9.7.2
   Parliament, statements made in and reports of   9.7.3
   particulars of claim, sample   6.11.2
   payment into court   9.9.6
      acceptance of, effect of   9.9.6
   plaintiff, words capable of referring to   9.6
   proceedings, reports of   9.7.3, 9.7.4
   public funding not available   9.1, 9.2
   public interest   9.7.2
   'publication'   9.4
   publisher, showing that not   9.7.5
   remedies   9.8
   reputation, damage to   9.2, 10.2, 10.3
   settlement   9.9.3, 9.9.4, 9.9.6
   slander   9.3
   statement in open court   9.9.4
   summary of disposal of claim   9.10
   tape recordings and CDs   9.3
   trade libel   21.6.6
   true statement   9.7.1
Designer (set)   17.3
Digital technology, *see* CD, CD-ROM etc
Director (film)   15.4.2, 17.3, *see also* Programme production (film and TV)
Directors' Guild of Great Britain   15.2.2
Disclosure of information, *see* Confidence, breach of

Index

Distribution, *see* Programme production (film and TV)
Dramatic work
   copyright in   1.3, 1.4.3, *see also* Copyright
Drugs, *see* Medicines

EC
   broadcasting Directive   20.2.3
   comparative advertising draft Directive
      21.6.1, 21.6.3, 21.6.8
   copyright infringement, and   2.9.6
   human rights   9.8.1, 9.8.2
   performers' rights, and   4.2.3
   rental and lending rights Directive   8.2.4, 8.8.5, 15.2.2, 17.5
   restrictions imposed on contract by   5.2.4, 5.2.5
   trade mark, and exhaustion of rights   21.4.4
   transfrontier television   11.6, 20.2.3
Employee
   copyright, and   1.11.2, 3.2.2
      advertising agency   21.5.1
      photographs   3.7
Endorsement agreement   22.7
European Convention for the Protection of Human Rights   9.8.1, 9.8.2
   contempt of court, and   14.1
European Convention on Transfrontier Television   11.6, 20.2.3

Fair Trading, Office of
   complaint on advert referred to   20.3.1, 21.2.3
Film   15.1 *et seq*
   actor, engagement, credits etc   15.4.1, 16.3.12
   broadcast   17.2.1
   censorship or certification, general   18.2.2
   cinema, shown in
      British Board of Film Classification   11.7, 17.6, 18.3.2
      distribution agreement for   18.2.1
      local authority licensing   11.7, 18.3.1
      obscenity, and   11.7
   clearance   17.3, 18.3, *see also* Rights clearance
   copyright in, *see* Copyright; Copyright infringement
   copyright works used in   17.3, 18.3
   defamation in   9.3
   designer's rights (set)   17.3
   director   15.4.2
   distribution   18.1, 18.3
   excerpt, use of   17.2.1
   indecency and children   11.9
   insurance   18.2.2
   producer   15.4.2
   production and pre-production, *see* Programme production (film and TV)
   script   15.3.4, 16.3.4
   soundtrack   6.2.4, 17.2.1, 17.3
   special effects personnel   17.3
   treatment or idea for, protection of   13.1.2, 15.3
   video, *see* Video recording
Foreign language version   17.3, *see also* Abroad
Forfeiture
   order for
      obscene article, of   11.1, 11.3
      racial hatred, of material etc stirring up   12.1.2

Goods
   see also Merchandising
   misdescription of   21.2.2
   misrepresentation as to, as passing off   21.3.1
   shape or packaging, as trade mark   21.4.1
      offence to apply identical sign   21.4.2
   trade description, *see* Trade description
Goodwill
   damage to, *see* Defamation; Passing off
Group, *see* Musician(s); Recording contract

Hotel
   use of product in   6.2.4, 6.2.5, 18.2.1
Husband and wife
   joint owners of copyright   1.10
   undue influence, and lenders   5.4.3

Import
   copyright infringement, and   2.9.1, 2.9.6,
Indecency
   gross, with child   11.9
   photograph of child, and   11.9
Independent Television   15.2.1
   finance   15.2.1
   Network Centre   15.2.1
Independent Television Commission   19.5.2, 19.5.3
   Code of Advertising Standards   19.5.2, 20.2.1, 20.4
Injunction
   contract, for breach of   5.5.2
   copyright, for breach of, *see* Copyright infringement
   defamation, to prevent   9.8.2, 21.6.6
   moral rights, for breach of   3.5
   passing off, to prevent   21.3.2

Injunction *cont*
    performers' rights, for breach of   4.6.1
    trade mark infringement, for   21.4.3
Insurance   16.3.10, 17.6
    film, of   18.2.2
    musician, for   7.3.2
Intellectual property, *see* Copyright
Investor
    film, in   16.2.2, 16.3.2

Jingle
    trade mark, as   21.4.1
Journalist, *see* Contempt of court; Newspaper; Reporting restrictions; Television
Jury deliberations
    publication of, as contempt   14.4

Laches, doctrine of   5.4.4
Letter of intent   5.3.4
Libel, *see* Defamation
Libel, trade   21.4.4, 21.6.6
Licence
    copyright, of, *see* Copyright
Literary work
    copyright in   1.3, *see also* Copyright; Copyright infringement
Lock-in agreement   5.3.2

Magazine   11.2.2, 19.2, *see also* Newspaper
Mail order
    royalties on sales   8.8.1
Malicious falsehood   10.1–10.3
    comparative advertising, and   21.6.6
    defamation distinguished   10.1, 10.3
    definition   10.2
    economic interests protected by   10.2
    legal aid for action   10.2.2
    'malice'   10.2.2
    special or actual damage   10.2, 10.2.3
        when proof not required   10.2.3
    trade libel   21.6.6
    untrue statement   10.2, 10.2.1
Manager
    see also Musician(s)
    commission   7.3.4, 7.4.2, 7.4.6, 8.6
    undue influence   5.4.3
Mark
    see also Trade mark
    misrepresentation as to, as passing off   21.3.1
Matrimonial and introduction service
    advertising on television   20.4

Mechanical Copyright Protection Society   6.2.2, 6.2.5
    contract with BPL   6.2.5
    royalties, administration of   8.5.3, 8.7.2, 8.9
Merchandising
    agreement   22.7
    musician, endorsement by   7.4.3, 7.4.6
    recording contract, separate agreement for   8.4.2
    television programme, financing   16.2.4
Mini disc   8.2.1
Minor
    contract with voidable   5.4.2
Misdescription
    trade, in course of   21.2.2
Misleading advert   21.2.3
Misrepresentation   21.7.4
Moral rights   2.9, 4.1 *et seq*
    advertising, and   21.5.2
    assignment not possible   3.1
    breach, remedies on   3.5
    clearance   17.3, *see also* Rights clearance
    derogatory treatment, right to object   3.1, 3.3
        exceptions   3.3.2
        meaning of 'derogatory treatment'   3.3.1
        waiver   17.3
    false attribution, right to object   3.1, 3.4
        'attribution'   3.4
    identification as author/director, right to   3.1, 3.2
        assertion of   3.2.1
        exceptions   3.2.2
        waiver for credit in agreed form   17.3
    integrity right   3.1, 3.3, 17.3
    joint authors   3.1
    paternity right   3.1, 3.2, 17.3
    photographs   3.7
    privacy right   3.1, 3.7
    waiver   3.1, 3.3.1, 3.6, 3.7
        form of   3.6
        need for   17.3
Multi-media   8.2.1, *see also* CD-ROM
Music publishing contract   6.1
    release   15.4.4, 17.2.1
    restraint of trade, and   5.4.4
Musical work
    see also Copyright; Copyright infringement; Performance, rights in
    commissioned   17.2.1
    composer, *see* Musician(s)
    copyright in   1.3, 1.4.4, 6.2.4
        composer as first owner   6.2.1
    equitable remuneration   6.5
    exploitation   6.1, 6.2.1, *see also* Recording contract
        Internet   6.2.6
    licensing   6.2
        blanket (PRS)   6.2.4

Musical work *cont*
  licensing *cont*
    MCPS   6.2.5
    Music Alliance, The   6.2.3
    pubs, concert halls, etc, for   6.2.4, 6.2.5
    synchronisation licence   17.2.1
  management agreement for, *see* Musician(s)
  mechanical rights   6.2.2, 6.2.5
  musician, *see* Musician(s)
  performance of   6.1
  performing rights   6.1, 6.2.2, 6.2.4
    inquiry of administration of   6.2.4
  Performing Rights Society   6.2.4
    fees   6.2.4
    function   6.2.4
    membership requirements   6.2.4
    overseas use, and   6.2.4
  permission to use   6.2.1
  publisher, role of   6.2.2
  record industry, *see* Sound recording
  recording   6.1, 6.2.5
    right distinguished from performing right   16.2.5
  royalties   6.2.4, 7.4.6
    'mechanical'   8.5.3
    record company, from   8.5.3, 8.7–8.9
  song   1.4.4, 1.10
    copyright and permission for use   6.2.2, 17.2.1
    lyrics   1.10, 6.1
    recording of, separate agreement for   17.2.1
    writer's permission to use   6.2.2
  video, on   6.3.1, 6.3.3
Musician(s)
  agent for   7.4.6
  business medium for, choice of   7.2
  composer
    copyright owner, as   6.1, 6.2.2
    income and royalties of   6.2.4, 7.4.6, 8.7.1, *see also* Recording contract
  group   7.1 *et seq*
    departure of member   7.4.7, 7.6, 8.11
    indemnification   7.6
    joint and several liability   7.6
    manager for, *see* 'management agreement' below
    partnership, ads   7.2
    recording contract provisions   8.11–8.13
    see also 'partnership' below
  individual   7.2
  insurance   7.3.2
  management agreement
    accounts and accountant   7.5.1, 7.5.3
    activities clause   7.4.3
    advances   7.4.6
    artist's obligations   7.6
    assignment of benefit of agreements, undertaking against   7.5.4
    boiler plate clauses   7.7
    breach   7.7
    duration   7.4.5
    ending   7.7
    exclusivity   7.4.2
    force majeure   7.7
    form of   7.4.1
    group, for, *see* 'group' above
    income for artist   7.4.6, 7.5.2
    independent, need for   7.3.2
    insolvency   7.7
    intellectual property right   7.5.4
    merchandise endorsement   7.4.3, 7.4.6
    payment obligations   7.5.2
    performance obligations   7.4.5
    producer, money paid to   7.4.6
    promotion of artist   7.3.2, 7.7
    renewal, provision for   7.4.5
    terms of   7.4.1, 7.7
    territory covered   7.4.4
    undue influence, and   7.3.2
    warranties   7.5
  manager   7.3
    account to artist   7.3.4, 7.5.3
    agent, as   7.3.2, 7.6
    agreement with, *see* 'management agreement' above
    appointment   7.3.1, 7.4.2
    authority   7.3.3, 7.4.6
    business expenses   7.4.6
    commission   7.3.4, 7.4.2, 7.4.6, 8.6
    confidential information, respect of   7.3.4
    duties   7.3.2, 7.3.4, 7.4.5
    functions   7.3.1, 7.3.2, 7.4.3
    good faith   7.3.4
    indemnity   7.3.4
    no conflicting agreements   7.5.4
    rights   7.3.4
    skill and care   7.3.4
    termination of appointment   7.3.4, 7.4.5, 7.4.7, 7.7
  merchandising   7.4.3, 7.4.6
  partnership, in   7.2
    dismissal, retirement etc   7.6, 8.11
  producer, artist as   7.4.6
  recording agreements, personal signing of   7.3.3, *see also* Recording contract
  rental rights (PAMRA)   6.5, 8.2.4, 8.8.5
  television programme or film, for   15.4.4
  tours   7.3.2, 7.4.6
  trade union for musicians   6.4
  usage rights (PPL)   6.3.2
Musicians' Union   6.4, 15.2.2
  film music fee, and   15.4.4
  membership and recording contract   8.4.2

Name
    copyright, and   1.4.2
    misrepresentation as to, as passing off   21.3.1
    recording contract, and   8.4.2
    trade mark, as   21.4.1
        use of own not infringement   21.4.4
National Lottery
    advertising on television   20.4
Newspaper
    advertising, *see* Advertising
    blasphemy prosecution, leave required   12.2
    contempt of court, *see* Contempt of court
    copyright, *see* Copyright
    court proceedings, reports of, *see* Reporting restrictions
    defamation in   9.4
        circulation figures, effect of   9.8.1
        correction or apology, effect of   9.9.3
        fair comment defence   9.7.2
        Parliamentary and judicial reports, and 9.7.3, 9.7.4, *see also* Defamation
    journalists' sources, protection of   13.1.4
Novel, *see* Book

Obscenity   11.1 *et seq*
    broadcast or cable programme   11.6, 11.8
    children
        audience, as   11.9
        gross indecency with, offence of   11.9
    cinema, film shown in   11.7
    criminal offences   11.1, 11.2, 11.3
        possession etc of obscene article for publication for gain   11.3
        publishing obscene article   11.2, 11.3
    defences   11.4
        innocent publication/possession   11.4.3
        'learning', meaning for public good defence   11.4.1
        public good justifying   11.4.1, 11.6
        'repulsive, filthy, loathsome or lewd' not obscene   11.2.3, 11.4.2
    definitions   11.2
        'article'   11.2.1
        'deprave and corrupt', tendency to   11.2, 11.2.3, 11.4.2
        likely reader   11.2.4
        possession or control of article 'for gain'   11.3
        'publication'   11.3
        'taken as a whole'   11.2.2
    forfeiture of offending article, order for   11.1, 11.3
    magazine article   11.2.2
    television programme   11.2.1, 11.3, 811.4.1, 11.6
    Code   11.6
        satellite broadcasts   11.6
    video recording, and   11.8
On-line exploitation   8.2.5, 8.8.5
Option
    clause in contract   5.2.4
    extending length of recording contract, for   8.3.2
    producer taking over writer's work   16.3.4
Overseas
    use of compositions   6.2.4

Parliamentary proceedings
    defamation, and   9.7.3, 9.7.4
Parliamentary reports   9.7.3
Partnership, *see* Musician(s)
Passing off   21.3
    action for, prerequisites for valid   21.3.1
    comparative advertising, and   21.6.4
    damage to plaintiff required   21.3.1
    defences   21.3.3
    misrepresentation examples   21.3.1
    name, and   21.3.1
    remedies   21.3.2
Performance   2.6
    see also Copyright infringement; Performance, rights in; Recording contract
    first   4.2.2
Performance, rights in   4.1 *et seq*
    broadcast/cable of performance   4.3.1
    consent of performer   4.3.1, 4.3.2, 17.4
        need for, in contract with performer   4.3.2
        Tribunal, from   4.7
    contract basis   4.1, 4.8
    damages   4.6.1
    defence to infringement action   4.7
    delivery or seizure of copies   4.6.1
    distinguished from performance right   4.1, 6.3.5
    duration   4.5
    educational establishment, and   4.7
    exploitation   4.8, 17.2.1
    fair dealing for criticism etc   4.7
    fees for use   17.2.1
    free public show   4.7
    import, dealing etc with illicit recording   4.3.1, 4.6.2
    incidental inclusion   4.7
    independence from copyright   4.1
    infringing acts   4.3.1
    injunction   4.6.1
    'performance'   4.2.2, 4.2.3
    performers' rights   4.3
    permitted acts   4.7
    personal nature of   4.5
    protection of, regime for   4.2

Performance, rights in *cont*
   qualifying individual and country   4.2.3
   record company, and   6.3.5
   recording contract, and   8.1.2
   recording of performance, or exploiting
      recording   4.3.1
      offence   4.6.2
   recording rights, rights of persons with   4.4, 18.4
   remedies for breach   4.6
      civil   4.6.1
      criminal   4.6.2
   remuneration   6.1
   rights created   4.2.1
   'substantial part'   4.3.1
Performing Registration Centre   6.3.2, 6.5
Performing Artists' Media Rights Association   6.5, 8.2.4, 8.8.5
Performing Rights Society   6.2.4
Phonographic Performance Ltd   6.3.1, 6.3.2
Photograph
   child, of
      indecent   11.9
   copyright in   1.4.5, 1.4.6
      'author' for   1.9.1
   infringing copyright in film etc   2.3.2
   privacy of person commissioning   3.1, 3.7
Political adverts   19.5.3, 20.4
Press, *see* Advertising; Contempt of court; Magazine; Newspaper; Reporting restrictions
Price
   misleading information on   21.2.4
Privacy   13.1–13.3
   alternative to defamation injunction application, as   9.8.2
   contract should cover   13.1.3
   data protection   13.2.1–113.2.8
      data processing   13.2.3
         conditions for   13.2.4
      data subjects, rights of   13.2.6
      manual records   13.2.2
      media exemption   13.2.7
      penalties   13.2.8
      sensitive data   13.2.5
   elements of   13.1.1
   employees of well-known personality   13.1.3
   human rights   13.3
   personal information   13.1.3
   protection of idea, and   13.1.2
   public knowledge, disclosure prevented until   13.1.1
   third party receiving information, position   13.1.1
Privilege   9.7.3, 9.7.4
Producer   8.8.6, 15.4.2, *see also* Programme production (film and TV)

rights and contents clearance   17.1 *et seq*, *see also* Rights clearance
Product placement
   ITC Code prohibits   16.2.4
Production agreement   15.1
Production company
   see also Programme production (film and TV)
   finance raising   15.1
   independent, use of   15.1
Production costs   8.5.2
Programme production (film and TV)
   abandonment of project   16.3.5
   actors   15.2.2, 15.4.1
      casting   16.3.7
      credits   16.3.12
      see also Performance, rights in
   advertising expenses   18.2.2
   broadcasting bodies   15.2, 15.2.1
      BBC   15.2.1
      Channel 4   15.2.1
      ITV   15.2.1
   censorship fees   18.2.2
   commissioned works   15.2.1, 15.3.4, 16.2.1
      delivery to commissioner   16.3.7
      editing approval, commisioner's right   16.3.11
      literary work   17.2.1
      music   17.2.1
      payment by commissioner   16.3.8
   content clearance   17.6
   contracts
      forms of   15.1
      production agreement   15.1
   copyright assignment or licence   15.3.3, 16.2.5
      apportionment   16.3.4
      copies, provision for   18.2.2
      distributor entering   16.3.2, 18.2.2
      editing and cutting, provision for   18.2.2
      existing works   15.3.4, 17.2.1
      new works   15.3.4, 16.2.1, 17.2.1
      public domain material, and   15.3.4
      sub-licence of rights, provision for   18.2.2
   copyright protection and confidentiality (ideas etc)   15.3.1–15.3.4
   credits   16.3.11, 17.3, 18.2.2
   development   15.1, 15.3
      agreement   15.3.3
   directors   15.2.2, 15.4.2, 16.3.7
      moral rights   17.3
   distribution   17.1–17.6, 18.1 *et seq*
      accounting   18.2.2
      agreement   16.3.2, 16.3.3, 18.2.2
      films (cinema)   18.3
      specialist company arranging   18.2.1
      termination of licence for   18.2.2
      video recordings   18.4
   distributor   18.2

Programme production (film and TV) *cont*
  distributor *cont*
    advance   16.2.3, 16.2.8
    commission   18.2.2
    discounting advances   16.2.3
    expenses   16.2.7, 18.2.2
    infringement notification   18.2.2
    obligations   18.2.2
    payment to rights owner   18.2.2
    pre-purchase of rights by   16.2.3, 16.3.2, 16.3.5
    sales agent finding   16.2.6
    sub-distributor   18.2.2
    warranties by   18.2.2
  editing   16.3.11, 18.2.2
  exclusive rights, grant of in agreement   18.2.2
  exploitation   15.1, 16.2, 17.1–17.6, 18.1–18.5
    limited rights   17.2.1
    see also 'distribution' above
  fees and commissions   16.3.9
  finance   15.1, 15.2.2, 15.3.3, 16.1, 16.3.2
    budgeting   15.4.2, 16.3.6
    cash-flow   16.1, 16.2.3, 16.3.2
    deferments   16.2.7
    example   16.2.8
    exceeding budget   16.3.5
    investors, from   16.2.2, 16.3.2
    full commission funding   16.2.1, 16.3.2
    lender   16.2.2
    loan and other agreements   16.2.8
    merchandising, from   16.2.4
    methods   16.2
    'net profits'   16.2.7
    repayment of advances   16.2.8
    sale of rights generating income   16.2.5
    sponsor, from   16.2.4
  financiers, *see* 'finance' above and 'production agreement' below
  force majeure   16.3.5
  formats   15.3.1
  hiring   15.1, 15.4, 16.3.7
  ideas
    backer   15.3.3
    developing   15.3.3
    protecting   15.3.1
  independent production companies   15.1, 15.2.2, 16.2
  insurance   16.3.10, 17.6, 18.2.2
  investment   16.2.2, 16.3.2
  lawyer's involvement   15.1, 16.1, 17.6
  licences, *see* 'copyright assignment or licence' above
  musicians   15.2.2
  option, producer taking over writer's work   15.3.4
  PACT   15.2.2, 15.3.3, 15.3.4
  performers' rights   17.1
  personnel   15.4
  producer   15.4.2, 16.2, 16.3.2
    insolvency   16.3.5
  production agreement   16.3
    breach   16.3.5
    clearances   16.3.9, 17.1 *et seq*, *see also* 'copyright assignment' above
    co-production   16.3.2
    credit obligations   16.3.12
    financial matters in   16.3.6
    indemnity of licensee and distributor   16.3.8
    parties   16.3.3
    programme specification   16.3.7
    reason for   16.3.1
    termination   16.3.5
    warranties   16.3.8
  production matters   16.1–16.3
  rental rights, deemed assignment   17.5
  rights clearance, *see* Rights clearance
  script   15.3.4, 16.3.7
  stages of   15.1
  take-over   16.3.5, 16.3.6
  technical staff   15.4.3
  titles   16.3.12
  underlying rights   15.3.4, 17.2.1
  unions and guilds   15.2.2
  writers   15.2.2, 15.3.4, 17.3
Promotion
  see also Sponsorship
  artist, of, manager's duty   7.3.2, 7.7
  record company, by   6.3, 8.4.2, 8.5.1, 8.5.4, *see also* Recording contract
Public interest
  defamation, and   9.7.2

Racial hatred   12.1
  broadcast material   12.1.2, 12.1.3
  criminal offences   12.1.2
  defences   12.1.3
  definition   12.1.1
  distribution of material   12.1.2
  ethnic, meaning of   12.1.1
  forfeiture of material   12.1.2
  non-broadcast material   12.1.2, 12.1.3
  threatening, abusive or insulting words or behaviour   12.1.2
  written material   12.1.2
Radio   6.2.4
  see also Broadcast
  advertising   20.2.1
Record
  see also Recording contract; Sound recording
  budget line labels   8.8.2
  compilations   8.8.3

Record *cont*
    copyright   6.3.1
    dealer price and uplift   8.9
    LPs and singles, covering in contract   8.2.1
    mail order   8.8.1
    organisations involved with industry   6.3.2–6.3.4, 6.4, 6.5
    phasing out of vinyl   8.9.1
    production costs   8.5.2
    releasing and promoting   6.3, 8.5.1, 8.5.4
    royalty on   8.8.1, 8.9–8.9.2, *see also* Royalties
Record club
    royalties on sale through   8.8.1
Record company
    see also Sound recording
    performers' rights, and   6.3.5
    royalties on copyright works ('mechanical royalty')   8.5.3
Recording
    contract, *see* Recording contract
    exclusive rights, rights of person with   4.4
    performance, of, *see* Performance, rights in
    sound, *see* Sound recording
Recording contract   6.3.5, 8.1 *et seq*
    accounts, keeping   8.10.1
    advance   8.1.2, 8.3.2, 8.6
        cross-collateralisation   8.6
            meaning   8.6
            size of   8.6
    advice on   8.1.1, 8.2.5
    choice of company   8.1.1
        record company or independent production company   8.1.1
    confidentiality   8.4.2
    consent   8.1.2, 17.4
    contractual matters   8.2.5
    costs
        music publishing royalties, of   8.5.3
        recording, of   8.5.2
        see also 'promotion' below
    delivery under, time for, delay etc   8.3.1
    duration   8.3
        fixed term   8.3.1
        minimum commitment   8.3.1
        option to extend   8.3.2, 8.5.1, 8.6
    exclusive   8.1.2, 8.4.2
    exploitation, company's commitment   8.5.1
    fee or incentive payment   8.6
    funding   8.5.1
    group, provision for member leaving   8.11, 8.12
        going solo   8.11.2
        income after departure   8.11.3
        notice requirement   8.11.2
    merchandising rights, separate agreement for   8.4.2
    name of artist   8.4.2
    need for   8.1.1
    net sales, and royalties   8.9.2
    obligations
        artist, of   8.4.2
        company, of   8.6, 8.10.1, 8.13
    on-line distribution   8.2.1, 8.8.5
    overseas release   8.5.1
        royalties on   8.8.4
    performers' rights   8.1.2, 8.2.5
        qualifying person for protection, artist as   8.4.2
    promotion   8.4.2, 8.5.1, 8.5.4
        cost of   8.5.3
        free releases to industry   8.9.3
        live appearances, etc   8.5.4
        video for   8.5.4
    publicity   8.5.1
    release of artist   8.12, 8.13
    release of recordings   8.6
        no release by company   8.5.1
        quality, time etc   8.5.1
        unsuccessful   8.8.5
    rental rights   8.2.4
    re-recording, restrictions on   8.4.3, 8.13
    restraint of trade in   5.4.4, 8.3.1, 8.4.3, 8.5.1
    retail selling price of products   8.9
        packaging costs, VAT, and royalties   8.5.2, 8.9.1
    royalties (to artist)   8.1.2, 8.3.2, 8.7–8.9
        accounting for   8.10
        amount of   8.7.1, 8.7.2
        basis for   8.7.3, 8.9
        calculation   8.7.2, 8.9, 8.10.1
        compilations, on   8.8.3
        different rates for less than full price sales   8.8.1–8.8.4
        flat rate or scaled   8.7.3
        mistakes   8.10.1
        obligation to pay   8.7.1
        Published Dealer Price   8.9
        producer's   8.8.6
        rates   8.7.2
        recoupment from   8.5.2, 8.6
        reduced for broadcast advert   8.5.4
        reserve for unsold records   8.10.2
    royalties (for owners of underlying work)   8.5.3
    sales   8.7, 8.8
        clubs, through   8.8.1
        low price 'budget line'   8.8.2
        net   8.9.2
        retail and dealer price   8.9
    sound recording, for   8.2 *et seq*
        copyright   8.2.2, *see also* Sound recording
        definition   8.2.1
        exploitation methods   8.2.1
        moral rights   8.2.3
    termination   8.11.2, 8.12

Recording contract *cont*
   territory   8.1.1
   tours   8.5.4
   warranties
      artist, by   8.4
      company, by   8.6
Religion
   advertising   20.2.3
   ridicule of Anglican faith as blasphemy   12.2
Rental rights   6.5, 8.2.4, 17.1, 17.5
Reporting restrictions
   fair and accurate report of legal proceedings   14.2.1
Reputation
   damage to, *see* Defamation; Passing off
Restraint of trade   5.4.4
   doctrine   5.4.4
   examples   5.4.4
   group, member leaving   8.11.1
   recording contract, and   8.3.1, 8.4.3, 8.5.1
   remedies   5.4.4
   severance   5.4.4
   terms of agreement, scrutiny of   5.4.4
Rights clearance   17.1 *et seq*
   author, waiver, credit etc   17.3
   contents clearance   17.6
   copyright   17.2, 18.3
      assignment or licence, deciding on   17.2.1
      existing works   17.2.1
      underlying works   17.2.1
   Copyright Regulations 1996: rights considerations   17.5
   director, waiver, credit etc   17.3
   insurance cover   17.6
   moral rights   17.3
   performers' rights   17.4
   script   17.6, *see also* Script
Royalties
   copyright licence, under   1.12.3
   musical work, for   6.2.4, 7.4.6
      mechanical royalties from record company   8.5.3
      on-line exploitation   8.2.1, 8.8.5
   payment method, as   5.2.7
   recording contract, under, *see* Recording contract
   reserve provision   8.10.2
   video recording, and   18.4.3

Satellite television   2.6, 11.6
   advertising breaks   20.2.3
   distribution agreement for   18.2, 18.5
   'domestic satellite service'   11.6
   'non-domestic satellite service'   11.6
   service neither domestic nor non-domestic, prosecution of   11.6

   sports on   22.2
Script
   content clearance   17.1, *see also* Rights clearance
   film   15.3.4, 16.3.4
Sculpture   1.4.5, *see also* Copyright
Secrets, *see* Confidence, breach of
Services
   misdescription of   21.2.2
Sex, *see* Obscenity
Shape
   goods, of, as trade mark   21.4.1
Singer, *see* Musician(s); Performance, rights in; Recording contract
Slander, *see* Defamation
Smoking
   Code for advertisers   20.3.2
Solicitor
   see also Advice (professional)
   fiduciary relationship with client   5.4.3
Song, *see* Musical work
Songwriter, *see* Composer; Musical work
Sound recording
   British Phonographic Industry Ltd   6.2.5, 6.3.1, 6.3.4
   copyright in   1.3, 1.4.4, 1.5, 6.3.1, 8.2.2
      'author'   1.9.2, 8.2.2
      definition for   1.5.1
      ownership   8.13, *see also* Copyright; Copyright infringement
   counterfeit and bootleg, combating   6.2.5
   exploitation   6.3–6.5
   forms of   6.1, 6.3.1, 6.2.1
   Performers Registration Centre   6.3.2, 6.5
   performers' rights   4.1, 6.3.5
      recording contracts and royalties   6.3.5, 8.1.2, 8.2
   Performing Artists' Media Rights Association   6.5
   Phonographic Performance Ltd   6.3.1, 6.3.2
      fees   6.3.2
      licensing by   6.3.2
      usage rights assigned to   6.3.2
   record company
      obtaining licence etc of copyright   6.3.1
      performers, contract with   6.3.1
      royalty to composer etc   6.3.1
   recording contract for, *see* Recording contract
   video, on   6.3.1, 6.3.3
Spare parts
   advertising of   21.4.4
Sponsorship
   advertising   22.6.2
   agreement   22.2–22.6
      broadcast rights   22.3.1
      designation in   22.3.1
      duration   22.3.3
      exclusivity   22.3.1

Sponsorship *cont*
  agreement *cont*
    extension of   22.3.3
    logo, use of   22.3.1, 22.4, 22.5
    organiser's obligations   22.5, *see also* 'organiser' below
    power to contract   22.2
    sponsor's rights and obligations   22.3, 22.4, *see also* 'sponsor' below
  ambush marketing   22.3.1, 22.6
    avoidance of   22.6.2
    meaning and examples   22.6.2
  broadcast coverage   22.3.1
    interference with   22.6.2
  broadcast sponsorship   22.6.2, 22.8
    ITC Code   22.8.1
  competing commercial interests   22.6.1
  endorsement agreement   22.7
  goodwill, third party advantage of   22.6.2
  logo   22.3.1, 22.4, 22.5
    protection of   22.6.2
  merchandising   22.3.1, 22.3.2, 22.5
    agreement   22.7
    unauthorised   22.6.2
  organiser
    appointment of sponsors, freedom for   22.3.1
    compliance with rules   22.5
    indemnity from sponsor   22.4
    insurance cover   22.5
    nature of, and grant of rights   22.2
  sponsor
    advertising   22.3.2
    categories of product   22.3.1
    compliance with rules   22.4
    fee payment   22.4
    marks, third party use of   22.3.1
    official supplier   22.3.1
    product control and approval   22.3.1
    seats for event   22.3.2
    secondary rights, examples   22.3.2
    supply of products, prizes, etc   22.4
    status and naming of   22.3.1
    title right   22.3.1
  television Code   22.8
    failure to comply   22.8.1
    product placement prohibited   16.2.4
    review of   22.8.1
    services to which applies   22.8.1
  trade mark protection   22.6.2
Sports event
  broadcasting of   4.2.2, 22.6.2
    broadcast sponsorship   22.9
  finance for, *see* Sponsorship
Sportsmen   4.2.2
  broadcast event, consent to   4.2.2

Tape
  packaging costs   8.9.1
  recording contract, in   8.2.1, *see also* Recording contract
  royalty on   8.8, 8.9
Television
  advertising   19.5
    ITC Codes   19.5.2, 20.2, 20.4, 21.6.7
    licensed services   19.5.2, 19.5.3
    principles and standards   20.4, *see also* Advertising
  BBC   15.2.1
  cable, *see* Cable transmission
  Channel 4   15.2.1
  children's programmes   11.6
    advertising   20.4
    advertising breaks   20.2.3, 20.4
  copyright matters, *see* Copyright
  defamation on   9.3, *see also* Defamation
  Family Viewing Policy   11.6
  'free'   18.5
  good taste and decency, and   11.6
  ITC licences   19.5.2
  ITV   15.2.1
  obscenity, and programme on   11.2.1, 11.3, 11.4.1, 11.6
    criminal offences, and   11.6
  performing rights, and   6.2.2
  Programme Code   11.6
  programme production, *see* Programme production (film and TV)
  releases dates for video, and   18.4.2
  reporting of court proceedings, *see* Reporting restrictions
  rights clearance   18.3, *see also* Rights clearance
  sales agent for programmes   16.2.6
  satellite   2.6, 11.6, *see also* Satellite television
  sponsorship, and   22.6.2, 22.8
    ITC Code   22.8.1
    see also Sponsorship: television code
  Transfrontier Television, EC Directive on   11.6
Theatre
  see also Actor; Dramatic work; Performance, rights in
  union   15.2.2, 15.4.3
Tobacco manufacturers
  smoking, code for advertisers   20.3.2
Tour
  musician, for   7.3.2, 7.4.6
Trade descriptions
  advertising, and   21.2.2, 21.2.3
  false   21.2.2
    defence to offence of   21.2.2
  prosecutions   21.2.2
  scope of law   21.2.2

Trade libel   21.4.4, 21.6.6
Trade mark   21.4
   comparative advertising, and   21.4.4, 21.6.3
      infringement of mark, test for   21.6.3
      trade libel, may be   21.4.4
   definition   21.4.1
   delivery up, etc of infringing goods   21.4.3
   identification of registered mark   21.6.3
   infringing acts   21.4.2
   logo, for, and sports sponsorship   22.3.1
   Paris Convention   21.4.3
   registration   21.4.1
   remedies   21.4.3
   well-known   21.4.3
Trade secret, *see* Confidence, breach of
Trade unions   15.2.2
Typographical arrangement of published edition
   copyright in   1.6
      infringement   2.3.3, *see also* Copyright

Underlying works   1.5, 15.3.4, 17.2.1
   categories   15.3.4
Undue influence   5.4.3
   examples   5.4.3
   manager, by   7.3.2
   professional advice, and   5.3.5, 5.4.3
Unregistered design right   1.4.5

VAT   8.9.1
Video recording
   advertising   20.3

British Board of Film Classification control   11.8, 17.6
   categories   18.4.4
   exemption   18.4.4
   offence to supply without certificate   18.4.4
copyright   1.12.5
defamation in   9.3
distribution agreement for   18.2.1, 18.4
obscenity   11.8
payment to rights owner   18.4.3
promotional video for record etc   8.5.4
purchase   18.4.1
release dates   18.4.2
rental   18.4.1
royalties   18.4.3
sound recordings on   6.3.1, 6.3.3
violence in   11.8
Video Performance Ltd   6.3.1, 6.3.3, 8.5.4
Violence
   see also Obscenity
   advert, in   20.3.2
   video, in   11.8

Warranty
   collateral   21.7.4
   licence or assignment of copyright, in   1.12.4
   production agreement, in   16.3.8, 18.2.2
   recording contract, in   8.4
Writer
   see also Book; Copyright
   scriptwriter   15.3.4
Writers Guild of Great Britain   15.2.2, 15.3.4